# Signs of Freedom

*Theology of the Christian Sacraments*

# Signs of Freedom
## *Theology of the Christian Sacraments*

German Martinez

PAULIST PRESS
NEW YORK/MAHWAH, N.J.

Cover design by Sharyn Banks

Book design by Celine Allen

Library of Congress Cataloging-in-Publication Data

Martinez, German.
    Signs of freedom : theology of the Christian sacraments / German Martinez.
        p.  cm.
Includes bibliographical references and index.
    ISBN 0-8091-4160-4 (alk. paper)
    1.  Sacraments—Catholic Church.  2.  Catholic Church—Doctrines.
    I.  Title
    BX2200 .M353 2004
    234' .16—dc22

                                                                    2003016452


Published by Paulist Press
997 Macarthur Boulevard
Mahwah, New Jersey 07430

www.paulistpress.com

Printed and bound in the
United States of America

For Fr. Victoriano González, O.S.B.
MAESTRO

and for the Benedictine Community of Samos Abbey (Spain)

*"That in all things God may be glorified"*

# Contents

**PART TWO**
**THE INITIATION AND FOUNDATIONAL CHURCH**

## PART FOUR
## THE CHURCH AT THE SERVICE OF COMMUNION

# Abbreviations

CCSL    *Corpus Christianorum, Series Latina*

CSEL    *Corpus Scriptorum Ecclesiasticorum Latinorum*

DS      *Enchiridion symbolorum*, ed. H. Denzinger and Schönmetzer

PG      J. P. Migne, *Patrologia Graeca*

PL      J. P. Migne, *Patrologia Latina*

*SCh*    *Sources Chrétiennes*

# Introduction

The rapid cultural and social changes of the second half of the twentieth century have inevitably reverberated in the contemporary Christian consciousness. Change has affected the faith experience of believers and the very bedrock of their communal life—the sacraments. Decades of theological research, reforms, and renewal preceded and followed the Second Vatican Council. Then, in its wake, the shifting ecclesial landscape reversed centuries-old conceptions, practices, and attitudes about the sacraments. There was in the opinion of some theologians "a quiet sacramental revolution." The Rite of Christian Initiation of Adults (RCIA), for example, was promulgated in 1972. Its liturgies of initiation have forced sacramental theology to reorient and redefine itself. The Council laid foundations, many theologians developed a wealth of models, and various Christian communities led a flowering renewal of sacramental spirituality.

Some areas of theological study like Christology and soteriology achieved coherent visions after the council. Within the theology of the sacraments, however, there still prevails a wide divergence of views and approaches. Nevertheless, there exists a growing consensus on many basic issues, some of which were emphasized even before the pre-Vatican II era, like the necessity of strong christological and ecclesial foundations and the need to integrate word and sacrament. In the long run, the progress of adequate sacramental understanding and a vibrant liturgical practice will require a series of methodologies and fresh pastoral approaches. The incorporation of cultural factors and the creation of multidimensional approaches to sacramental expression will be required. The continuing engagement of theologians in the process speaks to the fact that a more mature sacramental synthesis lies ahead, essentially holistic in its liturgical foundations and yet open to current religious consciousness.

This book attempts to synthesize and see beyond more recent theological work on the sacraments from an ecumenical perspective, and in particular garners some gifts of understanding from the Eastern Church's traditions. Envisioned for both scholarly research and pastoral ministry, this book presents the key issues of a renewed sacramental theology in light of today's cultural challenges to sacramental practice. This theology is grounded in a biblical, patristic, historical, and theological background. It tries to articulate especially the christological, ecclesial, individual, and social aspects of the sacraments as a dynamic and organic whole, emphasizing their spirituality, that is, a mystery to be lived and fully experienced by the believer.

The book has four parts: (1) the sacramental meaning of Christian existence; (2) the sacraments of initiation, baptism-confirmation, and the fundamental sacrament, the Eucharist; (3) the sacraments of healing, penance, and anointing; and (4) the sacraments that construct and preserve the Christian community's unity, marriage, and orders. The book begins by investigating the key interpretative elements of the sacramental experience and its symbolic character. The chapters that follow in part 1 provide more concrete perspectives of Christian sacramentality. The four parts cited above offer a roadmap for exploring the individual sacraments. They are grouped together according to their role of manifesting the deepest meaning of our lives within the Christian mystery. Thus the perspective from which they are examined is ecclesiological and eucharistic. The Eucharist, understood as the central mystery of Christian existence, provides a foundation for reflecting on the whole sacramental economy of grace. Finally, the presentation of the four parts concludes by returning to the central theme of the book—the sacraments as freeing and transforming symbols of the living God.

To offer a synthesis of the theology of Christian sacraments in the twenty-first century, one needs to draw from many sources: the New Testament's biblical catechesis; the vital writings of the patristic age; the great scholastics; the interpreters of the Reform; the remarkable progress and developments in the twentieth century, and current challenges to traditional sacramental theology and practice emerging from postmodern thought in our global world. All of these sources, interpreted in a coherent way, can bring together the lessons of sacramental tradition and advance ecumenical approaches to actual sacramental expressions. Focusing on sacramental spirituality results in an interpretation of current issues that is broad, inclusive, and ecumenical. This is an appropriate theological context for the new millennium, given the now truly worldwide Christian community's sacramental tapestry—a new and dynamic tapestry that adds depth to the ministry of the Church and the life of believers experiencing the presence of God in daily life.

I want to express my gratitude to the special people whom God brought to me and who were in various ways my teachers and supporters. The content of this book took shape over several years of my teaching on liturgy and sacraments at Fordham University. It has benefited from the exchange of ideas with students from many nations, who with their enthusiastic classroom sharing both challenged and instructed their teacher. The content is likewise rooted in practical experience within multicultural parishes where a strong sacramental outlook characterizes celebrations, particularly those of Hispanic people whom I serve as spiritual leader.

I initiated this book during a leave with a faculty fellowship generously given to me by Fordham University. My heartfelt gratitude to Fr. Vincent Novak, S.J., my dean, and the faculty of the Graduate School of Religion and Religious Education with whom I share a labor of love in the educational ministry. I sought advice and received valuable suggestions from two friends: an exceptional theologian, Michael Lawler, a professor at Creighton University; and a model of pastoral wisdom, Michael Kerrigan, C.S.P., pastor of St. Peter's Church in Toronto. I am also indebted to several colleagues in the priesthood who, in reading different chapters, provided many timely corrections that made my English smoother: Richard Gemza, Patrick Mooney, and Walter Mitchell.

Finally, I wish to acknowledge those whose work made possible the professional quality of this book: the staff at Paulist Press, especially Fr. Lawrence Boadt, C.S.P., Mr. Paul McMahon, and Dr. Christopher Bellitto, whose generous editorial assistance helped bring the text to completion.

## PART ONE

# The Sacramental Way of Life

# 1

# A Sacramental Universe

In the introduction we spoke of a worldwide sacramental tapestry. But the tapestry metaphor applies to all liturgical celebrations and to sacramental theology itself. Intricate and complex, they are woven with the bodily threads of humanity fulfilling its vital needs and celebrating a lived experience of the ineffable mystery. The threads of faith and human creativity represent the basic rhythms of the experience of God in the midst of everyday life. Typically, over time, a colorful cloth tapestry hanging on a wall will wear out. Its intricate threads will disappear or become loose. It will no longer mirror the human mind that created it. The ancient yet always new sacramental tapestry is similar. It ever needs renewal and must constantly be made whole again.

This chapter looks at the symbolic and sacramental tapestry from two different perspectives. First, it presents ten interpretative elements of the life of the sacraments. The complexity and multidimensional nature of sacramental experience require that one adopts elements of interpretation that will allow both a unified approach and a renewed sense of the power and beauty of celebrating the sacraments. Second, it explores the anthropological basis of the sacraments. In this chapter's second part, the powerful capacity of symbolism to mediate the sacramental meaning of human existence will be emphasized. As a consequence of this capacity we are awakened to the mystery.

## Interpretative Elements of Christian Sacramentality

Fresh challenges face the sacraments today. At the special consistory in Rome in May 2001, Cardinal Godfried Daneels (of Mechelen-Brussels)

stated that "the Western churches of established Christianity are passing through a profound crisis of sacramentality." Yet, newly reformed
sacramental rituals reveal signs of growth and vitality. In order to
understand the fresh challenges to sacramental life and to enhance the
signs of new vitality, we need an integral and consistent approach to the
liturgical experience of the sacraments. We must see them as a coherent whole, but with many dimensions. Obviously, sacramental interpretation is an ongoing task. Like life itself, sacraments demand coherence
within their various dimensions.

The interpretative elements about to be presented derive from
consideration of the dynamics of sacramental liturgical enactment as
found in the tradition. Subject to refinement as they are, they do not
pretend to embrace all the themes of a contemporary hermeneutic for
approaching the sacraments. Nonetheless, the elements enumerated
represent major current emphases with important implications for the
renewal of sacramental life institutionally and personally.

Reflection on these elements begins this study of Christian sacramentality, the central purpose of which is to assist spiritual revival and
help pastoral evolution of a valid contemporary sacramental life for a
world that yearns for spiritual and transcendent experience. These ten
interpretative elements will guide our systematic theological and liturgical exploration. They are:

1. The power of symbols

2. A holistic view of life and a sense of the divine mystery

3. The integration of sacraments and life

4. A baptismal consciousness

5. The centrality of Eucharist to Christian life and ministry

6. The all-embracing and transforming sacramental mystery

7. The constants of tradition

8. The primacy of the spiritual

9. The sacraments as prophetic signs

10. A cultural and interdisciplinary approach

## 1. The Power of Symbols

The topic of symbolism is vast. Here we will highlight the theology of symbol, its role in sacramental theology, and its liberative potential.

Symbolic thinking constitutes an essential precondition for sacramental mediation. In fact, from Augustine's time (354–430) sacraments have been called "symbols," "symbols of a sacred reality" (Council of Trent, 1551).[1] The symbolic mode of being actualizes the mystery and allows the believer to experience it in the depth of his or her existence. It rejects the rationalistic and utilitarian thinking that blinds one's vision of the spiritual and transcendent. The believer in the community at prayer is the center of the Christian symbolic universe. An experience of ineffable mystery, contemplative awe, and mystical interiority does not occur in a shallow and merely functional mentality content with bare minimalism and ritual validity. Symbolism, which makes the holy mystery of God real to the community, is the lifeblood of sacramental liturgy. Whether it be vital or anemic depends on the community's commitment to its corporate symbols in all their beauty and wealth of expression.

## 2. A Holistic View of Life and a Sense of the Divine Mystery

Openness to transcendence as it validates creation's oneness is an essential presupposition for a holistic view of sacramentality. All life's dimensions—person and society, world and history—are dynamically interrelated and constitute a single sacramental whole. Endowed with a symbolic power, creation and our humanity can be an epiphany of God. All life is experienced as ultimately "holy" through the incarnation of the *Logos*. The sacramental universe is steeped in this Christian sacramental principle. It offers not only a holistic meaning to salvation, but also an overarching vision within which one perceives sacraments as interrelated and meaningful, necessary and integral to *real* life.

However, pragmatic secularism has progressively eclipsed the original and basic sacramentality engrained in the depths of the human person. Secularism is the cancer of sacramentality's wider and deeper meaning, since it removes the mystery lying at the heart of all life's aspects and deletes the cultural support of faith. In today's secularized society sacraments have yet to become meaningfully operative in the lives of most Christian people. For many, the sacraments are individual supernatural commodities, objects of spiritual consumerism, rather than a continuing force that nurtures an experience of conversion and freedom, growth, and transformation.

The sacramental dimension remains, however, an essential characteristic in many cultures, most evidently in those of Latin America, Africa, and Asia. Due to an enduring holistic world view and awareness of the divine, Christians in these cultures may rightly be called "naturally sacramental people." The real presence of the divine expresses itself in the many practices of communal popular religion. These practices often represent joyous festival experiences in and outside "the temple." They give meaning to the expression of faith and provide a cultural context of holy mystery for sacraments and sacramentality. The specific meaning and matrix of all seven sacraments—their social and aesthetic, festive and liberative dimensions—have to relate to an overarching sense of sacramentality that extends to every facet of life. People who have no awareness of the divine mystery in their personal lives will not be drawn to the dynamics of the sacramental mystery.

## 3. The Integration of Sacraments and Life

Even with a world view that perceives signs of transcendence, the believer needs to experience Christian sacraments as the expression of life's deepest mysteries and to experience life itself as sacramental. This presupposes a continuing and personal spiritual growth *before, during,* and *beyond* the experience of sacraments. The spirituality of daily life and sacramental spirituality are not distinct but inextricably complementary, leading to and flowing from one another. Vatican II describes this integration as follows:

> All [the laity's] works, if accomplished in the Spirit, become spiritual sacrifices acceptable to God through Jesus Christ: their prayers and apostolic undertakings, family and married life, daily work, relaxation of mind and body, even the hardships of life if patiently borne. In the celebration of the Eucharist, these are offered to the Father...along with the body of the Lord.[2]

An ongoing renewal steeped in traditional Catholic sacramental imagination and envisioning the future is needed in order to bridge the gap between worship, people's experience of faith, and local mission. The word of God is primary and precedes the sacrament in fostering discipleship. Thus, the connection between sacramental liturgies, spirituality, and secular life is essential for the Eucharist to become actually the "source and summit of Christian life."[3]

## 4. A Baptismal Consciousness

With the eucharistic mystery, baptism is the foundation of all the Church's sacramental life and ministry. From this perspective all sacraments are initiatory. Through baptism the believer is endowed with a Christian identity, world view, and calling to live out the gospel. Many of the theological and pastoral challenges the Church encounters among its people can be traced to a lack of consciousness of what it means to be baptized. For example, a spirituality genuinely relying on baptismal consciousness becomes the ground for a sacramental and spiritual understanding of marriage. In the same way, young people can hear a call to ministry. Baptism is the ontological foundation for laity and ordained alike to share in the priesthood of Christ. The call to holiness, to mission, and to service in our daily lives has baptismal and eucharistic foundations.

## 5. The Centrality of the Eucharist to Christian Life and Ministry

The Eucharist, the fulfillment of Christian initiation, is the bedrock underlying the path of the Christian vocation. First and foremost, we need to acknowledge the mystery of the real presence. The awesome and transforming mystery of the real presence of the risen Christ is given to us in the eucharistic banquet. Actualizing Christ's death and resurrection, the Eucharist contains the inexhaustible riches of the Church. It is the central mystery, one and the same with the mystery of the Church. Vatican II reclaimed this patristic view and, as noted above, envisaged the Eucharist as the source and summit of Christian life and ministry. The restored Rite of Christian Initiation of Adults, in which the Eucharist represents the crowning experience, could make a great difference in the community's life and ministerial structures.

The Eucharist is the center and foundation of all sacramental life, ministry, and evangelization. This presupposes a eucharistic spirituality —the living out of the gift of divine life—which builds a strong corporate identity and vision of the Church. Thus, the experience of "God-for-us" and "God-in-us" through sacramental liturgy creates a community of missionary outreach.

## 6. The All-embracing and Transforming Sacramental Mystery

The Christian mystery is not a category; it is the total Christ-event. The absolute mystery is the living God manifested in the blessed Trinity and communicated to humanity in the Word made flesh. This mystery became the saving event of Christ and the new life in the Holy Spirit. It is expressed symbolically in the liturgy within which sacrament is celebrated. Christ manifests himself in his body, the Church, and actualizes himself in the Eucharist. The ultimate reality of grace is in the Christ's Passover, the axis about which all sacramental life turns. From this perspective, sacraments are an organic liturgical whole, rather than juxtaposed sacred objects. They are many-faceted ways of being for the same body of Christ, in ecclesial or in eucharistic form.

Mystery is an open-ended, developmental, and encompassing reality. It provides the major interpretative key to the sacraments experienced existentially, in their actual liturgical setting and celebration as part of life, extended through time. It also yields a unifying vision of the sacraments, in that it grounds their interrelationship mutually and organically. Further, it explains the nature and depth of each sacramental event in terms of its specific wider liturgical and existential meanings. For instance, we can understand the journey of Christian marriage within the broad sacramental mystery founded on Christ, related to Eucharist, its source and heart. In contrast to the narrow, static, and legalistic view of the canonical "sacrament of marriage" held by many in the past, "mystery" seeks core values, the profound meanings of sacramental marriage.

## 7. The Constants of Tradition

A sacrament is not of itself an inalterable ritual act. Rather, it is an ever-changing liturgical event shaped by religious and cultural ideas. We see a sacrament's foundation in biblical sources and trace its evolution through a complex history. The following chapters approach this evolution by positing paradigmatic shifts in the light of which one can discern the constants of tradition. Paradigms serve as hermeneutic devices, setting agendas for historical eras, while remaining exemplary and seminal models of tradition for the future. The core elements of tradition, which continue across a broad spectrum of historical models, make up the essential constants of sacramental practice. From them we can and must draw not just lessons from the past for handing on living tradition, but lessons for indicating paths for the future. Where the loss or devaluation of these constants may have ushered in a crisis of sacramental meaning, their critical re-appropriation (not a mere retrieval or archaic repetition of past traditions) provides a grounding for sacramental wholeness and renewal. Moreover, to use the first millennium's theological adage, these constants of an actual liturgical celebration confirm the need to integrate critically the *lex credendi* (the law of belief) into the *lex orandi* (the law of prayer).

## 8. The Primacy of the Spiritual

The reforms resulting from the Second Vatican Council were necessary. From them came a new understanding of the sacraments and of participation in them. This new understanding challenged established theological assumptions and traditional religious and pastoral attitudes. It laid the groundwork for a renewed sacramental vision and practice within a new sacramental paradigm. Nevertheless, a real and existential paradigmatic shift does not occur without a true experience of conversion. If the continuing reform were not to encompass a living, personal liturgical spirituality, it would say little to the concrete renewal of Christian life. A liturgical sacramental spirituality is essential for shaping the shared vision of an outward-looking Church. Such a vision stands in contrast to that of a Church of maintenance. It fosters a sense of direction in parish ministry.

The primacy of the spiritual experience is crucial. It allows for the deepening of the theology of the sacraments and the development of the life of the sacraments. Because they are profoundly personal by nature, the sacraments are divine gifts that reveal God's glory, God's mighty deeds, in the present. They are spirituality at its roots and enjoy Christ's holiness as their final aim. The dynamism of the sacraments presupposes personal spirituality—the believer "on the way," *becoming* rather than *doing*. The primacy of the spiritual acknowledges the paramount importance of liturgical and sacramental spirituality within the Church and in its mission as it radiates into the world.

## 9. The Sacraments as Prophetic Signs

The sacraments, above all the Eucharist, must play a central and integrating role in the Church's mission and in the life of Christian people. This interpretative element envisages sacraments as prophetic signs of freedom. It expands their scope beyond that of privatized practices for mere individualistic concerns, or of sacred rituals belonging to a community centered on itself. Sacraments are declared to be communal actions of a Church proclaiming Christ's liberating news. The Church is a servant of God's reign and a sign of unity among all people. In fact, the Church's prophetic power is nothing other than the prophetic power of the sacraments it celebrates. In the light of the gospel, the interior and personal dimension of conversion compels the believer to confront the sinful structures of society and to "restore all things in Christ" in the hope of future fulfillment. In particular, the Eucharist prophetically symbolizes the mystery of cosmic and liberative transformation ushered in by the paschal mystery of Christ.

## 10. A Cultural and Interdisciplinary Approach

Celebrating the very rhythms of life, sacraments are inextricably tied to cultures. Yet, to be understood properly and to respond adequately to people's deepest needs and concerns, sacramental experience must be integrated into a particular culture. Sacraments must become incarnate in cultural forms; they must undergo inculturation in the likeness of "the Word-become-flesh." In this way they can confront a culture, animate it, and infuse it with their redemptive grace. The never-ending process of interchange between cult and culture calls for continuing rediscovery of the basic sacramentality that lies inherent in the world's cultures as they value experience, ritual, and story.

The Church must embrace cultures. They are the source from which sacramental imagination draws inspiration—a key source for the Christian sacraments in a postmodern world. This basic sacramentality can express itself in a variety of ways, such as, for example, in the multicultural forms of popular religiosity, in the atmosphere of *fiesta*, in an awareness of the divine in creation, and in contemplative and mystical interiority.

In this dawn of the third millennium, other issues like the experience of being a woman in the Church and questions related to postmodern thought seriously challenge current sacramental theology and practice. Meeting this challenge by exploring sacramental reality in its liturgical and real-life settings will require branching out into new dimensions and calling upon various disciplines, methods, and interpretative tools. Inspiration must come from other fields of research, including contemporary human sciences. For instance, cultural anthropology is an important avenue to understanding the function of human ritualization, especially at a time when the old socio-cultural support of key passages of life—birth, puberty, betrothal, and death—has to a great extent been lost.

## Symbols, Sacraments, and Mystery

Recovery of symbolic and sacramental ways of expressing life's meaning and destiny enjoys new urgency today. At the same time, there appears to be a cultural shift in the same direction. Without agreement on the interpretation of symbol, diverse domains of the human sciences continue extensive exploration of the world of symbolic meaning. Prominent among the investigating disciplines are the phenomenology of religion, theology, psychology, and anthropology.[4] Contemporary theology has come full circle, reclaiming the patristic language of symbolism with which the Church's theology of sacramental mystery began. "The whole of theology," as Karl Rahner wrote, "is incomprehensible if it is not essentially a theology of symbols."[5] This statement applies above all to sacramental theology: sacramentality is a modality of symbolism.

All religions have rituals. All religions have their own "sacraments," ritual events that are the cradle and core of religious faith. Sacramentality, then, broadly understood, is an essential element of universal religious consciousness. A descriptive definition of the person could thus be "the sacramental being" and human life, as "sacramental life," since it has a sacramental sense. John Macquarrie puts it this way: a sacramental sense has a "secure basis in the very constitution of humanity."[6] Given this wider religious perspective, human nature in its threefold dimension of person, cosmos, and history reveals a potentially sacramental reality, a reality from which a vision of transcendence and present mystery emerges. This reality is a sacramental universe.

Although secularism spreads itself everywhere in today's Western cultures, a universal sacramental sense pervaded the ancient world. In William Barclay's words, it was "saturated in sacrament."[7] St. Irenaeus affirmed that "nothing is a vacuum in the face of God. Everything is a sign of God."[8]

It is not possible here to examine every underlying constituent of sacramental symbolism—what comparative religion shows us, the sacred signs of the Hebrews and Jews, or even the contributions of a postmodern age. The chapters ahead attempt rather to deepen understanding of the sacramental principle in general, and to shed light on particular issues emerging from the background of the Bible and from sacramental liturgy, filled as it is with signs. Reflecting on the relationship between symbolism's human roots and the sacramental meaning of all of life is essential to understanding the sacraments.

In what follows we will examine the implications of symbolic mediation for sacramental theology. The mystery of the human person requires this mediation, not only as a creature of embodied spirit, but as one who relates to others, searches for freedom, and is open to transcendence. We reflect progressively on the symbolic reality of Christian sacramentality, moving from *symbol* to *sacrament*, to *mystery* by looking at (a) sacramental transparency and (b) doors to mystery. The viewpoints are both anthropological and theological.

## Sacramental Transparency

The sacramental significance of human reality expresses itself through symbols. Symbols are the essential elements of religious communication. They allow people to grasp human reality in its deeper meaning. They open the vast dimensions of what is incomprehensible mystery and lead people into it. Aware of transcendent reality, human beings link transitory existence through symbols to the "Total Being" we call God. The world of symbols is essential to the fundamental understanding of ritual and sacramental expressions, indeed of all human life.[9]

*Signs and Symbols*

Symbols differ from signs in that they point to and share in a reality beyond themselves. Signs, such as, for example, traffic signs, represent fixed, external, conventional, unchanging meaning. Nevertheless, the word "sign," as a generic term, is frequently used as a synonym for "symbol," especially in liturgical and sacramental terminology. Theologians may talk about sacraments as signs of the mystery of Christ.

There is no complete agreement about the meaning and function of symbols in the prolific literature and divergent fields of study treating them. However, the etymology of the word "symbol" assists in understanding the term. It derives from the Greek *symballein,* meaning to place together the two matching halves of an object. In practice, two people would each hold a half and then be able to recognize one another by matching the two parts. Thus the *symbolon* would mediate their identity and guarantee the legitimacy of their relationship. We now take symbols to be things, events, or even persons with immediate and intuitive, often multiple, meanings: a beloved schoolteacher, a shiny ring, sharing a meal.

Modern anthropology confirms the social and cultural relevance of ritual symbolism. In stressing that the symbolic and the sacramental lie deeply embedded in the profound structures of human existence, the behavioral sciences and theology usually concur on one important matter: the revelatory and universal value of symbols.

The revelatory and universal value of symbols and their creative and transforming power stems from the fact that, as modern anthropology asserts, we are "symbolic animals," in Ernst Cassirer's terminology, *animal symbolicum.*[10] To be human means to coexist and to participate with others in interrelating and intercommunicating. These, the interpersonal dynamics of human existence, are the generic context in which sacraments function as conveyers of meaning. To be human implies interpersonal relationships that are essentially actualized through symbolic communication. Of itself, through its very meaning and dynamism, human existence lies open to Absolute Being. As embodied spirits, we are symbolic beings in our mode of being and our ways of thinking, acting, and communicating. The making of symbols profoundly anchors the human structure. It is a religious and cultural constant. Obviously, symbols demand critical interpretation and honest use to prevent ideological distortion.

Human existence cannot be explained in terms of itself; it points to the beyond, it is transparent, laden with transcendence; it bears the holy! God is awesomely omnipresent in the world, the place where human beings meet God. The human person is created as the visible sign and image of God (Gen 1:26). God's presence permeates the cosmos. Human history mediates God's self-communication to human beings. As Paul says, "Ever since the creation of the world his eternal power and divine nature, invisible though they are, have been understood and seen through the things he has made" (Rom 1:20). It was perhaps Paul Claudel who said that all reality is a book that speaks to us of God. The created world mirrors the divine. In the humanity of Christ the full mystery of God and God's giving of self to us are revealed. We speak of the sacramental significance of the whole of reality because the mystery of God infuses the whole of reality.

*Symbols and Sacraments*
Symbolic living is therefore an essential dimension of human and so of Christian existence as well. Because sacraments are symbolic, the grammar of symbol is an essential key for understanding sacramental language. Symbols are the building blocks, the sacramental rituals, by which we reenact the story of salvation and express our personal and communal spirituality.

A holistic approach to the presence of the sacred in the world helps to fill in the gap between the Christian vision expressed in the Church's sacraments and everyday life. Our lived experiences are not merely "secular," but also possess sacramental meaning. Through the experience of the sacred these experiences can become transparent; they can reveal themselves to be icons of the divine presence. Leonardo Boff, in writing on the sacraments, introduces his symbolic approach to sacramentality with personal stories. He uses these to evoke the sacramental meaning of some of the most ordinary elements of familiar experience, such as, for example, homemade bread, a Christmas candle, a local schoolteacher. Drawing on the implications, he states: "In the ephemeral, [human beings] can read the Permanent; in the temporal, the Eternal; in the world, God. Then the ephemeral is transfigured into a sign of the presence of the Permanent, the temporal into a symbol of the reality of the Eternal, the world into a great and grand sacrament of God."[11]

For instance, within the larger framework of a liturgical context, an *object* (bread) can become a *symbol* of person (body). This in turn is transformed into a communal *ritual* (banquet) and the ritual is molded into a grace-filled *sacrament* (Eucharist). Within this perspective achieved in faith, men and women see the creative power of God and his salvific plan, not only for the whole of what is man or woman—for body and spirit—but also for all of the cosmos and its history. By expanding our religious consciousness and enriching our daily lives, sacramental rituals become the dynamic core of the experience of faith. In one sense, therefore, sacraments are to be seen from the perspective of the symbolic world; yet, in another sense, all human existence, whether individual or collective, endowed as it is with a symbolic structure, is to be understood in the light of the sacramental celebrations of the total Christian mystery.

## Challenges

On one hand, cultural contexts condition our perception of reality. The greatest failure of modern secularism stems from its pragmatism and individualism. It has devalued symbolic imagination and scorned the sacred as fading supernaturalism irrelevant to human existence. When objects and people, indeed the planet earth itself, have little significance, they cannot bear a deeper meaning or serve a symbolic and sacramental function.

On the other hand, the modern suspicion of symbolic ritual and the sacramental sense cannot be attributed to the process of secularism alone. It might arise from the celebrating community itself. In commenting on the seeming irrelevance of some liturgical practice, Leonardo Boff notes: "We cannot hide the fact that in the Christian sacramental universe there has been a process of ritual mummification."[12] The modern person may well have become suspicious of minimized and rigid rituals, such as, for example, a scanty washing at baptism, a mechanical performance at Mass, or a lack of liturgical leadership. The rituals are celebrated in "holy" buildings, but are separate from the holiness of daily life.

A broader perspective of symbolic sacramentality is now replacing an abstract, juridical, and restrictive idea of the sacraments that viewed them simply as "channels giving grace." The mentality of juridical validity has dominated the Western Church for a millennium. By contrast, a larger sacramental sense envisages every authentic human experience as potentially revealing divine reality. Sacraments then are symbols pointing to God's grace ever present in all of life. Karl Rahner speaks from this cosmic perspective of God's grace and about the need to perceive other avenues of grace: "Now it is a lasting and tragic misunderstanding for us to turn these sacramental signs once more into a circumscribed enclave, such that it is in this alone that God is present and that the event of his grace takes place."[13] Human reality, made holy through Christ's incarnation and rooted in the mystery of his resurrection, is already sacramental. In practical terms, this perspective connects our ordinary living experiences with the Church's sacramental worship. It yields the basic and deeper meaning of those experiences. In fact, sacramentality makes those experiences transparent, since they are able to communicate something beyond themselves.

Symbolic and sacramental expressions have more than a mere instrumental value. They essentially manifest and participate in the reality symbolized, precisely because reality itself, laden with divine presence, is symbolic. Sacraments respond to the profound symbolic nature of human experience and the human person's openness to transcendence. In this way, contemporary theology recovers symbolic thinking, a primary focus of the ancient Christian writers.

Influenced by Neo-Platonic culture, many church fathers, such as Augustine, considered all visible realities symbols of the invisible, the spiritual, and the transcendent. Recapturing the patristic vision, Alexander Schmemann sees that people no longer recognize symbolism as an essential dimension of the sacrament and calls this a theological tragedy:

> If, for the Fathers, symbol is a key to sacrament it is because sacrament is in continuity with the symbolic structure of the world...And the world is symbolical...in virtue of its being created by God; to be "symbolical" belongs thus to its ontology, the symbol being not only the way to perceive and understand reality, a means of cognition, but also a means of participation. It is then the "natural" symbolism of the world—one can almost say its "sacramentality"—that makes the sacrament possible and constitutes the key to its understanding and apprehension.[14]

From the viewpoint of historical theology, sacramental theology has come full circle. After the eleventh century, there was a shift from symbolic thought to dialectic thought, based on Aristotelian logic. Today, a phenomenological and symbolic approach holds sway.[15] All this implies a basic move from the narrow understanding of formal ritual functions on which theologians focused in the past to the larger sacramental meaning of our human and Christian lives. "Once we give 'sacrament' its older and broader meaning, we realize that in the Church, the 'universal sacrament of salvation,' everything is somehow sacramental, that is, everything is the vehicle of a meaning and an efficacy belonging to a different order from the realities of direct experience, and that this is so because the Church of Christ is a sign and anticipation of the 'mysteries of the kingdom.'"[16]

## Doors to Mystery

Sacramental liturgies are a rich universe of symbols whose complexity and multidimensional meaning must be understood and interpreted. Today we pay much more attention to broad interdisciplinary insights. Still, a contemporary understanding of the symbolic-religious structure of human life can help deepen our understanding only if we get beyond the theories and functions of symbolic ritual. We need to delve into sacramental symbolism. Even more, we must experience it as mystery. Its basic function is mystagogic—within it we find that the Spirit leads us into the mystery and we receive life from it.

In the second half of the twentieth century, reintroduction of biblical and patristic perspectives led to a vision of the sacraments that relied on salvation history and was at once liturgical and existential. Today we must develop a sacramental theology from this vision.[17] At the same time, we must face new challenges from the world of cultural diversity and from contemporary insights offered by thinkers such as Chauvet, Power, and Osborne.[18] In this book, the twentieth-century vision will set the foundation for our effort to develop a new theology.

An overview of some themes in the current understanding of symbolism and its implications for sacramentality will help in next considering the sacraments as prophetic signs.

*1. Symbols are means of transformation.*
Research from many different fields of study indicates that symbols possess the potential for religious, cultural, and social transformation.

This innate power derives from three functions of the symbolic form found in every facet of life.

First, symbolic forms mediate, communicate, and develop the deepest of human experiences. Paul Ricoeur explains that symbols are opaque, hence their inexhaustible depth. With regard to a fuller sense of religious experience, he states, "the symbol gives rise to [critical] thought; yet thought is informed by and returns to the symbol."[19] Symbols are powerful vehicles for shaping our consciousness on many levels. They address the totality of human existence. In Paul Tillich's words, "sacrament grasps our unconscious as well as our conscious being. It grasps the creative ground of our being."[20] Sacraments interpret the fundamental religious experience of a person or a group. In doing so, sacraments have the potential to develop in us a critical self-awareness. They motivate us toward the full realization of our stature as spiritual beings.

Second, symbols engage the whole person as he or she relates to a community in imagination and will, heart, and mind; they bring about holistic personal and communal change. Social anthropology indicates that the loss of symbolic communal celebrations—such as initiation into a religious culture, rites of passage, and so forth—and the religious and social rituals associated with them can result in a crisis of identity for the spiritual and social life of individuals and the community. Bernard Cooke has observed that "because symbols have this power to touch the entire range of our consciousness—rational thought, imagination, emotions, dreams—they are privileged means of expressing our most personal and important and disturbing experiences, they are a powerful force in shaping the way we think and feel."[21]

Finally, symbols can shape the way we act. Symbolic forms express and promote the shared values of the community and its identity. They lead to personal and communal action. Roger Haight points out that symbols transform persons because they mediate a transcendent reality. Religious symbols mediate an experience that calls for total response and implies openness to change and conversion. They therefore bring about transformation. "Symbols appeal to and elicit a total response of a person. Thus they appeal as well to the will; they motivate and empower action; they influence and direct behavior. Symbols are principles of the action which in turn becomes the most elementary bearer of the response of faith."[22]

*2. Symbols open up new dimensions of reality.*
The human person is a symbol-making and symbol-perceiving being. In fact, the fullness of reality can be expressed and comprehended only through the communicative and mediating function of symbols. Things, persons, and events become symbols not of other things but of human and transcendent reality. Intense moments, like a beautiful sunrise, the birth of a child, or the death of a loved one, become symbolic and are perceived symbolically. They resound profoundly in people and lead to experience of the holy. Such moments are deservedly called sacramental.

From a phenomenological perspective, sacramental symbols are revelatory actions that evoke the presence of the sacred in all of life. In Karl Rahner's theology, human corporeality is the beginning of the world of meaning. The body is the primordial symbol, and for the person—"spirit-in-the-world"—the world itself becomes a symbol. In this way Rahner stresses the reality of our openness to the absolute mystery of God. Symbolic reality *(Realsymbol)* is the rendering present, the self-realization, of one being in the other. Another writer, Frederick Dillistone, summarizes Rahner's thought on the Christian mystery as it expands further: "The Logos, the Father's real symbol, expresses himself in the incarnation through the real symbol of his human nature ... The Church ... is the real symbol through which the Incarnate Word expresses himself in human history... The concrete individual sacramental signs are the real symbols through which the Church expresses herself as the fundamental sacrament of God's grace."[23]

*3. Symbols participate in the reality and in the power they express.*
Although different from the reality to which they point, symbols participate in that reality. As Paul Tillich explains:

> The sacramental material is not a sign but a symbol. As symbols the sacramental materials are intrinsically related to what they express; they have inherent qualities (water, fire, oil, bread, wine) which makes them adequate to their symbolic function and irreplaceable. The Spirit "uses" the powers of being in nature in order to "enter" man's spirit...A sacramental symbol is neither a thing nor a sign. It participates in the power of what is symbolized, and therefore it can be a medium of the Spirit.[24]

In the summary of Karl Rahner's thought above, the *Logos*, the Church, and the sacraments appear as symbols that participate in, contain, and make present the different realities they express. Christ, Church, and sacraments are three different levels of sacramentality. Yet, the Christian world view would be incomplete without a fourth level, a still deeper and wider level of sacramentality, namely, the universal cosmos. (This universal cosmos of course includes the little cosmos, the human person and his or her history as it is rooted in the grace of God.) Again Rahner proposed a new way of thinking about sacraments, one that recaptures the symbolic and sacramental vision of ancient Christianity already presented above: "Instead of seeing in them a spiritual movement outward from the sacramental system to an effect in the world, we should look for a spiritual movement of the world toward the sacrament."[25]

Rooted in creation, Christian symbolism and sacramentality contains and expresses the mystery of the Word made flesh. Christ's dwelling among us has opened up all the created world's matter and flesh to the effects of God's redemptive mystery. In fact, the role of Christian symbolism and sacramentality is to release the sacramental potential of God's creation. Filled with God's presence, the universe is a sacramental place. Christ is the proto-symbol, the supreme symbol. Sacramental symbols, then, are his saving presence, historical and actualized. They are vehicles of divine grace.

*4. Symbols are invitations to participate in the mystery.*
Symbols express and make effectively present the incomprehensible mystery of faith through their mediating, communicative, and revelatory function. This function of introducing one into mystery is called mystagogy. In fact, Christian initiation is a symbolic process by which we are led into the mystery. Symbols allow different levels of participative and incremental entry into the mystery. They point to the mystery that they veil and unveil, bear and evoke. In doing so, they invite the participant to transcend the material image, to enter and contemplate.

The power and mystery of the symbol make present a realized sacred reality. Drawing insight from biblical language, Michael Lawler envisaged the sacraments as "prophetic symbols": "To say *symbol* is not to say *not real*, but rather *fully real*, that is, representatively and concretely and effectively and personally real."[26]

True freedom and holiness are possible only when our inner spirit reaches beyond itself and opens itself to the experience of transcendent reality. This is an essential dimension of our human existence. In Saint-Exupéry's words, "what is essential is invisible to the eye."[27] The heart alone, the revelatory locus of conversion and transformation, can see it. We grasp this dimension through the symbolic movement of life celebrated in worship.

*5. Symbols are to be lived out.*
Only through interiorizing the mystery of the symbol can we find meaning. When we live out our ritual symbols, that is to say, when we cherish them, experience them, and open ourselves to their inexhaustible significance, our lives become transformed in the process. A basic symbolic spirit of this sort demands confidence in the power of symbols and thoughtfulness in living them out. For instance, the symbol that is the gathering of a worshiping community exists not merely to evoke a religious *obligation* in the process of fulfillment but also to declare festive *celebration* of every element of life in its deeper values and graced dimensions. A worshiping community motivated by a spirit of celebrating ordinary life, not by mere social convention, reveals signs of love and unity to others. These are the true and relevant signs of a real sacramental Church.

The same is true of other liturgical symbols, like eucharistic bread and baptismal water. They are not to be seen as static things, but as dynamic expressions of life and the divine gift in them. In today's secular society it is common to speak of alienation from religious symbols and their increasing irrelevance for many. The answer to this challenge lies, not in the symbols' lack of power, but in the lack of commitment to them through effective faith participation in grassroots communities. The sense of the sacred in men and women is atrophied. If God's people receive an awakening to the sacred mystery available to them in the symbols, then communities can become cradles of symbolic creativity, cradles in which symbols will thrive and become alive.

Creativity does not mean creation out of nothing or at will. "Symbols cannot be invented; they cannot be produced intentionally," Paul Tillich declares.[28] They live and die in relationship to a particular community, a concrete culture, in which symbols create themselves. They are living symbols when they evoke participation by revealing to people their basic religious experience and thereby enable them to enrich their lives. They die in a cultural climate of logical pragmatism and materialistic secularism.[29] The answer to the symbolic crisis and the lack of a developed symbolic imagination lies within the community. Creativity is a complex phenomenon that depends on renewal and freedom within the community. It requires individual and corporate commitment not to a thing, but to actions involving the communal relationship of faith existing in the participants and the mystery they celebrate.

Behind the fragmentation of symbolic meaning and consequent spiritual emptiness, there is a crisis of faith. Through the Spirit, faith enables us to live out the full and rich meaning of our Christian symbols. They then become alive and open to the ever-changing horizons of the human mystery. In summary, we cite an author in *The New Westminister Dictionary of Liturgy and Worship,* Anthony Thiselton:

> Symbols are born when they resonate at the deepest level with experiences of truths which are important for the corporate life and identity of a community. Operative symbols often maintain an integrating and stabilizing power for the community, but they may also lose this power, and wither away into mere poetic-symbolic metaphors.[30]

The symbolic reality of the world and human sacramentality, including the Christian sacraments, are inseparable. In Bernard Cooke's words, we are not only "symbol-making and symbolically existing beings, but we exist sacramentally."[31] Each of the two facts is an essential dimension of "the irreducible character of the sacred" (again, Cooke's words), which points to the absolute transcendence of human existence. Consequently, this sacred experience cannot be reduced to a nontheological phenomenon. Sacramental symbolism links the person to the Total Being. Not symbolizing the sacred leads to an overly rationalistic and technocratic society susceptible to wide-ranging alienation, as Jung, Cassirer, and other authors have affirmed.[32]

Overcoming the shortcomings of the individualistic rationalism of modernity, scientists today from many academic disciplines emphasize the enormous potential of symbolic processes for human creativity and transformation. Responding to the challenge of a world consciousness of planetary crisis and the hunger for spirituality and peace, we conclude that weakening awareness of the divine mystery transparent to us in the cosmos and the consequent lack of commitment to symbolic rituals lie at the root of the spiritual crisis in the West.

A challenge therefore presents itself to the Church to create new and broader symbolic expressions. These must integrate Christian experience and the culture and speak meaningfully to today's religious experience about the transcendent mystery of life. They have to offer a critique of all exploitative and alienating ideologies, whether local or global, and incarnate a vision of "totality" in today's fragmented culture of disbelief.

# 2

# The Development
# of Christian Sacramentality

A comprehensive examination of the socio-historical evolution of the Christian sacraments can be a liberating experience, especially given the growing awareness of a global Christianity. Historically, the Church retained a pastoral focus by adapting to particular cultures and religious experiences. A contemporary search for pastoral renewal draws upon the primal sacramentality of the New Testament and major historical points that produced paradigmatic shifts in the conceptualization and expression of the sacramental Christ-event. The paradigmatic historical shifts in culture and religious ideas provide a benchmark for analyzing the evolution of sacramental theology. These include: (a) the emergence of Christian sacramentality in the New Testament; (b) the patristic concept of mystery as the total Christ-event; (c) the medieval and modern Roman-Catholic synthesis; (d) the Evangelical-Protestant challenge; and (e) the impact of the Second Vatican Council on the global Church.

## Signs of Christ for the Journey

The New Testament is central to understanding Christian sacramentality. Jesus appears as the visible glory of God and reveals the ultimate glory of humanity. The New Testament testifies to the distinctive reality of Christ himself as "the image of the invisible God" (Col 1:15) who "is the reflection of God's glory and the exact imprint of God's very being"

(Heb 1:3), for "in him the whole fullness of deity dwells bodily" (Col 2:9). In Jesus the divine and human, freedom and salvation become one, fully actualized, and visible. Jesus in his humanity is the sacrament of God's love. This statement of modern sacramental theology, an *a posteriori* reflection on biblical sources, focuses on the fact that the humanity of Christ is the source, center, and ultimate meaning of Christian sacramentality.[1] Modern theologians have expressed this most basic sacramentality of Jesus Christ with expressions such as "first," "arch," and especially primordial sacrament.[2]

The dimensions of the sacramental reality of Christ can be summarized from the triple perspective of *his person, his ministry,* and the *key moments of his public ministry.* First, Christ is a sacramental person because he signifies and points to God in his being. He is God-with-us, the total fulfillment of the mystery of salvation. He, "though he was in the form of God...[took] the form of a slave, being born in human likeness...and every tongue should confess that Jesus Christ is Lord, to the glory of God the Father" (Phil 2:6–11). Through the incarnation "the Word became flesh" (John 1:14). The second person of the Holy Trinity became the visible and living symbol of God's total availability to humanity. Then in his life and public ministry the son of God is the perfect human offering to the Father. As Jesus says in John's Gospel, "Whoever has seen me has seen the Father" (John 14:9) and "I came that they may have life and have it abundantly" (John 10:10). In his incarnation and ministry culminating in the liberating love of his *Pasch,* Christ was the effective, palpable sign of God's presence. He became the servant of humanity, bringing the good news to the poor, healing the brokenhearted, giving sight to the blind and freedom to the downtrodden (Luke 4:18).

Finally, Christ is sacrament in the key moments of his prophetic ministry. In New Testament accounts and specifically in John's Gospel, Jesus' baptism and eucharistic supper are core to his sacramental ministry. The sacramental significance of these moments is rooted in the paschal mystery. The baptism of Jesus is baptism in the Spirit of God, in which Jesus is acknowledged as God's beloved son and God's sacrificial lamb.[3] His eucharistic supper and the other meals he celebrated with his disciples are the fountainhead of eucharistic celebration in the New Covenant. In both rituals Christ is the supreme sign and the total reality of our encounter with God. The mystery of Jesus' life, ministry, death, and resurrection is the preeminent locus of the experience of God. God's saving power is through and in him: "But so that you may know that the Son of Man has authority on earth to forgive sins—he then said to the paralytic—'Stand up, take your bed and go to your home'" (Matt 9:6). "Although these actions are performed in a human way, they are divine actions by their nature. This is true of the miracles, the forgiveness of sins, the giving up of his Body to eat and his blood to drink, and, above all his death, resurrection and glorification, the paschal mystery from which everything derives its meaning and value."[4]

## Origins of Sacraments

The symbolic actions of the early Christians flowed from and were directly linked to the messianic power of Jesus' ministry and praxis. Specifically, the Easter and Pentecost event gave meaning and power to the earliest ecclesial and sacramental experience. From the beginning it was as the body of Christ and community and work of the Holy Spirit that the Church was a sacramental Church. The origin of the Church and the origin of the sacraments are inextricably linked because the former is a basic premise for understanding the latter. Jesus provided the vision rather than a blueprint for basic Church structures or ritual details. Establishing the Church and making it capable of grace-filled actions was God's work within the community of believers who experienced the fullness of God's promise in Christ.

The basic sacramental actions arose prior to Christian conceptualization of ritual life and sacramentality. Some sacramental actions originated directly from Christ's mandate, such as the Eucharist, while others were responses to the vital needs of the Church, as for instance the imposition of hands on a community leader. Christian symbolic elements drew from existing cultural expressions such as fellowship meals, baptisms, and anointings. The originality of the Christian experience lay in the mystery of the new divine-human covenant, the paschal Christ, historically manifest in the sacrament of the Church.

Both baptism and the Eucharist were intimately connected in the Christ-event. From the outset, the "breaking of the bread" and the baptism of water and the Holy Spirit were the heart and nucleus of the sacramental life of the Church. The Christian rituals manifested the fullness of God's love in Christ rather than its conceptualization. Christ had disappeared from their sight (Acts 1:9), but was alive in the lives of the believers as Lord and Christ in his resurrection (Acts 2:36).

The community viewed the "passage" of the Lord to the Father as the core of the baptism of water in the Holy Spirit within the nascent and initiating community: "Do you not know that all of us who have been baptized into Christ Jesus were baptized into his death?" (Rom 6:3). As the first baptized, Christ was the paradigmatic reality of Christian existence. And the memorial "breaking of the bread" testified to the glorified Christ's presence in the lives of Christians and communal gatherings. Paul attests to the eucharistic memorial in one of the first accounts: "For as often as you eat this bread and drink the cup, you proclaim the Lord's death until he comes" (1 Cor 11:26). The memorial also celebrated the dynamic and life-giving power of God's action within the Christian community. Despite the absence of references in the New Testament to any penitential ritual, the action of reconciling sinners acquired sacramental status within communities.

The New Testament provides an extensive range of references to symbolic acts. They emerged from the faith experience of the disciples and were central to the building up of those communities under the creative guidance and saving action of the Spirit of Christ. The community also ritualized the receiving of the gift of the Spirit by the imposition of hands (Acts 8:17); anointing of the sick (Jas 5:14); exclusion from (1 Cor 5) and reintegration into the community; and the commissioning for specific ministries (1 Tim 4:14; 2 Tim 1:6).

The experience of power and freedom guaranteed by what God has done in Christ and continues to do in his present self-manifestation through the activity of his Spirit characterized the ecclesial life of the New Testament communities. From its inception the Church developed as an eschatological assembly of believers. "The disciples then proclaimed the death and resurrection of Jesus and the sending of the Spirit as the breaking in of a new age that they made present through the proclamation and the sacramental celebration in Spirit."[5] Specifically, the Easter joy at the eucharistic celebrations (Acts 2:46) reflected the community's eschatological conviction of salvation "until he [the Lord] comes" (1 Cor 11:26).

## New Testament Sacramentality

What is most striking in early Church sources of sacramentality is the spirit of its practice. The community avoided sacramental formalism and the conventionality of social ceremonies. Within this ecclesial context, Christians did not "receive" the sacraments; they celebrated the mystery. The New Testament records the baptism of rebirth in the Spirit and the eucharistic *agape* of the presence of the risen Lord as liberating Easter events. As sacraments of Christian freedom, baptism and Eucharist were based on the essential oneness in Christ (Gal 3:28).

The spirituality of sacramental freedom stressed the actual transforming power of God in the rituals. Baptism and Eucharist were signs of the encounter of the living Spirit of God-in-Christ at the heart of personal and community life. While proclaiming the liberating newness of the Christian experience, Christians drew from prevailing cultural and religious realities rather than inventing different symbols and rituals. In his study of these sources within the multiform theology of the New Testament, Michael Quesnel emphasizes the converging points centered on the sacramental presence of the risen Lord. Sacraments are seen as authentic signs of the love of God. They are engaging signs and testify to the resurrection. He concludes his study with an important statement for today's sacramental practice: "The Sacramental dimension of Christianity is certainly one of its greatest originalities because it takes into account the integral man in his disposition, as well as in his body and in his communitarian life. To minimize it is to risk minimizing the resurrection."[6]

## Sacraments of Christian Freedom

The New Testament omits terms such as "mystery" or "sacrament" to describe a symbolic action. The Greek word *mysterion*[7] is mainly a Pauline concept, and *sacramentum* was used after the third century. Nevertheless, these terms provide a key to understanding a Christian sacramentality rooted in biblical sources. We will consider the original concept of the Christian mystery first and then the historical development of sacramentality in ancient Christianity to the fifth century.

## Christian Mystery

For St. Paul, mystery meant essentially the Christ-event, both in the eternal dimension of God's hidden design revealed in Christ (Col 1:27) and in the person of Christ (Col 2:2) as the temporal revelation of the divine salvific economy: "this mystery, which is Christ in you, the hope of glory" (Col 1:27). The Pauline letters connect the biblical mystery to Christ's *kerygma* (announcement). The mystery is the historical fact of Christ proclaimed by believers announcing the crucified Christ (1 Cor 2:2), and the mystery of God in Christ (Col 2:2). It is manifested by his revelation (2 Tim 1:9–10), and "presence" among his people (John 1:9–14).

Human reality filled with God's presence, "God-with-people" (Rev 21:3), is the historical presence of God that Christ epitomizes. This salvific history has a sacramental structure, for it reveals and makes present to humans the salvific plan fully manifested in Christ. Christ, the Incarnate Son, is the original mystery-sacrament of God's loving presence and action. The revelation of this mystery to the faithful indicates that "the community of believers takes part in the sacramental structure of Christ's event."[8] In fact, as the Gospel of Matthew says, "where two or three are gathered in my name, I am there among them" (Matt 18:20).

The community of believers participated in the sacramental reality of Christ, "the mystery of God" (Col 2:2) through different symbolic actions following their conversion: "Repent, and be baptized every one of you" (Acts 2:38). Specifically, when the Emmaus disciples recognized the Lord and he disappeared from their sight, the event was filled with sacramental significance. Such symbolic actions expressed the mystery of salvation and became the *mysteria* or sacraments of the Church.

The community adopted the term "mystery" from Greek philosophical tradition. It was a term that was used in secret cults, especially in its plural form *mysteria*, prior to the Christian era. Initially used by Greek philosophers, such as Plato, the term was introduced into the Old Testament apocalyptic texts, such as Daniel, and later into other books of the Hellenistic period. In using the term *mysterion* in the singular, Paul and the Synoptics followed the apocalyptic interpretation. At this early stage the term was not used in reference to Christian rites such as baptism and the Eucharist because Christians wanted to avoid the religious overtones of the term in the "esoteric rites of the mystery cults."[9]

The crucial link between mystery and its sacramental meaning originated from the participation of believers in the dynamic presence of the Christ-event. As Church of Christ, Christians became sharers in the divine lordship and the reality of grace manifested by the kingdom of God: "To you has been given the secret [or mystery] of the kingdom of God" (Mark 4:11). Paul based his conceptualization of mystery on the apocalyptic background of the Old Testament. Mystery pointed to the eschatological fulfillment of Christ realized in the community of his followers. This new eschatological vision made worship in the early Church radically Christian.[10] Believers shared in the "mystery" of the kingdom through faith in the proclaimed word and in the "memory" of the risen Lord kept alive symbolically and in action.

## Spiritual and Prophetic Sacramentality

Christ's jubilantly celebrated resurrection and imminent return inspired and fashioned a new style of worship that could be rightly characterized as eschatological. The christological mystery that transformed the Jewish disciples into witnesses of a new age was the symbolic creative power of the new order of worship. This theological and symbolic thinking effected a radical shift from Jewish as well as Gentile cultic worship.

The New Testament cultic concepts applied to Christ and the whole of Christian life rather than isolated ritual practices. The community eliminated references to cult, sacrifice, divine service, and priesthood. Christ was the temple, the altar, and the sacrifice. Also, believers imbued with the gift of the Spirit became acceptable offerings. There was no human sacralization of people, objects, or places because the fellowship was established by the eschatological reality of Christ. While drawing from prevailing realities, early Christians affirmed their independence from conventional sociological ritualism in favor of a spiritual and prophetic worship (1 Cor 16:22; Rev 22:20).

By the third century, a new eschatological conception had made it possible for the Church to take roots in culture. Christian writers such as Clement of Alexandria, Justin, and Tertullian typified the new movement of openness to culture and creativity within sacramental theology. Clement of Alexandria (ca. 150–215) used religio-philosophical terminology in an attempt to reconcile Christian *kerygma* and Neo-Platonist thought. Arguing against the mystery cults, he stressed the transparency of the christological mystery. Christ was for him the Mystagogue who initiated the believer into the mysteries of eternal truth.[11]

The resurrection event, now at the center of history in Christian consciousness, became the symbolic ritual paradigm around which the worship activity revolved and the basis for future worship structures. According to Jean Galot, "since the *parousia* was falling back to a more remote horizon, the Resurrection of Christ appeared with brighter radiance, as eschatology in action, a happening which directed the present and the future."[12] The re-conceptualization of *mysterion* by Greek-speaking writers inspired a new sacramental theology and practice. The "sign-synthesis" of the *mysterion* of the *Kyrios* (Lord) laid the foundation for a new orientation to the Christian *koinonia* (communion of the people of God). It also addressed the religious aspirations of converts from the mystery cults of Hellenistic antiquity.

## Mystery and Sacrament

The evolution of the sacramental mystery reflected the theological association of the economy of salvation in Christ with its symbolic ritual expression in the Christian communities. Mystery was applied to ritual actions, such as Easter ("mystery of the *Pasch*"), or the Eucharist. After the third century the Latin West translated mystery *(mysterion)* to sacrament *(sacramentum)*. Enhanced by a contemporary, flexible, and remarkably open-ended terminology, a profound and comprehensive sacramental vision developed during the patristic age and continued until the end of the fifth century. This terminology was not limited to mystery or sacrament.

Origen (ca. 185–254), whose theological thought was nourished by scripture, synthesized the early sacramental traditions. The *mysterion* concept linked scripture, Church, and Eucharist. Origen's biographer, Eusebius of Caesarea (267–340), used "mystery" in reference to the Eucharist, "the memorial of the great sacrifice of Christ," mandated by Christ and celebrated by the people. He explicitly related to the core of the contemporary sacramental vision:

> First our savior and Lord himself offered sacrifice, and now all
> the priests of all nations who derive their priesthood from him

do likewise, when in accordance with the canons of the Church they enact *the mysteries of his Body and Blood* under the symbols of bread and wine.[13] (italics added)

By the middle of the fourth century, Church vocabulary of the *mysteria* (mysteries) applied to baptism and Eucharist within the unifying conception of the mystery of the Church. Believers viewed the dynamic actualization of the economy of salvation in Christ, the sacramental rituals, as the *mysteria*. The primary purpose of the celebration of the mystery was to make historically present the accomplished reality of grace in the consecration of the believer.

Stressing this precise idea of consecration and commitment on the part of believers, Tertullian (160–240) avoided the literal translation of *mysterion* with the Latin word *sacramentum* (from *sacrare*, action by which something or someone becomes sacred). He initiated the vocabulary that prevails in Western sacramental theology. Originally *sacramentum* was a legal term with religious implications. It meant an oath taken by a person, especially a soldier or civil servant, pledging allegiance to his leader or to the emperor. For Tertullian, who was a lawyer and the son of a Roman officer, baptism and the Eucharist, as rites of Christian initiation, had the character of a consecration binding a person through a covenantal relationship to a new way of life in Christ. Attacking the initiatory rites of the mystery cults, he integrated biblical typology and secular imagery to Christian initiation elements.

Tertullian's focus on faith and its moral implications showed the richness of the concept of mystery. It also demonstrated the importance of uniting the mystery and sacramental focus. In fact, as Hotz affirms, the realization of *mysterion* produced the *sacramentum*. "Both concepts, initially used as synonyms, were never identical from the beginning but only analogous."[14] However, subsequent centuries neglected these theological and pastoral insights.

## Patristic Sacramentality

With the dawn of the Constantinian era (313), previous sacramental thinking resonated with the dominant historical-cultural context. The change from a charismatic approach to more elaborate ritualization was evident by the fourth century. This ritualization represented a different ecclesial and sacramental paradigm. The cosmic conception that centered on the *Kyrios* in patristic theology as well as in folk religious practices became the very matrix of the symbiosis between cult and culture.

Fourth- and fifth-century Christianity produced a new era of sacramental structures and a dramatic transformation of ritual patterns as the historical evolution of sacraments demonstrates. The need to integrate the Christian experience with local cultures and to clarify Christian beliefs and practices in response to the new Christian world were major factors behind sacramental developments.

The theology of the *mysterion* was the hermeneutic key that unlocked the nucleus of belief and created a more complete sacramental practice and theology. Christianity successfully supplanted the Greco-Roman pantheon and transformed it into a Christian ethos by sustaining the hope of salvation. It enriched the life of that society with the creative power of sacramental symbols. Now a genuine contextualization of the Christian mystery expressed in a rich variety of local cultural idioms emerged.

The vision of oneness and integrity in the mystery provided more meaning to the sacraments seen as the actualized, definitive, universal gift of salvation. This vision embraced all human and cosmic reality. Within given socio-cultural limitations, sacramental theology was liberating because it was grounded in a holistic existential condition in a meaningful way. Believers experienced freedom in the sacraments in terms of a symbolic encounter with the community as celebrant, and in the Spirit of Christ, who transforms, sanctifies, and gives freedom and life rather than in terms of causality (as in the Scholastics).

By incorporating the Neo-Platonic theory of symbols, the sacramental theology of St. Augustine (354–430) made further progress in the cultic interpretation of the notion of sign. Augustine represented a patristic sacramental synthesis that focused on the sacraments as signs of freedom. Utilizing human means—water, bread, and wine that have acquired a sacred meaning—the Church continually celebrates the freedom of the person. And Christian celebrations are "sacraments of Christian freedom."[15] The Augustinian idea of freedom has a theological dimension. Sacraments should be simple and more meaningful for Christians because they actualize Christian freedom.

Signs are the windows to human knowledge because created realities symbolize the invisible, the spiritual, and the eternal. In the language of creation people are able to read the divine message. However, God's revelation established new and clearer signs, "sacred signs" endowed with an eschatological meaning. "When signs refer themselves to divine reality they are called sacraments."[16] The word as sign is added to a material element, like water or bread, in the sacrament. The divine and visible "word" effects what the sacrament symbolizes, for it is the symbol of Christ as the agent of the sacramental action.

Augustine focuses on baptism and the Eucharist while including the larger sacramentality of all religious realities. Mystery includes the presence of the spiritual reality of the saving action of Christ within the Church and initiatory sacramental actions into that reality: "What is celebrated visibly...is understood vitally in Christ."[17] Christ is the Word-symbol of God, "the Wisdom of the unchanging God." Augustine's thought reflects the inspiration of the Pauline and Johannine Christologies. He stresses the need for personal faith and for communion with the community of the Church. His sacramental realism, a turning point in the clarification of the understanding of the mystery, had an immense influence on Western Christianity.

The fathers of the Church transformed ancient world views by expressing the Christian *kerygma* in terms of the cultures of their time. They were the theologians of the sacramental mystery in Christ, "the mysteries and sacraments of the flesh of Christ,"[18] of the "magnificent salvific mystery."[19] The quotations are from St. Leo (d. 461) and St. Ambrose (d. 397), who, as was the case with other Christian writers, interpreted the sacraments within the framework of biblical typology and symbolism.

## The Seven Sacraments of Christendom

The biblico-patristic sacramental vision builds on symbolic thinking and the biblical idea of mystery. However, the terminology applied to the sacraments remained varied and fluid long after the time of the great masters of the patristic era. Until the ninth century, authors such as Isidore of Seville (d. 636) and Paschasius Radbertus (d. 865) in the West stressed the mystery character of the sacraments. This was the heart of the common tradition in which Western and Eastern Christendom found a principle of unity. Although patristic sacramental creativity lost its centrality in the West, its heritage remained vital in Eastern worship.

In the eastern provinces of the Roman Empire, biblical *mystery-sacrament* theology retained its efficacy, producing the longest continuum in the sacramental tradition. The Byzantine tradition arose at the close of the early Church period when Constantine made Byzantium (Constantinople) the capital of the empire. Sacramental worship represented the very heart of the Greek and Byzantine ecclesial vision. It was centered on the mystery of the *Kyrios,* the Lord, who founded the unity and harmony of the cosmos.

## Scholasticism: Symbol to Dialectic

In the Latin West, the adaptation of the Aristotelian philosophical framework by the Scholastics of the thirteenth century created a new theological paradigm. The passage "from symbol to dialectic" (H. de Lubac) that led to a "logical" and static concept of sacrament characterized the new shift. The Aristotelian language of "substance" replaced ancient symbolic thinking. It was used to explain the real presence as in the case of the Eucharist. The question of the operation of the sacraments (the notion of cause versus the role of sign) dominated theological speculation so that "there was an inevitable tendency to ask how a sacrament works rather than why a sacrament is given."[20]

Thomas Aquinas produced the most complete sacramental synthesis by integrating Aristotelian categories with the sacraments and incorporating the Augustinian emphasis on sacred sign. Sacraments are efficacious signs of grace, for they cause what they signify. "Matter," the visible element as water, and "form," the words of the priest, are the structural elements of a sacrament that effect grace *ex opere operato.* In their symbolism, sacraments proclaim faith and express worship as signs of Christ's presence and of the unity of the Church.[21]

Scholastic sacramental theology addressed an overemphasis on the internal experience of the divine. It attempted to clarify the sacramental concept in the intellectual categories of the time. The specification of the actual number of the sacraments and their efficacy was an important development during this period. This is especially evident in the christocentric focus of Aquinas's theology. Peter Lombard (d. 1160) identified the seven sacraments; they were sanctioned by the second Council of Lyons (1274).

The age of Scholasticism (1055–1414) neglected the ancient tradition with its baptismal and eucharistic consciousness, its biblical and ecclesial roots, as well as its Spirit-related theology. It also disregarded the depth of the symbolic world view and the centrality of the paschal mystery. The Orthodox theologian Alexander Schmemann has perceptively described this medieval sacramental shift:

> The fatal error of post-patristic rationalism was the isolation of the sacrament from the liturgy as total expression of the Church's life and faith. It meant, in fact, the isolation of the sacrament from the symbol, i.e., from that connection and communication with the whole of reality which are fulfilled in the sacrament. By becoming a closed and self-contained "means of grace," a drop of reality in a sea of symbols, the sacrament deprived the liturgy of its proper function—to connect the sacrament with the Church, the world, and the Reign, or, in other terms, with its ecclesiological, cosmical and eschatological content and dimension.[22]

After the patristic age, the unified sacramental system structured and developed from the initiatory rite in the ancient Church became fragmented. In his study of the fundamental relationship among sacraments, Jungmann observed that "between the fourth and sixth centuries a true crisis of the penitential discipline of the Church developed."[23]

The theology of the role of the Spirit and the word became marginal in the Latin tradition. This development undermined the eschatological perception of the vision of the pilgrim Church. In addition, within Christendom in the Middle Ages, the hierarchy came to hold a hegemonic sacramental role. As Paul Tillich pointed out, "the hierarchy represented the sacramental reality on which the existence of the Church, state, and culture as a whole depended."[24]

The following time frame indicates the emergence of each separate sacrament as a formal rite. Historical theology attests that for each sacramental rite there pre-existed an actual ecclesial experience.

| SACRAMENTS | HISTORICAL SOURCE | YEAR |
|---|---|---|
| Baptism and Eucharist | New Testament (Easter) | A.D. 27 |
| Reconciliation | *Shepherd of Hermas* | 150 |
| Anointing | Apostolic Tradition of Hippolytus | 200 |
| Orders | Apostolic Tradition of Hippolytus *(episcopos, presbyteros, diakonos)* | 200 |
| Confirmation | Faustus of Riez | 500 |
| Marriage | Decree of Gratian | 1150 |

Theodore Klauser rightly characterized the High Middle Ages as a period of dissolution, elaboration, reinterpretation, and misinterpretation.[25] Since worship was not the action of a celebrating community, believers retreated to individualistic forms of spirituality outside communal worship. Over-sacralization and legalistic overtones combined with adopted analogies to the Jewish temple reached their zenith at this time. Jungmann rightly named these centuries before the Reformation "the flowering of autumn" when "there was a mighty facade and, behind it, a great emptiness."[26]

## Council of Trent

The Council of Trent (1545–1563) represented a strong self-reaffirmation of the medieval sacramental and hierarchical Church within its scholastic theological framework rather than a radical sacramental renewal. However, Trent did clarify the doctrine of the sacraments with some retrieval of patristic sacramental insights. This was true especially in regard to the Eucharist. Although overlooking the cultural and religious movements of the Renaissance, the council countered the Reformation and curtailed the flagrant abuses of the late medieval years. Trent represented a reaffirmation of traditional views and a self-reform within the Church. It articulated Catholic doctrine with extreme lucidity and invigorated pastoral care and spiritual piety. The council also stressed the importance of faith for sacramental participation.

The establishment of the Sacred Congregation of Rites by Sixtus V in 1588 represented to some extent a return to the Gregorian reform of the eleventh century. This model, called "Roman" in the official books, separated the total language of the symbolic forms from any local or historical creativity. While preserving the permanent structures, the restoration led to a standardization of liturgical practice and failed to foster a biblico-liturgical spirituality. Divorced from its direct biblical foundation, popular Catholic spirituality developed into extra-liturgical piety and devotionalism. The Roman Catholic liturgy lost its direct cultural and social relevance.

## The Reformation and Sacramental Practice

The Reformation brought about a radical break with the past—at least the medieval past—and, consequently, a break with the structural continuity of worship. It repudiated clericalism and medieval sacramental theology and practice. The reformers stressed the biblical foundation of sacrament, albeit interpreted in a literal way. While retrieving the power of the word and the need for a living faith, the process de-emphasized the sacramental and symbolic. Specifically, Protestant worship dramatically marginalized sacraments to the word. "That was certainly not what Luther, Calvin, Cranmer, or Wesley anticipated or desired," observed the Methodist scholar James White,[27] but it led to displacing the sacraments themselves. In fact, "the sacramental system was shattered." White adds:

> Reconciliation as a sign-act of setting one's conscience right before God was virtually abandoned, or rather, it was grafted on to the Eucharist making that sacrament even more penitential. The sacrament of healing, already seriously deteriorated into last rites, was abandoned though the human needs it ministered to obviously did not disappear. In Reformed and Free Church traditions, funerals tended to be secularized or omitted. Weddings and ordinations survived the least changed.[28]

At the dawn of modernity secular humanism produced a creative and emotional movement emphasizing the Christian liberty of individual conscience. Emerging religious fervor generated ethical and theological theories about the person and God, the Church and the sacraments.

Late medieval hypertrophic symbolism and piety, deemed magical and legalistic by the reformers, failed to inspire a theological vision of salvation history or provide a meaningful spirituality. "Consequently," as Paul Tillich puts it, "there is only grace, reunion with God. That is all! Luther reduced the Christian religion to this simplicity. Adolph von Harnack, the great historian of dogma, called Luther a genius of reduction."[29]

Lutherans focused on biblical proclamation and the nurturing of the faith of the people through the word. This undermined the eucharistic prayer of the early Christian tradition. The Lutheran movement centered on a fellowship "communion rite" that emphasized Christ's eucharistic presence. But the movement rejected the concept of "Mass as sacrifice." Lutheran worship in future generations would produce a completely new image of worship with richly didactic and musical elements.

The reformers' common stance against the ultra-sacrificial medieval theology focused on sacrificial categories and the eucharistic presence. In the judgment of James White, "Surely the greatest simple tragedy of the Reformation was the conflict between Luther and Zwingli over 'the concept of presence.'"[30] Luther failed to appreciate the theological value of liturgical structure, notably the actualization of the total salvific mystery and its eschatological dimension in the liturgical action. Calvin's theology of the Eucharist was relatively comprehensive given his profound patristic knowledge, especially his perception of the role of the Holy Spirit and the reality of the covenant. Similarly, John Wesley (1703–1791) tried to recover the notions of eucharistic presence and sacrifice of the early centuries.

Drawing upon biblical sources and tradition, many contemporary Protestant denominations seek models of sacramentality to express the mystery of God in the world. They are reviving the spirit of the early Church through the renewal of a biblically founded sacramental consciousness "so that the ancient face of the Church might be in some way restored and made whole."[31]

## Vatican II and Beyond

The Second Vatican Council affirmed the sacraments as a celebration of Christian mystery and presented them from the perspective of

salvation history. A primary contribution of Vatican II to the understanding of sacraments was the retrieval of biblico-patristic concepts of
mystery-sacrament. By reinterpreting sacraments from biblical sources,
the council challenged the faithful to appreciate the Church as the
sacrament of salvation: "Rising from the dead [Jesus] sent his life-giving
Spirit upon his disciples and through him set up his body which is the
church as the universal sacrament of salvation."[32] From the perspective
of mystery, the council linked all reality to the concrete event of Christ
and his universal sacrament of salvation, "at once manifesting and actualizing the mystery of God's love for humanity."[33]

Because sacraments are the essential elements of worship, worship
is a sacramental reality. Vatican II explicitly linked the sacraments to
salvation history, the center and climax of which is the paschal event. As
the universal sacrament of salvation, the mystery of the body of the
Church contains all the sacramental actions. They derive from Christ as
the head of the Church. Proclaiming and accomplishing the salvific
ministry of Christ, sacraments are an exercise of that ministry. Thus,
"the purpose of the sacraments is to sanctify people, to build up the
body of Christ, and, finally, to worship God."[34]

The sacramental theology of the council is christocentric and ecclesial. Because he is actively present, Christ is the personal salvific efficacy of the sacrament, that is, Christ in action ("He himself baptizes").
This presence is realized in different ways, particularly in the Eucharist.
Sacraments provide the privileged moment of the believer's participation in the fullness of redemption through the presence of the sanctifying power of the only savior and priest, Christ.

This salvific economy is also evident in the trinitarian and Spirit-
related perspective. The Holy Spirit as life, holiness, and perennial
renewal of the Church effects the sacraments. Sacraments bear and
give life as the embodiment of the presence of the one salvific reality of
the Spirit.

From the paschal mystery, the ultimate salvific event unifies and
makes concrete the sacramental vision because "from this source all
sacraments and sacramentals draw their power."[35] Each sacrament is a
concrete participation in the same unique mystery at pivotal moments
of the personal and ecclesial journey. And because the Eucharist is the
presence and summit of the celebration of the paschal mystery, all

sacraments relate to this central sacrament. As eminent signs of the final consummation of all things in Christ, sacraments are prophetic signs of future glory.

Vatican II stressed the relationship between faith and sacraments within the perspective of evangelization. They are "sacraments of faith," and thus "they not only presuppose faith, but by words and objects they also nourish, strengthen, and express it."[36] Through faith the believer is empowered and sanctified by grace in the mysterious self-communication of God through the sacraments.

## Contemporary Sacramental Theology

Prior to and after Vatican II, theologians emphasized the search for a new symbolic vision of the person and the study of historical and biblical sources. These dimensions stressed essential yet complementary aspects of sacramental meaning. In subsequent years, sacramental theology was at the forefront of theological research. It brought about a shift from the abstract and objective idea of the sacraments as exclusive "channels of grace" to a vision of symbolic actions and events of God's living presence in all of life. In searching for authentic sacramental understanding and practice, theologians developed different approaches. Among other post–Vatican II developments, Odo Casel stressed mystery-presence, Schillebeeckx the interpersonal encounter, and Karl Rahner the world and the word. Other approaches emphasized the esthetic dimension and God's glory (von Balthasar), the concept of symbol (Chauvet), liberation (Segundo), postmodernity (Osborne), celebration (Reinhold), cosmic and human sacramentality, the experience of women (feminist theology), and the emergence of a multicultural Church.

Despite the shortcomings of Odo Casel's research on the "mysteries" of Hellenism, his work on the concepts of mystery in early Christianity had great theological influence. Its substance became part of the council's constitution on the liturgy. Casel also retrieved the central concept of "memorial" *(anamnesis),* the action by which God's salvific will is present in the worshiping community and points toward the eschatological fulfillment.[37]

Schillebeeckx presented the sacraments as the "encounter" with God through the glorified Christ present in the re-creating activity of

the Holy Spirit.[38] He focused on the Christ-sacrament as the manifestation of God's love for humankind, a manifestation culminating in the
paschal mystery. Christ is the central sacramental reality and visible
manifestation of all ecclesial sacramental actions. The Church actualizes the sacramental presence of the risen Lord in the world through
history by involving believers in the original sacrament of Christ. In
addition to articulating the Christ-Church-Person mystery, Schillebeeckx affirmed the importance of active faith as integral to the individual's sacramental participation.

Rahner employed the interpersonal encounter model to portray
Christ as the radical sacrament and the Church as the fundamental
sacrament for the salvation of the world. Sacraments are acts by which
the Church actualizes its essence fully for the salvation of the people of
God. Rahner's sacramental vision is relatively broader, because it
encompasses a theology of creation that stresses the centrality of sacramentality. The world is sacrament and is graced at its roots, for God is
really present in the world through humanity's ongoing communion and
cooperation with God in history. Jesus Christ is the source and fulfillment of the liturgy of the world, expressed symbolically in sacramental
worship. And sacraments, which realize God's saving work, are both
acts of Christ and acts of the Church, which continues his redemptive
work in time and space. Rahner also explicated the mutual relationship
between the word of God and the sacraments that embody it. Sacraments are word-events revealed in Christ to be celebrated by the
Church as the sacramental word of Christ. As a "kind of sacrament,"
the Church is "the bearer of that eschatologically victorious word that
creates salvation."[39] A sacramental sign is an effective sign.

Both Schillebeeckx and Rahner emphasized God's absolute mystery
and the transcendent source of salvation. They also bridged the sacred
and profane in recognizing that God graciously draws near to us and
salvation occurs in the midst of our daily activities. Worship can and
should be the basic meaning of everything we do, an experience of
interpersonal communion with the absolute, holy mystery.[40] The
insights of these modern theologians and many others represent a leap
forward in our understanding of the essential and existential meaning
of sacramentality in relation to the word of God and evangelization, and
its effect on the renewal of styles of worship and of sacramental life.
They have also contributed to the furthering of ecumenical dialogue.

## Ongoing Sacramental Renewal

Recent reinterpretations of the sacraments require us to focus on the christological mystery as the dominant theme and on a praxis ecclesiology. These reinterpretations are multidimensional. Sacraments interpret the Christian economy of salvation within the global richness and complexity of contemporary cultures. The Second Vatican Council not only inaugurated a new era of Roman Catholic ecclesiology, it also represented a truly catholic and potentially "global" council. Beyond the medieval and post-Tridentine ecclesiology, another religious paradigm has emerged. At the heart of it, the power of the sacramental tradition has become the best hope for the concrete renewal of Christian ecclesiology.

The "revolutionary" openness to a world Church allows the development of a complex process of inculturation. By integrating faith and culture, inculturation expresses a basic principle of the mission of the Church in all its dimensions, especially in the areas of the evangelization of culture and social transformation, ministry, and sacramental renewal. In this sense, inculturation is the ongoing process of integrating the sacramental experience into the culture of the local people.

Inculturation bridges the gap between Western liturgical tradition and various historical and cultural traditions. "The Church is faithful to its traditions and is at the same time conscious of its universal mission; it can, then, enter into communion with different forms of culture, thereby enriching both itself and the cultures themselves."[41] The very nature of sacramental worship and its ultimate goal, the evangelization of all cultures, necessitates an ongoing dialogue between gospel and culture grounded in the reality of the incarnation of Christ. In particular, the evangelization of the Western secularized and fragmented culture of disbelief requires radical renewal. The 1972 restoration of the Rite of Christian Initiation of Adults (RCIA) provides a basic model for that renewal in that it focuses on the baptismal foundation of sacramentality with which Christian faith begins.

The history of sacramental practice shows that it has the potential for transforming society and cultures when it embraces the concrete realities of human existence called to conversion in the light of Christ. Religious life and mission might be possible in certain instances despite irrelevant rituals, but not without an experience of God. Nevertheless, history demonstrates that a vital corporate life of worship is the matrix for a transforming Christian vision of reality and the building of a unified spiritual culture. Ancient Christianity, in particular, is a telling example of the formative and transformative power of Christian sacramentality. Referring to the birth of Western Christendom, Christopher Dawson observed: "The Church possessed in the liturgy a rich tradition of Christian culture as an order of worship, a structure of thought and a principle of life."[42]

# 3

# Basic Dimensions
# of Christian Sacramentality

The sacraments celebrating the paschal mystery of Christ stand at the heart of the life of the Church. The 1985 Synod declared: "In the presence of the Word of God the Church celebrates the mysteries of Christ for the salvation of the world." The statement expresses the core of the liturgical and sacramental mystery and provides a basis for exploring the origin, diversity and number, nature and dynamics of the sacraments from the anthropological, christological, and ecclesial perspectives of subsequent discussions. These perspectives offer a key for envisioning sacramental renewal.

The present study extends beyond the traditional elements defined by the Church, especially those outlined by the Council of Trent (1545–1563). These traditional elements are the dogmatic constants of the post-patristic tradition of the Church: The sacraments are sacred signs, all instituted by Christ, that confer the grace that they signify; they are seven in number and are necessary for salvation, especially baptism; God's offer of grace acts in them by the very fact of the actions being performed *(ex opere operato);* baptism, confirmation, and holy orders confer an indelible sacramental character, or seal, and thus they cannot be repeated.[1]

## The Origin of the Sacraments

We will begin by presenting three principles at the root of Christian sacramentality. Then we will draw upon historical insights regarding the order and significance of the seven sacraments. All Christian traditions agree on the fact that Christ is the origin of the sacraments. The differences arise in regard to the extent and meaning of this affirmation. The *Catechism of the Catholic Church* roots sacraments in Christ's life and its culmination in the paschal mystery, the foundation of the Church's sacraments. As St. Leo the Great (d. 461) stated, "what was visible in our Savior has passed over into His mysteries."[2] Thus, the Catechism retrieves the core of the biblico-patristic tradition by stressing the context of salvation, human history, and the Easter event. These are paradigmatic loci for interpreting the institution of the sacraments.

## Sacramental Principles

Modern interdisciplinary scholarship on the sacraments presents a comprehensive description that avoids both juridical concepts and the strictly historical idea of the institution of the sacraments in previous theologies. However, theological differences arise from individual interpretations. This demonstrates that the fundamental question of the origin of the sacraments is complex and needs to be considered from all major perspectives. In what follows, three interrelated and complementary perspectives will be considered: (a) the dynamic relationship of Christ-Church-sacraments, (b) the continuum of the paschal mystery from the Lord's Supper to Pentecost, and (c) the praxis of the early Church as the community of the Holy Spirit.

## Christ, Church, and Sacraments

Focusing on the dynamic relationship of Christ-Church-sacraments highlights the three levels of sacramentality in God's salvific economy. Essentially, sacraments originate from the institution of the Church. Christ, the "original sacramental word of ultimate grace" (Rahner) instituted the Church as the fundamental sacrament, and the sacraments themselves as the "self-expressions" of the Church.[3] In Rahner's words, the "institution of a sacrament can . . . simply ensue from the fact that Jesus founded the Church with its nature as original sacrament."[4] Schillebeeckx adds another dimension to the dynamic sacramental relationship between Christ, the Church, and the sacraments as specifications of the original sacrament. "Christ himself, in some cases specifically, in others merely implicitly and without particularization, determined the sevenfold direction of the signification which is brought out in the ecclesial saving acts that are the sacraments."[5]

## Paschal Mystery

The second perspective refers to the continuum of the paschal mystery from the Lord's Supper to Pentecost. The liberating and victorious *Pasch* of Christ provides the paradigmatic source and foundation of the sacraments. The link of both Church and sacraments (baptism and Eucharist) to the pierced side of Christ on the cross (John 19:34) was a central theme in biblico-patristic theology. As the preface for Pentecost in the Roman missal proclaims, "Today you sent the Holy Spirit on those marked out to be your children by sharing the life of your only Son, and so you brought the paschal mystery to its completion."

Reduced in the past to the passion of Christ, this above perspective reflects a modern retrieval of a biblical concept ("Christ our Passover," see 1 Cor 5:7) developed by the ancient tradition starting with Melito of Sardis (d. ca. 190). By "paschal mystery" he meant the total history of salvation, or "the cosmic mystery of Easter"; "the new and ancient, eternal and temporal, perishable and imperishable, mortal and immortal."[6] The context provides a unifying foundation for the sacramental organism in its creational, christocentric, and Spirit-related dimensions.

The concept of the paschal mystery extends to the Church and sacraments through which the salvific economy remains visible and is accomplished in time and space. Thus, the paschal mystery becomes the "source event" of sacramental liturgy. John Corbon writes: "This unprecedented power which the river of life exercises in the humanity of the risen Christ—that is the liturgy! In it all the promises of the Father find their fulfillment (Acts 13:32). Since that moment, the communion of the Blessed Trinity has been spreading ceaselessly throughout our world and flooding our time with its fullness. Henceforth *the economy of salvation takes the form of liturgy.*"[7]

## Life and Spirit

The concept of a faith community living out the historical dimensions of the gospel in the power of the Spirit is a critical theological perspective.

The Christian sacraments responded and celebrated the liberating praxis of the historical Jesus. In addition, the early community, empowered by the Spirit of the risen Lord, reflected on this praxis and recognized particular gestures as uniquely sacramental. The numerous meals of Jesus' ministry were certainly related to his institution of the Eucharist. During meals, Christ made manifest God's mystery of salvation and progressively disclosed to his disciples the covenantal Eucharist. However, the Eucharist in the full sense of its meaning and celebration is a post-resurrection event.

There is a general consensus among biblical scholars that New Testament narratives referring to baptism and to the Eucharist may differ from Jesus' actual words at the institution. Rather, they represent a post-Easter faith interpretation, the embodiment of his mandate by the early communities, and the inspirational core of their developing practice. In a conclusive statement on the eucharistic texts, Betz affirms:

> The New Testament institutional narratives were not first formulated by their witnesses, but as a part *(ein Stück)* of the gospel prior to the gospels—and indeed the oldest part—stem from the community worship. Their linguistic coloration reaches back into the Palestinian community. They portray the Last Supper of Jesus, not in a historical way with all its significant details, but simply in the light and the perspective of what was of value for the liturgical celebration of the community.[8]

In building up the body of the Church in that foundational period, the disciples acted "in the name of the Lord Jesus" and "through the power of the Spirit." Their actions, therefore, cannot be understood as simply repeating words or imitating actions. Rather, they give vital expression to the mission of the only mediator before the Father, the ultimate source of the sacramental event.

As a summary statement on the origins and life of the sacraments, the following emphasizes the importance of stressing the reality of the trinitarian mystery, and in particular the role of the Holy Spirit in the sacramental event:

> When we speak of Christ as the symbol and sacrament of God's presence, we are drawing out the implications of the Trinitar-

ian belief. To clarify this truth within its New Testament context, two complementary Christologies must be recognized. Logos ("descending") Christology begins with the redemptive task of Jesus and the ensuing mission of the Holy Spirit. Spirit ("ascending") Christology emphasizes the sanctification of the humanity of Jesus created by the Godhead as such, that humanity having been elevated to union with the Word who assumes it. If we respect the message of both Christologies, the action of the Spirit clarifies our understanding of Christ as the basic sacrament of God's presence.[9]

## Significance and Symbolic Meaning of Sacrament

The shift from a broad and concrete understanding of ritual event in patristic writings to relatively abstract and technical conceptions of the sacraments occurred when medieval scholastic theology adopted precise definitions and vocabulary for the sacraments. Three major issues arose regarding sacraments: the marks, efficacy, and specific number. From the Augustinian definition "visible sign of invisible grace," Peter Lombard (ca. 1110–1160) distinguished sacraments from other sacred signs by introducing the concepts of causality and efficacy of a sign. He asserted that "One speaks of sacraments in their proper sense when a sign of God's grace, which is a form of invisible grace bearing its likeness and being its cause, is present."[10] Along with Peter Lombard and other theologians of the time, the father of canon law, Gratian (twelfth century) established the number seven. In the subsequent century, drawing upon older traditions, Thomas Aquinas integrated the seven sacraments into a vision of the meaning of human existence embraced by the mystery of Christ. Sacraments are the extension of the mystery of Christ, and their efficacy derives from his passion. Thomas's anthropological approach is only an argument of convenience relative to the number seven, an appropriate number that represents all of human existence. In fact, "spiritual life resembles certain conformity with corporeal life."[11]

These theological developments determined the sacramental world view and practice that characterized the Roman Catholic Church until Vatican II. They were codified at the Council of Trent in 1547.

We can better understand these developments if we see them as reflections of the prevailing quest for doctrinal clarification taking place in the social context of the time. The medieval symbolic mind gave great importance to numerical patterns. The number seven was a symbol of perfection because it was the sum of three, meaning divinity, and four, meaning created perfection. Numerical patterns and specifically the mystical significance of the number seven were a reflection of a larger cultural background. "The pre-Christian philosophers, the Jewish Platonist Philo, and Augustine ascribe to the number seven the symbolic meaning of totality, universality and inclusiveness."[12] Albert the Great (d. 1280), who taught Thomas Aquinas, wrote: "seven were the virtues, seven the gifts, seven the beatitudes, and seven the sacraments."[13]

In contrast to the tradition of the first millennium, this sevenfold vision of the economy of grace saw the sacraments as independent realities loosely related to the baptismal and eucharistic center rather than as an organic and complex body of mysteries.

The insistence of the Council of Trent on the number seven is important in terms of reaffirming the principle of Christian sacramentality in general and also in ecumenical terms, since the reformers recognized only baptism and the Eucharist as true sacraments. The purpose of Trent's teaching was to safeguard the essential sacramental rites according to the common doctrine of the Church. It depended theologically on previous medieval developments. The council avoided sanctioning the whole of the Church's tradition of the sacraments, but rejected the possibility that there were "more or less than seven." In enumerating the sacraments, the council unambiguously identified purportedly authentic sacraments while describing the significance of each one: baptism, confirmation, the Eucharist, penance, extreme unction, holy orders, and matrimony (Session VII, Canon 1).

In conclusion, Trent's teachings should be interpreted in a qualitative sense, in terms of the necessity of an all-embracing sacramental economy of salvation communicated through different signs at "all the stages and all the important moments of Christian life,"[14] rather than in a quantitative or reductive way. The consensus among modern theologians, including those of the Orthodox Church, is virtually unanimous in stressing the symbolic meaning of the number seven.

## Seven Sacraments: An Organic View

The question of the diversity and number of sacraments, like the question of their institution, was formally raised after centuries of historical development. It was an *a posteriori* question that was used by medieval theologians in their search for the meaning and function of the sacraments. The bewildering process of sacramental clarification mirrors the debate and final acknowledgment of the inspired books or canon of scriptures within the Church.

As demonstrated earlier, sacraments originate from the source event of Christ and his Church. Furthermore, like the communal stages of ritualization found in all religious cultures, sacraments are not arbitrary inventions, but respond to profound structures of the human spirit. All sacraments celebrate the unique saving mystery of Christ, although access to the mystery depends on an individual's disposition and the needs of the Church with God's grace. Therefore, the present study is conducted within the triple and complementary perspective of person, Christ, and Church. The reflection that follows looks first at the sacramental structures of life and second at the organic world view of sacraments and sacramentality.

### Sacramental Structures of Life

Sacraments exist for people. They originate from life and transform life because they are embodied in the existential and historical structure of human beings. They are anchored in the most basic human experiences, for "what is involved in sacrament is what is most basic to our very being as humans," and thus they "have some special relationship to the fundamental process of humans being human."[15] Sacraments spring from pivotal human experiences and have an intrinsic anthropological dimension to which they relate. Christian sacraments have equivalent rituals in many other religions; these rituals include initiation into a community, rites of passage and healing, celebration of a sacred meal. Religious ritual behavior is a universal phenomenon that follows certain patterns. As religious anthropological experts assert, it relates to something in the foundations of the human soul.

The Christian sacraments share in some of these ritual patterns and symbolism.

The celebration of basic human experiences creates a diversity of sacramental moments. The experiences can relate to such things as biological stages (from birth to death) or institutional needs (such as authority or service). They are moments of human transformation through the presence of God's self-giving. They involve the total person in a mysterious way and at a deep level of consciousness, even when the person is not aware of them. In Pauline terminology, sacraments are *kairoi*, or moments of grace, like rebirth in the Spirit of God (baptism) or participation in Christ's priesthood (ministry). Various experiences essential to the person and the community make up the complex sacramental organism.

Far from devaluing the Christian ethos, the human dimension incorporates a Christian vision of creation and relates to the foundation of the incarnational and paschal mystery of the sacraments. The world as the arena of our experience with God calls for symbolic expression, especially at key moments of our personal and communal journey. In fact, the human journey initiates sacramental moments. "These nodal points are the sacraments of life *par excellence* because in them is transparently condensed the life of the sacraments: the presence of the Transcendent, of God."[16]

The diversity of sacraments reflects ritual content, meaning, and symbolism in the celebration of these prime junctures of life in community. The perspective of the sacramental nature of the Christ-event is essential both in terms of the unity and the diversity of the sacraments, as previous discussion on the primordial sacramentality of Jesus Christ demonstrates. The paschal mystery recapitulates Christ himself and his salvific ministry in the integrated vision of the seven sacraments.

Every sacrament draws its meaning from the salvific words and actions of Jesus' public ministry. As Osborne notes, Jesus is the most basic component of every sacrament, and he becomes therefore,

> the baptized one,
>
> the confirmed one,
>
> the really present one,
>
> the reconciler,

the priest,

the lover,

the healer.[17]

Except in the case of the eucharistic institution at the Last Supper, identifying Jesus as the root-sacrament is the expression of a central truth rather than an indication that he actually instituted them by certain words and actions in a particular historical setting.

As exemplary source events, the mysteries of Christ and his prophetic ministry give new meaning to the fundamental needs of humanity. These source events include his own baptism as anointed with and led by the Spirit, the *agape* of his body and blood "given up and poured out," his exercise of forgiveness, his love for sinners and mission of reconciliation, his power over evil and sickness, and his vision of conjugal love. Nevertheless, the soteriological and existential meaning of these events and actions is demonstrated by the central memory of Easter and Pentecost.

The words and actions of Christ's visible humanity passed over into his sacramental mysteries and are continued by the Church "until he comes." In constituting itself in history, the body of the Church has a diversity of fundamental situations and vital needs that require successive sacramental actions. It is an organic diversity, because all sacraments depend on, have their center in, and lead to the Eucharist, the fullest expression of the organism of the Church.

> In this organism a single vital sap, a single flow of life from him who is at once head and fullness (or fulfillment), a single life-giving breath (the Spirit) that works differently in the different members, makes it possible for the whole to grow harmoniously, through the ministry of all, to the full stature of the perfect Human Being.[18]

Each sacrament is a particular projection within the diverse situations of the life of the Church of the one and total sacrament, Christ. Theologians have compared the latter to the single white light of the sun which, as it passes through a prism, produces the former as a spectrum of colored light beams, the sacraments.

## An Organic World View

It is important to develop both the christological and the anthropological foundations of the sacraments noted above in order to grasp the larger picture of the sacramental organism. They are inseparable in an actual celebration. The sacraments refer to the great events of Christ's life from which they all draw meaning and power. For this reason, they have been called acts of Christ or signs of the mystery of Christ. Simultaneously, sacraments are worldly realities, because they embrace the whole range of the stages and events of human life and utilize earthly elements like bread or water. They celebrate the rhythms of human existence. As symbolic and festive actions, sacraments express the rhythms of human life, because they relate to the key moments of the human process. Revealing and realizing the dimensions of God's reign, sacraments relate to the core of the person's entire structure of experiences.

Christ is the heart of the living organism of the sacraments, and consequently the main referent in terms of importance and centrality. Although sacraments primarily celebrate the paschal mystery, its ritual expression encompasses different signs and corresponding content. Specifically, the Eucharist is the primary expression of the realization of the reign of God and the paschal mystery. And although dependent on the christological dimension, different human experiences and historical process have different degrees of poignancy and meaning. Thus, initiation into the shared values and identity of a community is of greater importance than the ritualization of any other stage of life. Clearly, the living substance of a baptismal consciousness has to a great extent been lost, manifesting a great spiritual vacuum in Christianity today. And yet in the absence of baptismal consciousness, sacraments such as marriage and holy orders may falter spiritually.

As stated above, christological and anthropological foundations establish the organic interdependence of all the sacraments and their relation to the life of the Church and the world. As Schmemann affirms concerning the early Church, "sacrament was not only 'open' to, it truly 'held together' the three dimensions or levels of the Christian vision of reality: those of the Church, the world, and the Reign."[19] In this sense, sacraments are interdependent and are mutually inclusive "organisms."

The christological foundation shows *a circular system* of sacraments organized around the central nucleus of the Eucharist.[20] The

Eucharist is the primary sacramental action flowing from the paschal mystery like a river of life, the life and body of Christ. It is therefore the source of the salvific efficacy of all sacramental actions. Thomas Aquinas taught that, "The sacrament of the Eucharist is, in an absolute sense, the greatest of all the sacraments...all the other sacraments are ordered to this one as to their end."[21]

The anthropological foundation establishes *the linear system* of the sacramental organism through life's stages and rhythms. Baptism is the gateway to the sacramental structure. It provides the essential basis for future sacramental life, which includes certain phases and events as well as the daily living experience of the people.

The major sacraments of the tradition of the Church and early Christianity were Eucharist and baptism with confirmation. As sacraments of the risen Christ, and by the power of the Holy Spirit, they initiate and bring to maturity the individual Christian and build up the body of the Church. The Eucharist is the axis of the sacramental hierarchy.

Current sacramental theology stresses the importance of considering the sacraments in terms of rhythms rather than as isolated realities: in fact, they are internally and organically related. The above description of the organic view of the sacraments can be seen in the following schema:

## Sacramental Organism

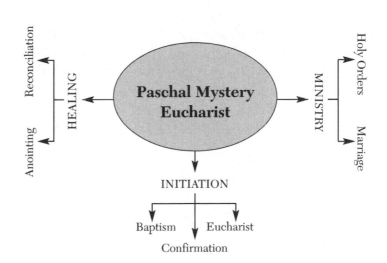

No schema captures the complexity and richness of Christian sacramentality in its integral whole. Similarly, sacramental definitions and concepts fail to adequately express the living mystery of Christ in us. *A sacrament is mystery in action.* The following ecclesiological categories articulate major areas of this mystery in action, the living of the same mystery from its source, the paschal mystery. The sacramental structures include initiation, foundations, healing, and ministry, and the service of communion, all of which are brought to fulfillment through the paschal celebration of death.

## SACRAMENTAL STRUCTURES OF CHRISTIAN EXISTENCE
### *LIVING THE PASCHAL MYSTERY*

### *THE INITIATION CHURCH*

**Master Symbols of Paschal Freedom:** ritual structures of transformation through a process of progressive spiritual growth and conversion to Christ. Initiation, the work of the Holy Spirit, is a scripturally grounded action experienced through symbols and the support of a community of faith. Following is the threefold structure of the Great Sacrament of Christian Initiation:

**Baptism-Confirmation**: incorporating into the priesthood of Christ the whole people of God (Church) in a personal relationship with him as teacher, sanctifier, and leader, through the action and gifts of the Holy Spirit, to witness to the freedom of the children of God in the family, in religious communities, in the Church, and in the world.

**Eucharist**: being nurtured to live out Jesus' own prophetic initiation and enter his life of communion and sacrifice; being empowered to witness to the love of God in this world.

### *THE FOUNDATIONAL CHURCH*

The Eucharist is the heart of the Christian existence, a call to growth and maturity into the word and the body of Christ. It is also the perpetual sacrament of Christian initiation, by which we are being transformed to live out Christ's total self-giving presence in the Christian community and in the world. The Eucharist is the summit and font of Christian sacramentality and the Church's ministry.

## THE HEALING CHURCH

**Master Symbols of Re-conversion to Holiness and Wholeness:** ritual structures counteracting the realities of sin and sickness.

**Reconciliation**: reconciling persons with God and neighbor, renewing the process of their conversion and reorienting their lives toward the freedom of God's reign.

**Anointing and Healing**: restoring the physical and spiritual health of the seriously impaired person who shares in the paschal mystery through suffering.

## THE CHURCH AT THE SERVICE OF COMMUNION

**Master Symbols of Life Self-giving and Leadership:** deep ritual structures of the stages of initiation and incorporation into a community of love (domestic Church) and service (church leadership).

**Marriage**: bonding a relationship of self-donation for life in the vocation, communion, covenant, sacrament, and partnership of marital life and love rooted in Christ, lover and spouse.

**Holy Orders and Ministry**: serving and acting in the person of Christ —head, teacher, sanctifier, and leader—as member and servant-leader of his body, announcing the gospel, building the community, and presiding at worship.

## THE FULFILLED CHURCH

**Symbols of Paschal Fulfillment:** Ritual structures of hope through the stages of dying. *Viaticum:* comforting the dying and feeding them for the passage through death to eternal life. *Funeral:* celebrating the paschal mystery of new life through the passage of death.

These sacramental structures represent the common link among sacraments and establish the mutual relationship of their specific functions within the Church. The Eucharist is central to the realization of the Church as sacramental event: the Church makes the Eucharist and the Eucharist makes the Church. The paschal mystery is the fountain and medullar axis of the sacramental organism. And the presence of the paschal mystery in each sacramental event makes the sacraments the paradigm of Christian spirituality.

The proposed schema has certain limitations, however. The life of the Church extends beyond sacramental ritual, and worship encompasses life as a whole, beyond formal rites. Thus, a sacrament is a total experience endowed with the power to give ultimate meaning to the world's history and to the experience of God in ordinary life. These sacramental themes depend on a particular understanding of the Church. They vary according to various and broader-based traditions.

There are other ways of categorizing sacraments. Specifically, the Eucharist as a repeatable sacrament of initiation can be viewed as a sacrament of daily living. Marriage also fits this category. Furthermore, a greater variety of complementary ritual actions, not sacramental in the technical sense, could be included within the above schema. Some have been developed recently, such as ministerial commissioning, or rites of passage (adolescence, mid-life, and late-life). Others, such as religious profession, are as ancient as the sacraments themselves. Furthermore, the use of sacred signs or sacramentals, always present in the Christian experience, demonstrates the Church's belief in an all-embracing concept of living sacramentality.

The traditional Catholic concept of character or "seal" is another way to differentiate the sacraments. Three sacraments, baptism, confirmation, and holy orders, are consecratory and imprint an indelible spiritual mark on the recipient, consequently eliminating the need for recurrence. In a one-time event, the consecrated person is called to share the priesthood of Christ in a permanent relationship.

The concept of "seal" draws upon New Testament sources. "But it is God who establishes us with you in Christ and has anointed us, by putting his seal on us and giving us his Spirit in our hearts as a first instalment" (2 Cor 1:21–22; cf. Eph 1:13–14; 4:30; Rom 4:11). St. Augustine developed this doctrine against the heretical practice of rebaptizing. He insisted on the radical and irreversible effects of the signs of baptism and ordination. In the sixteenth century, the Council of Trent based its definition of the doctrine of character building on historical tradition. Recently teachings of the Church have reasserted the theology of character. "This configuration to Christ and to the Church, brought about by the Spirit, is indelible; it remains for ever in the Christian as a positive disposition for grace, a promise and guarantee of divine protection, and as a vocation to divine worship and to the service of the Church."[22]

## Sacraments as Encounters of Freedom and Grace

In what follows we will explore the inner nature of the sacraments, their purpose in the divine economy of salvation, and human response through faith and commitment. We will consider sacraments from the point of view of *faith, salvation,* and *eternal life.*

As stated earlier, sacramental reality is total. It celebrates the full Christ-event in the cosmic biblico-patristic sense, although it goes far beyond the celebration and even the consciousness of believers. It provides a vision of "totality," because it embraces the whole of life. As a transformative power, sacramental life permeates history and culture, person and society, both present and future. Sacramental reality is human, cosmic, and historical as well as invisible, spiritual, and transcendent.

The sacramental event is a gift and a call—God's self-gift of grace to us calling us to the ways of his reign. It is the divine presence and encounter that manifests, realizes, and celebrates the saving action of Christ and the work of his Spirit in people's lives. A sacrament is an effective and vital sign of the transforming and sanctifying power of God made present in the human experience of daily living.

These descriptions of sacrament illustrate its breadth and complexity and indicate that, as mystery, the reality of a sacrament is multidimensional. For theological clarification, two definitions will be explored. The first derives from a text of St. Augustine, who described sacrament as a sign of grace: "A visible sign of invisible grace."[23] The second is both traditional and modern because it reflects the broader and original meaning of sacrament, which Vatican II recaptured from the biblio-patristic sources: "A sacrament is a worldly reality which reveals the mystery of salvation, because it is its realization."[24]

The latter definition applies to Christ, Church, and sacraments, although in different ways and according to three different aspects of sacramentality. Christ in his humanity is the only mediator and source of grace. Sacraments are worldly and effective signs of God's grace. This definition implies the essential elements of the traditional Catholic doctrine, as stated by the Council of Trent: "Sacraments contain the grace which they signify." It also includes the idea of effectiveness, because the worldly reality realizes the salvation that is signified according to the economy of salvation.

The divinization of the human person is the goal of the mystery of lived sacramentality. Thus, the heart of sacramental theology, rooted in the human reality, has to express the ongoing relationship of God's self-giving. God touches first the person's heart, but expects a human response. He invites us to the intimacy of divinity, a profoundly liberating experience. "Sacraments are 'powers that come forth' from the body of Christ, which is ever-living and life-giving. They are actions of the Holy Spirit at work in His body, the Church. They are 'the masterworks of God' in the new and everlasting covenant."[25]

### Signs of Faith

The mission of Christ and the apostles, as well as the mission of the prophets before them, was the radical renewal of humanity, conversion through acceptance of the word of God. This was the heart of Jesus' and the apostles' preaching of the good news: they "welcomed his message and were baptized" (Acts 2:41). The sacramental actions were born from this mission; they embodied it and demanded a living faith, which in turn found expression in them.

The presence of faith is very important, not only because it has a central position in the economy of salvation, but also because sacraments are fundamental expressions of faith *(sacramenta fidei)*. As Christian churches acknowledge in modern times, behind the sacramental crisis there is a crisis of faith. This crisis is only too evident in Western secularized society. If today's sacramental structures are to touch the lives of people, they need to embody again Jesus' praxis of renewal and transformation from the roots that a lived faith allows. Faith is an integral part of the sacramental process. It precedes, accompanies, and flows from the celebration.

New Testament texts referring to baptism and the Eucharist show that faith was essential in the practice of the primitive community. The sacrament was viewed as a gift of grace, and the experience of the sacrament implied a confession of faith. Converts received baptism by professing the Father, the Son, and the Holy Spirit (Matt 28:19), and the paschal faith, a gift of God, led to baptism and participation in the breaking of the bread (Acts 2:41–46). Several texts imply the following sequence in the life and growth of their mission, as in Acts 2:37–38: announcement of Jesus' *Pasch*, faith and conversion, sacramental celebration, and the reality of God's salvation through his Spirit.

Faith is a complex reality. It is primarily a gift of God that empowers the person to surrender to God's offer of salvation in a personal relationship of love and trust. Faith also implies a humble attitude and a vital commitment to follow the way of Christ and to live according to his Spirit. It inspires both discernment of the present reality and commitment and solidarity toward others: "The only thing that counts is faith working through love" (Gal 5:6), because "faith by itself, if it has no works, is dead." (Jas 2:17). In the second millennium, the idea of a rational or intellectual sense or mere assent to a doctrine devalued the covenantal and personal meaning of faith.

The Christian living tradition attests to the conviction that there is no sacrament without faith and no faith without sacrament. Their symbolic movement is the two-way movement of Christian life. Both are actual encounters of God's offer of salvation. In speaking of the sacraments, Vatican II describes this intimate relationship: "[The sacraments] not only presuppose faith, but by words and objects they also nourish, strengthen, and express it. That is why they are called sacraments of faith."[26]

First, a sacrament *presupposes* faith because faith is the root and foundation of the symbolic action that leads to the mystery. Faith originates in the good news, a blessing for those who accept the apostolic witness (John 20:29). The Emmaus disciples (Luke 24:1–32) exemplify the nature of sacramental faith. It is God's gift ("their eyes were opened") that allows the mysterious encounter ("and they recognized him"), but he had to leave them to allow the celebration in faith of the living memory ("he vanished from their sight").

Faith *precedes* the sacramental celebration and is *required* by it, not only in the objective sense of its power of sanctification that originates in God whom we cannot please without faith (Heb 11:6), but also in the subjective sense of the natural receptive attitude of the participant. Faith enables the person to transcend the apparent value of the human action. Because of faith, the action becomes a mysterious vehicle of God's encounter, an action that allows the person to accept the word of God and to live in an experience beyond words and objects. Thus, faith is not just a previous condition, but the fundamental attitude needed for the initiatory process of conversion by which the person becomes part of the vivifying paschal source, Christ.

Second, sacraments *nourish* and *strengthen* the participant's faith. This is one of their primary goals. If liturgy is the school of faith, sacraments are its cradle. The Church gives birth to faith through the baptism of the Spirit that seals the faith of the believer. But sacraments are also the heart of the community of faith shared primarily through them as "corporate works done in faith."

Third, as corporate work, sacraments *express* both the faith of the Church, which precedes the faith of the participant, and the life in faith of the participant who professes the faith of the Church.

A sacrament is an ecclesial event and always has a communitarian dimension. "When the Church celebrates the sacraments, she confesses the faith received from the Apostles—whence the ancient saying: *lex orandi, lex credendi* [the law of prayer, the law of belief]."[27] This is the objective or ontological meaning of the faith required by the sacraments. They are sacraments of the gospel that give rise to the Church and are ultimately founded on the paschal event. Therefore, this symbolic action has to be "in the name of the Church" and vitally connected to it. Through faith related to actual human experiences, sacraments empower and enliven people's lives. Outside of this connection, celebrations can degenerate into individualistic sacramentalism. As Segundo points out: "Our difficulty and our crisis with respect to the sacraments does not stem from the sacraments or their decrepit liturgical entourage. It stems from the fact that we do not see the necessary correspondence between what they signify and the reality of the Christian community in the world."[28]

## Signs of Salvation

The affirmation that sacraments are efficacious signs of grace is a fundamental principle of Catholic sacramental theology. Grounded in a biblical background, this medieval affirmation represents a theological reflection that inspires the teachings of the Church. It also includes three other traditional affirmations of faith: (a) the sacraments confer the grace that they signify; (b) their efficacy rests in the actions being performed; and (c) they are necessary for salvation. These affirmations of the Council of Trent should not be narrowed into rationalist categories of utilitarian efficacy, but should be understood from the basic gratuitous experience that comes from God and graces all human life.

### Grace

The biblio-patristic affirmation of faith is essential because the stress on automatic and juridical efficacy obscures the meaning of grace as a free and transforming gift. Grace is not granted against a participant's will. In popular understanding, this rational approach has often degenerated into faithless mechanical sacramentalism.

Grace is God's self-gift to humanity and to the individual person. This personal self-communication of God to humans was revealed in the salvific *oikonomia,* the dispensed mystery (Eph 3:9): "God's love has been poured into our hearts through the Holy Spirit that has been given to us" (Rom 5:5). The New Testament employs a comprehensive view of grace, utilizing a rich terminology (such as gift, life, mercy, and action) and applying it to the life of the trinitarian mystery in the believer. Grace is God's loving liberality and the new life for the Christian, a salvific design that transforms human experience and also makes human beings "participants of the divine nature" (2 Pet 1:4). This divine self-communication is seen in the New Testament as bearing the spiritual potential for the transformation by and action of the Spirit, all of which imply the human response of faith. In the thought of Odo Casel, Christ himself is primarily that grace, the eternal today of God actualized through the sacramental mystery.[29]

Sacraments are events of grace because they are the total mystery of Christ in action communicated to us—in Paul's terminology, to be in him and to live in him, so that "Christ is formed in you" (Gal 4:19). This form of "Christification" is brought about by our sacramental encounter with the redemptive *Pasch* of Christ through baptism (Rom 6). Through it one can live a new life in the Spirit: "You were washed, you were sanctified, you were justified in the name of the Lord Jesus Christ and in the Spirit of our God" (1 Cor 6:11). There are various sacramental texts, especially in the writings of St. Paul and St. John, that speak of the gift of sanctifying grace through the vivifying presence of the Spirit, that is, the total gift of grace.

New life in Christ and the Spirit has a sacramental structure. It begins with incorporation into the Church by baptism and with the guiding presence of the Spirit, who is the source of every sacramental grace. The believer, bearer of the Spirit of God, is gifted and empowered to share the mission of Christ in the world and to participate as a member of the celebrating community in the Eucharist. Strengthened by these and other means of sacramental communication, the faithful "are called by the Lord to that perfection of sanctity by which the Father himself is perfect."[30]

The above reflection leads to the classic principle of Catholic sacramentality: "sacraments confer the grace that they signify." They are mediations of God's uncreated grace. The power of grace, though, comes from the salvific history recapitulated in Christ's way of being: his relationship to the Spirit, his giving of himself, his loving, serving, forgiving, and restoring—all of which are freeing. Christ's total solidarity with the human condition—except in sin—exemplifies the diverse and concrete ways in which God's universal grace is made present. These are sacramental projections of the undivided reality of grace.

God's grace is always available. It is effective in different ways. Moreover, it has the potential to bring about the total integration of the human being, which results in complete freedom in Christ. Considered in its source event of the *Pasch* of Christ, the condition of grace and salvation has a double character. Grace is ontological, that is, universal and real, "once and for all," accomplished by the man-God Christ as the beginning of life and a new freedom (Gal 5:1). The ineffable mystery of liberating grace, which is already acting in the hearts and lives of people, makes us children of God. It is sacramental because actual grace does not exist outside the sphere of the Christ (in the cosmic sense) or without concrete and historical realization in various human situations. "As we wait in joyful hope," there will always be new conditions that call for liberation by grace as an empowering and transforming force. Grace enables us to be authentically free within human limitations. It prefigures, moreover, future universal liberation both in the individual and within society. The risen Christ is truly present in the world.

## Grace and Sacraments

The second affirmation of Catholic belief presented above—the efficacy in the actions being performed—also has to be considered against the background of the ontological and sacramental character of salvation and grace. Sacraments confer grace "by virtue of the performed action" *(ex opere operato).* By their very nature, symbols are performative and expressive. As sacramental actions they are acts of the symbolic language the Church uses to express its mystery in virtue of the saving work of Christ. By the power of the Spirit, the sacramental word and symbol contain and exhibit Christ's revelation and action in the world and in history.

The interpersonal action of grace can be considered a cause as well as a condition. As a cause, the effective event of grace depends exclusively on the free and creative power of God promised through the mysterious action of Christ's Spirit in the Church rather than on any particular ritual. God's unconditional availability in Christ is encountered anew and made visible as a sign of grace. And the holiness of the people is not the holiness of the ritual. An action cannot be an effective encounter of grace without the personal response of faith, which is in itself God's gift. In stressing God's free initiative, we preclude any extrinsic or manipulative interpretation of sacramental efficacy.

In the thirteenth century, Thomas Aquinas noted that sacraments act "by the action which Christ himself performed."[31] Medieval theologians commonly used this argument to counter heretics for whom sacramental validity was exclusively dependent upon the merits of the minister and the subjective faith of the recipient. The Council of Trent adopted this expression to stress the infallible sacramental action of grace, in this case against the Protestant belief that sacraments were mere external signs to stir up faith, and that only faith was necessary for the grace of justification.[32] Trent also highlighted the need for faith, "without which no one has ever been justified."[33]

God's free offer of grace is neither conditioned by the human will nor limited to sacramental moments. God's self-communication is omnipresent to his creation, "made new" in Christ, "the beginning and the end" (cf. Rev 21:5–6). The whole of creation is immersed in the mystery of God. In this sense, Rahner speaks about the universality of grace and its larger cosmic history. Thus, God's offer of grace is always available and always present. "The world is permeated by the grace of God . . . The world is constantly and ceaselessly possessed by grace from its innermost roots, from the innermost personal center of the spiritual subject."[34]

## Sacraments and Salvation

Finally, sacraments, and in particular baptism, are necessary for salvation. With this statement the Council of Trent reaffirmed the traditional view of the sacraments as pivotal within the Christian process of salvation. This was to counter the reformers' stress on word and faith as sufficient and exclusive *(solo verbo, sola fide)* components of salvation. Trent affirmed the intrinsic connection between the salvific work of Christ and its celebration in baptism.

Considered from its source as the unconditional offer of God's self gift to human beings in the eternal and present event of Christ, salvation is universal. "For since Christ died for all . . . we must hold that the Holy Spirit offers to all the possibility of being made partners, in a way known to God, in the paschal mystery."[35] In practice, it is not possible for every human being to come to the knowledge of God's revelation to the world in Christ and experience him in his sacramental mysteries. For this reason the teaching of the Church affirms that salvation is also possible without a real encounter of the sacraments of faith, because "God showed mercy to all humankind" (Rom 11:31). As Vatican II stated: "Those who, through no fault of their own, do not know the Gospel of Christ or his Church, but who nevertheless seek God with a sincere heart, and, moved by grace, try in their actions to do his will as they know it through the dictates of their conscience—those too may achieve eternal salvation."[36]

## Signs of Eternal Life

In their dynamic structure as signs of hope, sacraments are endowed with an eschatological symbolism and thus have the potential to express the eternal mystery of the person in God. As acts of Christ, they make present in the midst of the community the dimensions of God's reign, which in turn reveal the depths of the mystery of the person. Sacramental revelation encompasses the threefold dimension of God's reign: as liberating memorial rooted in the past, graced realization in the present, and hopeful anticipation of the future. As signs, sacraments in fact symbolically proclaim, actualize, and celebrate the dawning of the messianic era.

Building on Thomas Aquinas, classic theology interpreted the dimensions of the reign by stressing the threefold symbolic function of the sacraments. As *commemorative signs* of the great biblical events they center in Christ, who is both the origin and foundation of the present reality of God's spirit. As *demonstrative signs* they manifest the historical reality of grace at work. As *prefigurative signs* they anticipate prophetically the fulfillment of future glory. In the words of St. Thomas, "a sacrament is a sign that commemorates what *precedes* it—Christ's Passion; *demonstrates* what is accomplished in us through Christ's Passion—grace; and *prefigures* what that Passion pledges to us—future glory."[37] This threefold sacramental reality announces the prophetic promises held out for future glory, "already here" but "not yet" within the historical and transitory existence of the human person.

A sacrament is a prophetic sign of the world to come because it signifies what the world is meant to become. It symbolizes the call, the potential, and the process of becoming until the person's destiny with God is reached. The dimensions of the mystery of God proclaim the ultimate possibility of the mystery of the person. A "sacrament bodies forth a utopia that has its basis in the risen Christ and represents man's fulfillment. A sacrament, says Moltman, is already running ahead of itself and of our experience. It thereby brings a dynamism into play, creates a hope, and sets man on the road to his realization and fulfillment."[38]

Although it has been neglected in some modern studies of eschatology (narrowly conceived as the study of the last things), this threefold dimension of the sacramental sign represents a central teaching of the Christian tradition. By focusing on the last things, namely death, judgment, heaven, and hell, theologians have overlooked the very basis and horizon of Christian eschatology, the Christ-event of Easter. Christ is the realized *eschaton,* absent and yet present in the Church through his Spirit. It is "in the Spirit" that sacramental actions are signs of eternal life. Through him the entire Christian existence is sacramental and shares in the absolute future of Christ.

A great malady of our secularized world is the loss of an eschatological consciousness. Influenced by secularization, the Christian community and its celebrations suffer from the same malady. In contrast, New Testament accents are consistently eschatological. Christ is presented as the eschatological prophet who fulfills the messianic expectations of the new Israel. Early Christianity internalized this consciousness and saw itself as the definitive gathering of the community of the "later times" (Dan 7).

St. Paul's message is also strongly eschatological. Christ's Easter sheds a new light on the meaning of time. In him the old world has passed away and the new has come (2 Cor 5:17). Time is radically relativized, because he is "the fullness of time" (Gal 4:4; Eph 1:10). In fact, he is now the total revelation of God's plan for humanity. As God directs history toward its final goal, humanity hungers for the definitive inauguration of God's reign, "so that God may be all in all" (1 Cor 15:28). The eschatological hope between the event of Christ already in "the end of ages" (1 Cor 10:11) and at the same time not yet fully realized until its final "epiphany" (2 Tim 4:8) maintains a dialectical tension because of the resurrection of Christ and the coming of the Spirit.

Under the influence of this paschal experience, the *ekklesia* (the people of God) interpreted the symbolic actions of Christ and his disciples, namely the "breaking of bread" and the baptism of the Spirit, as eschatological symbols. The Church called believers to conversion through acceptance of the promise of God in Christ, baptism, and reception of the gift of the Spirit (Acts 2:38–42). The same people shared the *agape* of the reign, the Eucharist as pledge of the resurrection (John 6:54). The eschatological accents that permeated the communal prayer of early Christians are clearly evident: "*Marana Tha,* Come Lord" (1 Cor 16:22; Ap 22:17, 20).

Vatican II tried to recapture the christological, ecclesial, social, and historical dimensions of an eschatology already operative in salvific history. The Constitution on the Church in the Modern World especially stresses the unity of the secular and religious realities in the mystery of Christ. It avoids a dichotomy between spirituality nurtured in sacramental life and secular involvement and recognizes the social and cosmic dimensions of the eschatological horizon. The constitution respects the proper balance of all these elements and takes seriously the Christian responsibility in the rebuilding of the secular order. In this regard it states: "Let there, then, be no...pernicious opposition between professional and social activity on the one hand and religious life on the other. Christians who shirk their temporal duties shirk their duties toward their neighbor, neglect God himself, and endanger their eternal salvation."[39]

This healthy tension toward the future "as we wait in joyful hope" is also presented in the constitution on the liturgy. Sacramental liturgy is once again seen as an icon that remembers *(anamnesis)* Christ's *Pasch* and anticipates the *parousia,* the unveiled presence of total fulfillment. It contemplates the existence of the person, in the present, within the universal presence of the resurrected Christ lived *in sacramento;* and in the future, as an unimaginable encounter *facie and faciem* with God. Thus, in sacramental life the eternal mystery of the person finds ultimate meaning in Christ.

# 4

# Sacramental Mystery
# and Christian Spirituality

The rediscovery of sacramental roots in spirituality is the Christian response to the great yearning for mystery, meaning, and freedom in the modern world. Various theological factors account for this rediscovery. There has been a general trend toward greater integration between scripture, sacraments, and theology, on the one hand, and sacraments, human existence, and spiritual life on the other. Ritual reform and theological research have placed sacraments at the center of ecclesial life in its ministerial, spiritual, and educational mission. Thus, the Church has today a fresh sacramental face. Its fruits will be manifest as sacraments become a genuine expression and realization of the ministerial and spiritual life of Christian communities.

This chapter explores the sacramental roots of spirituality in ordinary life, its relationship to sacraments, and the characteristic features of sacramental spirituality.

## The Sacramental Dimension of All Life

The ambivalence in world views and personal values translated into a crisis of sacramental practice has also affected individual capacity for sacramental life. Specifically, the process weakens the capacity of the modern person for understanding the meaning conveyed by traditional sacramental symbols (meal, community, ministerial mediation) and their implications (communion, conversion). In addition, psychological conditioning and sociological trends affect people's ability to appropriate traditional sacramental symbols and Christian values.

The change in religious consciousness requires the Church to develop an appropriate theology and praxis of sacramental celebrations incarnate in the concrete and ordinary experience of the people. Sacraments are an indispensable source of spirituality because they manifest the mystery of the reign of God in key human experiences. Consequently, we need to have a holistic sacramental spirituality, experienced as integral part of real life and expressed prophetically in the language of our culture.

Considerable advances emerged following the theological developments and renewal of Vatican II. The council's primary purpose was to revitalize the vision of sacramentality as constitutive of the whole of Christian existence and as a manifestation of God's grace in all aspects of life. God's gift of salvation is at work in the secular world and its history, the arena where the experience of faith is lived and celebrated. Sacraments should be viewed as grace-filled actions rooted in key human experiences through which the living presence of God is revealed and realized at the heart of life.

Karl Rahner associates the redefinition of grace events in both secular and liturgical life "as a Copernican revolution in modern man's understanding of the sacraments."[1] God's self-gift is continually offered to all as an invitation to share in the new creation in Christ. In the process, God empowers and heals both human experiences and day-to-day sacramental encounters. The human story is linked to the divine as people radically encounter, through faith, God's presence in the ordinary and mundane.

Human life is graced by the mystery of God. As people of hope we believe that all creation and human experience are potential sacraments of communion with God. However ambiguously, both creation and experience embody the mystery of the divine. D. Staniloae's contention sheds light on the Western quest for sacramental spirituality: "The entire world should be appropriately seen as the visible part of a universal and permanent sacrament, and all human activity as sacramental communion, divine."[2]

In the sacraments we express what we already are and what we are meant to become. The sacraments manifest pre-eminently the gift of divine life working in the very web of our lives. Although the mystery of God is also veiled in the sacramental signs, through them we can hear his voice, we can contemplate his glory, we can touch and live the supreme experience of the mystery of God in us.

As Rahner has stated, the world is graced at its roots (his notion of the "supernatural existential"), and consequently "the world and its history are the terrible and sublime liturgy."[3] Sacramental liturgy is the symbolic expression of what he calls the "liturgy of the world," whereby salvific grace happens in the midst of secular lives. This sacramental theology of the world does not diminish the importance of worship. Michael Skelley, in interpreting Rahner, says: "The more actively we participate in the liturgy of the Church, the more actively we will participate in that silent and secret liturgy, which is the deepest meaning of our lives. And then the entire universe will be transfigured in our communion with God."[4]

One of the features of early Christianity was the unity between sacramentality and human existence. Every baptized person shares in the priesthood of Christ (1 Pet 2:5) and thus all of his or her life is potentially a priestly act. Christ broke the barriers of the sacredness of the temple that separated human beings from the holiness of the totality of all creation and everyday things. The life of Christians is an authentic liturgy because through Christ and with Christ they "continually offer a sacrifice of praise to God" (Heb 13:15). St Paul adds: "Present your bodies as a living sacrifice, holy and acceptable to God, which is your spiritual worship" (Rom 12:1). Christian life should be seen in an eminently cultic perspective. It is a eucharistic thanksgiving for the revelation of the love of God the Father, in the election in Christ to holiness (Eph 1:4–6; 5:2) through the indwelling of the sanctifying Spirit.

The Second Vatican Council reaffirmed the universal call to holiness by stressing the link between sacramental and secular life. This represented a return to the biblical sources and to the patristic theology of mystery, re-emphasizing the foundational basis of spirituality in sacramental experience and celebration. Vatican II viewed the sacraments, particularly the Eucharist, as the celebration of human life and the source and summit of all Christian life. It envisaged a sacramental theology that integrates the sacraments and life in general, overcoming the traditional separation of the sacred from the profane, of the spiritual from the secular. This dichotomy was the result of an individualistic way of understanding spiritual life, an approach that divorced the liturgy from spirituality, spirituality from secular involvement, and secular involvement from liturgy.[5]

## Sacraments and Spirituality

Sacraments are at the forefront of the contemporary renewal of Christian spirituality. Current movements of spirituality intersect in the ecclesial life of the sacraments and are rejuvenated by it. Vatican II's fundamental emphasis was on the "mystery of salvation" in Christ whose presence we encounter both personally and communally. The process established the foundations for an integral ecclesial spirituality: the Easter-Pentecost event celebrated sacramentally and lived out daily by the baptized. What emerged from the council was a doctrinal and pastoral convergence that reshaped Catholic thinking and was gradually adopted by many traditional Protestants.

The pioneers of the liturgical movement sought to rejuvenate and deepen the spirituality of the faithful and transform the social order by rediscovering the sacramental core of the liturgy. Similarly, Vatican II envisaged an ever-increasing vigor within Christian life. The sacraments are the foundational and indispensable source of the true Christian spirit and the primary means by which "the faithful are enabled to express in their lives and manifest to others the mystery of Christ and the real nature of the true Church."[6]

The council's statements affirm the theological truth that the actualization of the mystery of Christ in the sacramental celebration and in the life of the community is the central and fundamental reality. This reality is the source and climax of the perfect expression of the spirituality of the Church. Sacramental liturgy should provide the basic spirituality for the Christian community, the faithful. It is the paradigm for all forms and schools of Christian spirituality.

Spirituality is a relationship with God and an orientation toward the divine. Spirituality empowers the person in all the dimensions of his or her life and has elements that are common to most religions. Specifically, Christian spirituality concerns the faith experience of Easter, actualized in the life of the baptized by God's gratuitous self-communication through the Spirit. This faith experience is motivated by love, establishes an intimate relationship with God, and is rooted in, nurtured by, and shaped through the sacramental celebrations.

In the New Testament the concept of spirituality is linked to a Spirit-related reality. A believer's union with the Lord is realized by the indwelling of the Spirit of God: "Anyone united to the Lord becomes one spirit with him" (1 Cor 6:17). Consequently, rebirth in the Spirit through baptism allows the Christian to worship in spirit and truth (John 4:24). In fact, baptism is the doorway of spiritual life.

The universal call to holiness and emphasis on sacramental spirituality of Vatican II significantly transformed the conception and expression of spirituality. However, an integration of life and worship goes beyond an acceptance of these two basic tenets. Eucharist and the sacraments become the orienting and transforming center when they intersect with Christian ministry and are reflected in the whole of life.

The sacraments of baptism and Eucharist integrate the various dimensions of spirituality as foundations to holiness in the world, public mission, and service to the whole people of God. The Church refers to liturgy as the "source and summit" of Christian life because it is the "normal setting" for and "a more encompassing term for the sacrament."[7] Sacramental spirituality is liturgical spirituality. Liturgy celebrates sacraments as a profound source of Christian spirituality, and "acts of Christ" through the symbolic self-expression of the Church. Referring to Christ's power, Peter Fink states: "Sacraments achieve their effect by signifying, and their signifying power works to transform us into Christ, in Christ's way of being, Christ's way of praying, Christ's way of acting, Christ's way of loving, healing, forgiving, serving."[8]

Vatican II prophetically articulated this central and incarnational role of liturgy as "the summit toward which the activity of the church is directed . . . the source from which all its power flows."[9] Sacramental liturgy is normative because it expresses the permanent memory of the total Christ-event through the Church. It is also the preeminent school of the community of faith and Spirit-led discipleship: "And since we are that Church in whom Christ lives, the liturgy . . . is the most perfect expression and realization of the spirituality of the Church."[10]

The sacraments penetrate all dimensions that make up the existential and ultimate realities of the Christian journey, including the personal and social, prophetic and institutional, historical and cosmic. In sum, "the total Christ-event that is the liturgy, and in which we are constantly involved, extends far beyond the consciousness of faith and the celebrations of believers. It assumes and permeates all of history, as well as all human beings, and each of them, in all their dimensions, and the whole cosmos and all of creation."[11]

## The Essential Characteristics of Sacramental Spirituality

Sacramentality is rooted in the profound structures of a humanity divinized in Christ, the primordial sacrament. Thus sacramentality is the ultimate force of all spiritual experience. Sacraments lose spiritual efficacy to inspire and transform people's lives if they become religious formalities. A review of the central features of sacramental spirituality highlights the full mystery of sacramentality as it celebrates God's work, and also as it nurtures the Christian community. These features are *trinitarian, paschal, Spirit-related, baptismal, evangelical, and formative-transformative.*

### Trinitarian

All Christian liturgy is trinitarian in structure. Participation in the trinitarian mystery, frequently seen through different prisms, always constitutes a source of spiritual dynamism in the Church. The New Testament links the sacrificial Eucharist to the revelation of the salvific economy of the Holy Trinity. In Hebrews, Christ as *pontifex par excellence* offers a spiritual and voluntary sacrifice of prayer and supplication (Heb 5:7; 9:14; 10:7, 10).

"God is revealed in Jesus, and Jesus himself is the nature of God's relationship to the world."[12] The *Logos* is God's definitive mediation continued through the Holy Spirit, the artisan of sacramentality within the Church. The sacramental mystery in liturgy is the work of the Triune God. The Catechism explains: "The Father always hears the prayer of his Son's Church which, in the epiclesis of each sacrament, expresses her faith in the power of the Spirit. As fire transforms into itself everything it touches, so the Holy Spirit transforms into the divine life whatever is subjected to his power."[13]

As noted above, the spiritual life of a Christian is a liturgy because through Christ and with Christ he or she "continually offer[s] a sacrifice of praise to God" (Heb 13:15). Christian life from a liturgical perspective is a Eucharist that reveals the glory of the living God in the election of Christ in holiness (Eph 1:4–6; 5:2) through the indwelling of the sanctifying Spirit. This trinitarian and liturgical perspective was fundamental in ancient Christianity.[14] Worship ontologically transforms Christian living, since secular activities are immersed in the sanctifying action of worship.

There is a correlation between awareness of transcendent reality and sacramental mediations as bearers of that divine reality. The alienation of secularized modernity stems from the denial of the mystery that is both transcendent and sacramental. Alexander Schmemann addresses this issue from an Orthodox world view of "the world as sacrament." He sees all persons as priests standing in the center of the world receiving it from God and offering it to God. The world becomes meaningful only when seen as the "sacrament" of God's presence. He maintains that "the world was created as the 'matter,' the material of one all-embracing Eucharist, and man was created as the priest of the cosmic sacrament."[15]

The sacramental view of creation and human life as bearers of salvation and mystery is central to sacramental theology. Because sacraments arise out of human interaction with the world and God, our experience of God is sacramental. The appreciation of sacraments as encounters with God builds on a similar recognition of ordinary life as a sacramental encounter with the holy. In these encounters the human heart cries out for union with God because God speaks first. Thus, sacramental spirituality is properly a dialogue, "but it is a dialogue in which God must speak first; otherwise there can be no conversation. God opens the mystery of divinity and the human heart to receive that revelation."[16] The Johannine writings endorse the view of the world renovated in Christ as "sacramental."

## Paschal

The total Christ incarnated in our flesh, cross, and glory, and forever present through God's Spirit is the foundation of Christian spirituality. The sacraments, as acts of Christ, our Passover, are the beginning, pledge, and consummation of the Christian journey. Baptism and Eucharist are the central symbolic memory (*anamnesis*) of the paschal event. They are the eternal present, the celebrative *hodie* (today) throughout the time and space of God's total self-gift to us in Christ. Vatican II rooted the source of all Christian sacramentality in the gratuitous and transforming power stemming from the paschal mystery. Spirit-filled with love, believers encounter divine life in the God who joins us in word and sacrament, and who reveals himself acting in the *Pasch* of our everyday life. Believers enter through the sacraments into Christ's resurrection, the hope of the world.

The Christian ideal is based only on one person, Christ, rather than on an abstract expression, whether philosophical, mystical, or ethical. Also, it is not the result of one's initiative or will, or the reward of one's ritual self-righteousness. The Christian's goal, as St. Ambrose, says is "to encounter Christ in His mysteries."[17] The liturgy, therefore, supports sacramentally the christological focus of Christian spirituality. As noted by the Second Vatican Council: "Receiving the offering of the spiritual victim, he may fashion us for himself as an eternal gift."[18]

### Spirit-related

Easter and Pentecost are the foundational events of Christianity. Contemporary theology stresses that the Eucharist's origins are basically post-resurrectional. The paschal framework applies to all sacramental actions, as it includes the outpouring of the Spirit at Pentecost and his active presence in the community of believers. "Jesus poured forth his Spirit as an integral part of his paschal *transitus* [passage] to the Father, both on the cross (John 19:30) and on Easter Sunday itself" (John 20:22).[19]

According to the New Testament, Christians represent the actual holy temple of worship that the Holy Spirit creates. Human life rooted in Christ is a sacrificial offering to the Father in the Holy Spirit. The Eastern churches have kept this theology alive by recognizing the Holy Spirit as the artisan and enabler of the sacramental actions. The work of the Spirit in the *epiclesis* ("calling down upon") actualizes Christ's priestly action in the sacraments and creates the unity between the life of worship and ordinary life. The presence of the Spirit of the risen Christ in worship constitutes the dynamic soul striving toward perfection, because through him (Spirit) all our life is elevated and transformed into a spiritual journey. And through the action of the Spirit, the giver of faith, worship accomplishes the dynamic relationship between creed and life. As an Easter octave prayer states, "...[that] they may grasp by deed what they hold by creed. "

## Baptismal

A baptismal consciousness is of paramount importance for every aspect of Christian life. Baptism establishes a believer's covenantal relationship with Christ. It is the historical continuation of the prophetic action of Christ as savior of the world. Baptism, including eucharistic initiation, is the wellspring of sacramental spirituality and the foundation of our common call to witness to Christ within a faith community. The sacramental experience, especially its eucharistic center, stands at the heart of both holiness and mission. Since baptism is the foundation of God's call to holiness and mission, the Eucharist is the center, "for in the most blessed Eucharist is contained the entire spiritual wealth of the church."[20] And bearing witness to God's love for the world is a necessary consequence of the sacramental experience of that love.

A shared baptismal consciousness developing from the new rites of adult initiation (RCIA) encompasses all spheres of life and Christian praxis. The process leads to a shift from the old clergy-laypeople opposition to the new *communio* vision of community-ministries whereby all believers share in Christ's priesthood. In this regard Vatican II envisioned a partnership between priest and laity in the ministry of worship, service, and evangelization. "The service of laity in the world is not purely secular service, it is salvation service which at the same time is ecclesial service. The laity's secular service also shares in the Church's sacramental-symbolic character as the universal sacrament of salvation."[21]

## Evangelical

Worship is the sacramental wellspring of evangelization because it proclaims the reality of the risen Lord. As both word and event, sacramental worship constitutes the greatest self-expression of the Church's central mission of evangelization. The word becomes the saving event and God's self-revelation to the community. God's nurturing and prophetic word transforms participants into evangelized, and evangelized into evangelizers.

The life of the Church is made possible through two essential and symbolic realities: word and sacrament. And while faith gives rise to community, the community is always called to be *ekklesia* (always in need of the real living out of Christ's mission). The word of God and sacrament are intimately related and complement each other. In the words of Karl Rahner: "The power to preach the word of God by the authority of God and his Christ, and the power to administer the sacraments to men are two basic constituents of its [the Church's] essence."[22]

The power of evangelization rooted in authentic sacramental life depends on making the intrinsic interrelationship of word and sacrament real and dynamic. As the central mission of a faith community, evangelization needs to be rooted in sacramental experience and faith-filled proclamation. Both faith and the sacramental mystery empower people with an evangelical and prophetic vision, a new spirit and freedom that is a true Christian spirituality. There is an "unbroken continuity" rather than opposition between God's word and sacraments. Michael Schmaus has observed that "even the use of signs is fundamentally a saving preaching of the word. The use of signs is part of the Church's task in preaching the Word, not vice versa."[23]

The ecumenical Dombes Group has cogently presented the interrelation between word and sacrament, the prophetic character of the sacrament, and the sacramental character of the word. It asserts that: (1) the sacrament has an intrinsic relationship to the word; (2) the sacrament is constituted by the word; and (3) the sacrament is the word of salvation.[24] Sign and word are, therefore, essential elements of the symbolic movement of God's self-giving to the community.

Scripture is fundamental to the liturgy, because the liturgy takes most of its elements and its contents from the Bible. The Bible in fact has always been and will always be the authentic sacramentary. As St. Jerome poignantly notes, "ignorance of the Scriptures is ignorance of Christ"[25] and, therefore, ignorance of the sacramental mystery. The liturgy is the faithful guardian of scripture and above all its best interpreter. "Sacred scripture is of the greatest importance in the celebration of the liturgy,"[26] since liturgical spirituality is biblical in all respects.

## Formative-Transformative

Sacramental liturgy is the "school of the Church," because it accomplishes the dynamic relationship between creed and life. Pfatteicher notes how it "provides a framework within which the deepest mysteries of Christianity await discovery."[27] The primary effect of the Eucharist and all the sacraments is that, as the third eucharistic anaphora says, we "may be filled with his Holy Spirit and become one body and spirit in Christ." It engages the whole person and community in a symbolic and real way. It is both action and contemplation, the vehicle of meaning and transformation that has the potential to integrate disparate concepts and culture, the personal and social, the spiritual and secular. It is through worship that all those aspects of the total mission of the Church intersect. By God's grace, the formative-transformative power of worship touches the inner core of our lives.

Inner freedom and true evangelization of every sphere of life require genuine intimacy with the living God. Sacraments are signs of the reign of God, signs that elicit a response—particularly conversion—to Jesus' preaching. Conversion *(metanoia)* involves the unconditional return of the person to God through a profoundly new way of relating to the world around him or her. Sacraments initiate and support personal conversion to Christ, the baptized and the anointed one by the Holy Spirit (cf. Mark 1:9–11), who became immersed into God's own being. The faithful become immersed in Christ, anointed in his Spirit and united with God. A person can descend to the depths of self and rise to the heights of God. There is no spiritual growth without sincere conversion accomplished by the Holy Spirit in real life and in the sacramental events.

Personal conversion is the fruit of God's life and action in us. Communion in the body and blood of Christ transforms believers into what they receive. In the sacraments we encounter the fullness of love and life. The encounter with the liberating love of Christ, made present and real in the experience of the believer, is a source of healing and sanctification. It is a formative and transformative action in the inner life of the Christian. When our thoughts and ways match our words, sacramental spirituality becomes personal. By means of sacramental worship, soul and body, total self and community, human society and cosmos are raised and assumed into the heart of the Church, Christ.

Sacraments express, form, and build the corporate identity of the lives they transform. The creative and dynamic link between the sacraments and community is reflected in the New Testament and in the praxis of early Christianity. St. Paul stresses the organic unity among the community members begun in their initiation through baptism and continued through their transformation into Christ's body by the Eucharist (1 Cor 11, 12). Augustine attests to the same profound unity, especially between the eucharistic body and the ecclesial body: "He entrusted to us in this sacrament his own Body and Blood which he turned into ourselves."[28] "Hence, if you are Christ's body and members, your own mystery is placed on the Lord's table: you receive your own mystery. You say amen to what you are and by saying it you subscribe to it."[29]

Any authentic spiritual process builds up the body of the Church. Since the Church is the "sacrament of unity," the spirituality originating in sacramental life and supported by it is ecclesial. The sacraments are symbols of ecclesial freedom and transformation. They are redemptive symbols by which the Church heralds the good news, proclaims God's justice, and lives out the hope of future fulfillment. In sum, since the Church is a universal sacrament of the unity of all humanity, sacraments are the Church's vital actions in the transformation of the world.

The great potential of sacramental worship for the evangelization of the modern world, as well as its cultural transformation, stems from its capacity to respond to a world hungry for a spirituality that is relevant to the struggles, hopes, fears, and aspirations of peoples and cultures. The Church requires a broader sacramental expression of the mystery of God in the world because sacramental wholeness is Christian holiness:

The signs of sacrament, like bread, wine, and water, and the human actions of sacrament, like the loving pledge of a man and a woman, or the "touch" of healing words—these things speak loudly to us about the conversion of what is nature and what is human by the mystery of the God who comes to us to change us and our world. The very fact of the sacraments and their mundane focus on what is essential in life is eloquent testimony about the *mysterion* of God alive in the world as transforming power.[30]

As worship initiates personal conversion and empowers believers to transform social structures, it also proclaims prophetically the fullness of the imminent reign of God. The ultimate goal of sacramental participation is Jesus Christ in us, for "it is no longer I who live, but it is Christ who lives in me" (Gal 2:20). What we see and touch now is only a "shadow of what is to come; but the substance belongs to Christ" (Col 2:17). Sacraments are in fact eschatological symbols. They contemplate human existence within a vision centered and focused on the eternal mystery of God.

## PART TWO

# The Initiation
# and Foundational Church

# 5
# Baptism:
# Rebirth in the Christ-Event

Common to all religions initiation is a developmental concept that describes the incorporation of an individual into the shared values and beliefs of a community. The theological significance of Christian baptism stems from the full significance of Christ's baptism. Baptism was the basic rite of initiation in Palestinian Christianity for those who accepted Jesus' way of life and lived it in the communion of believers. Their integration into the Christian communion also included the experience of the mystery of the Spirit's work and the practice of the eucharistic mandate. The whole of the New Testament testifies to all of these ecclesial actions, namely baptism, the imposition of hands, and the Eucharist. They became the initiating Easter sacraments in early Church practice, culminating a process of faith conversion. All Christian life and its world view was lived from this spiritual center.

This chapter analyzes baptism within a framework of initiation as the Christian way of life in the world. It is a way of life that flows from the spiritual implications of baptism and the Eucharist. This is apparent from a New Testament point of view and in the developing practice and ongoing interpretation of the earliest Christian communities. The chapter on the origins of the Eucharist supports this approach.

The discussion in this chapter considers baptism from the following perspectives: (1) its biblical, theological, and spiritual foundations; (2) the lessons that have arisen as a result of their historical evolution; and (3) the Church's core beliefs and the permanent sacramental structure and dynamics of the process of Christian initiation. There is a growing realization of the need to recover in the twenty-first century a renewed sense of the baptismal spirituality that characterized ancient Christianity. This and the following chapters on confirmation and the Eucharist focus on the central and foundational role of an ongoing Christian initiation for the spirituality of the believer and for the structures of the Church.

## The Foundational Charter

The New Testament baptismal themes constitute the basis of the Christian vocation and the foundational charter of the "universal call to holiness." Baptism actualizes God's salvific plan for humanity by allowing the person to enter symbolically and concretely into the central mysteries of Christianity. All these themes focus on the "event of Jesus of Nazareth." Christ was baptized in the Jordan. This crucial event in his salvific ministry summed up prophetic and messianic expectations and announced the transforming and liberative paschal event accomplished by Jesus' self-gift on the cross. The New Testament is a telling example of the sacramental link between Christ's baptism and ours—as Christ is, so are we. This is evident in the synoptic gospels, but especially in the writings of Paul, who in the sixth chapter of Romans relates the baptismal event to the Christ-event.[1] These New Testament themes with their corresponding images provide the basis for Christian baptism. In what follows we will discuss the content of these themes and examine theological and spiritual dimensions drawn from them.

### Biblical Foundations

The symbolic action of baptism initiates the Christian life journey. The baptismal event is of crucial importance in the New Testament. It is connected to the central apostolic mission of proclaiming the *kerygma*, an announcement of salvation rooted in the original experience of the risen Christ and his Spirit in the lives of the disciples. From its inception, the baptismal event became the model of the Christian way of life, because it constituted the embodiment of the new life of Jesus and his liberating presence as Lord and savior.

Baptism, in fact, is a post-resurrection concept in terms of its specific Christian features and its theological interpretation. This applies, in particular, to the source event of Jesus' own baptism, as interpreted by the Church's post-paschal Christology. Drawing inspiration from a theological reflection on Jesus' baptism, the post-resurrection experience of the risen Lord shaped the apostolic ministry of the proclamation of the good news of salvation in Christ. It also shaped the community of those who received the gift of faith through baptism with its outpouring of the Spirit. According to New Testament narratives, Jesus' baptism was fundamental to all Christian baptisms. The narratives provided the paradigm of Christian calling and discipleship.[2]

## Christ's Baptism, the Paradigmatic Center

All the evangelists give an account of Jesus' baptism and the theophany at the Jordan. They present it as a key moment in his ministry, and as the source event of Christian baptism. Mark (1:9–11) focuses on the revelation of Jesus as the Son of God: "You are my Son, the Beloved," a statement echoed by the other narratives. This is a post-Easter announcement of his paschal mystery as we can see in the centurion's words at the moment of Jesus' death: "Truly this man was God's Son!" (Mark 15:39). With a similar acclamation, Matthew (3:13–17) also presents Jesus' divine origin after his baptism. John the Baptizer empties himself before Jesus as "servant of the Lord," saying "I need to be baptized by you, and do you come to me?" In Luke (3:21–22) Jesus is baptized among the people preparing for the messianic times. He appears at the center of God's activity and in communion with him ("when Jesus...had been baptized and was praying," Luke 3:21).

The Fourth Gospel sums up the theological meaning of Jesus' baptism while omitting specific references. Enriched by a long Easter tradition, this gospel (A.D. 90–100) focuses on the paschal Jesus as the redeemer of the world through the image of the "Lamb of God who takes away the sin of the world" (1:29–34). This image seems to evoke both the *suffering servant* (Isa 53) who, endowed with God's spirit (Isa 42:1), is slaughtered like a lamb who bears our sins, and the *Passover lamb* of sacrifice (John 19:36).

The two images point prophetically to Jesus' redemptive mission, accomplished by the sacrificed "lamb of God" whose side was pierced with a lance: "and at once blood and water came out" (John 19:34), a baptism of death for the new life of the world. At a more mature level, the Fourth Gospel reaffirms the new reality of the baptism in the Spirit of the synoptic gospels. In the testimony of John the Baptizer, Jesus is presented as God's chosen one in whom the Spirit is manifested in all power. He remains and thus grounds a new baptism with the Holy Spirit: "The man on whom you see the Spirit come down and rest is the one who is going to baptize with the Holy Spirit."

Inspired by a higher Christology characteristic of the Johannine community, these theological reflections on baptism shaped the vision of the early Christian communities. They can also inspire a profound baptismal spirituality in the twenty-first century. Conversion is complete, for "John gives us a picture of the baptized as one fully transformed by the paschal mystery of Jesus, who is permeated by the Spirit, chosen by God, destroying evil, bringing new life."[3]

Both the Synoptics and John's narratives reflect the New Testament nucleus, "water and spirit," from which the Spirit-filled post-paschal community develops the vision of living the life of the reborn. Baptism, a normal practice after the events of the resurrection, was probably not an expressed mandate of the historical Jesus. Jesus himself did not practice the purification and penitential baptism of John the Baptizer (John 4:2).[4] In fact, the earliest pre-paschal texts omit the commission to baptize. Rather, they emphasize the preaching of God's reign of unconditional love and forgiveness and its confirmation with healing.[5] The teacher's great commission in Matthew's Gospel to make disciples from the Gentiles by baptizing them (Matt 28:16–20) is in fact a later liturgical formulation: "The Trinitarian formula accompanying Jesus' command adds to the suspicion that the risen Jesus' language has been shaped in light of the experience of the early Church, in this case by a baptismal formula (cf. *Didache* 7:1–3)."[6]

According to current scholarship, the other baptismal saying of Jesus (Mark 16:16) is a second-century composition absent from the original Gospel of Mark. As Gerhard Lohfink states in reference to the decisive .text of Luke 24:47, "It is quite clear that Luke did not find within the large spectrum of the tradition of early Christianity any reference to Jesus' mandate to baptize."[7] Just as Jesus' own baptism was central to his messianic ministry, so the resurrection and Pentecost experiences were fundamental to the new Christian existence symbolized by the baptismal action. Baptism came to be seen as the universal sign of salvation through which one entered the new eschatological community in the Spirit of the risen Christ.

Jesus, in his own baptism and in his own "passing" to the Father, was in this sense "the baptized *par excellence*," and thus the only source and foundation from which the mystery of Christian baptism originated. Early post-paschal references speak of a normal procedure of baptism, "in the name of Christ." The risen Lord's explicit command to baptize included in the late texts of Matthew and Mark mentioned above represents an authentic Christian conviction of the first Christian generation concerning the christocentric grounding of baptism. In contrast to the Eucharist, it is difficult to indicate the precise moment of this sacrament's institution. Whether Jesus' disciples performed actual baptisms during his public ministry or whether they revived the Baptizer's water ritual after the resurrection remains unverified.

## Water, Spirit, and Paschal Mystery

The elements of water, Spirit, and the paschal mystery recur in the development of New Testament biblical theology, especially in Paul. These three elements are interrelated within the mystery of Christian initiation and represent the basic framework of the baptismal belief of the New Testament. This belief is the source of eternal life, as the first letter of John states in relation to a cross-centered and Spirit-related Christology. The author of this letter speaks of three witnesses, or the trilogy of the new life in Christ: "the Spirit and the water and the blood" (1 John 5:8).

*Water*
Neither baptismal terminology nor the symbolic value of a religious bath originated in Christianity. The ritualization with water is part of the experience of the sacred in many religions. This is particularly true in regard to basic types of purification and initiation through ritual washing practiced by different religious sects well before the time of Jesus in the Near East. Current scholarship dismisses any immediate influence of Hellenistic religious teachings on Christian baptism.

The fundamental structure of Christian worship comes from Judaism, and baptism in particular derives from Jewish practice. The symbolic Christian meaning of a water baptism undoubtedly has its roots in the messianic bath practiced by the Baptizer. The use of water for purification of objects and persons is well documented in the Hebrew Scriptures, and the practice of ritual ablutions was widespread in Palestine. A reflection on the meaning of washing is found in the prophetic description of the messianic age as, for example, in Ezekiel 36:23–28.

Three divergent types of ritual washings are documented at the time of Jesus: (a) the baptism of Jewish sects; (b) Jewish proselyte baptisms; and (c) the baptism performed by John at the Jordan. The influence of the first type is less than certain, for—as was the case with the Essenes' community at Qumran—the repeated washings were not initiatory. In contrast to Hebrew purification patterns, the proselytes' immersion bath performed around the Passover involved a ritual including the idea of incorporation and indoctrination into another religion. It could have influenced the Christian ritual event of initiation, especially with the new converts from the Hellenistic missionary communities.

The Baptizer's "baptism of repentance for the forgiveness of sins" (Mark 1:4) exhibited similarities to early Christian baptism in that it was initiatory and performed once in a lifetime as a means of salvation. This cleansing bath of immersion implied a *metanoia* (repentance) and prepared all Israel for the imminent coming of God's reign. The idea of belonging to the eschatological people of God in the messianic age (Isa 40:3–5) satisfied the needs of a people who were waiting for deliverance (Luke 3:15). It placed John in the pages of the Synoptics as the messiah's precursor, "[making] ready a people prepared for the Lord" (Luke 1:17).

Historically, from the beginning of Christian initiation, water baptism was the central symbol of the convert's incorporation into the one body of Christ. Enriched with a wealth of imagery to form a rite of initiation, especially within Hellenistic Christianity, water-baptism became the embodiment of the Christian *kerygma* and a means to express the developing context of sacramental mystery.

Two technical phrases, "to baptize" and especially "to be baptized," were used, particularly for immersion. They indicated a decisively new reality: "You are alive to God," and a new creation: "You are the body of Christ." The scanty New Testament references fail to specify whether baptism was performed by pouring or by immersion.[8] Although the classic Pauline text, "buried with him...walk in newness of life" (Rom 6:4), suggests an *immersion bath*, the author of Titus uses the image of *pouring* (3:5–6) to refer to God's salvation "through the water of rebirth and renewal by the Holy Spirit [which] he poured out on us richly through Jesus Christ our Savior."

Water is also an important baptismal theme in John's Gospel, especially in the case of Jesus' dialogue with Nicodemus: unless a person is "born through water and the Spirit" (3:5). It presents the risen Christ as the living spring of the Spirit. By virtue of this spring the person is regenerated by divine action as a child of God and reborn to eternal life. The water symbolism appears often in the Fourth Gospel and dominates the Christian symbolism of initiation and election, as is evident in the first epistle of Peter. Proclaiming the greatness of the baptismal vocation, Petrine catechesis relies on biblical typology, namely the flood, an image of destruction of the old and liberation of the new humanity as a type of "baptism, which...now saves you" (1 Pet 3:21). The new Noah is the risen Christ who through the paschal water restored the unique dignity of the spiritual household of God:

> But you are a chosen race, a royal priesthood, a holy nation, God's own people, in order that you may proclaim the mighty acts of him who called you out of darkness into his marvellous light. Once you were not a people, but now you are God's people; once you had not received mercy, but now you have received mercy. (1 Pet 2:9–10)

*Spirit*

As an external sign without meaning would be empty, so water without the Spirit cannot be a Christian sign. The visible and invisible together create life, an incarnational reality in the womb of Church-mother. The invisible working of the Spirit is the soul of the new being of the baptized person and of the Church itself. Jesus baptizes his disciples with the Holy Spirit (John 1:33), gives them the power to take away the sin of the world, and after receiving the baptism of his passion (Luke 12:50) creates a new community through the Holy Spirit at Pentecost. Although distinct, Spirit and water are vitally related in the narratives of the New Testament. Theologically, the Spirit data concerning Christian baptism govern the water data, and the water-bath is a function of the Spirit.[9] Both together, as sign and reality, actualize the hope of salvation of the convert through the confession of faith and associate him or her to the person, life, and lordship of Christ.

Early Christians made a distinction between the water of purification, like John's baptism, and the baptism by which the believer is gifted with the Spirit. For this reason, John's disciples were re-baptized (Acts 19:5). It is the effusion of the Spirit that unites all in the new freedom of Christ: "In the one Spirit we were all baptized into one body—Jews or Greeks, slaves or free—and we were all made to drink of one Spirit" (1 Cor 12–13).

The presence of the gift of the Spirit, promised by Jesus and associated with the reception of baptism, appears early in the New Testament. Peter's speech after the event of Pentecost states: "And be baptized every one of you in the name of Jesus Christ so that your sins may be forgiven; and you will receive the gift of the Holy Spirit" (Acts 2:38).[10] This text reveals an early tradition in the expression of the apostolic *kerygma* that contains the two essential meanings of baptism: (a) a symbolic action accomplished "in the name of Christ" by the authority and power of Jesus through which sins are remitted, and (b) the permanent and universal endowment of all believers with the life-giving Spirit.

Baptism appears, therefore, as the event of Christ and as the event of the Spirit. It is grounded in the resurrection of Jesus and the promise of the Spirit at Pentecost. In fact, Paul identifies the risen Christ with the Spirit (2 Cor 3:17) and the baptismal event with the Christ-event, for a Christian is "baptized *into* Christ Jesus" (Rom 6:3) and is intimately bonded to Christ. This union can happen only in the life of the Spirit.

*Paschal Mystery*
Christian baptism establishes a radical bond of unity and a relationship of total solidarity between the initiated and the initiator, the paschal Christ. Baptism is a salvific moment. It accomplishes an ontological transformation and demands a corresponding moral identification with the mystery of Christ's life, passion, and resurrection. This is the recurring theme of the baptismal theology of most Pauline letters, the cen-

tral idea of the paschal mystery—immersion into a reality of death and
rising to a glorious life.

> When you were buried with him in baptism, you were also
> raised with him through faith in the power of God, who raised
> him from the dead. And when you were dead in trespasses and
> the uncircumcision of your flesh, God made you alive together
> with him, when he forgave us all our trespasses. (Col 2:12–13)

Evidently, there is in the New Testament an evolving understanding
of the paschal dimension of baptism as the interpretive symbolic key of
salvation history. The incipient sketch of the Synoptics, especially the
*logion* (declaration) about the "Beloved" at Jesus' baptism and Peter's
inaugural speech in Acts have their climax in the classic text of baptismal
theology, Romans 6:1–14. Here and in other Pauline texts, baptism is
the paschal symbol of incorporation into the mystery of Christ: "baptized into Christ Jesus."

This reality, signified by baptism as the sign of "Christ our *Pasch*,"
goes beyond an external association with the person of Jesus. It is a personal conversion that is existentially and mystically equivalent to "dying
with" and "rising with" him, and it expresses the salvific aspect of
Christ's *Pasch* made symbolically present in the life of the baptized.

The paschal mystery is therefore central to the baptismal theology
of the New Testament, the foundation of its soteriological, ecclesial, and
spiritual dimensions. Regis Duffy sums up these dimensions. Theologically, "Paul achieves an amazing integration of (1) the problem of sin,
(2) the connection of redemption, justification, and initiation as actualized by the paschal mystery, (3) the ecclesial dimension of baptism, and
(4) the Christian moral life as ongoing baptismal commitment."[11]

## Theological and Spiritual Foundations

We have explored the reality of baptism in the New Testament where it
is presented as the gift and embodiment of the life-giving power of the
Spirit as Paschal Lord. Baptism by water and baptism by the Spirit
were seen as one. This one divine act effects not only the symbolic transformation of the free person; it is also the foundation of the holiness of

the priestly dignity of the one ecclesial body: "All of you are one in Christ Jesus" (Gal 3:28). Baptism goes far beyond a traditional initiatory ritual. As the foundation of all sacraments, it symbolizes a new covenant and creates a new freedom that is made possible by Christ's glorious cross. It is a new reality, a shift that transforms the mind and heart of the believer. The New Testament expresses this reality through many images, such as new birth, new person, new creation, and new light. In fact,

> Baptism is a polyvalent sign and, at the same time, an essential point of convergence. It is the encounter of a divine intervention and a human acceptance. It unites and symbolizes in the same action God's grafting to human life and the person's commitment to divine life. Even before the Eucharist, which completes its effects, baptism is the sacrament of reunion and reconciliation: the seal of the covenant in the faith.[12]

The following discussion expounds on this baptismal experience and its implications for the faith of the early Christian communities. These implications, found especially in the Gospel of John and the letters of Paul, provide a profound theology and a rich spirituality. They are integral and inseparable parts of the same paschal structure. The essential themes of these implications are: (a) new birth and new creation, (b) dying and rising with Christ, (c) life in the Spirit as God's children, (d) and the priestly dignity of the one body.

## New Birth and New Creation (Spirit-related Dimension)

Humankind has to be re-created in the Spirit. The Holy Spirit is the incorruptible seed of new birth that effects the re-creation of all things accomplished by the coming of Christ. Christ came from above to bring salvation and returned to heaven through the exaltation of the cross. Likewise, the Christian has to be born "from above," not only in the natural way of the life-giving water, but above all from the source of the life-giving Spirit.

Jesus' encounter with Nicodemus presents baptism as rebirth, a classic theme of the Christian theology of baptism. Christ proceeds from God and comes into existence by the power of the Holy Spirit. Therefore the believer must be born from above, that is to say, must be born of the Spirit. Both expressions have an equivalent significance and stress spiritual and real regeneration through the initiation experience. The Lamb of God sacrificed for the sin of the world and bearer of the Spirit (John 1:29–34) brings new life to the baptized.

While Jesus is the source of the living water (John 4:10), the Spirit is the agent of Christian regeneration. As in other New Testament sources, the connection between baptismal water and the gift of the Spirit is presented simultaneously. In fact, the identification of Spirit and water reappears in John 7:38–39 where it is given the full christo-logical sense of Jesus as the source of the Spirit/living water.[13] This is the existential beginning of the journey of the believer sharing in the new creation and living the ideals of the reign of God.

For this reason, the Fourth Gospel stresses the christological necessity of the begetting of God's children by the pouring out of God's Spirit at baptism: "No one can enter the kingdom of God without being born of water and Spirit" (John 3:5). Rudolf Schnackenburg comments on how the passage focuses on the "begetting from the spirit," the new creation through the Spirit of God, and consequently on that funda-mental salvation event bound by the Lord to the sacrament of baptism rather than viewing baptism from the standpoint of the external rite and requirement.[14]

The concept of regeneration and the birth of the children of God is developed from the experience of that saving-event, that is, from the eschatological newness lived in faith by the believers. The Spirit, brought forth from the spring of the risen and glorious Christ, became the permanent presence that empowers the believer to radical new-ness. Thus, the ideas of regeneration and rebirth permeate the New Testament, albeit in the more developed works of its theology: "But when the goodness and loving-kindness of God our Savior appeared, he saved us, not because of any works of righteousness that we had done, but according to his mercy, through the water of rebirth and renewal by the Holy Spirit" (Titus 3:4–5). The first letter of Peter, woven with the liturgical and catechetical elements of a baptismal tradition, expresses a similar theme: The Father "by his great mercy…has given us a new birth" (1 Pet 1:3); "You have been born anew, not of perishable but of imperishable seed, through the living and enduring word of God" (1 Pet 1:23).

The baptized person represents a new creation as a result of the salvific work of Christ and the ensuing life of freely chosen conversion to the way of holiness. This transformation of the believer is the fruit of Christ's love. It gives the believer the grace to live for others as well as for himself or herself, and for the one who died and was raised to life: "If anyone is in Christ, there is a new creation: everything old has passed away; see, everything has become new!" (2 Cor 5:17). This new creation in Christ implies passing from sin to life, being made free from the law, and entering into a covenant with God who gave us his Spirit as the pledge of our future inheritance.

## Dying and Rising (Soteriological Dimension)

The pattern of living and dying is ever present in the world. This realization carries within it great symbolic meaning. It opens up the breadth and depth of the initiatory mystery. Through the water-bath of baptism, which signifies death to sin and resurrection in Christ, death is effectively transformed into a mystery of life. Baptism is a celebration of life, a life in the Spirit, and the sacrament of the glorious death/ resurrection of Christ. It signifies the double effect of the baptismal grace of dying and rising: dying to the human condition of sin represented by the "old person," and rising to the life of grace of the "new person." This implies an actual association with the resurrection of the Lord. St. Paul expressed this mystery in the classic text of his letter to the Romans:

> Do you not know that all of us who have been baptized into Christ Jesus were baptized into his death? Therefore we have been buried with him by baptism into death, so that, just as Christ was raised from the dead by the glory of the Father, so we too might walk in newness of life.
>
> For if we have been united with him in a death like his, we will certainly be united with him in a resurrection like his. We know that our old self was crucified with him so that the body of sin might be destroyed, and we might no longer be enslaved

to sin. For whoever has died is freed from sin. But if we have died with Christ, we believe that we will also live with him. We know that Christ, being raised from the dead, will never die again; death no longer has dominion over him. The death he died, he died to sin, once for all; but the life he lives, he lives to God. So you also must consider yourselves dead to sin and alive to God in Christ Jesus. (Rom 6:3–11)

The mystery of baptism implies a symbolic participation in a totally new reality inaugurated by the resurrection of Christ. Through the process of baptismal initiation, the Christian enters into a new relationship with the divine source of life and becomes "alive for God." This mystery encompasses inextricably linked soteriological, ethical, and eschatological dimensions.

In the soteriological context of Romans 6, Paul presents primarily a theology of redemption. Baptism is a saving event. Being buried with the Lord through faith, water, and Spirit demands a total identification with the order of values established by Jesus, who lived and taught the will of God. The radical christological foundation of baptism stems from the whole of Jesus' human journey. It produces a new vision of human-divine relations and creates a new set of human relations and a new lifestyle.

Finally, faith in the resurrection is the ultimate ground of our hope in the final victory over sin. Baptism is the beginning of a process of daily dying and rising guaranteed by the communion of the believer with the cross by which "having died with Christ we shall return to life with him." Through baptism, Christians experience an anticipation of the resurrection, because the cross has made this possible.

### Life in the Spirit as God's Children (Existential Dimension)

The experience of the saving Spirit of God with its unmistakable marks in the life of the believer is inseparable from Christian initiation. Rebirth and re-creation in the Spirit through baptism allows the person to be spiritually transformed and receive a new vision in the light of Christ. Every person possesses a spirit and thus has a spirituality, that is, lives with a certain spirit. However, Christian spirituality means a life freed and empowered by "the breath of God" *(ruach)*. A Christian cannot live without the "life-giving Spirit" of Christ (1 Cor 15:45).

In the New Testament, the experience of the risen Christ and the experience of the saving Spirit of God are inseparable. Paul stresses the salvific and eschatological event of the resurrection by which Christ is forever alive and active through the present Spirit. Hence current theology expressed the need for a unifying vision of the mediation of Christ as the primordial sacrament of God's presence and the sanctifying action of the Spirit in every sacramental action. This represents a Spirit-Christology. The *epiclesis* (the invocation of the Spirit in a sacramental action) in liturgy has traditionally, at least in Eastern churches, expressed this vision of a Spirit Christology: "The Spirit sanctifies in every sacramental action so that the gathered Church may more truly be the body of Christ and thus do the work of Christ."[15]

The Spirit is the primary gift of the Father through the Son. It precedes and challenges the community and the person to a change of heart and mind and attitude. This leads to living a new life in the Spirit. According to the New Testament, the effects of the Holy Spirit in believers include divine filiation, sanctification and reconciliation, freedom and empowerment, as well as charismatic gifts for the building up of the community.

With baptism we become God's children in Jesus Christ through the divine Spirit. Every baptized person is called by name to hear God's irrevocable pledge of divine filiation: "You are my beloved son/daughter; my favor rests on you." This is the wondrous gift and the fundamental birthright of all Christians adopted "as children" (Gal 4:5) by the inward giving of God's Spirit.

From an existential and spiritual perspective, following Jesus and life in the Spirit are the same. We are part of Christ's destiny because we have been adopted by him, and "if we live by the Spirit, let us also be guided by the Spirit" (Gal 5:25). Baptism, in fact, celebrates the communication of the gifts of the Holy Spirit through which the believer is consecrated. This reality initiates Christian existence in the communion and the union of the Christian with the Spirit (St. Paul), forever the abiding presence in the believer (St. John). In conclusion, "baptism is the faith commitment to conversion. [It] unites the people of God, grafts in the destiny of Christ and entails being immersed, drowned and dead to the old person, emerging resurrected to the new person. Such is the life in the Holy Spirit."[16]

## A Priestly Community (Ecclesial Dimension)

The day of Pentecost established the priestly people of the New Covenant, the paradigm for the new humanity. These people form the one body of richly diverse members of the Church. They all share the same prophetic and priestly dignity. Both oneness and diversity are Spirit-given gifts. Incorporation into the body of Christ equalizes all the baptized as the new family of God: "As many of you as were baptized into Christ have clothed yourselves with Christ. There is no longer Jew or Greek, there is no longer slave or free, there is no longer male and female; for all of you are one in Christ Jesus" (Gal 3:27–28).

Priesthood is a basic element in the definition of a Christian and an existential dimension of human life. This priestly rank has nothing to do with any clericalization of the laity's mission, which is primarily one of involvement in family life and in the world. On the contrary, a Christian vision of the world itself as the epiphany and sign of God's presence broadens the concept of priestly dignity to all humanity. It applies it to every person as priest and minister to God's creation, to history, and to society in all possible areas of human endeavor. In this regard, the Eastern Orthodox theologian Alexander Schmemann sees the person as the priest of the world. He in turn characterizes the world as the cosmic sacrament.

> All rational, spiritual and other qualities of man, distinguishing him from all other creatures have their focus and ultimate fulfillment in this capacity to bless God, to know, so to speak, the meaning of the thirst and hunger that constitutes his life. "Homo sapiens," "Homo Faber"... yes, but, first of all, "Homo adorans." The first, the basic definition of man, is that he is the priest. He stands in the center of the world and unifies it in his act of blessing God, of both receiving the world from God and offering it to God—and by filling the world with this Eucharist, he transforms his life, the one that he receives from the world, into life in God, into communion.[17]

Baptism is the celebration of the unconditional love and life-giving power of God's Spirit that incorporates the believer into the dynamic reality of Christ "to be a holy priesthood" (1 Pet 2:5). This priestly power goes beyond a mere initiation into a body of doctrines. Rather, it is the source of the believer's vital energy for empowerment, to "be built into a spiritual house" (1 Pet 2:5). Priestly dignity is the foundation of the Christian vocation to be Christ's body showing forth his works in the world.

Baptism is the birthplace and consecration of the universal priesthood flowing from the *Logos*, the creator Christ, with whom the believer takes on the form of his likeness (Rom 6:5). Thus, the distinctive character of the Christian vocation has its source in baptism, which celebrates this vocation and identity rooted in the saving event of Christ who calls the baptized to "a new creation." According to the New Testament, this call to be a Christian is the vocation *par excellence.*

Priestly dignity is an integral part of the reality of the paschal sacrament of baptism. As Christ inaugurated his public calling at the Jordan, which culminated in his "baptism" on the cross (Luke 12:50), so the Christian lives the very life of Christ. In Romans Paul describes the witnessing of Christians in a cultic perspective of spiritual donation: "Present your bodies as a living sacrifice, holy and acceptable to God, which is your spiritual worship" (Rom 12:1). Ministry likewise is the exercise of a priestly dignity received at baptism. It means a non-cultic type of priesthood, as in the following text: "The grace [has been] given me by God to be a minister of Christ Jesus to the Gentiles in the priestly service of the gospel of God, so that the offering of the Gentiles may be acceptable, sanctified by the Holy Spirit" (Rom 15:15–16).

The first letter of Peter and the book of Revelation explicitly connect baptism to priesthood. Peter emphasizes the dignity of the Christian vocation. The texts proclaim the paschal Christ as the only priest, the source and basis of the priestly people of the new household of God: "Like living stones, let yourselves be built into a spiritual house, to be a holy priesthood, to offer spiritual sacrifices acceptable to God through Jesus Christ" (1 Pet 2:5).

> By sharing the life of the risen Lord, Christians become with him
> a household formed by the holy Spirit, to be a holy priesthood
> ...*spiritual sacrifices:* Christians, viewed corporately as a body

of priests, present their lives of faith and love to God as a sacrifice.[18]

The book of Revelation (1:6; 5:10; 20:6) echoes Exodus and Isaiah as Jesus fulfills the ancient prophetic promises. The Christian family is shown as king-priests who offer a sacrifice of praise. The resurrection has inaugurated the eschatological event by which Christ became the universal king: "To him who loves us and freed us from our sins by his blood, and made us to be a kingdom, priests serving his God and Father, to him be glory and dominion for ever and ever" (Rev 1:5–6).

Apparently, baptism is the sacramental foundation at the heart of Christian existence in the body of the Church. The New Testament exegesis and theology presented above are the essential elements of a baptismal consciousness and spirituality so urgently needed for the sacramental and ministerial renewal of Christianity. Progress in the renewal of the Christian mission, particularly the mission of the laity, depends on the conviction that ministry is the vocation of all the baptized. This includes ministry to herald the gospel in the world, in the family, and at work, as well as participation in the sacramental and spiritual life of the parish. It needs no extraordinary delegation from the hierarchy.

## Christian Initiation: Revitalizing the Tradition

The recovery of the baptismal tradition and consciousness of ancient Christianity in today's Church is the basic focus of this chapter. Such a recovery must be based on a thorough historical interpretation that requires, first of all, a consideration of the prominent role of baptism in the early churches and the overall context of Christian initiation. The historical tradition emphasizes the complete initiatory context: It recognizes baptism, confirmation, and Eucharist as interrelated parts of the one ritual celebration and fundamental expressions of the redemptive mystery. They form an organic and indivisible whole, a unified sacramental event, which from *a posteriori* reflection we could call the Great Sacrament of Christian Initiation. Baptism holds the key (not in terms of primacy, which belongs to the Eucharist) to the beginning and basic foundation of all Christian life.

### Origins (Until the Third Century)

New Testament cultic theology had to do with the mystery of Christ and the whole of Christian life rather than with ritual practices. The action of baptizing a convert is very simple. There is neither a description of this symbolic action nor any organized preparation for it. Many references to baptism are cited within catechetical and probably liturgical texts. They are to be found especially in Acts, the Pauline letters, and the first letter of Peter. Baptism is tied to the Christian mission and to the apostolic building up of communities. Mission is the crucial element in the dynamic reality of the early communities and in later developments of an organized liturgical process of Christian initiation. Matthew's pivotal text on Jesus' universal commission to the disciples testifies to the significance of the baptismal tradition for the primitive communities: "Go therefore and make disciples of all nations, baptizing them in the name of the Father and of the Son and of the Holy Spirit" (Matt 28:19).

Earlier testimonies show the charismatic activity of people filled with the Holy Spirit who are subsequently led to missionary work. This is the case of Philip, one of the seven (Acts 6), who, prompted by the Spirit, leads a Gentile Ethiopian official to conversion to the good news of Jesus and to baptismal immersion in the water (Acts 8:26–39). Baptism is celebrated in the earliest communities "in the name of Jesus" and him as the risen One who became "a life-giving Spirit." This is the Christian origin of initiation expressed throughout the New Testament as the continuation of the ministry of Christ, the giver of baptism and the Holy Spirit. "'Brothers, what should we do?' Peter said to them, 'Repent, and be baptized every one of you in the name of Jesus Christ so that your sins may be forgiven; and you will receive the gift of the Holy Spirit.'" (Acts 2:37–38).

The gift of the Spirit is associated with baptism throughout the New Testament even in the earliest Palestinian community.[19] The action of this divine gift, though, is not necessarily dependent upon the specific baptismal action. This is the case of the story of Cornelius's conversion, a crucial story, because it seems to be like a Pentecost for the Gentiles. Scholars view the incident as the nucleus of a baptismal catechesis based on a proclamation, with which all baptisms begin, the proclamation of Jesus' *kerygma* of universal forgiveness: "'Can anyone withhold the water for baptizing these people who have received the

Holy Spirit just as we have?' So he ordered them to be baptized in the name of Jesus Christ" (Acts 10:47–48).

Although not explicitly stated, this surrendering of faith to Christ with a full-bodied response leads those added to the Christian community through baptism to participation in "the breaking of the bread." This was an essential element around which the life of the early community revolved (Acts 2:42). The conferral of the Holy Spirit cannot be seen in these early New Testament sources as a separate sacramental act subsequent to the water-bath. Some scholars mistakenly associate the Western medieval sacrament of confirmation with the reference to the laying on of hands in certain texts. This will be analyzed in the section on Confirmation.

In summary, this was the integral and only ritual context of the New Testament's symbolic action of initiation: the water-bath, the experience of the Spirit, and subsequently the breaking of the bread.

After the New Testament, the oldest document is the *Didache*, a form of catechism dating from the end of the first century or the beginning of the second century. The first part of the work presents catechetical teachings on "the two ways" and some details on a ritual of baptism. The trinitarian formula has become the norm. The *Didache* stresses the use of living water and mentions that candidates and possibly members of the community are to fast before the celebration.

In the mid–second century, the *First Apology* of Justin (ca. 100–165) shows the direct connection between the water-bath of baptism and the communal eucharistic celebration. Besides the explicit affirmation of universal forgiveness of sins, seen in the *Didache*, Justin presents baptism as new birth and an illumination. Although baptismal celebrations ask for some kind of formal preparation, stressing especially the catechetical and spiritual components, an outline of the catechumenal process has not yet come into being. The two cited documents still represent, for the most part, the Judeo-Christian world of spiritual and prophetic worship with strong eschatological accents as well as a continuation of the apostolic period.

### Patristic Splendor (Third through Fifth Centuries)

A spirit of critical openness to new symbolic forms of creative structuring of worship arose gradually in the multicultural fabric of Roman-

Hellenistic society. Scholarly investigations into the interplay between historical and theological perspectives of tradition in early Christianity have documented the trend toward different institutional forms and various liturgical expressions. New developmental shifts represent change as well as pastoral and cultural adaptation, especially in view of the extremely varied situations of the Christian communities within the provinces of the Roman Empire.

In relation to the development of the Christian catechumenate, the following thesis of Robert Grant should be kept in mind: "A doctrine of theological or liturgical evolution which produces a picture of straight-line development in the past does not do justice to the complexity of historical evidence and simply consecrates the present situation, whatever it may be." The evolution of Christian initiation is one of "multiple choices in manifold situations" rather than a straight-line development. "What one sees is not progress but change, brought about as the Church responded to various kinds of occasions."[20]

What follows is an outline of major developments and essential features across a span of four centuries and the creativity of diverse ecclesial traditions. Special attention will be given in this presentation to the structure and theological meaning of the catechumenate.

A lengthy and formal preparation for baptism and the Eucharist is well attested in the West during the early third century, especially in Tertullian's *De Baptismo* and in the *Apostolic Tradition* of Hippolytus of Rome. Converts were called catechumens from the Greek word "to teach," hence catechetical learning, or catechumenate. They were also called "hearers" from the Latin *audiens, auditores.* The preparation was a complex process of initiation that, according to Hippolytus, lasted three years. The catechumenal journey represented above all a ritual and sacramental unity. It focused on the true core and principle of life of the Christian mission and already showed the fundamental structure for the Church's future celebration of the mystery. The catechumenate developed and flourished especially during the fourth and fifth centuries. Drawing from its essential features in various local churches, this was the pattern of Christian initiation:

*A. Admission to the Catechumenate*
Candidates were admitted after an investigation of their background. They were normally presented by other Christians: "New converts to the

faith, who are to be admitted as hearers of the word, shall first be brought to the Teachers (clerics or laypeople) before the people assembled. And they shall be examined as to their reason for embracing the faith."[21]

Toward the end of the fourth century in the West, the rites in some churches included these elements: sign of the cross on the forehead, rite of salt placed on the tongue (signifying healing and wisdom), a laying on of hands, and an exorcism. Clerics or laity as catechists instructed the catechumens in the basics of Christian doctrine, while the sponsors supported them as companions in the journey of faith. According to John Chrysostom, sponsors "ought to show their paternal love by encouraging, counseling, and correcting those for whom they go surety ...you, the sponsors, have learned that no slight danger hangs over your head if you are remiss."[22]

### B. Election and Preparation for Baptism

This second stage coincides generally with Lent, a season of preparation for Easter as well as of intense catechetical and spiritual preparation for baptism. In a series of meetings of instructions, which occurred daily in some places, several ceremonies took place: enrollment of the candidates, exorcism and scrutinies to free and purify the candidates, the explanation and handing over of the creed and Our Father. These ceremonies would involve prayer and fasting.

### C. The Rites of Initiation

In many churches these rites took place during the celebration of the Easter Vigil, thus underscoring Easter symbolism and its connection to initiation. Practices included: the *ephphetha* ("be opened"), which refers to "the breath of divine life and the spiritual perfume exhaled by those who renounce the scents of the world,"[23] *renunciation* of the devil and a *pledge* of loyalty to Christ, prebaptismal *anointing* of the whole body as a sign of spiritual strength, *prayer over the baptismal water,* and *baptism.* Naked inside the baptismal pool, the convert was asked "if he or she believed in the name of the Father and of the Son and of the Holy Spirit. Then the convert professed the faith that saves and was immersed three times in the water, and then came out."[24]

"Chrismation" (anointing with chrism) on the head with blessed oil followed baptism to signify the individual's sharing into the mystery of Christ's kingship and priesthood. The neophyte (meaning "newly

planted") was also given a *white garment* ("you . . . have clothed yourselves with Christ," Gal 3:27), a symbol of resurrection. After the baptismal bath, *the laying on of hands* by the bishop signified the gift of the
Holy Spirit; this symbolic action became the Latin rite of confirmation.
Initiation was completed and reached its climax with the neophyte's full
incorporation into the assembly and their sharing in the paschal
Eucharist. As St. Ambrose (ca. 339–397) wrote about the procession
from the baptismal fountain to the eucharistic altar, with everyone
holding candles in their hands, "they hasten to draw near to the heavenly banquet; they come in and, seeing the holy altar made ready, they
cry: 'you have prepared a table for me.'"[25]

Tertullian and Hippolytus referred also to a special rite that, in certain churches of the West, followed the first eucharistic participation of
the newly baptized. This new feature in the rite of initiation consisted
of giving the neophyte milk and honey in addition to the Eucharist. It
probably originated from an archaic Roman custom: newborns were
protected against evil spirits with these elements, which symbolized a
welcome into the family.[26] An attempt to integrate into the local culture
and its Christian transformation is apparent in the text. Worship developed locally under the leadership of a bishop, but there was ample
space for charisma and participation in the verbal and formal expressions of the celebrating community. However, despite the extraordinary
spectrum of liturgical practices, the essential unity of the initiatory pattern was established.

THE FOURTH AND FIFTH CENTURIES represented the golden twilight of
the church fathers, creators of the awe-inspiring rites of initiation[27]
and authors of mystagogic baptismal works. They were the progenitors
of an ecumenical Church rooted in history and imbued with a sense of
mystery and experience of the divine. Christianity successfully supplanted the Greco-Roman pantheon, transforming it and building a
unified spiritual world by enshrining in the Christian mystery the major
hopes of salvation and life of the people.

### Medieval Fragmentation (Fifth Century to Modern Times)

The sixth century marked a major change in the history of ritual initiation as the complex process of Christian initiation of adults shifted to

the more expedient baptismal ritual for infants. This new trend, quite diverse within local churches, began in the sixth century and was fully integrated by the twelfth century. The end result was the disappearance of the catechumenate and the gradual disjunction of the three parts of the *one* rite of initiation. The separation of the reception of the Holy Spirit by the laying on of hands as a distinct rite (confirmation) originated in the fifth century. The councils of Riez (439) and Orange (441) in Gaul (France) attest to this.

## Infant Baptism

The Christianization of the masses, albeit nominal, contributed significantly to diminishing numbers of adults seeking baptism. A second major factor was the emergency *(quam primum)* baptism of newborn children, especially after the diffusion of Augustinian (354–430) theology regarding the absolute necessity of grace for salvation and Augustine's anti-Pelagian position on original sin. Augustine's theology decisively influenced the Church's belief and practice. In the ninth century Walafrid Strabo argued that "all who are not delivered by God's grace will perish in original sin, including those who have not added to it by their own personal sin. And so it is necessary to baptize infants."[28] The prevalence of infant baptism meant a gradual disintegration of the catechumenal process and the shattering of the original unity and corporate vitality of the paschal sacraments of initiation. The spiritual framework and foundational basis of baptism were weakened.

In Rome, the initiation time was reduced to a brief period of two weeks in Lent, and the neophytes were infants who received baptism at Easter or Pentecost. Even in the time of Tertullian (ca. 150–220)—who opposed the practice—infants and children were being baptized. During the Middle Ages, changes in baptismal practices were complex and responded to a variety of situations. Nevertheless, "in Rome itself the primitive unity of Christian initiation was by and large substantially preserved until at least the twelfth century."[29]

## Medieval Tradition

Thomas Aquinas's rich theological synthesis on baptism drew upon the Latin fathers and especially on basic theological concepts developed by Augustine. Thus arose the idea of original sin, the necessity of baptizing

children "as soon as possible," and the view of the sacramental character that established the personal relation of the baptized with Christ
and his body the Church: "the everlasting character (of the sacraments)
is Christ himself."[30] Conditioned by his understanding of the person
and the current sacramental practices of his time, Thomas Aquinas nevertheless continued the line of thinking of the biblico-patristic tradition.
Thus, his theology embraced the christocentric, paschal, ecclesial, and
social dimensions of the sacraments.

The primary concern of the sixteenth-century reformers was not
liturgical *per se* but biblical and pastoral. Their baptismal theology, concerned with the essentials of the sacramental rite, reflected the common tradition and depended in general on Augustine. Baptism was
renewed as a public celebration. It needed the nurturing of the personal faith through the proclamation of Christ's promise of salvation
and the acceptance of God's word.

In the sixteenth century the Council of Trent elucidated the Catholic doctrine and invigorated pastoral care and spiritual piety. Nevertheless, its sacramental theology was drawn from Thomas Aquinas and
its reforms re-affirmed medieval ritual practices.

Defensive reactions and a limited knowledge of the biblical and
earlier historical tradition prevented a paradigmatic shift toward full
recovery of baptismal foundations by both the reformers and Rome.
These foundations were a key to the renewal of Church and sacraments, "so that," as Calvin stated in regard to the Reformation, "the
ancient face of the Church might be in some way restored and made
whole."[31] As contemporary theologian Regis Duffy wrote from the theological perspective of infant baptism, the missed opportunity on both
sides was to reconsider: "(1) how justification is connected to the ecclesial community, and (2) [how] justification engenders a dynamic
response in faith on the part of the believing community as well as its
individual members."[32]

The Second Vatican Council inaugurated a new era of ecclesiology
which, together with the consideration of the primordial mystery of
Christ, re-envisioned the correct vision of the sacramental rites of
ecclesial initiation. Beginning with the liturgical constitution *Sacrosanc-
tum Concilium* in 1963, Vatican II marked a paradigmatic shift, which
in sacramental terms can be called "the catechumenal paradigm." In
fact, the council reintroduced the patristic and classical tradition of the
adult catechumenate with the promulgation in 1972 of the Rite of

Christian Initiation of Adults (RCIA). Its principles, dynamism, and structures will be discussed at the end of this chapter.

## Sacramental Initiation: Current Interpretation and Retrieval

This section is divided into two parts, doctrinal and liturgical. The first part reflects on different basic truths implied in the theology of baptism as developed in the course of the historical tradition of the Church. The second part presents the fundamental elements, catechumenal structures, and dynamics behind the recent implementation of the process of the Rite of Christian Initiation of Adults.

### Baptismal Core Beliefs

Together with the above-mentioned New Testament metaphors such as birth and death, several basic truths constitute the baptismal core beliefs of the major Christian churches. Although these truths have been discussed in previous chapters, they are addressed again here because they are an integral part of the theology of sacramental initiation. They include the following themes: baptism is (1) a *sacrament of faith*, (2) *instituted by Christ*, (3) *necessary for salvation;* it is (4) administered *for the forgiveness of sins,* (5) represents *incorporation into the Church*, and (6) imprints *a spiritual mark*.

1. Baptism constitutes *the sacramental act of faith par excellence* because it is the total surrender and immersion of the believer into Christ's own destiny. The relationship between faith and sacrament, a constant in the New Testament, is intrinsic and, like the intimate structure of faith itself, is dialogic and dynamic. It is first of all indissoluble and interdependent rather than extrinsic. A person becomes a child of God by the gift of faith: "for in Christ Jesus you are all children of God through faith" (Gal 3:26). Led by God's gracious gift to baptism, he is grafted into Christ.

2. *The institution of baptism by Christ* is a constant belief of the Christian tradition, a belief shared by all Christian churches because it has a foundation in the New Testament and is connected to the apostolic

Church. An in-depth approach examines the biblical evidence in regard to the essential baptismal core of doctrine received from Christ and the Holy Spirit and transmitted by the Church,[33] as well as theological reflection on the intrinsic relationship between baptism and Jesus' humanity.

The theological root of baptism is Christ's will, not human tradition. As stated in a previous chapter, the New Testament's explicit references to Christ's mandate to baptize do not necessarily mean that the mandate was Jesus' explicit injunction. The established baptismal practice in the apostolic Church arose from the inspiration of the Holy Spirit reminding the Church of what Christ had practiced and taught. The New Testament Church had a communal consciousness of the mandate of the Lord himself: "Go into all the world and proclaim the good news to the whole creation. The one who believes and is baptized will be saved; but the one who does not believe will be condemned" (Mark 16:15–16; Cf. Matt 28:19).

Jesus is the primordial sacrament-symbol of baptism because he in his humanity is the first and fundamental sacrament of God through which the community of faith encounters the divine and the living embodiment of God's initiative of salvation in the world. This is a contemporary theological concept without precedent in patristic or scholastic theology.[34] It is the basis for a groundbreaking approach that provides a unifying vision of the divine schema of redemption and its sacramental actualization in the Church. Jesus in his humanity is the instrument of our salvation, but specifically in terms of a sacramental perspective he is the original baptism, *the* baptized in its deepest and fullest and most genuine sense, and consequently the very meaning of baptism.[35]

3. *The necessity of baptism for salvation* and the correlative but broader issue of damnation outside the Church, as elucidated by Boniface VIII in the high Middle Ages, is a well-documented constant of the Church's tradition. Fundamentally a christological truth, it was subject in the past to differing interpretations, depending on various historical ecclesiologies. In essence, it is a truth that stems from the consideration of three realities: God, the person, and Christ.

God's self-gift is unconditional and universal: "For the grace of God has appeared, bringing salvation to all" (Titus 2:11). This offer respects people's inherent freedom (faith assent) and is also conditioned by the practical possibilities of their awareness of God's salvific economy effectively actualized in baptism. Christ is the baptized *par excellence*, the revelation of God's universal and definitive offer of eschatological salvation: "No one can enter the kingdom of God without being born of water and Spirit" (John 3:5). Therefore, the necessity of baptism cannot be absolutized, for "God has bound salvation to the sacrament of baptism, but he Himself is not bound by his sacraments."[36]

4. *The forgiveness of all sins* by one baptism is an essential tenet of Christian belief rooted as it is in New Testament references to baptism: "Repent, and be baptized every one of you in the name of Jesus Christ so that your sins may be forgiven" (Acts 2:38). Concomitant with this affirmation is the reality of grace in the baptized by the work of God.

The rite of baptism for children explicitly mentions *original sin*. This is a concept based not only on St. Augustine's counterargument against the Pelagians, but also on later ecclesiastical tradition developed through interpretation of the classical texts of Genesis 3 and Romans 5. Paul certainly refers to the christocentric nature of salvation for humankind. The condition of privation of grace was formally elucidated in later dogmatic statements on original sin at the Council of Trent in 1546. However, in fairness to the biblical meaning of the goodness of all creation, the idea of original grace and the superabundant grace of Christ celebrated in baptism should be stressed.

5. Baptism is preeminently the sign-act of the believer's *incorporation into the life of the body of Christ, the Church*. This is clearly seen in the New Testament, where both baptismal and ecclesial consciousness are paramount as the structural foundation (together with the Eucharist) of Christian life. They are vitally interrelated in the New Testament where a theology of baptism and the Church (that is the Church in its baptismal character) is developed through the use of the image of the "one body," a familiar Hellenistic metaphor of a social unity. Against this biblical background a theology of baptism encompassed these three dimensions: (a) a corporate act to enter into the Church, (b) a sign of the unity and equality of the people of God, and (c) consecration to the life of service in the communion of the Church.

6. According to the definition of the Council of Trent, *the sacramental mark of baptism* is an indelible spiritual sign imprinted on the soul. St. Augustine taught the impossibility of rebaptism even in the case of those baptized by heretics. The medieval theologians who defined the specific nature of the "sacramental character" developed this concept further. It has its biblical background in the idea of the seal *(sphragis)*[37] of the living God put on the foreheads of his servants (Rev 7:2–8). God's gift is irrevocable and free, offered by his salvific will and thus preceding personal determination.

The christological (Christ's priesthood) and the ecclesial (body of Christ) perspectives provide a theological rationale for understanding the concept of sacramental character. The profound meaning of the baptismal character stems from the configuration of the Christian to the priesthood of Christ. This is the classical insight, which was elaborated by Thomas Aquinas in his all-embracing view of the sacraments and Christian worship.[38] The baptized participate in Christ's priesthood, which is derived from Christ himself.

Initiated in his incarnation and consummated in his *Pasch,* Christ's priesthood continues in its eternal worship of God through the priesthood of all believers who are therefore consecrated for divine worship. If viewed from a broader biblical perspective, the synthesizing perspective of Thomas Aquinas retains its efficacy because it deepens the sacramental character and places baptism at the center as realization of Christian existence.

The permanent effects of baptism as the seed of eternal life reach out beyond our earthly pilgrimage. Baptism is the re-creation and salvation of humanity rooted in the destiny of the risen Christ. Thus, the very nature of the baptismal character also implies an eschatological perspective:

> The Holy Spirit has marked us with the *seal of the Lord ("Dominicus character")* "for the day of redemption." "Baptism indeed is the seal of eternal life." The faithful Christian who has "kept the seal" until the end, remaining faithful to the demands of his baptism, will be able to depart this life "marked with the sign of faith," with his baptismal faith, in expectation of the blessed vision of God—the consummation of faith—and in the hope of resurrection.[39]

## Principles and Structures of Initiation

The formation of the rite of Christian initiation, which leads to the cele-bration of baptism, confirmation, and Eucharist, represents the revival of the ancient tradition. It recaptures the original dynamic relationship of these three sacraments as essential and inseparable aspects of the unique event of Christ. From the perspective of this vital source event, we can envisage all three as the Great Sacrament of Christian Initiation.

This section first presents the principles or fundamentals of the process of sacramental initiation and then looks at its structure accord-ing to the modern Rite of Christian Initiation of Adults. This restored rite corresponds in its ecclesial principles and catechumenal structure to the practice of the ancient Church.

Vatican II revived this sacramental practice. Thus, the Rite of Chris-tian Initiation of Adults today defines initiation as the full development into communion with the mystery through the three sacraments: "In the sacraments of Christian initiation we are freed from the power of darkness and joined to Christ's death, burial and resurrection. We receive the Spirit of filial adoption and are part of the entire people of God in the celebration of the memorial of the Lord's death and resur-rection. The three sacraments of Christian initiation closely combine to bring us, the faithful of Christ, to his full stature and to enable us to carry out the mission of the entire people of God in the Church and in the world."[40]

As we attempt to examine each of the three sacraments, it is essen-tial to focus on the complete process as a unified action of Christian ini-tiation, as an integrated, albeit complex, whole. Baptism, confirmation, and Eucharist are central but inseparable elements whose role and the-ology should not be understood in isolation.

The long and complex process of initiation that developed from the second to the fifth century for the training and instruction of new con-verts was called the "catechumenate." It provided the foundation for all personal faith-life deriving from the sacramental experience.

### The Principles

The catechumenal foundation situates the sacraments in a new theolog-ical and spiritual framework. It represents a paradigmatic shift from previous theology and practice. It also provides a symbolic structural key, or hermeneutic liturgical model, to interpret not only the intrinsic unity of the sacramental order but also the ecclesial, spiritual, and ministerial dimensions of the sacraments.

The following discussion presents a comprehensive view of the fundamentals of the catechumenal structure. The fundamental elements are: *Word, Conversion, Mystery, Rituals, Ministry, Adult,* and *Process*.

*The word of God is primary.* Its profound relationship to the sacraments has already been stated. The acceptance of the *kerygma* of Christ crucified and risen from the dead is the spiritual foundation for the Christian process of initiation. The path of the catechumenate has as its goal communion with the mystery of Christ through conversion by means of responding to the call of the word of God. This function of the word, lived and living in a context of prayer and community relationship, is foundational. It entails a radical change in spiritual life and raises questions about one's way of being in the Church.

The catechumenal shift takes us to the very roots of Christianity. The dynamic spirit of early Christian initiation arose, in effect, from experiencing the proclamation of the new Passover. This proclamation embodies the symbols of the new creation in Christ, namely, the sacraments and the communion experience of the first Christians. The modern rite, the RCIA, an authentic gift of the Christian heritage, has the same dynamic spirit. It creates the possibility of existential openness to the word within a community of faith.

Catechumens are transformed and grow by listening to and freely accepting the word of God. This change gives them life and a reason for being. The word of God's liberating love, to which the listener makes the gift of self, has regenerative power. God's word takes its place at the core of the community where it inspires the community's vision and practice. The response of a community that walks in the light of the word will always be hope: "But those who wait for the LORD shall renew their strength, they shall mount up with wings like eagles" (Isa 40:31). In the catechumenate, catechesis and liturgy enjoy a profound relationship. Both have their roots in the experience of the word. Each has the same finality for evangelical Christian formation. This is the goal of the catechumen's journey.

*Conversion is the heart of the initiatory process*. The main objective of Jesus' ministry, conversion, was intrinsically connected to the preaching of the apostolic *kerygma*. The common New Testament term, *metanoia*, stresses radical change of a person's heart as the central motivational factor. The believer experiences the need for an unconditional return to God. A shift in perceptions, priorities, and lifestyle follows. It is the response to the good news: "Jesus came . . . proclaiming the good news of God, and saying, 'The time is fulfilled, and the kingdom of God has come near; repent, and believe in the good news'" (Mark 1:14–15). The response originates in the depths of a person's heart moved by God's grace: "bring me back, let me come back" (Jer 31:18).

The ongoing openness of the catechumen to the experience of God's unconditional love makes possible the process of conversion to the person of Christ rather than to a mere doctrine. This demands total trust and surrender to God's mysterious action: "Just like the clay in the potter's hand, so are you in my hand" (Jer 18:6). Conversion is essential to sacramental life and is the hallmark of Christian initiation.

*Mystery is the lifeblood of the transcendental communion unfolded by the initiatory action*. The catechumen is led into the mystery so that the mystery can lead the catechumen. That action fosters a vital and dynamic faith and is the privileged vehicle for a personal communion with God the Father, revealed by the person of Christ in the light of the Holy Spirit. This trinitarian heart is sacramentalized in the experience of the initiatory action whose focal point is the paschal mystery of Christ. The purpose of initiation is to enter into Christ's *Pasch* so that the whole life of the Christian becomes sacramental.

*Rituals punctuate the whole process* and are the mysterious vehicles by which the mystery of Christ is symbolically effected. They provide the framework for the sacramental words and action, which lead the believer through the reality of self-transcendence to the concrete experience of God's salvific presence. The Church uses key symbols (waterbath, the laying of hands with chrismation, the sharing of bread, etc.) and formative elements (the community faith, the power of the word, etc.) that are foundational to and will be repeated in other sacramental celebrations after Christian initiation.

*Ministry and initiation share the same dynamics* as developmental processes. They cannot be reduced to a ritual, but require growth in the mystery of Christ. Sacramental initiation grounds ministry and Christian ministry effects initiation. First, baptismal initiation gives fundamental meaning to the Christian vocation and mission, including that of ordained ministry. It empowers the believer who shares the life-giving power of the priesthood of Christ. As the first letter of Peter says:

> Come to him, a living stone, though rejected by mortals yet chosen and precious in God's sight, and like living stones, let yourselves be built into a spiritual house, to be a holy priesthood, to offer spiritual sacrifices acceptable to God through Jesus Christ . . . But you are a chosen race, a royal priesthood, a holy nation, God's own people, in order that you may proclaim the mighty acts of him who called you out of darkness into his marvelous light. (1 Pet 2:4–5, 9)

Second, the initiatory process itself necessarily requires the missionary self-awareness of the baptized community, and this is expressed in the diverse ministries—such as those of catechist and sponsor—needed for the spiritual support and formation of the catechumens.

Baptism calls to discipleship, and true discipleship requires the witness of service. In fact, the catechumenal process of becoming Christian requires the sharing of the community's vision and mission to building God's kingdom and witnessing the love of Christ within the family and to a broken world. As a normative model and the foundation of all the other sacramental rites of initiation, the RCIA is the ongoing movement of faith and ministerial development for the entire parish. Consequently, the involvement of the community is key, precisely because the baptized community is the primary minister of initiation.[41]

*The RCIA focuses on adults*, but its form has to be adapted to the concrete realities of a parish, especially children who have reached catechetical age and who await initiation.

A person of searching faith who is capable of accepting the consequences of inner conversion is the primary subject of the Church's initiatory praxis. However, the reality of conversion and the newness of life in Christ are God's gift. God's mysterious action respects human freedom and requires a person's commitment.

*Process is basic to all types of ritual initiation.* The idea of a continuous process through various stages is not unique to Christianity. The dynamics of process are an essential part of human reality. Deeply embedded in this human reality, sacramental initiation entails a gradual and complex process. Mircea Eliade defines religious initiation as "a body of rites and oral teachings whose purpose is to produce a decisive alteration in the religious and social status of the person to be initiated."[42]

Cultural anthropology stresses three basic parts of the religious process of initiation: rites of *separation*, rites of *liminality,* and rites of *incorporation*. These structures provide meaning, integrate a person into a community, and symbolize the originality of the new life. The catechumenate corresponds mostly to the liminal stage, a threshold point in a catechumen's progress. Assisted by the community, catechumens experience God's gift of himself.

The process of Christian initiation is more than an educational program. Similar to other religious initiations, it has to respect the basic patterns that respond to the dynamics of human development. Beyond those basic patterns of human experience, Christian initiation is a grace-event anchored deep in historico-salvific reality. Christian initiation is a gradual process of discerning God's activity in our lives in light of salvation history's great realities. Biblical signs (such as the blind man) and paradigms (such as the Exodus) are models for the existential situations the human person ordinarily faces. These signs and paradigms should, therefore, first be interpreted as a key for today, as concrete signs of God in the labyrinth of our lives, and then accepted as being capable of generating new persons in the image of Christ.

The new spiritual vision and consciousness of community that characterizes the catechumenal movement originates in a person who is the Word rather than in a body of doctrines, programs, or structures. To the degree that the hearers open themselves to the word, the Spirit of the Lord creates community. The faithful grow as members of the community of the Church.

The RCIA is primarily a liturgical and ecclesial process that entails three interacting movements:

The action of a living God, inviting all people into communion; the action of a faithful yet weak community of the baptized seeking to respond to the Lord's call and the action of those desiring conversion, thus seeking admittance into the community through baptism, confirmation, and Eucharist. These three actions together constitute the initiation process, and in their joining they create the Church.[43]

## The Structure

The structure of stages, periods, and their meaning as described by the RCIA provides a ritual framework. It calls for adjustments, a sense of flexibility and creativity. Parishes must respond in concrete ways to the spiritual needs of the people. The catechumen journeys through liturgical rites, which are part of his or her conversion and growth in faith. These include:

- acceptance into the order of catechumens;

- election or enrollment of those ready for the sacraments (First Sunday of Lent);

- celebration of the sacraments of initiation (Easter Vigil).

The entire initiatory process has four distinct periods:

*1. Evangelization and Precatechumenate*
This initial period marks a special time of parish outreach and response to the evangelizing mission of the Church. Faithfully and constantly the Church proclaims the living God and Jesus Christ whom he has sent for the salvation of all. A welcoming Church responds to the individual's inquiry, as a search for God and an initial acceptance of faith.

*2. The Catechumenate*
This period begins with the candidates' formal entrance into the Church as catechumens. The presider signs the cross on catechumens' foreheads and welcomes them to the table of the word of God. Signing and the word of God express the action of Christ leading the catechumens on their journey of conversion and the awakening of their divine vocation. The community's support is essential, for "the Church embraces

the catechumens as its own with a mother's love and concern."[44] The period of the catechumenate varies in duration and corresponds to the progress of the individual. It is a time of catechetical formation, of deepening of one's faith relationship to Christ. Christian training during this period deals with four areas: (1) *catechesis* rooted in the word that proclaims the mystery of salvation; (2) *experience* of the Christian way of life in its personal, communal, and social dimensions; (3) *participation* in the liturgical prayers and traditions, temporarily excluding the liturgy of the Eucharist; and (4) *witnessing* to the evangelical mission of the Church as members of Christ's body.

The rite of election or enrollment of names is usually celebrated on the First Sunday of Lent. This initiates the final preparation of the catechumens, now the elect, for the sacraments of initiation.

### 3. Purification and Enlightenment

These rites include the recitation of the creed, the symbol of faith, and the Lord's Prayer. The baptismal and penitential character of Lent harmonizes with this intense period of conversion and spiritual growth. The process is marked by celebration and scrutinies, the rite of *ephphetha,* the choice of a Christian name, and anointing.

The catechumenal journey culminates with the celebration of the sacraments of baptism, confirmation, and Eucharist. It is a jubilant occasion, usually integrated into the celebration of the most solemn and holy night, the Easter Vigil. Through sacramental participation, the paschal mystery reaches its climax in the celebration of salvation history.

### 4. Postbaptismal Catechesis or Mystagogy

The fifty days from Easter to Pentecost celebrate the final phase of the ritual action of initiation in which the neophytes ("newly converted") are fully and joyfully integrated into the community as committed participants and acquire a comprehensive understanding of the sacramental and ministerial life of the Church. The initiating Church, and the newly baptized, "grow in deepening their grasp of the paschal mystery and in making it part of their lives through meditation on the Gospel, sharing in the Eucharist, and doing works of charity."[45]

Into what type of parish community are the neophytes to be integrated? This privileged fifty-day festival deepens their personal experience

of the mysteries through God's word and sacramental participation in
the fellowship of the Spirit. It also develops their missionary awareness
as sharers in the common priesthood of all the baptized.

This is not the end, but a new beginning for the neophytes, literally
"newly planted," or newly made Christians. The initiation ritual ends
with Pentecost, but baptismal consciousness continues for life. Purely
doctrinal catechesis will not suffice for developing this baptismal consciousness for life. The Eucharist is central in the mystagogical experience leading into the mystery of God, the mystagogue, and in under-
taking a life-long journey by God's mysterious presence. Therefore "a
parish's RCIA process needs to be developed out of its understanding
of the role and vision of mystagogy, and not vice versa."[46]

In summary, the catechumenal structure of adult initiation—the normal process of Christian conversion, gradual evangelization, and effective
integration of the believer into the Church—has these characteristics:

- It is a *gradual process* marked in ritual stages of a journey of
  conversion to Christ experienced in small groups with flexibility and adaptation as important aspects.

- It presupposes *communitarian participation*, especially
  through the support of the inspirational model of sponsors,
  in a new understanding of the parish as a ministerial community in which laywomen and laymen have crucial roles to
  play.

- Finally, it is *scripturally and liturgically centered*. It is a
  process by which faith empowers and leads the believer into
  the mystery of God's kingdom.

Mystagogy is the soul of sacramental life. Before we move on to the
other two parts of the rite of initiation, confirmation and Eucharist, let
us reflect on this poignant text on the spiritual and theological significance of initiation:

The neophytes are, as the term "mystagogy" suggests, introduced into a fuller and more effective understanding of mysteries through the Gospel message they have learned and
above all through their experience of the sacraments they have

received. For they truly have been renewed in mind, tested more deeply the sweetness of God's word, received the fellowship of the Holy Spirit and grown to know the goodness of the Lord. Out of this experience, which belongs to a Christian and increases as it is lived, they derive a new perception of the faith, of the Church, and of the world.[47]

# 6
# Confirmation:
# Communion in the Holy Spirit

An overview of the literature on both the theological understanding and pastoral praxis of confirmation in the churches reveals a wide variety of opinions. There is a bewildering range of interpretations concerning its biblical, historical, ecclesial, and ritual aspects. Addressing the questions concerning the nature of confirmation presents an opportunity to achieve theological clarity by disclosing the underlying mystery and context of confirmation as an integral part of Christian initiation.

This chapter takes a three-part approach. First, it examines the different phenomena inherent in the sacrament. The discussion focuses on the essential *mystagogical vision* needed for a deeper understanding of the nature of confirmation. Second, the *biblical foundations and historical origins* explain the shifts in theological meaning and emerging ritual patterns throughout Christian history. Third, the *theology* of confirmation clarifies issues regarding the *constants* of Christian tradition.

Confirmation is an integral action of the total event of Christian initiation. Therefore, the following remarks presuppose an understanding of the biblical and theological foundations, as well as the ritual developments of the symbolic action of baptism as developed in the previous chapter.

## A Mystagogical Vision

In recent decades, confirmation has undergone a great deal of theological scrutiny both by Roman Catholic and Protestant authors.[1] The research touches on a wide range of biblical, historical, and theological data, as well as pastoral, liturgical, and educational issues. Nevertheless, a consensus regarding the origins and tradition of the sacrament as well as ways of developing a richer, more contemporary pastoral practice has proven to be elusive. The difficulties of the debate are evident in three main areas: theological, pastoral, and ecumenical.

## Mystagogy, not Chronology

Since the eleventh century, Western scholastic theologians raised questions about the theological identity and rationale of confirmation as a separate sacrament. Without providing a theology of the sacrament, yet recognizing it as standing on its own, the Council of Trent in the sixteenth century declared confirmation a true and proper sacrament. Later reformers denied its sacramentality on biblical grounds. They highlighted the completeness of God's action and gift in baptismal initiation. The Eastern Orthodox churches retain the early Christian tradition of a unified rite of initiation, including baptism, confirmation, and Eucharist, that stresses the mystery of chrismation by the Holy Spirit.

A theology of confirmation entails integration of the theology of baptism. Both sacraments signify the unity of the paschal mystery of the event of Christ and the event of the Spirit at Pentecost. The bishops at Vatican II and Pope Paul VI reaffirmed this intimate connection between confirmation and baptism.[2]

Related to this unity, there arises the question of sequence in the celebration of the sacraments of initiation with respect to children. The practice of infant baptism and the traditional system of religious education somehow condition the age of confirmation. Should the original sequence of baptism-confirmation-Eucharist prevail versus the present sequence of baptism-Eucharist-confirmation? The Church gives priority to appropriate spiritual dispositions, and thus takes a moderate posture regarding the sequence. Continuity and the meaning of the sacramental rites, which develop in their relationship to the mystery of Christ, should supersede any practical consideration. Thus, the answer to the question of order is primarily christological, not pedagogical. The sacramental sequence is established by the mystery of Christ in its progressive actualization in the life of the believer rather than by pedagogical function related to age. Consequently, the controlling issue should be *mystagogy*, not *chronology*, *kairos* rather than *chronos*, the organic deepening of the mystery of Christ and his Spirit rather than educational stages.

This mystagogical perspective makes confirmation an integral part of the baptismal and initiation event and also a phase of completion as well as an introduction of the baptized into the eucharistic experience. Mystagogy, the final stage of the initiation process, leads to a deepening of the Christian mystery by which the believer personally experiences the gift of the Spirit. Mystagogy has to do with spiritual growth and empowerment rather than pedagogical catechesis. It provides a foundation for discipleship and a living personal relationship with God. This theology is at the heart of confirmation.

Understanding the specific sacramental nature of confirmation and its distinction from baptism (especially in regard to the prophetic Spirit attributed to confirmation as a supplementary gift of the same baptismal Spirit) requires a mystagogical vision grounded in the Spirit-event of Pentecost. Confirmation, like mystagogy, is the experience of a living personal relationship through the mystery. This experience renews and confirms the baptismal call because the experience of the mystery has to be personally appropriated by those baptized as infants. It has to be made explicit and effective in a new deeper way through the celebration of the event of the Spirit.

Confirmation is an important part of the sacramental economy. It focuses on the central mystery of the Spirit in Christ, the confirmed one *par excellence.* Already shared through baptism in the life of the believer, the Spirit-event is proclaimed throughout history as present in the Church and in the world. This christocentric and historico-salvific perspective is essential to the theology of confirmation. "We are celebrating what God has been doing and is continuing to do. What we celebrated at the baptism of an individual continues on a day-to-day basis. Confirmation celebrates one aspect of that baptismal event, which has gone on continually since baptism: the gift of the Spirit to an individual."[3]

## Communion in the Holy Spirit

The second aspect of the problem has to do with pastoral implications. This is a difficult area because the history of confirmation is complex and present practices even within Catholic countries are varied. Thus, there is the need for a pastoral theology of confirmation, rooted in the principles of the RCIA and inspired by the mystagogical vision described above. In practical terms, in addition to the question of order, another main concern is age. Generally, there are two identifiable patterns of confirmation in modern times: (1) a ritual flowing from a baptismal consciousness and serving also as an introduction to the Eucharist; (2) a ritual apart from baptism and understood in educational terms as a rite of passage into adulthood.

These different understandings and ritual contexts leave a vast area open to interpretation and critical analysis. How can our pastoral practice be rooted doctrinally in scripture and be faithful to the early historical tradition? How can the Church harmonize the role of confirmation—celebrating the gracious gift of God—and at the same time respond to a culture of great emptiness in which the Church needs to ritualize the coming of age of young people as mature Christians?

These and other questions need not be insoluble. *Divinae Consortium Naturae*, the 1971 apostolic constitution of Paul VI, which introduced the Rite of Confirmation, laid the premise for a richer pastoral practice according to the biblical meaning of early tradition and its unitary sacramental and catechumenal model. This model, which represents the true tradition of the Church, views confirmation from a predominantly baptismal perspective as the sacramental expression of an unfolding initiation and as the sealing of baptism. Educational aspects are secondary because confirmation is neither tied to adolescence nor a rite of passage or maturity.

Confirmation is about *calling* rather than about age—calling to a relationship with the Holy Spirit. Yet the question of age is a factor to consider, and practices in this regard have differed widely both historically and regionally. The 1983 Code of Canon Law, following the apostolic constitution of Paul VI, determines that "the sacrament of confirmation is to be conferred on the faithful at about the age of discretion."[4] The problem of the right age, which is up to the national conference of bishops, can be argued on many grounds, including psychological, catechetical, ecclesial. In general, the European episcopal conferences have proposed that the age of confirmation be between twelve and eighteen years. The American bishops have temporarily adopted an even broader age span, between seven and eighteen years. Discretion is left to diocesan bishops.

The general norms allow a pluralism of models and a variety of pastoral practices. A challenging and simple celebration inspires youth and acknowledges the biblico-baptismal significance of confirmation, a significance that takes on renewed meaning in our time. In summary,

> Baptism is seen as a beginning, as a first step in the initiation process; while confirmation is seen as the completion or fruition of that same baptismal commitment... Baptism is a celebration of the Easter mystery—the foundation of the Church, the seed time, the first fruits; confirmation is a celebration of Pentecost—the continuation and growth of the Church, the fullness of harvest. Baptism focuses on Christ; confirmation focuses on the Spirit.[5]

## Other Christian Models

There is also an important ecumenical dimension to consider in the two other models of confirmation present in the Eastern Orthodox and Protestant Anglican churches. Progress and convergence toward a common theological ground and praxis of confirmation depend primarily on a redefinition of the sacrament from the christological, ecclesial, and anthropological perspectives. It also relies on the emergence of the catechumenal paradigm of the 1972 promulgation of the RCIA, the simple, radical, and revolutionary approach to Christian initiation. This vision promises to shape centuries of sacramental and pastoral practice in all churches.

The Orthodox tradition represents the ancient and biblico-patristic practice of unified initiation. Confirmation is called chrismation. It consists of one simple anointing with the holy chrism, or *myron*, applied by the priest to the sensing organs of the baptized in the course of the same celebration: "The seal of the gift of the Holy Spirit. Amen." This sacramental action is understood as the mystery of chrismation by the Holy Spirit, just as the same Spirit came upon Christ at his baptism, an action seen symbolically as an anointing. This and other themes of the great prayers, especially the sacramental *epiclesis*, are essential to an authentic understanding of the Orthodox tradition of chrismation.

Protestant Anglican churches tend to view confirmation as an adult affirmation of the baptismal vows (usually spoken for them as infants) and stress its catechetical structure. Luther was concerned about the importance of the primary biblical sacraments—baptism and the Eucharist—and challenged the idea of confirmation as sacrament. Two Protestant themes of the modern sacramental reform that indicate some progress toward convergence are the views that: (a) Christian initiation ought to be complete at one point; and (b) Christian initiation ought to be a lifelong process. The Lutheran scholar Maxwell Johnson stresses the importance of the recovery of a baptismal spirituality and its implications: "All the debates about knowledge, preparation, and age for confirmation should be terminated. Perhaps then the Churches can get busy on life-long *mystagogy* and the life-long return to the font as Christians seek to live out in the Spirit the implications of their new birth!"[6]

Several Protestant churches have restored chrismation to infant baptism, keeping confirmation as a repeatable profession of faith before the community. In an unpublished paper, William Myers, professor at Chicago Theological Seminary, noted four approaches to confirmation: confirmation as school; as spiritual experience; as rite of passage; and as membership system. The churches continue to develop the sacrament and ritual of confirmation along theological and practical lines to encourage the fullness of Christianity in their members.


## Biblical and Historical Origins

Contemporary Catholic scholars differ on the ritual origins of confirmation as a second sacramental act. However, both New Testament sources and the historical evolution of the liturgical structures of Christian initiation hold the key for interpreting the origins of a post-baptismal rite of the Spirit. The New Testament provides a theological background on the meaning of the sacramental experience of the gift of the Spirit. For some authors it contains the roots and even the explicit evidence of a separate sacramental act. Paul VI in his apostolic constitution finds the beginning of confirmation in the references of Acts: "This laying on of hands is rightly recognized by Catholic tradition as the beginning of the sacrament of confirmation, which in a certain way perpetuates the grace of Pentecost in the Church."[7]

An appropriate methodology does not read the liturgical practices and theological positions of a later period into the New Testament.

Both biblical and historical sources are self-evident. Despite the many gaps in our knowledge of the early Church, it is crucial to verify the constants in the history of sacramental practices and identify their connection to the apostolic Church. These historical *constants* hold the key to interpreting the ritual origins of confirmation. As Kavanagh asserts, these origins "cannot dependably be determined by theological reflection, biblical exegesis (even of Acts 8) or catechetics."[8]

## Biblical Sources

Does the practice of the apostolic Church contain indications of a specific post-baptismal rite of the Spirit? Two different New Testament references have been cited in relation to the sacrament of confirmation. Acts 8:14–17 and Acts 19:1–7 might refer to a second (post-baptismal) act of the gift of the Spirit. Then there are the Pauline and Johannine passages (see also Acts 2:37–38) in which the water-bath involves the gift of the Spirit: "In the one Spirit we were all baptized" (1 Cor 12:13); "No one can enter the kingdom of God without being born of water and Spirit" (John 3:5). The Samaritan people in Acts 8 received the good news and were baptized by Philip, an unauthorized missionary. However, the apostolic leaders of the Jerusalem church, Peter and John, laid hands on the converts, and they received the Holy Spirit. Acts 19 relates a second case in which baptized converts at Ephesus received the Holy Spirit as Paul laid hands on them.

Traditionally, Catholics have seen in Acts the biblical indication of a post-baptismal sacramental act, while Protestants have interpreted the references of Luke and his view of the divine Spirit in the context of Pauline-Johannine theology. The traditional position is still maintained by Catholic writer Thomas Marsh who presents Acts as the primary and controlling source for interpreting the initiation practice of the early Church. He concludes his investigation of the New Testament sources concerning that practice as "two rites, baptism followed by imposition of hands for the gift of the Spirit (or, in other terminology, confirmation)."[9] Marsh does not seem to use the appropriate methodology cited above.

Recent biblical scholarship utilizes a broad-based ecclesial and exegetical framework to analyze the eventually fragmented rite while building on the New Testament, specifically Acts. According to this interpretation, the above-cited references in Acts express ecclesial belonging through the gift of the one Spirit. It is signified by the imposition of hands by the apostolic representatives. The Church is one and apostolic, namely "built up on the foundation of the apostles and prophets" (Eph 2:20). This ecclesiological perspective rejects the idea of an inchoate rite of confirmation in Acts.

The reading of Acts as a basis for a second rite is purely speculative. As an assumption based on two exceptional cases, it contradicts the ordinary praxis of baptismal initiation in the New Testament, including the reception of the gift of the Holy Spirit as a sign of the new age. The issue is not the rite but rather communion with the apostolic fellowship by which the "disciples" in Acts 8 and 19 gain access to the Holy Spirit.[10] In fact, the event of Pentecost, the day of outpouring of God's Spirit, is characterized in Acts as the baptism of the Spirit (Acts 1:5).

Acts is not a systematic presentation of the practices of the early Christians. The works of the Spirit are seen as free and unpredictable rather than as sacramental moments. The Gentile Pentecost, the coming of the Spirit in the household of Cornelius, is telling. In fact, "it would contradict the New Testament to try to make the presence of the Divine Spirit in human hearts dependent on the administration of a sacrament. But it would not be contradictory to regard a sacrament as the prayer for the Spirit's coming and acting in a special way."[11]

## Historical Developments

Both the Pauline letters and the gospels confirm these conclusions concerning the initiatory rite based on a contextual approach to Acts. In second-century Christian writings there are no references to a second rite of initiation separate from water baptism. Similarly, works of early liturgical literature, like the *Didache* and the *Apology* of Justin, describe the rite with no mention of the laying on of hands or unction. These ceremonies, which followed the dipping in water, probably appeared toward the end of the second century and are clearly documented in the numerous references of the third century, especially in Tertullian's works and in the *Apostolic Tradition* of Hippolytus of Rome.

Both authors provide a complete and unified pattern of initiation as an integral whole involving water-bath, anointing, laying on of hands by the bishop, and Eucharist. Tertullian's description has strong Spirit-

related accents, for, according to him, the believer is cleansed and forgiven through the water by the power of the Holy Spirit and enriched
with its gifts through the ensuing imposition of hands. In Hippolytus's
structure of the rite, between the initiation and the Eucharist, the presbyter anoints each of the newly baptized, pouring oil on their heads.
Then the bishop lays his hand on them, signs them on the forehead,
and gives them the kiss of peace.[12]

The multiplication of ceremonies based on cultural and scriptural
interpretations emerged after the third century. These post-baptismal
ceremonies (anointing-sealing and the imposition of hands) are seen as
the "completion," according to Theodore of Mopsuestia: "You come up
from the water of baptism to receive the completion."[13]

It would be anachronistic to call these ceremonies in Hippolytus
"confirmation." In fact, the contribution of the *Apostolic Tradition* to
the issue of "confirmation" is problematic. Interpretation cannot be
based on a retrospective look from later fifth-century forms of confirmation or from medieval theology and liturgical practice. In his study of
its liturgical structure, Aidan Kavanagh concluded that "confirmation"
is not found in the *Apostolic Tradition*. The post-baptismal anointing by
a presbyter is not Spirit-related but christological. Also, the episcopal
laying on of hands and the prayers by the bishop are rather a dismissal
of the neophyte who is preparing to receive the Eucharist rather than a
special bestowing of the Holy Spirit.[14]

These post-baptismal ceremonies, namely, anointing, sealing, and
imposition of hands, in different forms within local churches, became an
integral part of the total initiatory unity of the classic age of Christian
initiation in the fourth and fifth centuries. They were to be performed
by the bishop and associated with the gifts of the seal of the Holy Spirit,
a meaning that appears to be rooted in scripture: "God…has anointed
us, by putting his seal on us and giving us his Spirit in our hearts as a
first installment" (2 Cor 1:21–22). The one simple rite of initiation
involved three important and organically related symbolic moments: the
water-bath, the chrism, and the Eucharist. It would be anachronistic to
see at this stage a separate sacrament of "confirmation."

The fifth century represented the beginning of a long period of
evolution of the complex process of initiation that gradually produced
the fracturing of its successive components: the catechumenate and
the baptismal and post-baptismal rites. This evolution in the West

eventually led to the separation in time between the water-bath and the chrism. The change was mainly pastoral, and came about due to different circumstances, one being that baptismal candidates were primarily children. Another was the emergence and extension of the ministry of presbyters, especially in rural areas where the bishop remained liturgically the central symbol of ecclesial communion. A third circumstance was the anointing of heretics after reconciliation with the Church. Historically, praxis determined theory. And the separation of the two rites led eventually to the theological justification for two distinct sacraments.

The new shift toward an independent rite for the imparting of the Holy Spirit by the bishop was first manifest during the fifth century in Gaul, where the word "confirmation" was first used. Precedents for the emergence of a new praxis are also documented in Pope Innocent I's letter of 416 to Decentius of Gubbio. In it the independent post-baptismal signing on the forehead is given the technical term "consignation." Citing the rite's biblical basis in Acts 8, the letter makes reference to the exclusive spiritual power of the bishop for the conferring of the Holy Spirit.

Bishop Faustus of Riez (d. 460) gave the rite new liturgical meaning and a new theological basis in a famous homily on the feast of Pentecost. This marked the turning point of the medieval Catholic image of confirmation. The independent rite of the laying on of hands was justified on biblical grounds. It was also equated with the coming of the Spirit at Pentecost: "What the imposition of the hand bestows on each individual at the confirmation of neophytes is what the spirit bestowed upon all when he descended on the throng of believers."[15] Faustus emphasizes the separation between the effects of baptism and confirmation: "In baptism we are born anew for life, after baptism we are confirmed for battle; in baptism we are washed, after baptism we are strengthened."[16]

Both the Protestant reformers and the bishops of Trent (seventh session, 1547) appealed to late medieval sacramental developments. The reformers refuted the sacramentality of confirmation because it had not been explicitly instituted by Christ. It also appeared to devalue the role and content of baptism. They reduced confirmation to a non-sacramental rite of public witnessing to one's faith and commitment. It was celebrated as part of a maturing process, before the coming of adulthood. In its defense of the traditional teaching on the sacraments, Trent maintained that confirmation confers a character and it is "a true and proper sacrament."[17]

The profound renewal of Vatican II, especially its stress on the unifying vision among all the sacraments in relation to life, led to the development of the ecclesial context. The Second Vatican Council saw the Church as the community of the baptized. The council emphasized the need for experiential initiation in Christian faith and the reality of the missionary calling to the apostolate of the laity as implied in baptism and confirmation. By this sacrament believers "are more perfectly bound to the Church and are endowed with the special strength of the Holy Spirit."[18]

## The Theology of Confirmation: Reform and Its Future

Both in medieval and in modern times the theology of confirmation as outlined in the previous discussions provided an inadequate methodology for revealing both the sacramental nature and the spiritual meaning of confirmation. It isolated confirmation from its symbolic and liturgical setting. Clearly, a theological methodology that focuses on the *symbolic* setting of the rite discloses the sacramental meaning of confirmation. The essential symbolic sacramental action, which is rooted in the Church's traditions, contains and expresses that full meaning in a concrete and specific way. The classic axiom *lex orandi, lex credendi* applies here: "the law of praying establishes the law of believing."

### Reformed Rite

Liturgical reform implied an increased theological awareness of new, explicit references to the role of the Holy Spirit across all major sacramental actions, specifically in the initiatory sequence. Baptism celebrates the sharing in the mission of Christ, originating with the Spirit and fulfilled by the Spirit in the paschal mystery. Then the grace-laden way of confirmation celebrates the same mission in the Christian person, who is gifted and sealed by the Spirit to live out the same Christ's *Pasch.* As a fundamental gift constituting Christian identity, the mystery of the Spirit's presence and relationship with the believer can be translated in a wide variety of ways, including affirmation and growth in the faith through the communion of the Spirit and a living personal relationship with Christ in the same Spirit. With the Spirit-pledge we are becoming what we are and what we shall be, for "God . . . has anointed us, by putting his seal on us and giving us his Spirit in our hearts" (2 Cor 1:21–22).

In the reformed Rite of Confirmation (1971), the outpouring of the Spirit at Pentecost as gift and seal is the centering theme and specific sacramental element. This reform retrieved the symbolic value and meaning of the former patristic initiatory structure of a post-baptismal chrismation. In the biblico-patristic vision, the oil symbolizes the penetration of the Holy Spirit in the baptized, and signifies the irreversible belonging to Christ. The bishop is called the original but not the exclusive minister of confirmation. He invokes the divine spirit by the laying on of hands, anointing the forehead with the sacred chrism (the essential element of the rite), making the sign of the cross, and reciting the words of an adopted ancient Byzantine formula: "Be sealed with the gift of the Holy Spirit."

Throughout this chapter's analysis of confirmation's issues, biblico-theological foundations, and historical origins, several constants have become apparent. These constants are crucial and can serve as guideposts in the continuing discussion of the theology and pastoral praxis of confirmation. Confirmation has had a complex historical development in the Western churches and its theology has been shaped by contrasting biblical and historical interpretations. Because they can be traced back to early Church origins and through contemporary reforms, an understanding of the constants is essential for the present and future renewal of confirmation. The constants are: (1) *the baptismal context* as the place of confirmation within the sacramental structure; (2) *the communion in the Holy Spirit* as the Church's basic identity; and (3) *the pastoral praxis* of the Church as the interpretative key to historical changes.

In general, one could say that many of the recurring difficulties having to do with confirmation are due to ambiguous theological and pastoral interpretations. Theologically, one cannot apply to confirmation rigid and univocal concepts of both sacramentality and the sacramental role of the Holy Spirit. Pastorally, one cannot expect a single rite to fulfill all the needs associated with building Christian identity, such as indicating religious maturity or providing a rite of passage.

## The Baptismal Context

Although there is no basis in the New Testament for a second sacramental rite separate from baptism, the meaning and origin of a symbolic act and prayer for the gift of the Spirit are traceable back to the
apostolic period. The initiation rite of the early Church was an integral
whole that was envisaged as a single great sacrament of Christian initiation. It consisted of a triadic pattern of (a) baptism in water, (b) anointing, laying on of hands, signing with the cross, and (c) Eucharist.

Tertullian's works in the early third century exemplified this integrated ritual practice of a baptismal bath by the operation of the Holy
Spirit and a Spirit-related laying on of hands after the post-baptismal
anointing, concluding with signation. In later terminology, this second
cluster would become confirmation. The two rites are separated, but
obviously the gift of God's Spirit remains one. In a dynamic vision of
the sacraments, one complements the other in the same operation of
the Holy Spirit. Confirmation symbolizes the gift of the sealing Spirit
already received at baptism.

An essential characteristic of the biblico-patristic churches was
their baptismal consciousness, a consciousness that appears to be significantly neglected in modern times. Reclaiming the fundamental meaning and vitality of confirmation depends not only on retrieving a unifying context but also on regaining a strong baptismal consciousness from
which flow profound ecclesial, spiritual, and transformational consequences. Thus, confirmation is intimately related to the catechumenal
fundamentals of baptism and its mystagogical vision, as was discussed
in the previous chapter.

## Personal Relationship with Christ's Spirit

The communion in the Holy Spirit at confirmation re-creates the coming of God's Spirit to the world. It also communicates to the Christian
community as a new Pentecost. Furthermore, it actualizes the christological mystery, which is the foundation and meaning of all sacramentality. This Christ-Spirit relatedness is essential. The Spirit precedes
and follows confirmation. The rebirth in Christ by the Holy Spirit is the
grace of baptism; the communion in the Holy Spirit is the grace of confirmation. Confirmation realizes a concrete sharing of the salvific mys-

tery of Christ and communion in his Spirit in the life of the believer. These are integral realities of the same celebration of the paschal mystery. In fact, communion in the Holy Spirit is the specific grace symbolized at confirmation. "The symbol of the imposition of hands with Chrismation is at the same time representation and reality of the event of the Spirit of God in the person, already given to Christ, so that the person becomes anointed—consecrated—that is *alter Christus* (another Christ)."[19]

Confirmation is, therefore, the perpetual sacramental fulfillment and realization of the creative and life-giving Spirit pledged by the prophets: "I will pour out my Spirit upon all flesh...Even upon my slaves, both men and women, in those days I will pour out my Spirit" (Acts 2:17–18). It is seen as an end-time universal endowment, the Spirit-filled community of Christ's disciples. Thus, "the gift of the Spirit makes you a living stone in that dwelling place of God amidst humanity that we call the Church. The Church counts on you for its existence: Even though you are young, you're able and ready to become, like Jesus, one who serves. You will receive a gift, but it's a heavy gift; I'd call it a seed that can bear wonderful fruit."[20]

## Pastoral Praxis

Finally, the pastoral praxis of the churches shows a pluralism of pastoral and ritual models adapted to the ecclesial context of the times. Chief among those models are: (a) chrismation as one of the three essential elements of initiation celebrated in a single liturgical celebration (Orthodox Church); (b) confirmation celebrated immediately after baptism, or separated from it and celebrated at a later age (Roman Catholic Church); and (c) a non-sacramental maturity rite as public profession of faith (Protestant Churches in general). The Protestant model fails to incorporate the relatively broad-based concept of sacramentality of the biblico-patristic age as well as initiatory structure of the early Christian churches. The developing structure of the rite of initiation appropriated the *Apostolic Tradition* and later split to form a new sacramental rite. Historically, in all the traditions the core thread has been celebrating the sealing of the Holy Spirit.

Other secondary interpretations also developed from the pastoral praxis of confirmation. It was theologized as a separate sacrament, or as the completion of baptismal rite for a mature commitment of faith. As mentioned earlier, the beginning of the practice of separating the sacrament of confirmation from the sacrament of baptism emerged in fifth-century Gaul, where "confirmation" was administered by the bishop. The Scholastics such as Thomas Aquinas considered it a sacrament of maturity. Today's concerns about the challenge of inculturation and multiculturalism, the need for a rite of passage into adulthood (like the celebration of *quinceañera* among Latin-Americans), and other pedagogical considerations demonstrate the necessity of respecting a pluralism of models to be used in addressing a variety of current needs in the local Churches.

Nevertheless, these models depend on the primary baptismal context with its spiritual implications, to which the dynamics of confirmation are inseparably bound. It is imperative that all models make the relationship with the Holy Spirit in the community and in the heart of the believer the fundamental referent.

Herbert Vorgrimler spells out two erroneous concepts against which we must always guard: (1) to regard confirmation as the first and fundamental communication of the Holy Spirit to any human being; and (2) to consider confirmation as a kind of ordination to the lay apostolate. Together with baptism, confirmation is "fundamental for all 'states' and ministries in the Church,"[21] a gift and a task: "Send us your Spirit to make us more like Christ in bearing witness to the world."[22]

# 7
# Eucharist:
# Center of Christian Existence

In the judgment of Edward Kilmartin, "the prevailing official Catholic Eucharistic theology...no longer does justice to this central mystery."[1] He further advocates an integration of the law of prayer, *lex orandi*, and the law of belief, *lex credendi*. Kilmartin foresees the normative value of the first law re-emerging in the third millennium. An authentic eucharistic theology builds on the Church's liturgical law of prayer. Regardless of the legitimacy of Kilmartin's thesis, the Church requires a more comprehensive approach to the Christian eucharistic tradition.

The approach taken in this chapter differs from the typical modern Catholic synthesis in that it does not concentrate directly on eucharistic categories, but rather integrates biblico-patristic thinking with contemporary religious consciousness. The starting point and focus is the *sacramental mystery* of the Eucharist as an essential element of Christian worship. Thus, the Eucharist is both the spiritual foundation of believers in the Christian community and vital center of Christian existence in the Church. This existence has three essential dimensions: (1) God's reign as primal source; (2) Church as salvific reality; and (3) universal transformation as liberating goal.

The future of these three dimensions of the Christian reality—eschatological, ecclesial, and cosmic—is in the eucharistic mystery. The inexhaustible sacramental symbol of the paschal mystery is the core of the three dimensions. This chapter approaches the dimensions of reign, Church, and world from the broad and ancient concept of *sacramental mystery*—in three complementary parts: biblical, historical, and systematic.

The first section explores the christocentric foundation of the Eucharist to identify three principles of interpretation connecting baptism and Eucharist in the life of the New Testament communities. To provide a context for the discussion, the second section identifies biblical master images of the Eucharist within a historical perspective and describes key historical shifts. The third section proposes a global and dynamic vision of the Eucharist as symbol of transformation of all reality: primordial, sacramental, ecclesial, and cosmic. It also analyzes central issues such as the real presence within a similar framework.

## The Sacrament of the Reign of God

The grounding of the Eucharist in the image of the coming of God's reign began with biblical and ancient tradition. Current historical research and comparative liturgical theology recognize an intimate relationship between biblical master images and the Eucharist as both christological and sacramental.

This section is divided into two parts. The first part reflects on the mysteries of Christ as the foundation of the Eucharist. The second part develops New Testament themes of sacramental praxis through the primary and intrinsically related signs of baptism and the Eucharist.

### Christological Origins: Pasch, Reign, and Praxis

Various theological treatises approach the origin of the Eucharist from its historical roots in the New Testament, specifically by basing the Eucharist on the Last Supper, the meals of the historical Jesus, and meals with witnesses after his resurrection. These are certainly fundamental events with which the New Testament eucharistic accounts are closely and directly linked. The contemporary historical-critical method relates these accounts to the post-resurrection faith experience of the early community. Eucharistic accounts of the Lord's Supper emerged from the disciples' shared faith in the risen Lord and the Spirit's transforming power. The starting point for a more comprehensive understanding is the life of the early Christians themselves, people whose faith was rooted in the Easter experience. More specifically, the theology of the accounts and references to the Eucharist must be seen in light of three overarching sources of interpretation: (a) *Christ's Pasch*, the central event; (b) *the reign of God*, the core theme of Jesus' life and ministry; and (c) the larger framework of the *sacramental praxis* of the New Testament.

### Christ's *Pasch*

Current biblical scholarship and eucharistic theology disclaim the strictly historical and literal interpretation of the Last Supper as the foundational event of the Eucharist. Thus, the Church's statement that the Lord instituted the sacrifice of the Eucharist at the Last Supper is theological rather than historical. The Last Supper was without doubt a key moment in the eucharistic experience of the early Church, but it was a moment that depended intimately on the cross and resurrection. Consequently, although it is an essential element of the eucharistic mystery, it is subordinate to Christ's Passover. It provides a link in the longer chain of paschal events culminating in Pentecost.

The roots of the Eucharist stem from that unique meal before Jesus' sacrifice on the cross. Indeed the earliest tradition calls the already established *koinonia* meals "the Lord's supper" (1 Cor 11:20). The Eucharist embodies Christ's own life and ministry. The centrality of Jesus' historical meals during his ministry provides a context for understanding the Last Supper.[2] Nevertheless, a theological approach based on a paschal vision of the communities that experience the risen Lord's continued presence offers a more comprehensive meaning than a pre-Easter historical interpretation. Vatican II's eucharistic approach has to be seen from this broad vision of the christological mysteries:

> At the last supper, on the night he was betrayed, our Savior instituted the eucharistic sacrifice of his body and blood. This he did in order to perpetuate the sacrifice of the cross throughout the ages until he should come again, and so to entrust to his beloved spouse, the church, a memorial of his death and resurrection: a sacrament of love, a sign of unity, a bond of charity, "a paschal banquet in which Christ is received, the mind is filled with grace, and a pledge of future glory is given to us."[3]

Lived through the faith experience of the early disciples, the Easter event was the core of the first eucharistic celebrations, "the breaking of the bread." This paschal meaning—Christ crucified as the lamb of the Christian Passover (1 Cor 5:7)—bases the Eucharist on the Last Supper, Jesus' meals in his ministry, and Jesus as risen Lord with his disciples.

The Eucharist is a paschal memorial, and therefore a post-resurrection event in its theological meaning and reality.

> The Post-Easter community, led by the exalted Lord present in the Spirit, by continuing in a new form the pre-Easter meals and especially the feast of Jesus' death with his disciples (i.e., in the form of thanksgiving, "in memory," calling on the Spirit), rightly laid claim to those pre-Easter celebrations (and especially the last meal) as a gift of the Lord to the Church.[4]

The four institution narratives (Mark 14:22–25; Matt 26:26–29; Luke 22:15–20; 1 Cor 11:23–26) need to be interpreted from this paschal perspective. Based on thematic similarities, scholars distinguish the texts of Paul and Luke from the textual traditions of Mark and Matthew. Léon-Dufour bases the eucharistic theology of the accounts of the Lord's Supper on two complementary theological traditions in the early Church. The *cultic tradition* (the four accounts, but especially Mark and Matthew) presents the event of Calvary and Jesus' living presence. In contrast, the *testamentary tradition* (evidenced primarily in the Gospel of John) connects the Eucharist to Jesus' testament in the farewell speech. Written after the Gospels of Matthew and Mark and Paul's letters, Luke's works seem to express the cultic tradition, stressing at the same time Jesus' spiritual testament, as in Luke 22:19–38. However, the testamentary tradition is also present in Paul's account, which emphasizes the need for communion and service for the eucharistic table participants.[5]

Christ's Passover is the founding event of the mystery. The contemplation of the Eucharist from this perspective leads to a central and broad vision of the sacrament. The *"paschal memorial" principle* of interpretation is the first and most comprehensive key to the correct methodological approach to eucharistic origins.

## Reign of God

The New Testament consistently relates the christological mysteries to the ecclesial assembly through the Eucharist. The relationship directly relates the Eucharist to *the mystery of the reign of God*. The Synoptics link the paschal mystery, the substance of Christ's kingship (cf. Rev 3:21), and the coming of the eschatological reign to the institution of the Eucharist: "Truly I tell you, I will never again drink of the fruit of the vine until that day when I drink it new in the kingdom of God" (Mark 14:25). The Eucharist is both a taste and a sign of the reign.

The reign of God is the central theme of the good news, the *kairos* preached by Jesus, and the heart of his ministry in words and actions. This reign ushers in a new age of God's lordship and spiritual freedom for all humankind. God's reign is at the heart of history, a gift of hope given by the Lord of life and history. It is accomplished in the present among the listeners and within them (Luke 12:37; 22:30), and yet to be fully realized in the future (Luke 12:35–40). In these texts, Luke uses the imagery of a meal to illustrate the eschatological nature of the reign of God.

In biblical tradition, the reign of God is seen through the imagery of a festive banquet promised in the messianic times (Isa 25:6). Joachim Jeremias notes how "it is important to realize that in the East, even today, to invite a man to a meal was an honour. It was an offer of peace, trust, brotherhood and forgiveness; in short, sharing a table meant sharing life."[6] The banquet of the reign appears in the gospels as a comprehensive key to understanding the redemptive mission of Jesus, a mission revealed through signs of the presence of the reign, such as the "eucharistic" multiplication of loaves (John 6:1–14). Jesus is the bridegroom and banquet of life in the Gospel of John. In the Synoptics there is a parallelism between Jesus' action of nourishing the crowds and the accounts of the Last Supper.

The Eucharist is an effective sign of the reign of God because it is the offer of the gift of the person of Jesus, and thus of participation in the mystery of his reign. Luke's account of the Last Supper connects the Eucharist to the reign of God as banquet: "I have eagerly desired to eat this Passover with you before I suffer; for I tell you, I will not eat it until it is fulfilled in the kingdom of God" (Luke 22:15–16). Jesus reinterprets the significance of the Jewish Passover through the prophetic imagery of the eschatological banquet and the expectation of its completion in the reign of God. "The first stage of fulfillment is the Eucharist itself, the center of spiritual life in the kingdom founded by Jesus; the final stage will be at the end of time."[7]

This association between the reign of God and the Eucharist as eschatological banquet establishes the Eucharist as an essential symbol of the presence of the reign. Called to participate in the banquet of the reign (Luke 22:28–30), the Church continued and preserved the memory of its dynamic reality. The reign ultimately embodied Jesus' service and sacrifice: "For the Son of Man came not to be served but to serve, and to give his life as a ransom for many" (Mark 10:45). In fact, the Last Supper symbolizes the reign of God announced and made present by Jesus. The eucharistic gift is the personal sacrifice of Jesus himself offering anew his banquet of the reign.

The centrality of the reign of God in Christian discipleship and the paschal memorial were part of the religio-theological interpretations of early Christians. The New Testament *kerygma* emphasized the symbol of the reign and the reality of the risen Christ. "New Testament eschatology received a particular accent from the disciples' experience of the Lord as risen: they came to think of his resurrection as a kind of anticipation of the coming of the kingdom. Consequently we have here a reason for seeing this early breaking of bread as focused on the risen Lord, and arguably on his presence, in continuity with the meals in the resurrection narratives."[8] The Eucharist was not only the sacrament of the *Pasch* but also the perfect sacrament of the reign, because the Eucharist realized the believer's communion with the risen Christ "at his table in his reign."[9] The presence of the messianic reign *already come* gathered the *ekklesia* around the eucharistic memorial, drawing the *ekklesia* into the reign *to come*.

Alexander Schmemann termed the biblical background and theological perspective of the Eucharist "the journey of the Church into the dimension of the kingdom."[10] He also states in regard to the origins of the Eucharist:

We can now affirm that the Church's worship was born and, in its external structure, "took shape" primarily as a *symbol of the kingdom*, of the Church's ascent to it and, in this ascent, of her fulfillment as the body of Christ and the temple of the Holy Spirit . . . The Church—that "little flock" to whom it was the Father's good pleasure to give the kingdom (Luke 12:32)— fulfills in the Eucharist her ascension and entrance into the light and joy and triumph of the kingdom . . . It was from this totally unique and incomparable experience, from this fully *realized* symbol, that the whole of the Christian *lex orandi* was born and developed.[11]

## Sacramental Praxis

The *sacramental praxis* of the early community builds upon the New Testament eucharistic tradition of the paschal memorial and reign of God. Praxis or action appropriate to belief is the criterion for genuine Christian discipleship through the concrete living out and celebrating of the christological mysteries. It includes a theological dimension. The early Christians fleshed out in their lives and liturgical assemblies their paschal experience, thus effectively responding to the way they viewed Jesus' mission from which they developed their own eucharistic traditions. Thus, the first eucharistic references reflect the spirit and concrete experience of the community in living out the *Pasch,* that is, the historical praxis of Jesus and his reign.

The concept of praxis is important because the Eucharist presupposes a particular community living out its faith experience and incorporating its own religious story. This kind of sacramental praxis rejects any ritualistic, individualistic, or external religious interpretation of the eucharistic memorial. In fact, New Testament sacramentality shows a dynamic link between celebration and life. There "sacramental" signs are the celebration of the praxis of God's reign preached and lived by the Lord.

In reference to the cultic and testamentary traditions, Xavier Léon-Dufour stresses the implications of the former, based especially in John, chapters 13 to 17. The washing of the feet has a powerful symbolic meaning. It represents Jesus' loving service as a model for participants at the eucharistic table.

The Eucharist not only presupposes an ethical and solidary mind-set and praxis, but also demands certain practical

> consequences...For the New Testament, the points at which
> the Eucharist is open to people's lives are more important than
> theological explanations...Léon-Dufour points, first of all, to
> the rhythm of cult and the daily life among Christians, which
> can be linked up with the cultic and testamentary tradition in
> the accounts of Jesus' final meal.[12]

Thus, remembrance inextricably connects liturgical action and an attitude of service with Christian existence. The disciples remembered Christ's words over the bread and cup and his action of washing feet "on that evening as the climax of his entire life...thus [giving] their own gatherings a ritual character by celebrating the Eucharistic meal."[13]

Elements of the testamentary tradition are primarily present in Paul's interpretation of the true meaning of the Lord's Supper. He stresses the importance of "discerning the body," or organic unity that exists among the many participants forming one body, namely the body of Christ (1 Cor 11:23–30). Christ is the basis of the Christian community living in the one life of the body. And the community is the basis of the Eucharist as it leads the community into Christ's risen life.

This praxis interpretation is important because the eucharistic accounts and liturgical formulas manifest the lives of particular faith communities. The Eucharist, as open table of the reign brought to all, especially to outcasts, is God's *shalom* embracing the world. It signifies what all people are to become. David Power states that: "These various features of the New Testament evidence facilitate a praxis-oriented understanding of the Eucharist whereby it is seen in relation to the Church's mission in the service of God's kingdom and to the Church's aspirations to truth and justice for all peoples, in the memory and hope of Jesus Christ."[14]

Most important, sacramental praxis points to a broader view of the New Testament sacramental movement, namely the relation between baptismal and eucharistic faith. Drawing on the Old Testament and developing from the post-resurrectional Christian experience, this evangelical sacramentality highlights essential theological themes that we will explore in the following pages.

## *Christocentric Spirituality: From Baptism to Eucharist*

As the lamb of God, Jesus inaugurated the universal banquet of the reign of God in his *Pasch*. This was the original event of the Eucharist and also of the baptism of water in the Spirit. Early Christians saw signs of these in different aspects of Jesus' ministry. The key symbolic actions, baptism and Eucharist, became the primary signs of the presence of his reign. Cullman notes that baptism and Eucharist are for the Church's life what miracles were for Christ's public ministry.[15]

The sacramental experience of early Christianity, that is, the experience of being reborn through water and spirit (John 3:5) and sharing the table of the Lord (1 Cor 11:21), began with the Church. The Church relived through this experience the saving event of the resurrection. Soon those key symbolic actions became the mainstays of the Church's spiritual life and the way to Christian maturity prior to any theological articulation of sacramentality and its terminology. The New Testament does not speak of sacramental categories or of a norm of Christian initiation, but refers to the great symbols by which Christians lived out in freedom and celebrated with joy their new hope.

A unified and articulated sacramental experience of the mystery of Christ emerged after the second century. However, from the very beginning, baptism and Eucharist appeared as major signs of the mystery and became the pillars of the developing ritual experience of the Church's faith. The sacramental experience was the lifeblood of a future catechumenal process of initiation. The response to the proclamation of the Christian *kerygma* was expressed in the faith and conversion of the hearers and culminated in the celebration of baptism and the breaking of the bread (Acts 2:41, 42).

Those sacramental moments might appear in the New Testament as separate actions, but we have to keep in mind that the textual references to baptism and especially to the Eucharist are limited. Throughout the New Testament, baptism appeared inseparable from the reception of the gift of the Holy Spirit, and the eucharistic fellowship meals were privileged occasions for expressing the same central mystery, the Lord's *Pasch:* "Are you able to drink the cup that I drink, or be baptized with the baptism that I am baptized with?" (Mark 10:38).

The sacramentality of Christ is the key that unlocks Christian sacramentality. He is the way, the life, and the goal of Christian existence.

Christ is the sacrament because he is the sign, image, and icon of God, "the image of the invisible God" (Col 1:15), the definitive Word of God made flesh who lived among us (John 1:14), and the hidden mystery of God now revealed to his saints (Col 1:27).

Those sacramental moments, which the book of Acts seems to present with little formality and reflection, had an intrinsic and unifying relationship. They were seen as symbols of the renewed people of God at "the end of time." In what follows we will focus on this evangelical sacramentality rather than attempting to review the great variety of eucharistic references.

There are five major themes in the sacramental praxis of the New Testament communities, rooted as they are in a paschal vision flowing from baptism to Eucharist.[16] They are signs of

1. Incorporation into Christ: "Proclaiming His Death, Discerning His Body" (Paul)

2. Christian Discipleship and Mission: "Drinking His Cup" (Mark)

3. The Presence of the Risen Christ: "For the Forgiveness of Sins" (Matthew)

4. The Christian Journey: "Recognizing Him in the Breaking of Bread" (Luke)

5. Christ's Glory and His Spirit: "For the Life of the World" (John)

*Signs of Incorporation into Christ:*
"Proclaiming His Death, Discerning His Body"

"Being in Christ" is a key concept of Paul's theology. The Pauline texts present the content of sacramental baptism and Eucharist as inseparable realities of what constitutes Christian life. "From Paul's presentation, we see how baptism and Eucharist were very closely related in both life and theology. We see too how Paul reflected on gospel realities and challenges in light of the Old Testament, where baptism and Eucharist had a prehistory."[17] In particular Romans 6:3–5 and 1 Corinthians 11:17–34 stress that sacraments are effective symbolic mediations of the saving-event of the death of Christ. Both proclaim existentially the meaning of the paschal mystery of the Lord.

Buried with Christ in baptism and raised with him through the grace of justification by faith, the believer is incorporated into the crucified and risen Lord. The implication of the cross for the *koinonia* of Christ's believers could easily be passed over, as the Corinthians' eucharistic assemblies demonstrated. Both baptism and the Eucharist initiate and nourish the Christian in the path of conversion, in the following of and communion with Christ to his death. Through baptism we "were baptized in his death" (Rom 6:3). The existential meaning of the eucharistic celebration demands grasping the challenge of the cross, for "as often as you eat this bread and drink the cup, you proclaim the Lord's death until he comes" (1 Cor 11:26).

Sacraments are also signs of the new exodus. Paul sees in the symbols of baptism and the Eucharist the realization of the definitive exodus. Christ, much as Moses the liberator of Israel, brings about an integral and universal liberation. The typological value of the Exodus narrative applies to both baptism ("baptized into Moses") and the Eucharist ("spiritual food/drink"). These signs incorporate the baptized to the new rock, the risen Christ, the source of the living water, the beginning, the way, and the destiny of a free and salvific existence for the believer. In the journey of the believer, baptism and the Eucharist are the source of the all-embracing freedom of Christ for us who are living at the end of the age (1 Cor 10:11). They mark the stages of evangelical conversion that lead to complete fulfillment. The people of the Old Testament were "types" or living models for all people of faith in the new exodus. St. Paul stresses parallel situations: "Our ancestors were all under the cloud, and all passed through the sea, and all were baptized into Moses in the cloud and in the sea, and all ate the same spiritual food, and all drank the same spiritual drink. For they drank from the spiritual rock that followed them, and the rock was Christ" (1 Cor 10:1–4).

*Signs of Christian Discipleship and Mission:*
"Drinking Jesus' Cup"

Mark's Gospel highlights Jesus' call to the freedom of the definitive exodus. His own journey, culminating in the gift of himself through the

Easter victory, exemplifies it. Mark links Christian discipleship to the paschal *kerygma*—embracing the mystery of the cross. In particular, Mark 10:32–40 contains baptismal and eucharistic references that stand at the center of an authentic sacramental spirituality. The message of the cross has to realize itself as transformation of the disciples' attitudes and aspirations. Although the sacramental significance is more implicit than explicit, as in the case of 1 Corinthians 10:13 to which it is related doctrinally, the text is based on the Old Testament. It narrates the incident of Zebedee's sons, James and John, requesting a share in Jesus' glory. The dialogue demonstrates the implications of Christian discipleship in Jesus' paschal mystery. His "cup and baptism" on the cross effected the salvation of all: "Are you able to drink the cup that I drink, or be baptized with the baptism that I am baptized with?" (Mark 10:38). "In the context of the New Testament Churches it is obvious that the symbolism of baptism and the cup likewise referred to two of the sacraments, and it was understood moreover that these two sacraments place their communicants into special relationship with the Lord's passion."[18]

Baptism and the Eucharist are essential for the Christian journey. They invite the believer to participate in the redemptive immersion of Jesus who gave "his life as a ransom for many" (Mark 10:45). Baptism is the beginning of the messianic ministry of Jesus (Mark 1:11). It culminates in his embrace of the cup of the Father's will (Mark 14:36) and his celebration of the cup of the New Covenant (Mark 14:24). Mark focuses on the essence of the biblical significance conveyed by these two paschal images, the cup and the bath. He expresses the images in terms of the servanthood that should characterize Christian leadership.

*Signs of the Presence of the Risen Christ:*
"For the Forgiveness of Sins"

Christology and ecclesiology are foundations for the sacramental vision of the Gospel of Matthew. The theme of the reign of God unifies this gospel. In Jesus, the Messiah, the royal anointed one (Matt 1:16), the saving power of God has been revealed and a new age has dawned. The command to baptize (Matt 28:19) symbolizes the active presence of the risen Christ to the end of time (Matt 28:20). He established universal and unconditional reconciliation through his covenantal blood: to be "poured out for many for the forgiveness of sins" (Matt 26:28).

The themes in Matthew's Gospel converge in a living person, the Lord Jesus Christ, the subject of the prophecies, the Emmanuel, a name which means God-is-with-us (Matt 1:23). With him the reign of heaven with its invitation to humanity to accept God's plan became present. The community of disciples to whom the mysteries of the reign of God were revealed (Matt 13:11) became the new Israel, the ecclesial continuation of a worldwide mission begun by the Son of God.

The Gospel of Matthew is deeply ecclesiological, and therefore deeply sacramental.[19] It strongly emphasizes the communal dimension of sacramental life. Concern for the Church, the new people of God that includes Gentile converts (Matt 21:43), is a unique feature of this gospel. The Passover was the turning point. The risen Lord, endowed with power and authority, demonstrated the universal design of salvation. Matthew's theological vision culminates in 28:18–20: "All authority in heaven and on earth has been given to me. Go therefore and make disciples of all nations, baptizing them in the name of the Father and of the Son and of the Holy Spirit, and teaching them to obey everything that I have commanded you. And remember, I am with you always, to the end of the age."

At the Easter time of salvation history, the disciples were consecrated to a universal mission as witnesses to the saving presence of Emmanuel in time and space. Their mission was to be carried out through discipleship, the sacraments, and teaching of the word. The dawning of a new reality of grace was realized through the Church, and specifically through sacramental life as the great symbol of the union of the disciples with the Father, Son, and Holy Spirit.

The efficacy of this new reality of God's self-gift to humankind was guaranteed by the divine presence of the glorified Lord to the end of time. His body was to be eaten, his blood to be drunk; "the blood of the covenant, which is poured out for many for the forgiveness of sins" (Matt 26:26–29). Given by Christ as risen Lord, both baptism and Eucharist became signs of his divine presence.

*Signs of the Christian Journey:*
"Recognizing Him in the Breaking of Bread"

Luke's works, his Gospel and the book of Acts, also highlight the central theological theme of journey evident in Paul and Mark. Schurmann maintains that Luke's Gospel is structured around the idea of Jesus' journey, or the way of Jesus.[20] Similarly, contemporary Catholic exegesis views Luke's work as having a deep sacramental structure and content. "For Luke, the sacrament is not an appendage or an epilogue of the faith and conversion process following the word, but a decisive part and fundamental and supreme stage of that process."[21]

The reality of the Spirit is another essential theme in Luke's Gospel and in Acts. It also represents the theology of the primary sacraments. The messianic times inaugurated by Christ begin as Jesus is conceived and baptized in the Spirit. "I will pour out my spirit" (Acts 2:18). The Spirit dwells in him and his acts are filled with the Spirit. He is the Spirit. And the reality of the Church is the reality of the Spirit, as the book of Acts, called a gospel of the Spirit, demonstrates.

The presence of God's Spirit gives full meaning to Jesus' baptism at the beginning of his ministry. Likewise, the presence of the same Spirit gives birth to the Church at Pentecost (Acts 2:1–13). The Church became the sacramental reality of the reign of Christ because of the presence and action of the Spirit of the risen Christ. After Pentecost, the process of incorporation of new members into the community and its communal life follows a certain pattern (cf. Acts 2):

– The disciples witness to the risen Christ *(kerygma)*

– People repent and follow the "way" *(metanoia)*

– They are baptized, receive the gift of the Holy Spirit, and remain faithful to "the breaking of bread" (sacramental initiation).

The book of Acts presents the early communities as the Spirit-guided people proclaiming a way of salvation (Acts 16:17). The presence of the Spirit is paramount. In many instances, although it is not always stated explicitly, the Spirit is seen as the source of the salvific and sacramental action that accompanies the disciples in their journey. In his journey, the Ethiopian eunuch hears the good news and is baptized (Acts 8:26–40). The Spirit of Christ touches Paul on the road to Damascus and his life is turned around. He is filled with the Holy Spirit and is baptized (Acts 9:17–19). In the same way, through sacramental gestures, the disciples encounter the mysterious presence of the crucified and risen Lord in their journey—a sacramental journey of transformation. It culminates with the eucharistic breaking of bread: he was "made known to them in the breaking of the bread" (Luke 24:35).

Luke integrates the sacramental happenings into stories of faith. Different historical circumstances are narrated in a three-part structure: (1) the personal spiritual process, (2) the action of the Church, and (3) the gift of God.[22] The Passover is lived out through these signs, because they are the mystery of the presence of the reality of Christ and of his Church.

*Sign of Christ's Glory and His Spirit:*
*"For the Life of the World"*

The Fourth Gospel was written toward the end of the first century. It reflects several decades of the early development of the Christian experience of faith within the so-called Johannine community. John's original and symbolic Gospel stresses the deeper and spiritual meaning of Christ's divinity and mission and the believer's relationship to him. However, John's Gospel presumes the institutional aspects of the community. It omits a direct account of Jesus' actual baptism or of his institution of the Eucharist.

Two key themes that unify "the Spiritual Gospel" (Clement of Alexandria) and correspond, according to Brown, to the two great parts of John's Gospel are *signs* (1:19—12:50) and *glory* (13:1—20:31).[23] They are like the two pillars of an overall paschal theme revealing Jesus' glory as Lord and God (John 20:28). He comes from the Father, "the Word became flesh and lived among us, and we have seen his glory" (John 1:14). But he also returns to the Father, "with the glory I had with you before the world existed" (John 17:5). The paschal theme underlines the christocentric movement from glory (coming down from God) to glory (going back to the Father). This movement climaxes in the passage of liberation, the great sign of his passion and resurrection by which Christ accomplished his salvific work. Jesus' signs manifest his glory in the eyes of the believer "so that you may come to believe that Jesus is the Messiah, the Son of God, and that through believing you may have life in his name" (John 20:31).

John offers an ecclesial and sacramental interpretation of the salvific event from the perspective of the christological mystery. This mystery was revealed through the signs of glory and actualized in a particular Christian community. The signs of glory linked the Lord of the Church to the historical Jesus. The evangelist recounts Jesus' story, presenting him as *sign of the salvation history*. He is now acting as the Lord who is spiritually present and living in the Church and in the sacraments.[24] Oscar Cullman, citing the extensive references to baptism and the Eucharist, argues for a strong sacramental presence throughout John's Gospel.[25] This gospel, overall, is filled with eucharistic themes that demonstrate the evangelist's constant sacramental awareness. Eugene La Verdiere writes: "John's tendency is to presuppose the Eucharist, rather than speak of it directly, and to focus on its significance and implications for the life of Christians. There is more than one way for a story, discourse, or symbol to be Eucharist."[26] Specifically, John 6 and 19:33–34 make particular reference to the Eucharist.

The discourse of Jesus at Capernaum on the bread of life (John 6:26–65) is a key text for interpreting the Gospel of John as a unique eucharistic account. As in the case of the baptism in the Spirit, this sacramental movement originates in Jesus, the giver of life, "for the bread of God is that which comes down from heaven and gives life to the world" (John 6:33). In both instances Jesus is the bread of life, the fullness of the gift of God. He comes from heaven and must be accepted by faith, a faith that ensures eternal life (John 6:38–40).

As the living bread, Jesus reveals the mystery of sharing sacramentally in the gift of his own *Pasch:* "Whoever eats of this bread will live for ever; and the bread that I will give for the life of the world is my flesh" (John 6:51). The truth of this mystery cannot be grasped or accepted without the gift of the Spirit: "It is the spirit that gives life; the flesh is useless" (John 6:63).

Johannine symbolism offers another important sacramental reference at the supreme moment of Jesus' crucifixion: "One of the soldiers pierced his side with a spear, and at once blood and water came out" (John 19:34). This is a clear paschal theme. It stresses the salvific meaning of the blood of Jesus' sacrificial death and the water of the Spirit (1 John 5:6–7) flowing from his side. A well-founded tradition from the fathers of the Church saw in the text a paschal reference to baptism and Eucharist.[27] The blood and the water are signs of eternal life given to his nascent Church when Jesus was exalted as king upon the cross (John 19:17–21).

IN SUMMARY, then, the New Testament contains various themes and symbolic meanings relating to the fundamental experience of early Christians. It posits sacramentality as the liberating and vivifying way of the Easter Christ and his Spirit. This paschal vision reflected in the texts shaped the nascent praxis of Christian initiation. Christ himself addresses the question to the catechumen and to each believer: "Are you able to drink the cup that I drink?" (Mark 10:38) Thus, the mystery of the glorious cross is the heart of the believer's participation in the sacramental life of the Church.

For Paul, sacraments are ways to partake in the paschal reality, the death and resurrection of Christ. They are prototypes of the definitive exodus of the New Covenant. Mark also reveals the existential meaning of a disciple's immersion into Jesus' passion. For Luke, the universal outpouring of the Holy Spirit inaugurates the new age for those who follow the way of conversion to Christ through baptism and participation in the Eucharist. Matthew presents the Easter sacraments as actualized signs of Emmanuel, God forever present to the new Israel, the Church.

In all the narratives and references, a profound christocentric foundation links the sacraments of baptism and Eucharist. Clearly, they must be interpreted from a post-resurrectional vantage point. John's Gospel specifically challenges people to commit themselves in spirit and in truth to the baptismal and eucharistic mystery of Christ. "Living in us and we in him," he continues his presence and brings the freedom of salvation through the signs of the glory and of the Spirit.

## The Sacrament of the Life of the Church

The Eucharist has been central in the Christian tradition from the time of the early Palestinian communities throughout two thousand years of history. It has been at the heart of building community as well as the primary sacramental expression of Christian faith and experience.

Understanding history is key to eucharistic meaning and practice, which are enshrined in biblical images. Beginning with the New Testament, these images continued for centuries as traditions of the Church. The previous section focused on the theological interpretation of the Eucharist as *Pasch,* God's reign, and sacramental praxis. This section explores the images representing primary truths of eucharistic faith. It will examine how they were interpreted in different cultural periods and expressed the historical distinctiveness of sacramental theology and spirituality.

Today's ecumenical Christianity has a great deal to learn from the major turning points in Christian history, points at which the eucharistic celebration has been reshaped at the intersection of religious-theological ideas and socio-cultural phenomena. The following study of key moments in the eucharistic life of the Church utilizes the concept of paradigm as a hermeneutic tool to interpret the history of the Eucharist.[28]

A historical paradigm, or model of understanding, can both set the future agenda and enlighten present-day questions. In terms of Christian theology, a paradigmatic shift relates primarily to foundational origins, in this case to the historical origins of the eucharistic faith. As Paul H. Jones has stated:

> Meaning unfolds diachronically. That is, the meaning of any event or test is neither exhausted by nor limited to the originating event. Rather, meaning includes continuity with the founding event as well as the ongoing interpretation of the event as it endures through time. The meaning of the Eucharist is no different.[29]

In this respect, the eucharistic celebration through the testimony of the Spirit is the best interpreter of the Christian *kerygma.*

Historical paradigms are milestones of momentous departures, but they never represent totally new shifts within the permanent continuity of the eucharistic tradition. It is only against this background that the eucharistic doctrine and praxis of the Church can be reinterpreted. The following paradigms apply to the history of the eucharistic celebration: (a) the Jewish-Christian and Hellenistic; (b) the Greco-Roman and Byzantine; and (c) the medieval and modern Roman Catholic paradigm. (The Reformation challenge to classical sacramental teaching has already been presented in chapter 2).

## Key Foundational Images:
### From the New Testament to the Hellenistic World

Biblical research on the origins of the Eucharist based on modern scientific criticism provides today's Christianity with a greater wholeness and balance in understanding eucharistic faith. This faith was fundamental to the Christian communities from the very beginning. The eucharistic experiences of the early Church constitute the source and foundation of subsequent historical reflection and practice.

The biblical images of the Eucharist provide a basis for evaluating the validity of previous interpretations by Christians. These images emerge from analysis of the institution narratives and other eucharistic texts. Rooted in the Hebrew scriptures, the images of memorial, sacrifice, Passover, communion, and the coming of the reign offer a key to interpreting the meaning of the eucharistic tradition from its source. These key images are the horizon and wellspring of the ongoing interpretation throughout the centuries. The manner in which Christian generations interpreted and experienced these images has ensured the wholeness of eucharistic faith and the vitality of Christ's original mandate within the Church.

The following discussion places these key eucharistic images in the historical and biblical context of the early eucharistic sources to explore the richness of the New Testament's doctrinal content through them. It describes the particular features of the Eucharist beginning with the Jewish-Christian sources and continuing through the shift to the Hellenistic world.

### Eucharistic Narratives

The chronology of eucharistic narratives, Jesus' words, the type of supper meal, and the form of early Christian eucharistic practices are some important elements of a historical reconstruction. However, historical reconstruction of the eucharistic origins from the upper room does not yield definitive answers. As Léon-Dufour states: "The historically certain is imprecise, and the precise is hardly historically certain."[30] The "Lord's Supper" is the oldest name by which the event is identified (1 Cor 11:20). This event is also described as the "breaking of the bread" (Luke 24:35; Acts 2:42). For Luke, the risen Lord appeared at the "breaking of bread," which soon became the central action of the community, the source of life and the grounding of Christian mission. The term "Eucharist," meaning thanksgiving, appeared only at the end of the first century, but the verb *eucharistein,* meaning thanking, is present in all institutional formulas. The four eucharistic narratives, which were discussed in the previous section, reflect a particular tradition, highlighting Christ's sacrificial death, the essential meaning of sharing, the command of love and service, and the prayer dimension of thanksgiving and blessing, among others.

The previous section presented the two main versions or supper narratives of the institution accounts. They are commonly recognized in the writings of Mark and Matthew as well as Paul and Luke. From a linguistic analysis of these early liturgical formulas, and especially the redaction stage within the New Testament sources, some scholars see in the first letter to the Corinthians (circa A.D. 55) the earliest institution narrative (1 Cor 11:23–26). This narrative contains earlier Semitic elements from an oral tradition of an "Antiochene" Church dated around the year A.D. 40. Mark's (14:22–25) and Matthew's (26:26–29) versions are presented as a "Palestinian" tradition. Matthew's version, written around the year A.D. 75, drew from Mark's (ca. A.D. 68). Semitic linguistic traces indicate that these two versions are based on an earlier Aramaic original. Finally, Luke's version (22:15–20, ca. A.D. 80) contains pre-Pauline elements that trace back to the mid-40s.

The scholarly debate about the historical priority of Paul's tradition versus that of Mark has relativized the issue of chronology. It shows that there was a diversity and richness of traditions whose meaning converged substantially in interpreting the foundational reality of the Christ-event. As stated in the previous section, it is possible to distinguish the cultic or liturgical tradition of Mark-Matthew with its sacrificial accents, the testamentary tradition of John with no institution narrative, and the primarily eschatological tradition of Luke-Paul. There is essential agreement in the major characteristics of the four narratives because their notions and terminology are embedded in the common Old Testament background and express a unique christocentric foundation. In addition, there is a noticeable uniformity in the structure of the accounts, "this is my body…my blood," especially in the same sequence of four verbs: Jesus *taking* bread, *giving* thanks, *breaking* the bread, and *giving* it.

However crucial, linguistic analysis and historical reconstruction are only one means for the retrieval and interpretation of the theological truth itself. If the experience of the risen Lord as source-event holds the key to that truth, the full context of the greater narratives yields it. Thus, it is essential to understand the continuity of biblical traditions and their transmission from the Palestinian-Jewish communities to the ongoing development of theology and practice with the coming of Hellenistic Christianity. Furthermore, the inexhaustible significance of Eucharist also requires interpretation of the developing tradition of the Church.

## Master Biblical Images

The key images of the Eucharist are embedded in biblical tradition and effectively express the prophetic action of the Lord's Supper, the fountainhead of the apostolic tradition. These images mediate the process of transmission and forge a new meaning. David Power has called them "historical master images" and also "the root metaphors of a tradition." In fact, "much of the accounts' power lies in their use of the historical master images of covenant, *Pasch,* suffering servant and sacrifice. These images give the words and actions of Jesus at the Last Supper their density and eschatological value."[31]

The number of these images and their importance varies according to different criteria. *Memorial, sacrifice, meal, Passover, covenant, presence,* and *communion* stand out as central in both the Old Testament religious cultural categories and the essential notions drawn from the full context of the New Testament eucharistic doctrine. In terms of their theological significance, the first three (memorial, sacrifice, and meal) require special study. The other images, already referred to in the previous section, are discussed as allied notions.

Eucharist was the central force behind the birth and life of the Christian community. Three methodological considerations are necessary in interpreting the connection between the Lord's Supper and the post-Easter ongoing interpretation of the Eucharist. We will use these methodological considerations in interpreting the three eucharistic images or core realities of memorial, sacrifice, and meal.

*1. The movement from life to narrative.*[32] A text is interpreted in the light of the living faith and the actual practice of the early communities that gave rise to the account. This understanding uses an indirect historical approach and pays attention to the whole of scripture, in particular the religious experience of the post-Easter Christian followers. The essential role of the Holy Spirit is connected to the eucharistic practice, albeit implicitly.

2. *The eschatological vision.* The overarching thread of the eschatological language typical of post-exilic Judaism and the ministry of Jesus himself in his proclamation of the future reign of God are apparent. Thus, the meaning of the supper and the vision of the final and heavenly banquet are inseparable.

3. *The broader biblical context.* Later eucharistic sources and early fragmentary references complement and shed light on each other. Such is the case of John's Gospel, as Theodor Schneider notes:

> A later Johannine text might have more significance and be more substantive and valuable than another that is older from the historico-critical point of view, a brief *logion* which corresponds to the earthly life of Jesus. Consequently, in terms of theological description and the explanation of the content of the mystery of the Eucharist, a broad-based approach to the New Testament expressions is necessary, from the early Pauline letters until the relatively late letter to the Hebrews, or even to the later book of Revelation.[33]

*Memorial*
The complex image of memorial emerges from the New Testament as the keystone of the whole eucharistic edifice. Its importance stems from both its biblical foundations and its function as a basis for the entire tradition of theological reflection. Other images such as sacrifice, covenant, and presence are intrinsically connected to it. It appears only in the Paul-Luke traditions, a formula that in the Léon-Dufour translation reads:

> Do this in order to make remembrance of me, *eis anamnesin* (1 Cor 11:24).[34]

The origin of this formula (Hebrew and Hellenistic) has been debated, because it is absent from the Markan-Matthean version. Biblical scholars such as Jeremias and Léon-Dufour place the memorial exclusively within a biblical context. It comes from the root ZKR, meaning "remembering," which actually includes memory, action, and expectation. When God remembers in fidelity and Israel remembers in obedience, the redemptive events of Israel's history are "actualized" in the present. In this reciprocal remembrance, God takes the initiative and establishes a solid bond to restore the original relationship. Memory has a privileged role in Jewish cult. The accounts of the Jewish Passover (Ex 12) and the covenant at Sinai (Ex 24) are foundational to the memorial concept. Thus, the Exodus provides an essential parallelism to the New Testament formula:

This day shall be a day of remembrance for you (ZIKKARON).
You shall celebrate it. (Ex 12:14)

The Lord's Supper, in the early Christian eucharistic consciousness, "represented" *(anamnesis)* the foundational event of a "new covenant," although it was not a ritual Passover in the strict sense, but a religious meal with "Passover characteristics." The Christian community entered into communion with the living Christ in hope and anticipation of the future kingdom. This new covenant was based on a person—this is my body, *soma*—the total self-giving of Christ, whose death had a soteriological significance and was not simply an exodus: "for this is my blood of the covenant, which is poured out for many for the forgiveness of sins" (Matt 26:28). There is no agreement on the accurate meaning of the liturgical *anamnesis*. The traditional idea of "rendering present again" has more recently been translated as signifying that the believing community enters newly into the presence of the past saving event of Christ's Passover.[35]

### Sacrifice

The Israelite Passover was a ritual memorial and the memorial was inextricably bound to sacrifice. The Passover nature of the Eucharist, and especially the unmistakable presence of the biblical concept of "memory," provides a symbolic grounding for the theological interpretation of the sacrifice of Christ explicit in the narratives. This interpretation has formed a constant tradition. It is evident in the New Testament sacrificial imagery and terminology and in later patristic understanding.

Christ's sacrificial offering on the cross, "our paschal lamb" (1 Cor 5:7) and the one sacrifice for all, was the fulfillment of the gift of his entire life. In fact, the New Testament eucharistic interpretation was focused on the intrinsic sacrificial meaning of the christological mysteries. The symbolic signs of the table-fellowship were the prophetic announcement of the eschatological fulfillment of God's reign through the sacrificial surrendering of Christ in his death.[36] A complete shift of *anamnetic* meaning and, thus, a radical new interpretation of salvation history took place: "This cup is the new covenant in my blood. Do this, as often as you drink it, in remembrance of me" (1 Cor 11:25). Memorial and sacrifice are, therefore, key images of New Testament eucharistic theology. They can be summed up in a comprehensive way as the sacrificial memorial of Christ's *Pasch.* The self-offering of Christ in obedience to the Father continues to be celebrated on the altars of the world. On these altars, the self-offering of the Christian community (Rom 12:1) is the communion with the redemptive action of Christ and, as such, symbolizes the universal offering of the crosses of humanity called from slavery to liberation until Christ's return.

*Meal*
As a communal means of attaining communion with others, a fellowship meal is already an archetypal case of "natural sacramentality," especially through the double symbolism of bread and wine. In ancient cultures the meal had an essentially sacred character and in Hebrew life every meal was considered religious. Sacrifice and meal are inseparable in the biblical memorial. In the Old Testament, meals serve as a memorial of the manifestations of God and a locus of sharing in the divine mystery (Ex 24:11; cf. Ex 12:1–28). Léon-Dufour stresses this symbolic interpretation of Eucharist: "Bread and wine indicate the two dimensions of daily life and festival in human existence, the food itself represents the new life that is bestowed on the community"[37]

The previous section explored the triple origins of the Eucharist in the New Testament. The origins of the Eucharist can also be found in the table companionship practiced by Jesus. The banquets of Jesus were a centerpiece of his ministry. The festive banquet of his Last Supper was an anticipatory sign of his sacrificial offering. The three or four meals of the risen Lord with his disciples were a joyful experience of encountering a living person. "[We] ate and drank with him after he rose from the dead" (Acts 10:41). As for the actual structure of the eucharistic ritual, the gradual process from a fellowship meal to a liturgical rite occurred in four stages.[38]

First, the disciples continued Jesus' table-fellowship practices as a preparation for and a continuation of the celebration of the Lord's Supper. Obviously, these were complete meals, as was the Last Supper, which according to Jeremias was also a paschal seder.

Second, the eucharistic memorial was moved to the end of an ordinary meal, as in the case of the eucharistic *agape* of 1 Corinthians 11:21. There was still evidence of a strong connection between the sharing of a common dinner and the ritual celebration of Christ's action of self-offering.

Third, the community meal and eucharistic celebration were separated. The stress was on the meal elements as signs representing the Lord's eucharistic presence and the disciples' *koinonia,* that is, communion with one another and with the Lord. The celebration of these communities took at times the shape of a symposium, as Mark seems to indicate (Mark 6:34–44).

Fourth, by the time of Justin (second century), the eucharistic celebration had become an independent liturgical rite No longer a full meal, the eucharistic banquet was a fellowship *agape.* It became a symbolic reality that was gradually sacralized. This was the most radical change in the history of the Eucharist.

*Early Tradition*
New Testament cultic concepts had to do with Christ's self-offering and to the offering of the whole Christian life in communion with Christ rather than with ritual practices. On one hand, Christ was the temple, the altar, and the sacrifice. On the other hand, the only offering acceptable was a believer imbued with the gift of the Spirit. The presence of the Spirit of the risen One, experienced jubilantly in the assembly of those who expected his imminent return, inspired and fashioned a new style of worship characterized as eschatological. Thus, early Christian orthopraxis was inspired by a strong christological and Spirit-related

messianism. The structure of worship invited the celebrating gathering to interiorization as well as to mission.

The first three centuries from the *Didache,* an early manual of Christian practice, to the *Apostolic Tradition* of Hippolytus, at the beginning of the third century, represented a shift from the Jewish symbolic ritual matrix of the earliest Christian Eucharists to the wider Hellenistic cultural context and the idea of the *mysterion.* Scholars generally agree that the synagogue celebrations and the Jewish meal shaped the original structure of apostolic worship. The *Didache,* which dates from the turning of the first century, represented only a Christianized Eucharist with a new anamnetic content of Jewish blessings *(Berakoth).* Baptismal initiation led to eucharistic celebration *(Didache,* especially Justin).

The essential idea of the *mysterion* of the Greek-speaking writers developed within Hellenistic culture. This new sign-synthesis of the celebration of the mystery of Christ inspired a new theology and practice of the Eucharist. It constituted a new core of theological understanding expressed frequently through the memorial concept: sharing in the new creation and the paschal mystery of the cross, celebrating Christ's continued presence and his self-giving to the community.

The new eschatological conception of "today"—which entails the presence of the risen Christ—made it possible for the Church to take root in culture. This happened by the third century. It appeared as a parenthesis or a transitional era before Christianity left the privacy of the patriarchal household of the Greco-Roman family and became at home in the public basilica with the dawn of the Constantinian era (313).

### *Patristic Mystery:*
### *The Greco-Roman and Byzantine Church*

The twilight of the patristic era was a turning point for new religious and theological conceptions in the fourth and fifth centuries. The Greco-Roman world provided a unified background for the new cosmic and historical vision expressed in the Eucharist. Christianity underwent the most pervasive transformation of ritual patterns through a process that today we call inculturation. It enshrined the major hopes of salvation and life with the cultural symbols and idioms of the age. It was a process of contextualization of the total Christian mystery through an integrated style of worship based on grass-roots faith-grounded models of apostolic tradition.

The sacramental mystery was the hermeneutic key that unlocked the nucleus of christological belief based on the celebration of the Eucharist. Christ became the center, not only of history but also of the world. This new cosmic conception, centered on the *Kyrios* in patristic theology, became the very matrix of the symbiosis between cult and culture, producing a decisive shift in the formal image of the Eucharist. The vision of the cosmic Christ was at the center of the Christian world view. Eucharistic interpretation flowed from its christological and ecclesiological basis.

Though complex and varied, the formidable wealth of the patristic understanding of the Eucharist had a unity in the broad vision of the ever-present Christian mystery. Patristic authors like Augustine and other church fathers presented this mystery in their mystagogical cate-chesis. The master biblical images, such as sacrifice and memorial, con-tinued to play a central role. As in the case of the pivotal concept of *anamnesis,* the meaning of these images was expanded with the support of a new way of thinking—Neoplatonism.

Patristic eucharistic theologies were characterized by a deep unify-ing sacramental vision, a strong realism and mysticism, especially in emphasizing the sacramental presence of the total Christ and the oper-ative actualization of the salvific mystery *(anamnesis).* Augustine (d. 430) stood out in his ecclesial interpretation of Eucharist, which he saw as the expression of the Church in its fullness. He states: "And for this reason, because he suffered for us, he entrusted to us in this sacrament his own Body and Blood which he turned into ourselves. For we are also His body and what we consume is ourselves."[39]

In patristic thinking, the Eucharist was the perpetual celebration of the memorial sacrifice of Christ himself. This was an overarching theme of the ancient tradition. A Protestant scholar emphasizes this when he writes:

> The whole early Christian tradition, when speaking of the Sup-per, makes use of a sacrificial terminology... I find the New Testament terminology as well as the patristic unanimity too overwhelmingly in favor of the sacrificial theme in a balanced Eucharistic theology... Since the Eucharist is a sacrament of

the sacrifice of Christ and a channel of the Church's sacrifice, it must also be interpreted in sacrificial categories.[40]

The paradigm of the Byzantine tradition retained its efficacy at the close of the early Church period with Constantine's historic declaration of Byzantium as the capital of the empire. The uniqueness of this paradigm, which could be surnamed "the icon paradigm," stemmed not only from a different approach to culture and historical evolution, but above all from a different ecclesiological interpretation. It was rooted, like the liturgical mystery, in its own historical-theological reality. Thus, worship remained contextualized within the local cultures.

## The Roman Catholic Sacrament: Medieval and Modern

The patristic era came virtually to an end in the West with the fall of the Roman Empire. The structural ritual patterns and the foundational concepts of Christian sacramentality had come of age. In the following centuries, the Eucharist took a variety of forms, manifesting fundamental shifts and the development of certain religious-theological traits. Specifically, the devaluation of the patristic concept of *real-symbol* and the interpretation of the sacrifice of the Mass can be seen in terms of three distinct periods: early Middle Ages (600–1000), the time of Scholasticism and Thomas Aquinas (d. 1274), and the four centuries that followed the Council of Trent.

### Middle Ages

A variety of complex factors contributed to changes in the perception of the corporate, ecclesial, and liturgical dimensions of the Eucharist that characterized patristic theology. The process of Christian initiation culminating with the Eucharist gradually disintegrated and finally arrived at a regressive turning point. There was a steady decline in liturgical participation due to cultural as well as theological factors. People became mere spectators and their passivity was evidenced by infrequent reception of communion (required at least once a year at Easter by the Fourth Lateran Council in 1215). A major shift in focus in the high Middle Ages is demonstrated by the practice of elevating the host (around A.D. 1200) for people to see and the progressive emphasis on adoration of the Blessed Sacrament outside the Mass. The new worship tradition developed in a richness of devotional practices, such as the institution of the feast of *Corpus Christi* in 1264. A strong sense of profound reverence and awe, an intimate union with Christ's sacrifice and, during the great annual celebrations, a communal and festive spirit, characterized the eucharistic tradition of the West.

Chief among the changes that prevailed toward the end of the first millennium was the loss of symbolic intelligibility.[41] This led to a false opposition between symbol and reality. De Lubac's research has demonstrated two fundamental shifts that were to underlie future sacramental and eucharistic theologies. One was cultural: the passage "from symbolic to dialectic," especially after the eleventh century. The other was theological: the passage from the Church as "body of Christ" to "the body of Christ" as the eucharistic presence of Christ in the bread and wine. The former represented the patristic interpretation of the mystery, especially in Augustine with roots in Paul. The latter corresponded to a medieval emphasis on sacramental intelligibility. Thus the "objectivized" sacramental sign lost its liturgical context and its broader meaning. Another consequence was the allegorization of the eucharistic reality, which led to controversies over the identification of the physical and eucharistic body of Christ.

A crisis in the sacramental interpretation of "real presence" took place from the ninth to the eleventh centuries. In opposition to Ratrammus, Paschasius Radbertus (ca. 859–865) defended the complete identification of the historical body and the eucharistic body of Christ. The controversy was continued by Berengar of Tours (d. 1088), who denied the real presence of Christ in the elements of bread and wine while affirming a mere symbolic presence. Lanfranc, as archbishop of Canterbury (d. 1089), challenged Berengar's position, stating that "the earthly substances on the Lord's table are sanctified by divine power in a manner that is unspeakable, incomprehensible, marvelous; and that [these substances] are changed into the essence of the Lord's Body, even though the appearances of earthly elements remain."[42]

The sacramental vision of Thomas Aquinas recaptured some of the patristic riches of Christian tradition, especially Augustine. It also highlighted the importance of the sacramental sign as an instrumental cause effecting what it signifies. In line with the Aristotelian outlook of his time, St. Thomas used the sacramental principle to guide his eucharistic thinking. He saw the Eucharist as "the summit of the spiritual life and the end to which all the sacraments are ordained."[43]

The concepts of presence and sacrifice are central in St. Thomas's masterful explanation of the eucharistic mystery. Christ himself becomes present spiritually in the Eucharist *per modum substantiae,* that is, because of a substantial conversion, similar to the soul's presence in the body.[44] Understood metaphysically, this developed Aristotelian mode of thinking sees the substance as the ultimate and inner reality of being. Therefore, it is the "total substance" (not the accidents) of the eucharistic elements that is changed into the inner being of another, meaning the body and blood of Christ. Christ's presence is sacramental and real. It is ontological and thus existential. Reiterating patristic thinking, Thomas understood this mystery presence as the perennial and symbolic actualization of the eucharistic memorial of Christ's definitive sacrificial action on Calvary.[45]

For Thomas, a beneficiary of the monastic liturgical tradition, the Eucharist was central. This centrality, at least in terms of liturgical participation by the faithful, gradually declined while at the same time a eucharistic piety outside worship developed. If the monks enriched Roman liturgy with their contemplative profoundness and mystical experience, the later medieval period constituted a breakdown of the liturgical idiom of the mystery to be shared by a worshiping community.

## Trent to Modern Times

The goal of the Council of Trent in the sixteenth century was to defend the essential doctrines of the Church, especially the doctrine of the Eucharist, against the reformers. It provided a foundation for both its precise formulation and the restoration of its practice. In particular, the council safeguarded sacramental realism and re-affirmed with profoundness and clarity the real presence of Christ and the sacrificial and propitiatory character of the Mass as the two traditional pillars of Catholic belief. First, the Eucharist is the eminent, admirable, and most holy sacrament, because in it "there are truly, really, and substantially contained the Body and Blood together with the soul and divinity of our Lord Jesus Christ, and therefore the whole Christ."[46] Second, the Eucharist continues the only and definitive sacrifice of Christ on the cross: "For the Lord, appeased by this oblation, grants grace and the gift of repentance, and He pardons wrongdoings and sins, even grave ones. For the victim is one and the same: the same now offers through the ministry of priests, who then offered Himself on the cross; only the manner of offering is different."[47]

The fathers at Trent depended on scholastic formulations. They adopted transubstantiation as the most appropriate (aptissime) concept to express the substantial conversion of the eucharistic gifts. Despite the remarkable patristic and biblical richness of Trent's canons, the lack of a unified approach prevented the retrieval of certain aspects of the biblico-patristic tradition. Chief among these were the biblical meaning of "memorial," the role of the Spirit, the thanksgiving nature, and the original idea of a communion fellowship meal of early Christian communities. With regard to the sacramental actions of worship, the Mass was restored and its dogmatic content was indeed clarified.

The second part of the twentieth century saw a renewed approach in Protestant churches to eucharistic practice and a progressive ecumenical consensus. The recovery of the eucharistic heritage, in particular the biblical concept of anamnesis, made this possible. According to Anglican scholar William Crockett: "The Reformers, therefore, ended up opposing the ideas of 'sacrifice' and 'memorial' rather than understanding the Eucharist as sacrifice precisely because it is the anamnesis of Christ's sacrifice on the cross."[48]

The eucharistic celebration of the Lord's Supper, as remembrance and fellowship, has been steadily enriched in many ways, especially with the recognition and fuller appreciation of key eucharistic images from the New Testament. Protestant scholar James White has outlined them as: thanksgiving, commemoration, communion fellowship, sacrifice, presence, the action of the Holy Spirit, and the foretaste of the final consummation of things. He wisely points out that,

> all seven images have advanced to prominence or receded from it at various times over the course of history. Not one is contradictory; each supports the others. Eucharistic faith and practice achieve a balance among all seven. But so rich is the outpouring of God's self-giving in the Eucharist that the Church has rarely found it possible to maintain that balance. Hence, much of the turmoil of the Reformation was an attempt to achieve a better

reflection of the New Testament richness and variety in experiencing the Eucharist. But even those efforts today seem insuffi-
cient as modern biblical scholarship has discovered more about
the environment in which the early Church experienced the
Lord's Supper.[49]

The discussion in chapter 2 highlighted the contributions of the
pioneers of contemporary renewal and reform to eucharistic theology.
Wide-ranging patristic research and the new theological movements of
modern times—liturgical, biblical, and ecumenical—led to that reform
and provided a foundation for new directions. The pioneers clarified
central concepts of the eucharistic mystery, such as the nature of the
sacramental sign and the biblical memorial *(anamnesis),* which are
basic to an understanding of the sacrificial character and the real presence of Christ in the Eucharist. Those modern movements along with
many other recent developments that have evolved in dialogue with
contemporary socio-cultural trends have made possible the shift toward
a new ecclesiological paradigm. Hence, with the Second Vatican Council the Church saw the inauguration of a new era in its eucharistic life.

Many different approaches have developed in the decades following
the council. Where do we go from here? In the following section we will
discuss several key issues and appropriate directions for the future of
eucharistic theology already being shaped by today's global Christianity.


## The Sacrament of the Transformation of the World

The third major element of this reflection on the Eucharist is "world."
"World" enjoys a complex relationship with the previously discussed
elements of "reign" and "Church." The Eucharist can be sacrament of
the reign and sacrament of the Church only in relation to the world and
connected to it. It is the paschal and, therefore, central sacramental
symbol of God's self-communication for the creation of a new world
and the birth of a new humanity. God is at work with Christ who gave
himself for the life of the world. His sacramental body gives the life
that has power to overcome death. The Eucharist, then, embraces all
life and contains life's ultimate meaning. As the pertinent document of
the World Council of Churches states: "The Eucharist . . . signifies what

the world is to become: an offering and hymn of praise to the creator, a universal communion in the body of Christ, a kingdom of justice, love and peace in the Holy Spirit."[50]

Consequently, the approach taken here looks at the Eucharist from a global perspective—as the cosmic mystery. It focuses on four mutually inclusive themes: *sacramentality*, *eschatology*, the *real presence*, and the *"cosmic Christ."*

*1. Sacramentality*: The Eucharist is an initiatory sacrament that forms the foundations of the Christian world view. The organic link between the Eucharist and the other sacraments as well as the links between Eucharist, Church, and world must be regained.

*2. Eschatology*: Reality is grasped only from a view of the future. The Eucharist's eschatological dimension prophetically symbolizes the mystery of universal transformation, a mystery whose roots lie in the resurrection event. This key dimension furnishes a universal lens through which one may examine a most fundamental eucharistic truth, real presence.

*3. Real presence:* Both biblico-patristic anthropology and contemporary religious consciousness demand a reformulation of eucharistic theology. In particular, the doctrine of real presence requires some crucial shifts in understanding.

*4. The "cosmic Christ":* The cosmic order of salvation, the ultimate meaning of all things, the call given creation to become what God wills it to be in Christ is the final theme. From a christocentric world view, the Eucharist appears as supreme symbol of cosmic transformation in perfection. The cosmic Christ of patristic theology and twentieth-century thinkers such as Teilhard de Chardin (1879–1955) is considered here.

These interrelated themes provide a theological framework for integrating and reinterpreting traditional aspects of eucharistic understanding. These themes help us to reexamine the ecclesiological foundation of the Eucharist and important concepts like transubstantiation.

Biblico-patristic writings frequently use the term "cosmos." Even so, their theological use of the term involves a variety of meanings. It refers obviously to the whole created, material world. However, the whole of the cosmos includes the "little cosmos," the human person in the totality of his or her being and historical existence. This implies that the human person is destined for transformation and the fullness of salvation through the power belonging to the risen body of Christ in the Spirit. Salvation, therefore, possesses cosmic universality and organic unity. It embraces creation and body, person and community, the visible and the invisible, the present time and the end of history. Christian antiquity portrays Christ, the cosmic Lord, at the center of the cosmos. Consequently, "no creationless redemption" is possible (cf. Rom 8:18–30) and, in the final analysis, "no redemptionless creation" is possible (cf. Eph 1:10; Col 1:20).[51]

"Transformation" is a concept inherent in the nature and meaning of the eucharistic mystery and its celebration. It represents an essential dimension of contemporary cultural experience. Transformation presumes other concepts, such as the human quest for meaning and freedom. It can apply in different ways to the person, to the community, and to the world in general. Transformation, therefore, constitutes an important hermeneutical tool for opening the eucharistic mystery to contemporary religious consciousness. It is also more in tune with a modern-day dynamic interpretation of the person as part of the creative process at the heart of humanity itself and of human history. Furthermore, it assists in the retrieval of the more comprehensive, even global thought of patristic tradition, the cosmic order of salvation, the developmental vision of Irenaeus and other Christian writers of his time.

## Sacramentality: Baptismal Foundations

Karl Rahner writes: "The universe is destined for God and for transformation. As the cosmos has a true historical past with God, which is part of *anamnesis,* the cosmos has a real future with God."[52] The person stands in the middle of creation in its destiny for transformation. This is the Christian hope: "The whole creation has been groaning…and not only the creation, but we ourselves…groan inwardly while we wait for adoption, the redemption of our bodies" (Rom 8:22–23). The paschal event of Christ, at the very heart of the Christian world view, expresses itself and is celebrated in the sacraments, especially in the sacraments of initiation—baptism (with confirmation) and the Eucharist. These are the paschal and universal sacraments. They realize in history the all-embracing and all-transforming event of Christ.

## The Mystery of Transformation

Understanding the Eucharist from its baptismal foundation leads to regaining a baptismal consciousness. Such a consciousness is essential to a wholesome and transformative eucharistic theology; it is able to make the Eucharist "the source and summit of Christian life" in fact as well as in word. This major emphasis underlies what follows.

We have already discussed the christocentric foundation connecting baptism and Eucharist as it appears in the New Testament. The themes arising from passages that speak of partaking in the Passover of Christ, immersion into his passion, and the new age present the Eucharist as a transformative symbol in the nascent practice of Christian initiation. In fact, the Eucharist ever stands at the heart of Christian identity and growth. As he considered the initiatory potential of the Eucharist, Aidan Kavanagh affirmed that "in baptism the Eucharist begins, and in the Eucharist baptism is sustained. From this premier sacramental union flows all the Church's life."[53]

A proper approach to the Eucharist as transforming mystery has to evolve from the experience of God in our lives and in our world, just as that experience has to have relationship with what we actually celebrate in our eucharistic liturgies. More specifically, this approach has to show how Christ's Passover has transformed life's meaning and how this new paschal meaning, hidden in the midst of our daily struggles, effectively reveals itself and becomes present in our experience of the Eucharist. The paschal mystery provides the unitive and central focus of sacramental experience related to worldly experience. As stated above, baptism and Eucharist are the chief sacraments of the paschal mystery. This mystery is present in the life journey of the Christian from the moment of the initial bath in "living water." It culminates always with the "grain of wheat" at the table: the two sacraments are the symbolic fountainhead of the transformation Christ has promised.

The goal of Eucharist is God's glory in the present and future transformation of the believer and the community into the body of Christ. "It is through the Eucharist that the Church continually lives and grows."[54]

While this transformation truly occurs by the power of the Spirit in Christian initiation, it must receive existential realization through the personal and corporate vision of conversion that baptism and Eucharist signify. In actuality, this implies an adequate understanding of the intimate relationship of both sacraments as source and cradle from which flows the Christian vision of all that is. Obviously, such an understanding presupposes in the practice of initiation a centrality of the catechumenal "way"—that is, the ongoing Christian journey of radical transformation —for all believers, with baptism as its impulse and the Eucharist as its sustenance.

Both sacraments declare a dual relationship in which baptism, the water-bath, "flows" into eucharistic fellowship and, vice versa, the Eucharist flows back into baptism.[55] The Eucharist represents the fullness of initiation and is the heart of Christian maturity. Consequently, initiation is adequately understood only with the Eucharist. This memorial sacrifice is the thanksgiving celebration of Jesus' baptism of water and blood, the initiation into his Passover of self-giving by which he was exalted as the Wisdom of God for the life of the world. Here the initiation journey reaches its apex, not as something fully accomplished once and for all, but as mystery, a living-out in the process of becoming. The Eucharist, initiation's completion, is that to which the community must return, again and again, on its "way" in order to experience through life, over and over, transformation in the Spirit of Christ, the primordial source of initiation.

Furthermore, the interrelationship envisages Eucharist as a multifaceted and repeatable sacrament of ongoing and permanent initiation. As the sign fully expressing Jesus' central message, the reign of God, the Eucharist is the primary means for the transformation of a Church with the mission of transformation. The Eucharist culminates and permanently sustains the believer's life-long and all-embracing initiation into the revelation of Christ's saving, healing, and transforming ministry present in the community.

## The Life of the World

The church fathers consistently witness to the importance of approaching the Eucharist as initiation in this way. It is a major constant of their eucharistic theology. Later theological development echoes it as well. It sees the Eucharist as central to the spiritual life and the goal of Christian sacramentality. Simeon of Thessalonica (d. 1429), speaking from the wealth of Byzantine liturgical tradition, affirms that the Eucharist "perfects and seals every sacrament and every divine mystery."[56] The truth is that the Eucharist fully expresses in sacrament the power, depth, and magnitude of Christ's proclamation; it is the memorial of what the whole created order and its history are called to be in hope of the fullness of salvation. In other words, it is the eschatological sign in the Church of the world's re-creation, its creation anew.

Today's eucharistic renewal emphasizes relevance to the totality of a person's life in the Church and to a Church called to be alive in the world. This emphasis resonates with the vision and grounding encountered in the classical tradition behind the restored rites of adult initiation. With the retrieval of a "baptismal foundation and consciousness," the Eucharist can more and more regain its rightful central place as transforming mystery at the deepest level. The modern magisterium, the doctrinal authority of the Church, has continually emphasized the Eucharist's central importance, as the following text so magnificently illustrates:

> The Eucharist is the "source and summit of the Christian life." The other sacraments, and indeed all ecclesiastical ministries and works of the apostolate, are bound up with the Eucharist and are oriented toward it. For in the blessed Eucharist is contained the whole spiritual good of the Church, namely Christ himself, our Pasch.[57]

Grounded in this central mystery that is "Christ himself, our Pasch," and endowed with a new identity and mission, the Christian and the community are reoriented to the world. They are able to express in their lives the mystery of the Eucharist, whose ultimate goal is the sanctification of humanity: "I am the living bread…and the bread that I will give for the life of the world is my flesh (John 6:51). The celebration of this mystery, which cannot remain an end unto itself, comes to symbolize to the highest degree the Christian vocation's unrealized potential, the sanctified and sanctifying mission of the Church and the destiny of the world. Christian tradition from the time of the church fathers encapsulated this belief in affirming that the Eucharist is the pledge and sign of the definitive or—to use the patristic word—cosmic transformation.

## Eschatology: The Risen Christ and the Eucharistic Universe

The implications of the Eucharist need to be understood eschatologically. The eschatological dimension allows for cogently grasping Christ's eucharistic presence and activity. It is at the heart of eucharistic theology and praxis. Whether one speaks of transformation of bread or wine, person or community, world or history, the radical Christian meaning of transformation stems from an eschatological reality, the universal transformation already begun in Christ, a transformation that is the goal of creation. Because the Eucharist is the seed of the new creation in Christ's resurrection, it is the anticipatory presence of the *eschaton* and foreshadows that universal transformation. Thus the mission of the Church and the destiny of the person and of the world are all bound together in Eucharist as their unity, center, and potential for transformation.

Eucharistic celebration anticipates the future in the present. The *Didache* witnesses to this in its description of Eucharist with people crying out and proclaiming Christ's coming in the celebration with the shout, "*Maranatha!* Come, Lord!"[58] The relationship with past, present, and future is possible only because the Eucharist is Passover fulfilled (cf. Luke 22:15f.); it is so because it is the work of God whose outstanding characteristic is fidelity. Eucharist is both memorial and promise of resurrection. The eschatological event of the resurrection is the source event, summit, and center of the living history of salvation, and thus represents continuity and at the same time discontinuity between past and present. As memorial of the Easter mystery, the Eucharist is the real presence of the incarnate Word and risen Lord, albeit sacramentally. In this sense, G. Martelet focuses on the resurrection in understanding the different modalities of being of the historical, risen, and eucharistic Christ:

> The identity of the historical body of Christ with the Eucharistic body passed through the discontinuity of the resurrection. It is the resurrection that obliges us to call identical, and yet different, the body which is born of the Virgin, which suffers, which dies on the cross, which rises again in glory, and which is given to us in the Eucharistic meal.[59]

The irruption of Easter into human history reveals the Eucharist's eschatological dimension. But to see it one must view the resurrection in its totality. Again, the fathers of the Church offer a significant perception. They present the Eucharist as Christ's last and perennial *Pasch,* and this Passover as cosmic mystery:

> Easter is the common feast *(panegyrosis)* for all human beings, messenger of the Father's will in the world, divine rising of the Sun-Christ upon the earth, eternal feast for the angels and the archangels, immortal life for the entire world...heavenly soul of the universe, sacred rite of heaven and earth, herald of the old and the new mystery...This is the cosmic and universal mystery of Easter.[60]

A right approach to central eucharistic truths, such as the mystery of Christ's presence, and to the reinterpretation of traditional Catholic concepts, such as transubstantiation, must include this eschatological reality—namely that the presence of Christ in the mystery of the Church and Christian existence actualizes the cosmic and universal paschal transformation. It is through this mystery of the Church that the transforming power of Christ's presence seizes the person and seizes the world. Thus, Christ's presence transforms the ecclesial community, the eucharistic gifts, and the world.

The eschatological event of the resurrection grounds the eucharistic mystery of Christ's presence as this mystery makes that event effective and ever new. In fact, it is the mystery of transformed gifts that represent transformed people and world only because Christ's total self-giving unto death altered all reality in his new life of resurrection. The risen Christ's Spirit is present in the eucharistic assembly and in the lives of the faithful who live because of the Eucharist. That presence constitutes the dynamic energy and soul of the radical transformation of the Church's offering of the believer and the world into his glorious body.

### Real Presence: Theological Shifts

The Catholic tradition of the eucharistic presence of Christ rightly speaks of it as true, real, and substantial presence. Vatican II advanced and broadened that tradition by stressing the ecclesial context of this presence. It further distinguished four modes of Christ's real presence:

in the word, in the presiding priest, in the eucharistic species (most especially), and in the assembly. The church fathers had already affirmed the ontological presence of Christ in the eucharistic bread and wine by the power of his word and the Holy Spirit.[61] Their eucharistic interpretation, especially in Augustine's vision, flowed from the consideration of the ecclesial body of Christ, the whole Christ.

The substantialist explanation of scholastic theology does not connect with the Christian mystery as an organic whole. It has no significance in relation to the present understanding of humanity and the world and, in particular, the meanings of everyday Christian experience. In fact, it fails to convey a fundamental relationship within the dynamic mystery of salvation, the relationship between the transfigured body of Christ's personal presence in the Eucharist and his universal salvific presence in the mystery of the Church and the world. Gustave Martelet calls our attention to the shift in the High Middle Ages from the concept of "body" in Augustine's eucharistic theology to the concept of "substance" in scholastic analysis of the mystery. With the introduction of the new concept, a new eucharistic orientation emerged:

> The unity of Christ rests essentially on the mystery of the body, as is unmistakably evident in St. Paul. When, however, in order to justify Eucharistic realism theological thought moves in the context of substance, it abandons, without realizing it, a field of meanings.[62]

## Transformation versus Transubstantiation

Generally speaking, the concept of "transformation" was for the first millennium what the term "transubstantiation" was for the second. Ancient church terminology, however, was anything but static. On the contrary, it was extraordinarily varied and rich. Eucharistic conversion is expressed by the church fathers with various nouns and verbs meaning transformation, each with its own nuances. Still, the language they utilized remained sufficiently precise to express the radical change in the Eucharist and was often comprehensive enough to convey the manifold and all-transforming levels of the eucharistic mystery.

Most Catholic theology of the second millennium sought to explain that presence through scholastic concepts. "Transubstantiation" implies that there is a conversion of the substance of bread and wine into the substance of the body and blood of Christ (presence *per modum substantiae*). Using categories of modern phenomenology, some recent theologians have offered complementary alternatives to transubstantiation. They stress the reality that the eucharistic gifts signify with concepts such as transignification (change of meaning) and transfinalization (change of purpose). The magisterium, however, has judged the new terminology inadequate: "the reason why they [the species of bread and wine] take on this new significance and this new finality is because they contain a new reality which we may justly term ontological."[63] For this reason, a new theological approach and broader framework of the formulation of the mystery are necessary. These have to attempt to integrate earlier biblico-patristic wisdom theology and be sensitive to the contemporary and global religious consciousness.

Although never used by the Second Vatican Council, the term "transubstantiation" clearly underscores the idea of radical transformation, which will remain an important dogmatic notion for asserting the reality of deep inner change in the elements. Nevertheless, the critical failure it exhibits today is that it does not sufficiently convey the heart of the mystery that is Christ's unique presence in the Eucharist. We cannot readily speak in terms of the "mystery of transubstantiation" as does *Mysterium Fidei*. This overly technical word is not the basic issue of the Eucharist; it does not touch the core of its reality and content. In fact, in the judgment of some theologians, such as Karl Rahner, transubstantiation yields only a logical and not an ontological explication because the term adds nothing new to the original institutional formula, "This is my body."

However, this opinion seems unsatisfactory to other theologians, especially in light of the Council of Tent's declaration: "This change [by the consecration] the holy Catholic Church has fittingly and properly called transubstantiation."[64] The meaning of the Eucharist is inexhaustible and no terminology will ever adequately express the reality of the eucharistic change. It is not a matter of replacing one term with another, such as shifting from transubstantiation to transformation (a generic term); rather, what really matters is to value the complementary explanations that constitute the integrity of Catholic tradition.

Speaking from the standpoint of the Orthodox tradition's transforming sacramental world view, Alexander Schmemann outlines the implications that post-patristic rationalism's devaluation of symbol as reality had for the Christian experience:

> Even if, as in the case of the Eucharist, the sign is completely identified with reality, it is experienced in terms of the signs of annihilation rather than in those of fulfillment. In this sense, the doctrine of transubstantiation, in its Tridentine form, is truly the collapse, or rather the suicide, of sacramental theology.[65]

Theological reflection has to go full circle in order to establish a new range of meanings. It must go back to God's revelation of self and his presence that takes place through faith in human experience. The old theological formulations based on abstract and metaphysical categories are inadequate. Not only do they distort the eucharistic meaning of an all-transforming action of the "total Christ" (that is, Christ *and* the Church, in the view of the fathers), but they are alien to modern religious consciousness. Contemporary experience of the world has shifted that consciousness.

We need to move from the old separated categories to a new organic theological approach. This approach involves at least three shifts: (1) *from speaking of "substance" to speaking of "body"*; (2) *from dialectical thought to symbolic thought*; (3) *from elaborating narrowly on the individual's relationship to the sacrament to developing understanding of the ecclesial and cosmic body of Christ.*

### 1. From "Substance" to "Body"

The reality "body" enjoys paramount importance in various ways. Anthropologically, the human body cannot be conceived of apart from an essential relationship to the world. Christ's sacramental body-person establishes a totally new and different relationship to the world, but one that is no less real and profound. On one hand, it already contains the new creation; on the other, the eucharistic body remains the seed and promise of the transformation of the world, human existence, and history.

"Body" is the eucharistic institution's principal word. It expresses three essentially united aspects of the Christian mystery: the person of Christ; his eucharistic self-gift; and his believers in communion with him and with one another as Church. Furthermore, the image of the body is central for accentuating the interpersonal character of Christ's real presence and the intimate and profound bond of *koinonia*—communion of the Holy Spirit, a key word in the New Testament—uniting the partakers of the eucharistic banquet. From this stance, modern Catholic theologians have interpreted the Eucharist as an interpersonal encounter. The abstract language of substance is alien to the personalist understanding of "body" in biblical revelation.

In the New Testament, especially in Paul, body is an important theological concept. It can denote the totality of a person's human existence. Sharing in the body of Christ signifies sharing the life of Christ given up as sacrificial self-giving. Using similar metaphors, such as flesh and blood, John's Gospel indicates the believer's complete communion with the person and mission of Christ. He is the bread of life that ensures full salvation, the gift of himself freely given—"the bread that I will give for the life of the world is my flesh"; it is bread; it must be "eaten," for "unless you eat the flesh of the Son of Man and drink his blood, you have no life in you" (see John 6:26–65).

Inspired by Greek patristic tradition, Jean Corbon beautifully states the wonder of the mystery of Christ present here in his body as life-giving stream in the Eucharist:

> [It is] the passionate love of the Father who "surrenders" his Word and "pours out" his Breath even to the point of "this is my body, *given up* for you; this is my blood, *shed* for you" and "Jesus *gave up* his spirit." The passionate love of the Father for human beings (John 3:16) reaches its climax in the passion of his Son and is thenceforth poured out by his Spirit in the divine compassion at the heart of the world, that is, in the Church.[66]

The scholastic meaning of "substance" is also alien to the modern understanding of person and its sacramental meaning. The body is not an object, but a human being in relation to others (the foundation of community) and also in relation to the world. The body of Christ is a new way of being for the glorious Christ—with us and for us, and also within the world and its destiny.

## 2. From Dialectic to Symbol

The second required shift, from dialectic thought to symbolic thought, is implied in the first. It involves the inner and complex symbolic meaning of life itself, which the body represents. Symbols are the universal grammar of communication. They echo the way of *being* of the person in the world. Symbols always do so in relation to people's world view, and to the presence of the real. In eucharistic terms, only symbolic thinking can account for the celebration that embraces the deepest mystery of human life and its destiny, Christ's Passover, itself a primary symbol. Symbol is essential to the total expression of the mystery. Obviously, the meanings drawn from this complex symbolic vision are inexhaustible. To cite one impressive example, a meaning drawn by Paul Jones: "By identifying his body with the bread and his blood with the cup, Christ blends archetypical symbols for presence and nourishment to convey the new humanity's dependence upon himself for life."[67]

The Eucharist is the divine self-communication and the symbolic and real transforming presence of Christ. Henri de Lubac has shown how the fathers of the Church used a concept of substance that had a different meaning from that of later scholastic terminology. In their eucharistic terminology—terms such as "substance of eternal life," "vital substance," "substantial bread"—the emphasis is on life, mystery, and transformation.[68]

In this view, real and dynamic presence are linked together in the complex symbolic event that is the Eucharist. It represents the corporate body of Christ, the God-man, his whole self, lying down and rising again for the community that enters into and celebrates the memorial of the mystery of redemption. This is the ancient and biblico-patristic vision in which the symbolic does not oppose the real, but rather represents it. Consequently, the presence of Christ through the mystery of eucharistic conversion can be called real-symbolic. In translating this patristic vision into modern theological language, Henri de Lubac, quoted above, tells us it has to be interpreted in the way of "ontological symbolism."

## 3. From the Individual to the Ecclesial and Cosmic

The third shift, moving away from focusing on the individual's relationship to the sacrament to developing an understanding of the ecclesial and cosmic body of Christ, is central to the Eucharist's ecclesiological foundation. Here again, the body is the unifying concept that expresses the ancient tradition rooted in the Bible, especially in Paul. In this tradition the personal, the ecclesial, and the eucharistic dimensions of "the body of Christ" are one sacramental mystery. Yet, in some medieval developments the emphasis came to be placed primarily, if not exclusively, on the presence of Christ in the eucharistic species. The former tradition stressed the "total Christ," or the organic unity of head and body. Now the scheme of the triform corpus emerged: first, the historical and risen Christ's own individual physical body; second, the sacramental body, the Eucharist; and, third, the ecclesial body, the Church. Further developments toward the end of the medieval period narrowed the eucharistic meaning of the body to the objective and spatial real presence of Christ and its individual reception, while Christ's fuller presence in the ecclesial body and its implications were underestimated or even forgotten.

The retrieval of "body" in relation to Church as the primordial symbol of Christ's self-giving presence is essential to understanding the eucharistic mystery itself, both in relation to the Church and in relation to the world. As Gustave Martelet, in line with Teilhard de Chardin, says, the eucharistic mystery of the Church is also the eucharistic mystery of the cosmos. He adds:

> As the Eucharist is inseparable from the risen Christ, so it is inseparable from the mystery of the *Church* itself. By an admirable reciprocity, not only does "the Church produce the Eucharist" which appears to be the more visible effect, but the "Eucharist produces the Church," and this effect, though hidden, is also the most indispensable. "Because there is one bread, we who are many are one body, for we all partake of the one bread," says St. Paul (1 Cor 10:17).[69]

A balanced eucharistic theology must incorporate the *koinonia* that Paul proclaims in the eucharistic mystery (see 1 Cor 10:16; 1 Cor 11:17–34). He insists on a dynamic, vital, and intimate relationship between the ecclesial community and the Eucharist, a relationship that must show itself in those who celebrate the memorial of the Lord. For Paul, the implications of *koinonia* are threefold. First, there is to be unity in the community through common eucharistic participation. (In other words, being for the Lord and being for others are inseparable realities.) Second, Paul speaks of "discerning the body." For him this means to be aware of and to actualize the new reality, which is the organic unity established by the one body of Christ. He is not primarily calling the assembly to be aware of the real presence of Christ in the eucharistic elements, as is so often understood by those who hear or read this passage. Rather, he wants them to be transformed into *koinonia* and to show signs of love, in summary, to see Christ in the community. There is no Eucharist when the meaning of Christ's personal, existential, and sacrificial self-giving body nourishing the body of believers is effectively denied. "For all who eat and drink without discerning the body, eat and drink judgment against themselves" (1 Cor 11:29). Consequently, the concept of the one body (*soma*) is the interpretative key that opens the Eucharist's many ecclesial, social, and transformative implications.

In patristic terminology the sacramental body *(corpus sacramentale)* and the real body *(corpus reale),* meaning the Church, are also one. There the Eucharist is presented as the preeminent sacrament of the Church. In the Eucharist the community discovers and effectively re-creates the ultimate potential of its transformation into the likeness of Christ. Pope Leo the Great preaches: "We become what we receive."[70] Grace, the gift of God poured from the Spirit of Jesus, is at work.

Augustine stands out in not only echoing the Pauline sacramental and ecclesial theology of the body of Christ but also in developing the mystery's complexity through symbolic thought and with strong spiritual and realistic language. The *res sacramenti,* or inward eucharistic reality, is the total Christ, head and body. It is the unity of grace and the transformation of believers brought about by Christ's presence: "The one Christ, the full Christ, the whole Christ."[71] At the core of Augustine's theology lies the concrete life of his community, as in this address to the newly baptized:

> If therefore, you are in the body of Christ and his members, your mystery has been placed on the Lord's table, you receive your mystery. You reply "Amen" to what you are, and by replying you consent. For you hear "The Body of Christ" and you reply "Amen." Be a member of the body of Christ so that your "Amen" may be true . . . Be what you see, and receive what you are.[72]

The Eucharist is for Augustine the food the community must eat with faith in order to have life in full. It must be taken not in a private or individualistic way but in the most comprehensively personal, ecclesial, and universal manner possible. This vital food is divine life pouring into the community that encounters God, the life-source, through the presence of a living person, "whom you eat, whom you drink...Therefore he has given us salutary food from his Body and Blood...hence let those who eat really eat and those who drink really drink; let them hunger and thirst; let them eat life and drink life...To drink that, what is it but to live? Eat life, drink life: You will have life and life in full."[73]

## Real Presence and Sacrificial Thanksgiving

Eucharist, therefore, is an act of Christ, "who always lives to make intercession" for us (Heb 7:25), and of the Church, sharing in his life (1 Cor 10:16). Only when we consider the unity and flow of the relationship of Christ, Church, and Eucharist from a sacramental point of view can we understand the mystery of the real presence. Kenan Osborne puts it this way: "The foundation for real presence is not the Eucharist, but (a) the real presence of the *Logos* in the humanness of Jesus and (b) the real presence of Jesus in the Church. Only on the basis of these instances of real presence will the real presence of Jesus in the Eucharist make theological sense."[74]

From this contemporary sacramental perspective, we can restate the sacramentality of Christ, the Church, and the Eucharist in their interconnectedness. Christ, the only sacrament of God (and so the primordial sacrament), is the principal agent of the ecclesial community's eucharistic action through his Spirit. The Church, born from the paschal Christ and his Spirit, is then the basic and universal sacrament. As such it is capable of generating the paschal gift as its basis. The Eucharist unceasingly initiates and builds the community as the definitive Church and yet at the same time is also "becoming" the body of Christ. This dynamic relationship between Church and Eucharist, the sacramental body and heart of Christ, is cogently understood in terms of mutual causality: Church and Eucharist not only presuppose each other, they are constitutive of one other.

Drawing on recent advances in biblico-patristic, liturgical, and ecumenical studies, Johannes Betz has formulated with theological clarity three highly useful concepts concerning the meaning of sacrifice and real presence in the eucharistic celebration. They are: (1) personal and pneumatic presence; (2) memorial actual presence; and, (3) corporeal and real presence. The first—personal and pneumatic presence— stresses Jesus' actualized sacrificial offering of his own person through the Holy Spirit, that is, not as an offering of *something*, but of *someone*, his very self. Memorial actual presence—the second—clarifies the meaning of the eucharistic action as living memorial, making sacramentally present for us here and now the reality of Jesus' self-offering to the Father. The third—corporeal and real presence—insists on the unique sacrifice of the body of Christ made present as a corporeal person, his whole self, whom the community joins in a living encounter, to "present your bodies as a living sacrifice" (Rom 12:1).[75]

### The "Cosmic Christ": Body of Christ and Cosmic Transformation

The preceding discussion identified three essential dimensions or organic links in understanding participation in the Eucharist. They are body, symbol, and Church. Their inner and deeper meaning of these dimensions points to something beyond them, to all created reality, that is, to the world. The theological relevance of a eucharistic spirituality of the cosmos is not only obvious, it is an essential component, often forgotten, of sacramental understanding. Thus, the eucharistic mystery of Christ and of the Church (the subject of the two prior sections) is also and inseparably the eucharistic mystery of all that is, of the cosmos, destined to be fulfilled with the grandeur of God. Our reflection starts with the idea of the cosmic Christ, "formulated by the Greek Fathers, in ways, at times, so strikingly presaging Teilhardian thought, as when Maximus speaks, across twelve centuries of 'Christ . . . as a center upon which all lines converge.'"[76]

Speaking from his insight into the universal Christ, Teilhard de Chardin could say that, "Fundamentally—since all time and forever— but one single thing is being made in creation: the body of Christ."[77] This chapter's thesis is that the Eucharist is the sacrament of the world's transformation by divine grace. It is such as the primary symbol of Christ's Passover and of his Church. Likewise, it is the special symbol and reality of what all creation is called to become in God's plan. What now follows in these pages is an exploration of the relationship between the body of Christ and the whole of creation in order to validate the thesis. What is crucial is to show the Eucharist's all-transforming potential, its true nature.

## Cosmic Mystery

The church fathers' understanding of eucharistic transformation contained a broad and elemental perception of the cosmic mystery, the risen Christ's all-embracing and eschatological power, universally effective for all reality and actualized at the heart of the world by the eucharistic existence. Moreover, what is most striking is the fact that the various patristic terms, formulae, and images for the eucharistic mystery are not restrictive, but are often correlated at different levels with essential themes of the Christian world view. The spiritual and the material, human elements and divine gifts, person and community, present and future are all subsumed by the dynamic eucharistic mystery, and ultimately implied in the lordship of the cosmic Christ, "the fullness of him who fills all in all" (Eph 1:23).

As research done by G. W. H. Lampe shows, common patristic terminology, such as "conversion" and "presence," used for specifically eucharistic doctrine also refers to the broader "cosmic" theme of the universal renewal to take place through the transformed risen Christ as Lord of the last age.[78] Christ's redemptive work is made perpetually available in the eucharistic sacrifice, pledge of a future glory. Like Melchizedek's sacrifice, it has an eternal and trans-temporal dimension. The Eucharist is *umbra* (shadow), for it looks back; it is *imago* (image), for it looks forward to the future transformation; and it is *veritas* (truth), for it is the true body of Christ and contemplates its fullness.

The complexity and quantity of patristic teaching allows only selective references here to illustrate this. Irenaeus of Lyons (d. ca. 200) is useful for this. He stands out as a pivotal link in the chain of truly Catholic doctrinal tradition, both Eastern and Western. His theological thought builds on the notion of "recapitulation" found in Ephesians 1:10: God will bring everything together in Christ.

"Recapitulation"—the re-beginning and fulfillment of the entirety of humanity and the universe in the humanity of the incarnate Christ—constitutes Irenaeus's starting point. From this he develops an integrated view of the goodness of the created world and of the unity of creation and redemption. The mystery of "recapitulation" then melds the idea of the total body of Christ with the acceptance of a unique sacrifice that implies the ultimate unity of nature and grace. They intersect in and are symbolized by the Eucharist. For Irenaeus, the Eucharist is pivotal in the refutation of Gnostic dualism. He is able to underscore both the union and transformation of spiritual and material reality by explaining that the sacrament of immortality contains and signifies each. The following text exemplifies this point:

> How can they say that the flesh passes into corruption, and does not partake of eternal life, if that flesh has been fed on the Body and Blood of the Lord? Let them either change their doctrine or cease to make their offerings. But our doctrine is in perfect harmony with the Eucharist, and the Eucharist conforms with our doctrine. For we offer to God His own, and we consistently set forth the union and fellowship of flesh and spirit, and confess our belief in the resurrection of both flesh and spirit. For as the bread from the earth, receiving the invocation of God, is no longer common bread, but is a Eucharist consisting of two parts, an earthly, and a heavenly, even so our bodies receiving the Eucharist are no longer mortal, seeing that they possess the hope of the resurrection to eternal life.[79]

Even more striking is how Irenaeus integrates his dynamic eucharistic understanding into an overarching vision of humanity and world, brought together to greater fullness of being through continuous transformation. The incarnate *Logos* is the central foundation of the saving mystery that illuminates a universe restored in the victory of resurrection. This universe is called to fullness in Christ's *parousia,* that is, the unveiled presence of the Lord at the end of history. Inspired by Paul's cosmic Christology of salvation, Irenaeus stresses the lordship of Christ as it is encountered in the universe.

Irenaeus's Christian realism brought new depth to the theological understanding of redemption. He envisaged it as developmental. "For [Irenaeus] redemption is a process of the transformation of the world. Our destiny means the transformation of the human condition into divine life, life in the Spirit, and at the center of that process he sets the Eucharistic Change."[80]

That realism has three closely related dimensions: creation, Christ, and Eucharist. Creation—represented by bread and wine—receives the *Logos* of God (Christ) and becomes Eucharist through the anamnesis of the incarnation and the power of the Holy Spirit. As Christ gives himself in the Eucharist and nourishes us, we therefore become one with him and with all creation. The Christian assembly expresses and signifies this oneness of *koinonia*. Gustave Martelet summarizes Irenaeus's powerful thought:

> The Lord's Supper, therefore, is indeed a feast at which we eat the bread of absolute life and, by favor of the Spirit, drink from the well of glory. The Eucharist realizes *in us*, through the bread and wine, what the incarnation effected *in Christ*; or, to put it even more precisely, through the Eucharist Christ introduces us into that for which he destines us by his incarnation.[81]

Many other Christian theologians have to some degree shared this cosmic outlook across the centuries. It has always been particularly evident in Eastern Christianity, especially in the form of a profound sense of communion with all of life transformed through the Divine Liturgy, that is, through the Eucharist. The mystics and other Christian writers down to the present have deeply felt the interconnectedness of all things in creation and in human history and have had a sacramental view of the world sharing its creative source in the Trinity. Nevertheless, this view became obscured at many turning points in history, notably with the rise of rationalist enlightened modernity and with the fragmented culture of secularism.

## Pledge of Universal Transformation

Teilhard de Chardin powerfully recaptured the vision of divine omnipresence in the cosmos, history, and person with his fundamental intuition of a christocentric world view. Christ, the life of humanity and of the world, is the "Omega Point" or simple center and goal of the universe. God's providence continually transforms the universe, gives it meaning and coherence, and moves it in evolutionary and ascending movement to full perfection in Christ.

The eucharistic mystery plays an essential role in the Teilhardian cosmic vision. Teilhard speaks of the process as an in-gathering of the cosmos. But history's potential and the mark of its destiny finds itself symbolized in the eucharistic bread:

Since first, Lord, you said "This is my body," not only the bread
on the altar but (to some degree) everything in the universe
that nourishes the soul for the life of Spirit and Grace has
become yours and has become divine—it is divinized, divinizing and divinizable. Every presence makes me feel that you are
near me; every touch is the touch of your hand; every necessity
transmits to me a pulsation of your will. And so true is this that
everything around me that is essential and enduring has become
for me . . . the substance of your heart: Jesus![82]

Christ is the heart of the world. Establishing "the divine milieu"
(Teilhard's phrase), the eucharistic communion binds together the
world, our humanity, and Christ. The Eucharist prolongs the incarnation
in the world; the world is the "matter" of the sacrament. Union with and
transformation by the eucharistic "body person" of Christ declares both
the vital center and the promise of the universal transfiguration.

At every moment the Eucharistic Christ controls . . . the whole
movement of the universe . . . As our humanity assimilates the
material world, and as the Host assimilates our humanity, the
Eucharistic transformation goes beyond and completes the
transubstantiation of the bread on the altar . . . In a secondary
and generalized sense, but in a true sense, the sacramental
Species are formed by the totality of the world, and the duration of the creation is the time needed for its consecration.[83]

Vatican II dedicates chapter 7 of its Dogmatic Constitution on the
Church to the Church's eschatological nature and union with the
Church in glory. It speaks of the destiny of the world and its ultimate
perfection with the Church now in its midst as the universal sacrament
of salvation. "The universe itself, which is so closely related to humanity
and which through it attains its destiny, will be perfectly established in
Christ (cf. Eph 1:10; Col 1:20; 2 Pet 3:10–13)."[84] The Eucharist, leaven
of the new creation, shows forth the purpose and future of the universe
in that it allows participation in the divine glory of Christ. Jesus in glory
is active in the world and by nourishing men and women with his own
body and blood makes them share in his glorious life.

## Bread Broken for a New World

A cosmic vision points to the unfinished work of establishing God's reign of holiness in history seen as encompassing all the human and the spiritual, social, and cultural realities of the human person. Confronting every sphere of life, this vision has the capacity to restore the Eucharist to its much needed central role for the creation of a new world. Thus, the Eucharist truly becomes the central and fundamental experience of a Church called to be the universal sign of salvation. Salvation and creation are, in fact, one from the perspective of the mystery of Christ: "Through him God was pleased to reconcile to himself all things, whether on earth or in heaven" (Col 1:20). This vision of totality calls for the most inclusive and all-embracing Christian mission of salvation. Ultimately, the transformative power of the Eucharist for the life of the person, the Church, society, and the world derives from God's grace and our commitment to release its power. This comes from the very life of Christ, "the firstborn within a large family" (Rom 8:29).

A cosmic vision is all the more important today after the highly individualistic and passive views of the recent past when the Eucharist was experienced privately by many as food for the individual soul. There was not only a tendency toward individualistic piety; eucharistic celebrations themselves were often unconnected to ecclesial ministry and to the daily lives of the believers, and also unconcerned with questions relating to the human person. Cosmic elements, having a cosmic meaning, bread and wine become Christ's body. They represent the glorification of the Creator and communion with the whole of creation. In being given and received, they share the solidarity of humanity in God with the cosmos, in both its concrete historical reality and its eschatological destiny at the same time.

The Eucharist is the Lord's open table to feed the hungers of humanity and, for this reason, it is also the joyful festival of liberation. However, this celebration demands the right spirit, a spiritual profundity without which the essence of the whole celebration is lost. It is the Lord himself who invites all, bringing the good news to the poor...and proclaiming liberty to captives (see Luke 4:18). Thus, the Eucharist cannot seal itself off from the human hungers that always await humanity, whether originating from a sinful world or from the human heart. It announces and furthers the liberating praxis of Christ for us and with us.

Recapturing this potential means creating communities that are boldly spiritually aware of the "real world" encounters that intersect in the eucharistic celebration. These constitute the place for today's historical embodiment of God's reign. It is a reign that calls for total transformation by God's grace and the power of the Holy Spirit, not only of personal attitudes and values until the ultimate transformation of death, but also of social structures according to the mind of Christ. He is the only prototype of the new humanity come alive in the Eucharist. The Eucharist is the fundamental symbol of the cosmic universality of God's definitive reign. As Vatican II states, "for in the most blessed Eucharist is contained the whole spiritual good of the Church."[85]

We live in an increasingly complex and fragmented world, lacking a sense of the mystery of God as revealed in Jesus and of God's goal for us and the universe. Nevertheless, humanity's destiny still lies in God's hands. His Spirit is working in our time just as in any other to re-create the world. God will answer the cry of even a fragmented people. Awareness of the mystery that relates humanity to its Creator Source gave past generations the original center, or a comprehension of the totality. Obviously, such an awareness affects the believer. In Christian terms, the Eucharist (the living Christ himself) is the sacramental center of the cosmos, of history, and of the human person awaiting consummation in God. Rooted in the mystery that integrates life and faith, it celebrates the "real world" being transformed, people's lives being changed. Thus, the eucharistic celebration becomes the very matrix of the Christian vision of reality and of a unified spiritual culture.

Theology today recaptures the thought patterns integrating God and his creation, grace and nature, that characterize Irenaeus of Lyons and Teilhard de Chardin. Karl Rahner has described worship in "real" life with the felicitous expression, "the liturgy of the world." The human community's ongoing communion and cooperation with God in the world's history is itself a liturgy, the primary and original liturgy. Rahner expresses this beautifully:

> The world and its history are the terrible and sublime liturgy, breathing of death and sacrifice, which God celebrates and causes to be celebrated in and through human history in its

freedom . . . In the entire length and breadth of this immense
history of birth and death, complete superficiality, folly, inade-
quacy and hatred (all of which "crucify") on the one hand, and
silent submission, responsibility . . . attaining the heights and
plumbing the depths, on the other, the true liturgy of the world
is present—present in such a way that the liturgy which
[Christ] has bought to its absolute fullness on his cross belongs
intrinsically to it.[86]

In seeing concretely how Christ's body, living and glorious, works
by the power of his Spirit, one must pay special attention to two areas:
first, the life and the ministry of the Church (at whose heart lies the
Eucharist); and second, the concerns of society and the world today
(for the Eucharist establishes what they are meant to become). On an
intellectual level one can only make a modest beginning in the listing of
resulting themes, given the complexity of issues arising today from
within both Church and world. More by way of example, then, we propose these for emphasis among the many possible others: the search for
social justice and the experience of the divine in our materialistic world;
the holiness of marriage and family living; the process of inculturation
through evangelization and social transformation; the need for ecological responsibility in our time of planetary crisis. The connections
between Eucharist and these issues are intimate and strong. Making
explicit the relationship with contemporary social realities, if not to
everything else in our lives, is vital for a eucharistic spirituality of
wholeness appropriate for our time. The Christ who is really present in
the Eucharist, alive here and now, has the power to change lives,
indeed to re-create the life of our world. This happens only to those
who seek him.

Church teaching has, in fact, lent formal recognition to the transformative possibilities of Eucharist for society. The theme chosen for
the 42nd International Eucharistic Congress (Lourdes, 1981) was
"Jesus Christ, bread broken for a new world." Likewise Pope John Paul
II has recognized current social, cultural, and ecological problems in
his encyclical *Sollicitudo Rei Socialis* (On Social Concerns):

The kingdom of God becomes present above all in the celebration of the sacrament of the Eucharist . . . In that celebration

the fruits of earth and the work of human hands—the bread
and the wine—are transformed . . . through the power of the
Holy Spirit and the words of the minister, into the Body and
Blood of the Lord Jesus Christ.[87]

IN CONCLUSION, understanding the Eucharist as cosmic sacrament and
symbol of transformation—the primary focus of this reflection—
gathers together much of eucharistic theology. While only one aspect of
a complex mystery—indeed, a mystery of inexhaustible significance—it
is, nevertheless, an all-embracing and central one. This mystery rests on
the reality of the risen Christ, the wellspring of universal transformation, and on the action of the Spirit, the eucharistic artisan through
whom the Lord acts in transformation. These considerations have
treated transformation as fourfold: (1) primordial, in Christ's transfigured body through his Passover; (2) sacramental, in the conversion of
bread and wine into Christ, a gift to his Church; (3) personal and communal, in our becoming one spirit with him; and (4) cosmic, in the
entire creation's "groaning" in longing for the promised reign.

    If, then, all the mysteries of faith and life converge in the body of
Christ, the problems and hopes, suffering and aspirations of today's
world can and must be related to its celebration. Christ's glorious body
is in the Eucharist, the all-containing prototype of a new heaven and a
new earth, of all reality, all history, all grace, and redemption, "God-for-
us" and "God-in-us," the sacramental power to transform the life of our
world. It is the sacramental prototype foreshadowing the final destiny
in which God will become all in all through the one "who is and who
was and who is to come" (Rev 1:8).

PART THREE

# The Healing Church

# 8

# Reconciliation:
# The Sign of Conversion

The Church's primary ministry is to proclaim Christ's mystery of reconciliation. The sacrament of reconciliation is a concrete and vital expression of the Church's total ministry. It is a rather complex sacrament, one whose full significance cannot be grasped except in correlation with the actual lives of church members and their social situation. More than in any other sacrament, this is apparent in the profound changes in the theology and practice of the sacrament of reconciliation throughout history. The reality of sin and its interpretation have been major factors contributing to this complexity.

Modern radical cultural shifts have challenged the religious foundations on which the traditional practice of reconciliation was based. Whatever is vital to the human search for meaning transforms the person. This transformation presents new opportunities, as well as new dilemmas. Challenged with critical questions, the sacrament of reconciliation is showing much vitality in our time. For example, at the global level, as the lines of penitents at the confessional shorten in Europe and America, they grow longer in other geographical areas (such as Africa) and in other spiritually awakening Catholic communities.

This vitality is also apparent in the various names given to the sacrament. The discussion focuses on three traditional names in particular: *confession*, the disclosure of sins: *penance*, the steps of reparation and satisfaction with the goal of conversion; *reconciliation*, the renewal of loving relationship with God, the community, and others. Our discussion of the sacrament will use the term "reconciliation." The chapter will stress the *theological*, *historical*, and *pastoral* aspects of the sacrament.

First, the central mystery of reconciliation will be considered in its broad christological and ecclesial dimensions. Moral conversion, the foundation for true spiritual growth, is stressed throughout the chapter. Second, attention will be paid to the historic and theological shifts both in content and in the mode of sacramental celebration, and will draw lessons from the constants of tradition.

Third, the relationship between the doctrinal development of the sacrament and the Christian doctrine of sin will be explored in conjunction with current sacramental, ministerial, and spiritual challenges to this area and other problematic areas. No profound renewal can come about without a coherent and complete vision of the total sacramental mystery in which reconciliation finds an important role as a prophetic sign for today's person.

## The Mystery of Reconciliation

Jesus' ideals inspire a theology and spirituality of the mystery of reconciliation and reshape current sacramental praxis. The reflection below focuses on the larger and foundational christological and ecclesiological perspectives from which and within which the single sacramental celebration of reconciliation becomes relevant. The reflection concludes by examining the central place of conversion, both in scripture and in sacramental expression, as an experience of God's holiness through the believer's wholehearted acceptance of Christ.

### Jesus, the Compassion of God

Jesus' compassionate relationship with sinners was not only incredible to his followers, but also extremely offensive to the religious establishment. The ideals he preached and lived by supported the paradox of God's holiness and unconditional forgiveness toward sinners. This relationship of compassion can hardly be conveyed in doctrinal statements. The gospel provides a strong basis for understanding Jesus' compassionate attitude toward sinners. We see this in the parables, such as the parable of the prodigal son, and in Jesus' association and table companionship with outcasts, such as the woman at the well and Zacchaeus.

Jesus brought to these outcasts the healing and liberating compassion of God. We call this "grace": "He saved us, not because of any works of righteousness that we had done, but according to his mercy" (Titus 3:5).

Reconciliation in the New Testament, especially in the Christology of Paul, is a master concept that implies various elements. First, Christ's sacrifice on the cross was the event of our reconciliation, for "he has now reconciled...[you] through death, so as to present you holy and blameless and irreproachable before him" (Col 1:22). Second, this was a universal and permanent atonement for human sin, "once for all" (Rom 6:10). Third, it is God's loving initiative and gratuitous gift which has forgiven "the sin of the world," for "all this is from God...for our sake he made him to be sin who knew no sin, so that in him we might become the righteousness of God" (2 Cor 5:18, 21). Finally, the basic path and ultimate horizon that makes human reconciliation possible is God's reign, which Christ embodied, "for he is our peace...[reconciling us] to God" (Eph 2:14, 16).

By making Jesus' ministry present, sacraments celebrate the paschal mystery. The totality of this mystery can be interpreted, according to von Balthasar, as a celebration of the sacrament of reconciliation. Reconciliation represents the incorporation of the sinner to a situation in which Christ is the archetype: "the disposition of the crucified Christ who bears all the sins of the world and confesses them before the Father, receiving visible 'absolution' in the Resurrection."[1] This fruitful perspective not only makes the sacrament of reconciliation dependent upon the centrality of Christ's saving act, but also touches the heart of a universally accepted confession of the Christian faith. It expresses the redemption of humanity through Christ's glorious cross.

Around this affirmation of Christianity is structured the whole sacramental system. All the sacraments express the richness and vitality of the same mystery present in human life. Specifically, they are all actions of reconciliation. This is especially true in the case of baptism and Eucharist with which the sacrament of reconciliation is interdependent. The sacrament of reconciliation is an effective realization, through the contrition of the believer, of the restoring, forgiving, and healing grace of God in Christ's mediation. The centrality of reconciliation arises from its foundation in Jesus, the savior of the world. Furthermore, the issues around the sacrament of reconciliation and around the problem of justification, according to Osborne, are fundamentally interconnected. Justification is the theological term for the gift of God's mercy that brings about reconciliation (see Rom 5). Thus, "any theology of justification or any theology of the sacrament of penance which compromises this centrality of Jesus and this gratuity of God's grace is incompatible with Christian faith."[2]

## The Church, Servant of Reconciliation

Christ was the sinless reconciler, who, by conquering evil and death, sin and hatred, restored humanity to life. He accomplished this through his death and resurrection, which was the culmination of his prophetic power of forgiveness through preaching, compassionate healing, and relationship with outcasts and sinners. Jesus continues his definitive mystery of reconciliation through the ministry of the Church, the sinful reconciler. For, "all this is from God, who . . . has given us the ministry of reconciliation" (2 Cor 5:18). From the beginning, the command of reconciliation, conversion, and forgiveness to the community of disciples as ministers of reconciliation was explicitly expressed: "Receive the Holy Spirit. If you forgive the sins of any, they are forgiven them; if you retain the sins of any, they are retained" (John 20:22–23).

The above injunction parallels two other classic texts on the transmission of the power to forgive given to Peter and the apostolic community as a whole: Matthew 16:17–19 and Matthew 18:15–18. These texts use the images of "binding and loosing," which have a primary salvific and eschatological meaning in the Church and before God. Jesus gives Peter the "keys" of the reign of salvation and life against the gates of the underworld of death. Contemporary theology has recovered the ecclesial dimension of reconciliation. Rahner's thinking attaches more importance to this universal power of ecclesial reconciliation than to other considerations, such as those raised by a historical approach.[3] The power of the keys is, in fact, "a divine authorization to allow mankind to participate in the eschatological kingdom (the kingdom of heaven), that is, to open up access to salvation (the power over the keys that the steward of the house possesses)."[4]

The Church came to be, then, a mystery and a servant of reconciliation through conversion to the gospel message. As a universal sacrament of reconciliation, the Church's permanent task is to proclaim

God's peace through the ministry of believers as "ambassadors for Christ" (see 2 Cor 5:20), that is, as gift-bringers of God's peace. It also declares the fullness of divine forgiveness and holiness in the midst of the world.

In the early Church, the unconditional return of the estranged person to God's healing embrace resulted from the call to conversion preached by the apostles. Baptism followed the prophetic proclamation: "Repent, and be baptized every one of you in the name of Jesus Christ so that your sins may be forgiven" (Acts 2:38). Believers then became "the body of Christ" and members of "the people of God" although the reality of sin and temptation remained: "If we say that we have no sin, we deceive ourselves" (1 John 1:8). As a consequence, newness in Christ and the reality of ecclesial holiness (first conversion) was sometimes damaged by sinful situations within the community. There arose the need of a post-baptismal praxis of reconciliation (second conversion), because certain cases of grave sins required exclusion (excommunication) from the community itself.

An awareness of the need for constant vigilance and reconciliation is evidenced in various New Testament texts. The texts imply the existence of corrective procedures and symbolic gestures for intra-communal forms of reconciliation. What later became a historical constant with the emergence of a sacramental and liturgical act of reconciliation has here an embryonic basis rooted in the practices of the apostolic period. These practices represent the will of a loving and merciful God for his people and inspired the tradition of succeeding Christian generations. The spirit of the gospel challenged the disciples to unconditional forgiveness (Matt 18:21–35), to brotherly correction (Matt 18:15–17; Titus 3:10–11), to public reprimand and penance (1 Tim 5:20; 1 Cor 5:1–11), and even to reconciliation before the Eucharist: "So when you are offering your gift at the altar, if you remember that your brother or sister has something against you, leave your gift there before the altar and go; first be reconciled to your brother or sister, and then come and offer your gift" (Matt 5:23–24).

The New Testament offers no formal rite of reconciliation. However, various precedents indicate certain incipient practices of reconciliation within the communities of the first Christians. Such is the case for excommunication, or expulsion of a member who seriously sins against baptismal and corporate holiness (1 Cor 5:1–5), as well as the possibility of reconciliation with the community (2 Cor 2:5–11). These Spirit-filled communities (as Acts show) were profoundly aware, as reconciled people themselves, of the presence of the reconciling mystery of Christ in them and through them.

As the documents of the first centuries testify, a rite of reconciliation was progressively defined and developed. The ecclesial dimension of reconciliation grew also with a parallel depth of testimonies in Christian writing, as for instance in the telling example of Isaac of Stella: "The Church cannot forgive anything without Christ, and Christ does not want to forgive anything without the Church. The Church cannot forgive anything, but to the one who does penance, that is, the one whom Christ touched with His grace; Christ does not want to forgive anything to anyone despising the Church."[5]

## Conversion, the Cutting Edge of Reconciliation

The paramount and only goal of the sacrament of reconciliation is conversion. It is the ongoing baptismal renewal as a lifetime journey of struggling against sin and striving for holiness. For this reason, baptism has been called "the first conversion," or the paradigmatic model of one's whole Christian life, and reconciliation "the second conversion" (*paenitentia secunda*). The *Catechism of the Catholic Church* describes reconciliation as an uninterrupted task for the whole Church, which "clasping sinners to her bosom, [is] at once holy and always in need of purification, [and] follows constantly the path of penance and renewal."[6] The Lutheran theologian Dietrich Bonhoeffer captures perceptibly this crucial relationship: "Confession is the renewal of the joy of baptism."[7] This approach is very important because it shows the theological rationale and spiritual orientation of this sacrament. It also highlights the link between reconciliation and the Christian initiatory process. In light of baptismal consciousness (which includes the Eucharist), reconciliation is an integral part of the total reality of the Christian mystery.

Conversion is the existential process of a radical change in a person's vision, life orientation, and way of acting and relating. Normally this process does not occur as a dramatic experience, but rather is a lifetime movement of seeking the living God; the process is sometimes verifiable and most often mysterious. From a faith perspective, the realization of one's impotence before sin and "the desire and resolution to change one's life"[8] are the precondition for the presence of God's grace that empowers a person to open up to the divine call and mercy. The person experiences an interior change *(metanoia)* together with a repentant attitude, which translate into wholeheartedly different ways of life conduct *(epistrophe)* in one's return to God.

The call to conversion is a core element in the message of the prophets of Israel calling the people to renew their covenant with God. Important themes in that call include changing their hearts, turning to God, rebuilding the community, trusting the power of God, and entering into communion with their Lord.[9] The call to conversion remained central from the prophets of Israel to John the Baptist and from Christ to the apostles.

All the synoptic gospels convey the *logion* of Jesus that defines the decisive proclamation of his redemptive mission: "I have come to call not the righteous but sinners to repentance" (Luke 5:32). To "repent, and believe in the good news" (Mark 1:15) is an essential and universal precondition for entering the reign and sharing in the eschatological community of salvation. The believer's new existential attitude toward seeking truth and authenticity brings joy and freedom. Acceptance of conversion entails life changes and personal sacrifice: leaving everything, following Jesus (Luke 5:11), even taking up one's cross and walking in his footsteps (Matt 10:38). In fact, discipleship is not only a movement of "converting from" but is also directed at "converting to" God in embracing Christ's will. He is the basis, the way, and the goal of conversion. Jesus' ministry revolves around preaching and miracles, signs of the same goal of conversion to the reign of God.

Together with the proclamation of the risen Christ, the call to conversion was also central to the apostolic witnessing of the Twelve: "So they went out and proclaimed that all should repent" (Mark 6:12). Paul's missionary activity likewise centered around the same prophetic call (Acts 26:20). He developed its meaning with the theology of the new law of grace and of the fruits of the Spirit, using a variety of contrasting images, such as "death and life," "old and new man," "darkness and light." John's messages are similar and center on Jesus as the Son of God who brings life and reconciliation (John 3:36). John gives special emphasis to the power of the Spirit and love, leading toward union with God who is light (1 John 1:3, 5).

Reconciliation involves a return to communion with God and the Church while penance indicates the acts needed for that return. The sequential acts of the celebration of penance/reconciliation are steps leading to the way of conversion: contrition, confession, satisfaction, absolution/reconciliation. They have, therefore, to be related to the larger life process of conversion. James Dallen has shown the drastic reduction of the liturgical action in later history. The Church's involvement and the penitents' activity toward the goal of conversion were reduced to a minimum. This vision of reconciliation contrasts with the ancient tradition. Beyond the personal commitment of the penitent, inner conversion requires external, ecclesial, and sacramental expression. "After penitents ritualize their conversion by celebrating the liturgy of penance, the priest responds by proclaiming reconciliation: pardon is granted by God through the Church working through the priest's ministry."[10]

## The Lessons of History

Despite the new rites for the sacrament of reconciliation, the Church experiences difficulty in making this renewal understood and appreciated. The history of reconciliation will help us understand these new developments and can point toward further pastoral applications. If we use it intelligently and attend to pastoral experience, history can become the key to solving problems concerning the sacrament of reconciliation today. We should not merely restore ancient customs, but we need to reflect on the past in light of present realities.

Vatican II called for renewed sacramental rites that would accent christological and pneumatological dimensions, a desire partially realized in the new Rite of Penance. The council did not want a break with the past but sought renewal within a living tradition. Thus, the *Catechism of the Catholic Church* strongly recommends the practice developed later in the Church's history of confessing venial faults. The fundamental shifts of this sacrament throughout history provide a key to envisaging new ways of adapting to contemporary Christian consciousness and the needs of our Church in a global world.

## The Shift to Public Ecclesial Reconciliation:
## The Canonical Penance (Third to Seventh Centuries)

Neither in the New Testament nor in the texts of the second century do we find an official rite of reconciliation. The first Christians awaited the imminent return of their Lord in glory and expected their thoroughly prepared converts to live out the implications of Christian commitment in their daily lives. For those who had fallen away, it was seen as "impossible to restore [them] again to repentance" (Heb 6:4). However, there were penitential testimonies at the turn of the first century in continuation with New Testament spirit and practice. They were often related to liturgical moments, although not institutionalized. The *Didache*[11] (first–second centuries) explained that sin breaks ecclesial and eucharistic unity, but can be absolved by penance and communal confession before the eucharistic celebration. In the second century, the *Shepherd of Hermas* (*Mandate*, IV, 3, 1–7) spoke of only one possibility for pardon (a rule in effect until the seventh century). It noted the possibility of excommunication and emphasized the ecclesial dimensions of sin and reconciliation. These early writings offer indirect evidence of an ancient form of church reconciliation with the imposition of hands.

In the early third century, the *Didascalia of the Apostles*[12] spoke of how the bishop's imposition of hands and the prayers of the faithful received the excommunicated back into the Church in a sacramental rite. Tertullian (160–230) described in detail this rite of reconciliation, which the Church allowed but once. It was called *paenitentia secunda*. He also distinguished between forgivable and unforgivable or capital sins, such as idolatry, homicide, and adultery. Lesser sins could be forgiven by fasting, almsgiving, and prayer.[13] Cyprian (200–258) was even more severe.

During this period, the church fathers began classifying sins. Serious sins had to be confessed to the bishop. Sins that were an occasion of scandal were to be confessed publicly. Delegated priests also imposed their hands in reconciliation and, in exceptional cases, (according to Cyprian) deacons did the same.[14] The fourth century saw many references to a developing liturgy of reconciliation in patristic writings and in the decisions of regional and ecumenical councils. Ancient rigor and discipline were maintained. Baptism and reconciliation of sinners usually took place in a Lenten context.

Solemn forgiveness was granted but once in a lifetime, though Siricius (384–399) allowed the relapsed to attend church and receive Viaticum on their deathbeds. Meanwhile Innocent I (402–417) allowed the relapsed reconciliation but not communion, not even at the point of death. This rigorism soon reduced the sacrament's use. Ambrose (340–397) admitted that many sinners were scared off by the difficulty of public reconciliation.

Augustine (354–430) introduced a gradual but imprecise distinction between serious sins that required public reconciliation and lesser ones that could be forgiven by daily prayer. Above all, the Eucharist was a source of purification from these sins. Christians saw forgiveness not so much as *preparation* for eucharistic communion, but rather hoped for forgiveness as a *result* of eucharistic celebration. This is clear from the post-communion prayers of Leo I (440–461).[15]

The high point of solemn reconciliation ceremonies came in the fourth to sixth centuries and involved three steps.

1. *Formal entry* into the penitents' ranks: prayer and the bishop's imposition of hands on the kneeling, sackcloth-clad penitent.

2. *The penitential period* itself, which ran from a few weeks (Eastern churches) to a lifetime. Works of penance consisted of fasting, prayer, abstinence from public business, and the legitimate use of marriage, sometimes withdrawal to a monastery. Clerics who were considered sinners were deposed, and no penitent could become a cleric. Penitents were often excluded from the Eucharist. Rome sometimes allowed them to attend the liturgy of the word and even to stay for the eucharistic rite, but they could not participate in the offertory or receive communion. Rahner notes that, in practice, this severe procedure was limited to notorious sinners.[16]

3. *Reconciliation of penitents at the end of Lent,* celebrated with prayer and the laying-on of hands by the presiding bishop or priest. The Spanish liturgy mentioned the joyful participation of the whole congregation, which repeated the pronouncement of forgiveness over and over again like a litany.

## *The Shift to Repeatable and Individualized Confession:*
## *The Tariff Penance (Seventh to Thirteenth Centuries)*

The rite of reconciliation changed with the Middle Ages. With the fall of the empire and the influx of new people, the adult catechumenate and the penitential rites proved pastorally inadequate. From the sixth century onward Irish monks initiated individual and regular reconciliation rites. This system spread to the Celtic monastic foundations in France and Germany. The Celtic monks had been influenced by the Eastern monastic tradition. Other forms of reconciliation were developed in Benedictine monasteries (*Rule of Benedict*, chapters 23–30; 43–46), also under the influence of Eastern monasticism. Here the abbot (not necessarily a priest) could excommunicate and also oversee the reconciliation of an estranged monk.

During the fifth and sixth centuries, the East moved more quickly to private reconciliation rites. Byzantine monks, even non-ordained monks, were charged by bishops with this sacramental function and with spiritual direction, although the bishop alone presided at public penitential rites. Coptic rites provided for two penitential ceremonies during Mass, a solemn one at the beginning and another just before communion. These Coptic rites were later adapted for private use. Eastern Church liturgies often included general confession and collective absolution in petition form. These rites were not just for "venial" sins but also for serious ones. Public reconciliation was still required for canonical cases.[17]

A less rigorous practice apparently developed in Spain because Toledo III (589) called for a return to ancient penitential practice. The origin of a new type of reconciliation called "tariff penance" might have originated here. It stressed satisfaction (such as personal sacrifices, prayers, and money) as a means of obtaining purification and freedom from guilt for every type of sin. Penitential books with lists of sins and appropriate penances, which could be performed *after* absolution, date from the sixth century. Individual, repeatable reconciliation, promoted by monks, was widespread in Europe by the eighth century.

The widely used Romano-German pontifical (tenth century) shows that both public and private penitential rites were used all over Europe. Various rites were open to the penitent: (1) *traditional, solemn*—for reconciling penitents (Ash Wednesday); (2) *public*—presided over by a priest, for pilgrims; (3) *private.*

Gradually new elements appeared. Whereas in the ancient Church penitents formed a group for whom the community prayed, now these penitents were excluded entirely from the Church. Even clerics could be required to do public reconciliation. There was also a new sense of church solidarity in sin. This sense of a penitent Church gave rise to the ninth-century Roman custom of everyone receiving ashes on Ash Wednesday. Reconciliation lost its links with baptism and the Eucharist. Nevertheless, Thomas Aquinas provided an uncompromising and profound theology of the relationship between Eucharist and reconciliation. "If Christ, in His passion, is the fount and cause of the forgiveness of all sin, how can a well disposed person fail to be forgiven when receiving the same Christ in the Eucharist?"[18]

### The Emphasis on Confession of Sins and Priestly Absolution (Trent to Vatican II)

Scholasticism busied itself with the essential sacramental elements. Franciscans maintained the traditional value of prayers of *petition*, whereas Dominicans emphasized the minister's declaration of absolution as the essential sacramental act. Trent, reacting against the reformers' denial that reconciliation was a sacrament, insisted on the juridical power of the keys; the formula of absolution "I absolve you" became the sacrament's "form," and the penitent's confession and satisfaction its "matter."

The council emphasized the christological foundation of the sacrament, but failed to treat sufficiently its ecclesiological aspects. The pastoral consequences of neglecting ancient traditions are significant. Private auricular confession, of late medieval period—now established as the sole official form of reconciliation—lost its connection with the word and the Eucharist. The judicial aspect was stressed. The minister's medicinal and spiritual role was weakened, although the narrowed sacramental expression did not prevent in practice a pastoral ministry of spiritual direction.[19] The essential sign, imposition of hands, became a minor gesture. The public and communal dimensions of reconciliation were weakened.

## History's Lessons

Up to Trent, reconciliation had known a complex development both in doctrine and practice, with a variety of coexisting forms of reconciliation. After Trent, the development and continuous pastoral adaptation of the rite in previous centuries ceased. We cannot simply ignore Trent's canons, which curtailed abuses and clarified and reaffirmed traditional doctrine, but neither must we forget the early Church's authentic witness. History can be the key to a profound pastoral renewal. Historical evidence of the Church's tradition makes the following lessons worth remembering.

1. Reconciliation had always been a celebration of personal and *community conversion*, not an act in individual piety. Routine and superficiality in the rite were foreign to this process. The early Church sought simply to enshrine biblical *metanoia* in a complex process and the liturgical rite was interdependent with the basic context of ministerial and sacramental life.

2. The early Church emphasized a person's reconciliation *with God and the Church*. The patristic "communion of saints" entailed sin's pervading nature; hence reconciliation was to be *public* and *ecclesial*. Renewal must not end up in a new formalism, but should lead to a living, felt ecclesial event of spiritual renewal.

3. The ancient practice of reconciliation intimately joined *ascesis* and *sacramental rite*. When a juridical understanding (with its lists of penances for various sins) overshadowed the mystery of reconciliation in the high Middle Ages (beginning with the "tariff penance"), the liturgical expression was sharply narrowed and the crucial link was weakened. However, Lateran IV still emphasized the sacrament's pastoral focus. Also, the Eastern tradition preserved the minister's role as involving *discernment, spiritual direction,* and *prayer*.

4. There is not one, but there are *many concrete historical forms* of the sacrament and, therefore, there must be a legitimate pluralism suitable for today's pluralistic world churches. Ahistorical, abstract, and ideological ideas of the sacrament's renewal prove inadequate. History is the

best proof that the *sensus fidelium* has been very often ahead of the official discipline of the Church.

5. The early Church saw reconciliation in relation to *baptism*, and penitential rites in connection with the *word* and the *Eucharist*. The word offers light and strength for conversion. Even Trent recognized the Eucharist as a source of forgiveness: "By this oblation the Lord...pardons wrong-doings and sins, even grave ones."[20] No doubt for this profound reason Eastern churches, as noted earlier, have included penitential rites and formulas of general absolution within their liturgical canons. The Eucharist as source of propitiation and grace is a clear and constant claim of tradition, both in the East and in the West.

For centuries there was no sacramental celebration of reconciliation for sins that today might be considered less serious, with the exception of certain canonical crimes. Herbert Jedin—an authority on the Council of Trent—states, "Trent nowhere condemned, in explicit and clear language, the opinion that absolution can be given in global form after a general confession of guilt."[21]

## The Reform and Its Future

Through the centuries, people have held similar basic convictions about human sinfulness. They have always considered it as a humbling *reality* and a human *mystery* in their worldly experience. Human sinfulness is a permanent existential condition enshrined in human history and manifested in the personal impotence of shaping one's life: "For I do not do the good I want, but the evil I do not want is what I do" (Rom 7:19). The experience of personal sinfulness and guilt is universal—provided that somehow the person has a relationship with the "holy."

The presence of rites of expiation, purification, or restoration in all religions demonstrates the universal human longing for inner healing and liberation from the rupture of guilt and sin. A restored kinship with the ultimate gives meaning to human lives. Rooted in the same universal condition, the Christian experience is revealed in biblical revelation: God as the infinite source of holiness and the definitive reconciliation in Christ (a theme developed earlier). Thus, Christian interpretation and praxis are radically different from the views of cosmic religions.

Like the story of the prodigal son and the symbolic embrace of Christ's cross, the sacrament of reconciliation is a continuous parable of God's unquestionable forgiveness. This sacrament, in fact, transforms a humbling human predicament into a mystery of liberating grace.

The sacrament heals. However, the healing must come from within, through an acknowledgment of the personal reality of sin. It is this acknowledgment, the fruit of God's grace and the individual's sincere contrition, that liberates the person and makes sacramental reconciliation a joyful sign of freedom. Is this a crucial factor in the sacramental practice and its current decline among Catholics in Western countries? In order to answer this question, we will begin by discussing the meaning of sin. We will then present the Christian response to it through the sacramental celebration of reconciliation, stressing its medicinal and liberating effects. The conclusion will suggest some perspectives for future renewal. The following section builds on an understanding of the sacrament as an instrument for realizing a believer's journey of conversion and spiritual growth.

### Sin and Reconciliation

A theological understanding of sin has to include some major dimensions: a relationship to *God, self,* and the *community*. Following the classic Augustinian definition, the *Catechism of the Catholic Church* defines sin as "an offense against reason, truth, and right conscience; it is failure in genuine love for God and neighbor caused by a perverse attachment to certain goods. It wounds the nature of man and injures human solidarity. It has been defined as 'an utterance, a deed, or a desire contrary to the eternal law.'"[22]

*First, sin is an offense against the truth of God.* Sin is always related to the interpersonal love between God and human beings. It ruptures the covenantal relationship with him, destroying the personal bond of mutual fidelity. In the teaching of the magisterium, or the doctrinal authority of the Church, the essence of sin lies in the individual's "exclusion of God, rupture with God, disobedience to God."[23] When we disobey his truth about the way life is to be lived (as in the ten commandments), we take a stance against the very same meaning that gives direction to human existence and energizes its growth.[24]

*Second, sin is an offense against the truth of the person.* What the person thinks about himself or herself in relationship to God will condition his or her moral attitudes. If God's glory is our life, sin is the refusal to grow in perfection for his glory. The person's great dignity stems from the fact that he or she is, even in the weakest condition, a concrete image and reflection of God. Endowed with inalienable freedom, one becomes a true person in responsible relation to the other. The truth of God and the truth of the person are inseparable (Luke 10:25–37), as the prophet Micah poignantly articulated in a threefold assertion of the same moral truth: "He has told you, O mortal, what is good; and what does the LORD require of you but to do justice, and to love kindness, and to walk humbly with your God?" (Mic 6:8).

*Third, sin is an offense against the truth of the community.* Sin also has a communal and social dimension. To use Buber's interpersonal concept, there exists an "I-thou" (versus the alienating "I-it") relation of solidarity and moral responsibility between interior freedom and the communal and social reality, and also between the person and the human family. Free choices by individual persons are a vital part of real life in the communal and social as well as in the spiritual dimensions. From the perspective of socio-historical relations, sin shatters the family and social fabric. It becomes an obstacle to the growth of love and justice in society. Thus, it creates situations of injustice that have been rightly called "structures of sin."

## Current Challenges to Sacramental Practice

### 1. Sin as Violation of a Covenant Relationship

In discerning and characterizing human behavior in relationship to the three dimensions discussed above, the notion of sin has been expanded in the last decades beyond the traditional categories of mortal and venial sin. First, current moral theology stresses that sin primarily means a violation of a covenant relationship of faithful loyalty to a personal God. This covenant approach underlines the real function of reconciliation as sacramental celebration. It actualizes God's unbreakable fidelity in Christ who embraces the repentant sinner.[25] The context of a covenant relationship is essential in envisioning the primary purpose of reconciliation.

## 2. Awareness of Sin

A second crucial factor in the approach to this sacrament by the person of faith is a consciousness of sin. An individualistic culture of moral relativism undervalues the reality of moral values and disregards the need for Christian judgment. The awareness of sin passes through the mediation of the dictates of conscience, as the Church teaches: "By conscience, in a wonderful way, that law [inscribed by God in the person's heart] is made known which is fulfilled in the love of God and of one's neighbor... It is, however, only in freedom that people can turn themselves toward what is good."[26] Thus, the question of the frequent use of the sacrament of confession has more to do with an informed conscience and spiritual sensitivity to living out the gospel than with the reality of sin and the availability of the sacrament.

In fact, the drastic decline in the number of people going to individual confession has been attributed to the loss of an awareness of sin. Also, there has been a loss of a sense of "community," so that sin is seen as being between "me and God." The heart (conscience) can become hardened without a point of reference to the holiness of God. This prevents the person from recognizing a sinful situation. Only a relationship with God transforms and leads the person to repentance. As Augustine confessed: "The lovely things kept me far from you... you called and cried out loud and shattered my deafness... you put to flight my blindness."[27]

## 3. Cultural Influences

A better grasp of the complex subject of the practice of reconciliation requires coming to grips with the current reality of culture and its profound transformations. Today there exist dramatic differences among Catholic communities, at least in terms of the numbers of people approaching the confessional. On the one hand, there are religious groups characterized by a communal sense of the sacred ingrained in their world view. On the other hand, there are religious people within secularized and individualistic societies who lack a strong reference to the sacred in daily living. The cultural environment (with the particular influence of modern psychological theories) affects people's perception of sin because it changes their value systems and their spiritual attitudes. It also changes their view with regard to the relevance of the role of the Church itself as a medium of salvation.

Nevertheless, ambivalence with regard to these changes persists. For instance, it has been argued that the sense of sin in contemporary society has not been lost; it has just shifted. The considerable emphasis given to the problems of social justice and human solidarity shows that communities have grown in moral responsibility and maturity, at least in the social arena. Some of these problems are reflected in the American bishops' declaration prior to the 1983 Synod of Bishops in Rome: "We believe that the present state of affairs points to a widespread confusion on a number of basic questions: the nature of sin, personal moral responsibility, the meaning of 'fundamental option' or life orientation as a factor in personal morality, the role of reconciliation in spiritual growth and maturity, and the nature of the sacramental system within our sacramental Church."[28] Sociology also shows a strong, consistent trend among Catholics straying from the understanding of Church as a locus of moral authority.

### Celebrating Reconciliation

The paschal gift of forgiveness gives meaning to the present sacrament of reconciliation. It is a sign of "God's mighty deeds" for his people in the life of the Church. "The height, the breadth, the depth and the length of this mystery of God's forgiving grace is what the sacrament of reconciliation is meant to celebrate."[29] Both sin and reconciliation relate to "the mighty deeds," the former as presupposition, the latter as outcome. Most important in the sacrament is the fact that both relate to three essential dimensions: God, person, and community. These are the terms we used above to articulate the meaning of sin.

If sin has these three dimensions, so does reconciliation. Now we will focus on each of these dimensions to emphasize the triple structure of the interpersonal encounter of the sacrament, that is, (a) the *christocentric*, (b) the *ecclesial* and, (c) the *personal* aspects of reconciliation. This larger vision of Vatican II was called for in the reformed ritual published in 1974.

*Christocentric Dimension*
First, only God forgives sins (cf. Mark 2:7). God in Christ sets the believer on the path of freedom and heals the inner being of the con-

trite person. Throughout history, the sacramental sign of reconciliation continues Jesus' ministry of forgiveness and healing: "'Friend, your sins are forgiven you' . . . [The paralytic] went to his home, glorifying God" (Luke 5:20–25). Reconciliation is the unending mission of the compassionate Christ by the gift of God and the re-creating power of his Spirit present in the penitent Church.

### Ecclesial Dimension

Second, sin hurts the communion of saints—the body of Christ and the family of the Church. If a member is hurting, everybody suffers. And if a member is healed, the community is strengthened. Mediation for conversion becomes "an uninterrupted task for the whole church who, 'clasping sinners to her bosom, [is] at once holy and always in need of purification, [and] follows constantly the path of penance and renewal.'"[30] Similar to Christ's prophetic ministry toward outcasts and sinners, the Church's mediating role becomes effective when she is perceived as a community of compassion. This means that she cannot be unduly rigid, but must heal the wounds of guilt and restore the brokenhearted. Indeed, the Church has in this sacrament a great potential for its own spiritual reform. The sacrament is likewise a lifetime process of the believer's transformation to the ways of Christ.

### Personal Dimension

Third, God does not save without the human response of repentance. The sacrament liberates from the oppression of sin, but first it has to break the human heart. In ratifying the response to the challenge of the gospel, sacramental reconciliation is a sign of freedom when it is reflected in life. Repentance is a necessary condition for the reception of God's grace. The need for repentance, inner healing, and freedom from the slavery of sin is also part of human growth. It is essential to the Christian existence. Whether the believer is restored to the life of grace or simply spiritually healed, contrition (a broken heart, which is the soul of the sacrament), confession, and satisfaction are the acts of the penitent leading to reconciliation.

As a healer and the freeing sacrament of Christ himself, the priest welcomes the penitent with sensitivity and wisdom. The Catechism describes beautifully his ministry: "The priest is fulfilling the ministry of the Good Shepherd who seeks the lost sheep, of the Good Samaritan who binds up wounds, of the Father who awaits the prodigal son and welcomes him on his return, and of the just and impartial judge whose judgment is both just and merciful. The priest is the sign and the instrument of God's merciful love for the sinner."[31]

In retrieving the biblical concept of God's reconciliation in Christ, the council provided a new theological and pastoral key for interpreting the mystery and present power of sacramental reconciliation. The sacrament is seen as an act of ecclesial worship, and thus, "social and ecclesial in its nature as well as its effects."[32] The basic inspiration of Vatican II is expressed in the following statement: Through the sacrament of reconciliation the faithful are "reconciled with the church which they have wounded by their sins and which by charity, by example and by prayer labors for their conversion."[33]

## Sacramental Names and Ritual Models

The new fundamental meaning of reconciliation is apparent in contemporary Church doctrine. It is essentially envisioned as a sign of a graced encounter of reconciliation. The meaning of the sacrament can also be seen in contrasting the different names given to the sacrament and the new liturgical structures of the reformed ritual. The ritual reform was an attempt to integrate broader historical traditions. It was, in particular, a compromise between the Tridentine and Vatican II visions of the Church's ministry of forgiveness of sins. The three historical names given to the sacrament (confession, penance, and reconciliation) refer to different dimensions of the same reality of repentance: opening of one's soul and return to God's grace and the Church's eucharistic participation.

"Confession" refers to the sacramental action that takes place individually between the confessor and the penitent. The verbal declaration of sins involves a humble dialogue and encounter with God in the Church. It implies also the person's psychological need to open up, to be heard and confronted. Sharing one's wounds brings about the healing of the soul. Like unloading a burden, it can be a very liberating experience.

"Penance" is an ancient name that emphasizes a sacrificial attitude and the medicinal actions undertaken by the penitent in the process of conversion. It is a sort of reparation for offending God and for the damage caused to the community of faith and to oneself.

"Reconciliation" means returning to God and to the Church, knowing that one is fully forgiven. It is also an ancient name that touches the essence of the sacrament. The praxis of community reconciliation symbolizes the full meaning·of spiritual conversion and emphasizes the thrust of the Church's missionary role. These last two names, "penance" and "reconciliation," thus relate to the social and ecclesial aspects of the celebration of the sacrament.

Initiated at the beginning of the thirteenth century and confirmed by the Council of Trent, the old rite lasted for almost one thousand years. The new liturgical structures of the Rite of Penance (1974) broke the historical tradition of a single form of celebration. It constituted a major historical development in the theological interpretation and sacramental practice of reconciliation. The most important features of the Vatican II mandate are the retrieval of the ecclesial dimension of the celebration of the sacrament (communal reconciliation), the primary role given to the word of God as the power of conversion, and the possibility of the use of general absolution.

An awareness of the pluralism of sacramental models over the centuries led to the introduction in the new Rite of Penance of three different ways for the sacrament to be celebrated. First, *individual reconciliation* is the traditional, private form of confession. Second, *communal reconciliation* is celebrated in church with the parish community gathered together. During the celebration, the word of God is proclaimed, the priest calls the community to conversion, and there is communal prayer. At the end of the ritual those who wish to do so are welcome to make an individual confession and receive absolution. Third, in *communal reconciliation with general absolution,* the priest gives absolution to all present without individual confessions.

All three rites involve a genuine change of heart and spiritual growth. Contrition, the humble response to the greatness of God's love, is the heart of reconciliation. It is in discovering God's glory and love that a contrite heart experiences freedom and healing, forgiveness and compassion, spiritual renewal and joyous transformation: "Father, I have sinned against heaven and before you; I am no longer worthy to be called your son" (Luke 15:18–19).

## Perspectives for Renewal

In this concluding section, the current practice of the sacrament and its potential for the spiritual transformation of Christian communities will be considered. The revision of the Rite of Penance has had its successes. Still needed is long-term pastoral renewal and development. This new stage of renewal should bridge the gap between current sacramental practice and people's experience of faith. In fact, the present experience of faithful Catholic believers *(sensus fidelium)* is key to revitalizing the official discipline of the Church.

Today's sacramental landscape is well known, especially the widespread crisis in the penitential system of confession. Comparing the attitude of Catholics of a generation ago to current attitudes and practice, we realize that a majority of people are not availing themselves of the sacrament. Even before the implementation of the new rite in 1974, Francis Buckley observed: "During the last five years there has been a sharp drop in confession: about fifty percent in Europe and up to seventy five percent in some parts of the United States."[34]

The state of the sacrament thirty years later is not very different. However, it seems that this view of the situation does not apply to non-Western Catholic churches, some ethnic people in the United States, and particular Catholic groups in parishes everywhere. Statistics do not provide a glimpse of the future and sweeping generalizations preclude clarification of the complex issues involved in this sacrament. Thus, the discussion that follows will focus on the following issues: (a) the meaning of *sin*, (b) the use of *general absolution* and the need of missionary *outreach*, and (c) *the centrality of the Eucharist* and *other forms of forgiveness*.

### Sin and Contrition

Behind the blinding mirage of inculpability, there is a severe crisis of spirituality. Obviously there exists a direct link between a personal sense of responsibility for sin and the corresponding repentance in contrition. If, despite human rationalization and moral relativizing, sin remains a stark reality at the personal, communal, and social levels (as we saw earlier), the perception of its meaning changes with different historical contexts. Again, it seems that the actual link between sin and sacrament is shifting, theologically and sacramentally, in Christian consciousness.

Theologically, a clarification of the meaning and full reality of sin is needed. This has to include not only doctrinal development (as has been happening in the post-Vatican period), but also catechetical updating. There seems to be tension, if not doctrinal confusion, between the former and the latter, which might rely on pre-Vatican II doctrinal presumptions. In the National Conference of Catholic Bishops' 1990 study document on the sacrament of penance, reference is made to a "general confusion over what is right and wrong."[35] On the one hand, abstract concepts of the difference between mortal and venial sin will not support future progress. On the other hand, the narrow and negative view of a morality of guilt or infraction is at odds with the liberating message of Christ.

## General Absolution

From the sacramental perspective, another critical matter has to do with the appropriate means to experience God's forgiveness and grace in and apart from the celebration of the sacrament of reconciliation. This problem is multifaceted, involving two separate issues: (1) the availability of general absolution and (2) other means of accomplishing repentance and reconciliation. By addressing these issues, not only will the primary and secondary truths about this sacramental practice come to the fore, but also a richer vision of the larger process of sacramental reconciliation will emerge.

A communal confession in general terms with a public proclamation of absolution for the whole community without individual confession (Rite III) has become controversial. The rite is restricted to extraordinary situations of emergency. Bishops in different countries and dioceses have asked for greater flexibility (as in the 1983 Synod of Bishops in Rome). They have even presided successfully over reconciliation liturgies with general absolution. In response, various Vatican congregations and John Paul II himself opposed the practice, stressing that reconciliation of individual penitents is the only normal and ordinary manner of sacramental celebration.[36] The second form of a *communal celebration* (Rite II) is regarded as equal to the first in terms of normality of the rite.

General absolution has been envisaged pastorally as a celebration of the repentant Church returning to Christ, seeking conversion, and joyfully proclaiming God's merciful grace. It implies later individual confession of any grave sins. On the one hand, the practice of the third model of reconciliation (Rite III) should not overlook the vital importance and inherent human need to confess, to open the inner self, to acknowledge and dialogue, that is, the need for some kind of "spiritual direction." This is how the penitent experiences healing, spiritual nourishment, and profound peace. Hence, the Rite of Penance stresses the importance of individual, integral confession and absolution. The self-deceptive and individualistic opinion of "confessing to God only" that is widespread among so many uncatechized people disregards the ministry of the Church. It also denies the public face of sin and leads to spiritual emptiness.

On the other hand, only true contrition and the absolution prayer are essential for sacramental reconciliation. Yet, "confessing" is an integral part of the sacramental action. Overemphasis on scrupulous enumeration of sins and on the negative side of human behavior ignores the developmental and complex reconciling dimensions of Christian life. It narrows the entire process of the reconciling action, which is wider than auricular confession, and whose goal is to repair, to nourish, and to enlighten. Ladislas Örsy maintains that religious models require adaptation and a shift from focusing on a list of small sins to the awareness of evil inclinations in the heart: "Where there was no breach with God in the life of a person, it may be more important to focus on our deeper movements and habits than our individual acts."[37]

The primary effect of this sacrament is the restoration to life of those who have cut themselves off from a relationship with God through mortal sin, "a self destructive, rebellious act, coolly calculated, supremely selfish and permeated by malice."[38] Nevertheless, many confessors can bear witness to the absence of the unchurched and inactive Catholics, particularly those who have seriously ruptured their communion with God. Of course, they also gladly know occasional cases of "prodigal sons" returning home. As Dallen rightfully observes, "the root difficulty lies in achieving a credible experience of a penitent Church, a reconciled and reconciling community that mediates the experience of a merciful, compassionate, and loving God."[39]

General absolution might become a pastoral concern if it is not implemented thoughtfully. Nevertheless, a pastorally wise celebration of general absolution has a powerful potential for challenging the "lost sheep" to return to the fold. Is the Christian community effecting genuine and deep conversion through appropriate penitential ritual structures and context, building bridges of compassion, reaching out to embrace the estranged? Or is it shutting doors with narrow interpretations, pharisaic strictures, and paternalistic attitudes? In the spirit of the unconditional grace of Christ's compassion, is the Church effectively a reconciler toward today's Samaritans, Zacchaeuses, and prodigal sons? For example, priests themselves going to confession before hearing confessions in a communal celebration would be a strong and credible sign to the assembly.

The second issue mentioned above, regarding other means of accomplishing the sacramental role of reconciliation, is very important, because it places this sacrament within the proper contextual foundation of the mystery of reconciliation. "Every sacrament is in its own way a moment of reconciliation."[40] The healing purpose of the sacrament has occasionally been obscured in distorted rituals that have brought guilt and alienation to God's children rather than the wonderful and liberating gift of God's mercy.

## The Cleansing Power of the Eucharist

The Eucharist's cleansing power is particularly evident in the case of the Eucharist's efficacy to forgive all sins of a well-disposed believer. The Eucharist is central to ecclesial reconciliation. The teaching of Thomas Aquinas on this relationship (referred to in the previous chapter) is enlightening and represents a forgotten link to the ancient tradition of the Church.[41] This tradition shows that "the Eucharist is the perfection of the remission of sins because the cross, the mystery of reconciliation, is present in it alone. For centuries the Church lived on these truths, allowing the sacrament of penance its extraordinary role."[42] More specifically, the ancient sacramental tradition in this regard (already discussed) can be summarized in two points: (a) believers have the firm conviction that they approach the eucharistic table with a consciousness of their sins; (b) petitions of forgiveness and purification are not primarily a means of preparation for a worthy celebration of the Eucharist; rather, they are its outcome and given grace. All believers are called to conversion and transformation, because they are called to live as holy people who celebrate the Eucharist. Both sacraments represent two perpetual signs of God's love and the continuing ministry of Jesus' healing and forgiving words and actions.

Christ, the center and agent of sacramental reconciliation, invites the believer to share his passion so that he or she can live his resurrection. Reconciliation is only a particular expression of the mystery of wider reconciliation, "a sacrament of the superabundant love and mercy of a reconciling, justifying, divinizing God."[43] It is organically interconnected to the Eucharist, the central sacramental mystery of victory over sin and the summation of all sacramental moments of Christian reconciliation. Expressing this rich Christian tradition and wider vision, the *Catechism of the Catholic Church* speaks about the various means of obtaining forgiveness of sins, especially the Eucharist. As the Council of Trent teaches, "It is a remedy to free us from our daily faults and to preserve us from mortal sins."[44]

IN CONCLUSION, the present crisis of the sacrament within the Christian community at large is challenging the Church to ongoing development. The tremendous diversity of the past in discipline and concrete forms speak today about the need to adapt and develop new models according to the multiform Christian experiences and spiritual needs of contemporary global churches. The 1974 reform of the Rite of Penance calls for a long-term renewal, a Christ-centered and evangelical movement. Thus, the *Catechism of the Catholic Church* presents this sacrament as the process of conversion and repentance whose characteristics can be found in the parable of the prodigal son: "Only the heart of Christ who knows the depths of his Father's love could reveal to us the abyss of his mercy in so simple and beautiful a way."[45] The following have been and remain today fundamental goals of the Christian tradition of the sacrament: the community's generous reaching out to the alienated and "spiritually dead," the process of nurturing conversion of heart, and the healing and strengthening of the believer in the life of the Spirit.

The practice of frequent confession is today underestimated though encouraged by the Church. It is an important aspect of our rich

Catholic spiritual heritage. It has a healing and restoring purpose, by God's grace, of discernment and spiritual growth. Historically it was closely connected, in many instances (as it is today), to spiritual direction. However, mechanical and perfunctory ritual practices without sincere commitment are ultimately a deceitful sham. One can acknowledge his or her sins only with a mind and heart spiritually renewed. The person experiences God's grace and a deep hunger for Christ's redemption through the Church's ministry. Then reconciliation comes alive as mighty deeds of God's grace for the sake of a divided and broken world.

# 9
# Anointing:
# Christian Wholeness

L ike a buried treasure, the precious sacramental sign of healing
anointment has been neglected and even shunned in our pragmatic age of disbelief. An opposite trend, however, discloses a
broad movement of manifold healing practices within various groups
and religious communities on a grassroots level. Some problems may
be traced back to the old sacramental mentality; lingering fears, due to
the narrowing of the anointing of the sick to the practice of "extreme
unction," still remain. Other challenges impact greatly on priestly roles
within modern institutionalized medicine. In an attempt to clarify these
and other issues, this chapter envisions anointing of the sick within the
broad view of the Church's scriptural and sacramental tradition. The
sacrament should pristinely mirror Jesus' commission to cure in a total
salvific sense and be at the center of a Christian mission of wholeness.

The symbolic expressions attending to the various meanings of the
"fifth sacrament" have always been related to the three fundamental
questions of sickness, sin, and death. The sacrament's complexity stems
from various interpretations of these questions. These interpretations, in
turn, have historically reshaped the sacramental celebrations of anointing as the actual experience of the ultimately freeing and healing Christian mystery. The discussion that follows will aim at providing an integrative and holistic approach to the multifaceted dimensions of this
healing sacrament by addressing: (a) the ministry of Christ, the paradigm for Christian healing; (b) the historical models of anointing and
healing, and the need for contemporary integration; (c) the connection
between illness and healing in the Christian search for wholeness; and
(d) the Christian rite of passage seen from an eschatological perspective.

222

## The Healing Ministry of Christ

Many New Testament texts, especially the synoptic gospels, portray Jesus as a miracle worker, a compassionate physician, and a prophetic liberator. Miraculous healings (approximately twenty-five) play a prominent role in Jesus' ministry and reveal his attitude toward the sick. As John Meier states, "Nothing is more certain about Jesus than that he was viewed by his contemporaries as an exorcist and a healer."[1] The healing power of his actions, such as the miracle "signs" in the Gospel of John, is directed not only toward accomplishing inner renewal through faith and trust but also toward communicating with the body, thereby touching the whole person. Moreover, Jesus' non-judgmental gentleness and unconditional compassion inspired trust and hope, which gave meaning to human sickness and suffering. Finally, as a prophetic liberator "moved with compassion," Jesus showed signs of deliverance coming from God to the people in the midst of their affliction. He proclaimed the dignity of the person by rejecting both oppressive religious laws and the culture's judgment, thus overcoming human selfishness (cf. Luke 13:10–17).

This prophetic passion for the destiny of the person makes the ministry of Jesus a living gospel of compassion, evident in the narratives of his prophetic actions. These narratives represent the faith of the early Christian communities proclaiming definitive and integral salvation. Through Christ, God designs to break the power of evil and to re-create the human condition. In fact, "Jesus' miracles were not simply kind deeds done to aid individuals; they were concrete ways of proclaiming and effecting God's triumph over the powers of evil in the final hour. The miracles were signs and partial realizations of what was about to come fully in the kingdom."[2]

In fact, the prophets had seen sickness in all its manifestations as an expression of the power of darkness and the slavery of evil that would be overcome with the messianic promise (cf. Isa 35:5–6; 61:1–3; Jer 33:6). The relevant background regarding sickness, suffering, and sin needs to be clarified. Three major meanings of the experience of suffering can be emphasized in the prophetic context: (a) it is a consequence of the reality of *sin* and a *punishment* for it; (b) it is a *purifying* and *learning* experience; (c) it has a *redemptive* and *healing* value.

First, suffering as a visible expression of the mystery of evil is contrary to God's will, his purpose in creation, and his covenant of fidelity.

Thus, sickness and suffering were often considered the results of sin and infidelity to God's covenant (cf. Gen 3). Second, in reflecting on the reality of evil as a result of sin, the just person who trusts the Lord learns from suffering in a process of personal purification (books of Job and Tobit). Finally, within the prophetic perspective of solidarity among the chosen people of the covenant, suffering served the redemptive plan of God's salvation (cf. the idea of vicarious suffering, especially in Isa 52:13—53:12).[3]

Jesus as Spirit-filled healer stood in the prophetic tradition because of his ministry of miraculous cures and compassionate forgiveness. These are signs of God's sovereignty over the chosen people and the coming of his reign. Jesus rejects a fatalistic idea about the onset of sickness as personal and collective retribution for sin: "Neither this man nor his parents sinned" (John 9:1–3; cf. Jer 31:29–30). Nevertheless, God's favor calls for personal responsibility (cf. John 5:14). Thus, Jesus' prophetic teaching invites everyone to be a healing reconciler, to show compassion (Matt 5:7), especially toward the sick. To visit the sick is to visit Christ (Matt 25:36).

For Matthew, Jesus' miraculous cures realize the prophetic fulfillment: "He took our infirmities and bore our diseases" (Matt 8:17; cf. Isa 53:4). Then Matthew sums up the realization of this messianic promise in the unsurpassable healing words and wonder-working actions of Jesus: "Go and tell John what you hear and see: the blind receive their sight, the lame walk, the lepers are cleansed, the deaf hear, the dead are raised, and the poor have good news brought to them. And blessed is anyone who takes no offence at me" (Matt 11:4–6).

These external signs of healing reveal God's offer of holiness, which calls the human condition to wholeness. In the biblical mind-set, not only is the person thought of as an integrated unity of body and spirit, but holiness and God's favor are also included in bodily wholeness and integrity. This manifold perspective of inward and outward wholeness is apparent in many healing stories: the physically ill, such as the outcast leper whom Jesus touched (Mark 1:40–45), are restored not only to God's friendship, but also to the fellowship of God's community; the brokenness of evil is overcome and the sick are cured (Mark 6:13); the paralytic is freed from the immobility as well as from the burden of sin (Mark 2:1–12); and the blind man recovers both his sight and his faith (John 9:35–40). Christ's redemptive holiness of grace and salvation is seen in the victory over the bonds of all evil (Matt 10:7–8) and thus reaches out to the whole person in God's community. For the disciple embracing it, Christ's supreme deliverance from evil and restoration of life comes with his sacrifice on the cross, through the Easter victory (Luke 9:23–24).

## The Tradition of Anointing and Healing

Empowered by Jesus' ministry and a special mandate (Matt 10), the apostles continued his healing activity (Acts 3:6), availing themselves of the basic symbolic elements—such as oil—of their Mediterranean culture. In the context of their salvific mission to the world, the apostles used oil as means of both spiritual and physical healing (Mark 6:12–13). The aim of complete restoration of the person, which manifests God's glory, was directed to strengthen faith and initiate conversion. Already in the late first century, this anointing of the sick was gradually coming to represent a major symbol of the healing power that the community of disciples received from Christ.

In what follows, three major paradigmatic models corresponding to the *ancient*, *medieval*, and *modern Roman-Catholic and contemporary* churches will be discussed.

### Anointing as Total Healing (First to Eighth Centuries)

The classic text of James 5:14–16 reveals an existent and official—not merely charismatic or miraculous—ritual act expressing the Christian gift of healing.

> Are any among you sick? They should call for the elders of the church and have them pray over them, anointing them with oil in the name of the Lord. The prayer of faith will save the sick, and the Lord will raise them up; and anyone who has committed sins will be forgiven. Therefore confess your sins to one another, and pray for one another, so that you may be healed. The prayer of the righteous is powerful and effective.

The main symbolic elements of what seems to be an already established practice are apparent here: anointing with oil by community leaders in the name of the Lord, with prayers offered in faith for the healing and salvation of the person.

Anointing is a salvific gesture that brings about healing in the holistic biblical sense, although not necessarily the cure of a particular disease. This gesture of faith becomes a communal ritual action among Christians, at least in the Palestinian context. It is done by the presbyters, or college of "elders." These are the ministers of pastoral care present in the Judeo-Christian communities of Jerusalem (cf. Acts 15:2, 4, 6), and in other places. These local presiding religious officials renew Christ's own presence of healing power ("in the name of the Lord") through trusting prayer, which God always answers (see Jas 1:5–7), and the use of the medicinal oil. They aim to save through God's grace a believer who is seriously ill, understood primarily in the physical and spiritual sense. This salvation includes the forgiveness of possibly serious sins, but does not exclude eschatological implications. To save *(sozein)* and to raise *(egeirein)* are terms commonly used in healing narratives. Some of these terms are also associated with restoration of health and forgiveness of sins (see Mark 2:1–12).

Undoubtedly succeeding Christian generations continued the apostolic practice of a symbolic anointing for healing. Nevertheless, there is little evidence of explicit references to anointing during the second century. Rather, bishops at the time stressed the importance of the pastoral care of the sick and shared the common biblical conviction of the dignity of the human body within the divine economy of redemption.

The first references to anointing come from liturgical formularies of the blessing of oil for the sick. Such is the case in the *Apostolic Tradition* of Hippolytus in the early third century. It contains the liturgical rites and practices presumably current in the Church of Rome, but its influence extends to some Western and Eastern traditions. A formulary for the blessing of oil during the eucharistic celebration has the bishop pray: "Lord, just as by sanctifying this oil, with which you anointed kings, priests and prophets, you give holiness to those who are anointed with it and receive it, so let it bring comfort to those who taste of it and health to those who use it."[4]

References to the blessing of oil intended for use with the sick appear to be common in different churches. However, evidence that these references had to do with its sacramental purpose became only gradually clear throughout the Christian centuries. Many other testimonies of ecclesiastical writers and fathers of the Church confirm the tradition provided by the liturgical formularies. An unambiguous state-

ment elucidating the sacramental nature and rite of anointing of the
sick that contains valuable information about church practice is given in
a letter, dating from the year 416, from Pope Innocent I to Decentius,
bishop of Gubbio in Italy. In response to the question about the recipient and about the minister of anointing, Pope Innocent I wrote:

> Now there is no doubt that these words are to be understood
> of the faithful who are sick, and who can be anointed with the
> holy oil of chrism, which has been prepared by the bishop, and
> which not only priests, but all Christians may use for anointing,
> when their own needs or those of their family demand...And
> how can it be deemed proper to grant one kind of sacrament to
> those who are denied the rest of the sacraments?[5]

This letter is very important for the practice of this sacrament in
the future Roman tradition. Just before the emergence of the Carolingian reform, the writings of Bede the Venerable (d. 735) from the
church in England reveal a faithful continuation of the Roman practice
under the authoritative influence of Pope Innocent I. Bede praises the
healing power of anointing on the body, stressing at the same time the
relationship between sickness and sin. The sacrament forgives sins;
nevertheless, there remains the need to confess with a contrite heart
more serious sins to the presbyters. Anointing is seen as the ordinary
sacrament of the sick, which Bede relates to the two biblical texts of
Mark (6:12–13) and James (5:14–16) cited above. Bede stresses the
importance of presbyters in administering this sacrament, but does not
exclude the possibility of an anointing done by believers. Moreover, the
role of the bishop in the consecration of the oil remains essential.[6]

In all, these first eight hundred years reveal an overall constant of a
healing praxis the main sacramental symbol of which is the blessed oil.
The continuation of the healing ministry of Christ, physician and suf-
ferer, at once effecting the wholeness of body and soul, is the substance
of this historical constant. The liturgical rituals, usually limited to the
blessing of oil and the practice of anointing—whenever available in different local churches—were by no means uniform across the various
cultural contexts. In addition, the multivalent symbolic meaning of oil
in liturgy and also the relationship of anointing of the sick to the other
healing sacraments of penance and the Eucharist affected both the

interpretation and practice of anointing. Consecrated by the bishop—an essential condition—who would invoke the power of the Holy Spirit, holy oil *(chrisma)* was considered, in the words of Innocent I, "one kind of sacrament" *(genus est sacramenti)* for the sick person. Also, the practice of lay anointing demonstrates the existence of a non-institutionalized sacramental ministry of healing in which the ordained priest had undoubtedly a major, but not an exclusive role.

## Anointing as Extreme Unction (Ninth to Twentieth Centuries)

Beginning with the Carolingian reforms, a decisive shift took place at the turn of the first millennium in the theology, conferral, and celebration of anointing. There was a gradual evolution toward a rite of bodily purification and spiritual salvation for the dying. Emphasis was placed on the rite for the dying person performed exclusively by the priest, rather than on the liturgical blessing of oil for physical and spiritual healing. Nevertheless, the history of these centuries is one of multiple ritual practices in the manifold situations of local churches.

The gradual association of anointing with "death-bed" sacramental reconciliation was a major factor after the ninth century. Assimilated with reconciliation or penance in the face of death *(ad mortem)*, anointing then became the completion of public penance *in extremis*. Responding to the theological teaching of the scholastics, such as Peter Lombard (ca. 1095–1160) and Thomas Aquinas (1225–1274), the second ecumenical Council of Lyons (1274) adopted the term "extreme unction." Henceforth, it was predominantly seen as the sacrament of those departing from life *(sacramentum exeuntium)*.

In this way, Thomas Aquinas's theology relies on a deeper sacramental interpretation and a more positive and even integrative view of the "last sacrament." The principal effect of anointing is not to forgive sins, but to strengthen the spirit and body for passing through death to eternal glory. Thomas died before he could complete a discussion on this sacrament. Nevertheless, he made a major contribution in stressing the eschatological aspect of anointing: "This sacrament is the last and as it were all-embracing sacrament of the whole spiritual way of salvation, through which the human being is prepared to participate in the divine glory. Hence it is also called Extreme Unction."[7] The sacrament "blots out the remnants of sin and prepares people for the final glory."[8]

The Council of Trent achieved a more balanced and positive view within a larger sacramental tradition at its fourteenth session in 1551. It presented the sacrament both as extreme unction and anointing of the sick to be used especially for those who are so dangerously ill as to seem near death, but it also saw the sacrament's use for the sick. It spoke of the sacrament's primary scope as spiritual salvation through the fortification of the soul and, conditionally, the forgiveness of sins and bodily healing.

Trent struck a balance among earlier traditions and asserted the presbyter as ordinary minister. It aimed at refuting the Protestant reformers' position against the sacramentality of anointing. At the same time, it stood against one-sided views and some abuses that had appeared in later centuries. The sacrament's institution was seen in the will and ministry of Christ continued in the apostolic mission of healing. The scriptural basis insinuated in Mark (6:13) and explicitly stated in James's letter (5:14–16) bore witness to that institution. Likewise, the consistent practice of Christian tradition supported it. The council's affirmation of the specific sacramental effect of anointing, the grace of the Holy Spirit, is central. Anointing is then seen as a healing sacrament, perfective of penance, and a spiritual remedy for the penitent's sins at the end of the Christian's pilgrimage.

Trent's doctrine set the stage for the sacramental practice of succeeding centuries. However, despite the council's more open view for its use with the sick, the pastoral practice of extreme unction, or "last rites," prevailed until the theology and ritual practices of the Vatican II reform.

## Illness and Christian Healing

The Second Vatican Council represented a complete turning back to the biblical sources that inspired the healing ministry of the ancient Church. A strengthened sacrament of the sick emerged from the council and the ritual reforms that followed. First, the more global context of the sacraments, their new ordering, the regaining of their christological and ecclesial dimensions, and the more integral vision of the person had provided a background against which the past understanding and practice of anointing could be reassessed. Second, many other factors, such as biblical and historical scholarship, contributed to the clarification of the specific aspects of the tradition of healing anointing. The text of the revised rites promulgated under Paul VI in 1972 is a key statement. It changed the old practice of extreme unction and added new sacramental meaning to anointing of the sick: "The whole Church commends the sick to the suffering and glorified Lord so that He may raise them up and save them."[9] The new rite provides flexible guidelines about who should be anointed.[10]

Two major and interrelated aspects of the interpretation and practice of the sacrament are apparent. The first has to do with the name and purpose of anointing. The sacrament is more properly called "anointing of the sick" than "extreme unction." Therefore, its proper setting is illness, not the end of life. The second aspect refers to the sacramental effects of anointing. These effects have to do primarily with the sick and suffering person. He or she is configured to the glorious passion of Christ through the transforming presence of the grace of the Holy Spirit. The sacramental view focuses on the sick person in an inclusive way within the perspective of God's purpose of ultimate healing: the effect is primarily spiritual strengthening, and the physical well-being of the person if such is God's will. The forgiveness of sins is also a sacramental effect.

Illness represents a privileged moment of the believer's baptismal priesthood lived through a special vocation. Personal faith enables the sick person to accept the new call through the sacrament of anointing, which is a sign of freedom. This vocation is expressed beautifully in the liturgy: "May all who suffer pain, illness or disease realize that they are chosen to be saints, and know that they are joined to Christ in his suffering for the salvation of the world."[11] Suffering can be salvific. It is sanctified in the faith of those who associate themselves with the passion of Christ and, in this way, become ministers of evangelization.

A new historical model of the Christian tradition of healing emerged in the wake of Vatican II reforms. Nevertheless, a recent rediscovery of the power of Christian healing in a variety of forms, not necessarily sacramental in the formal sense, has occurred. This movement suggests that the riches the Master Healer revealed to the Church will never be exhausted. Important shifts in contemporary health care and other cultural developments have affected the practice of the anointing of the sick in the context of the Church's healing mission. All these factors have to be taken into consideration in order to foster a rich context for the Church's pastoral care and to more effectively integrate the different aspects of the sacrament.

The following propositions focus on a more holistic understanding of anointing of the sick in current pastoral care.

### 1. Christian healing is wholeness and holiness.

Contemporary Christianity relies on a holistic anthropology. The person is one, a psychosomatic unity, endowed with an inherent dignity, especially in the case of the weakest individual and his or her full existential dimensions. Health and illness, life and death are seen not as absolutes, but as interrelated aspects of human destiny in need of redemption. As a consequence, the new rite emphasizes the salvation-health of body and soul. The saving grace of the Holy Spirit is invoked to provide forgiveness of sins, comfort in suffering, strength to fight against evil, and courage and hope in embracing God's will. The prayer after anointing says: "Lord Jesus Christ, our Redeemer, by the grace of your Holy Spirit cure the weakness of your servants. Heal their sickness and forgive their sins; expel all afflictions of mind and body; mercifully restore them to full health, and enable them to resume their former duties."[12]

It is important to make a distinction between *healing*—"becoming whole" in the total salvific sense of body and soul—and *curing*—removing the physical illness. The former is ordinary and must come from within; it is God's ultimate gift and it presupposes freedom of faith in the recipient; the latter, an instance of which could be a miraculous cure—a sign of God's glory—is extraordinary and provisional. However, healing and cure are interrelated. Jesus' prophetic mission of liberation (Luke 4:18–19) was healing in the widest and most integral sense. Throughout history, the Church has responded with compassionate caring for the spiritual and physical welfare of the person as, for instance, in the rise of medieval "hostels" for pilgrims and the poor. They were, in fact, the first healing institutions of Europe.

Nevertheless, among many laypeople, the anointing of the sick is still far from being considered a sacrament for life and for healing. For some Catholics, the sacrament poses an unwelcome predicament, at least as long as there is a ray of hope in medical science. They see it as something reserved for the dying—thus heralding death—or, as Empereur puts it, a "sacrament of consecration for death."[13] Perhaps this is due to inadequate catechesis about the meaning of the sacrament, or to the lack of a liturgical context of ministerial healing in the parish, which should involve lay ministers. Another reason could be the practice of a mechanical and privatistic use of ritual anointing, which might be neglected until the extreme situation arrives.

*2. Healing ministry, medicine, and health are interconnected.*
The biblical world view from Jesus the healer to James the apostle was therapeutic in the holistic sense. This world view included the total human being and the person in the inter-human and human-divine dimensions. The ministry of healing has remained ever since an essential role of the Christian leader. The community of believers shares in this ministry.

However, different anthropological and philosophical views throughout history have devalued the importance of this healing role. On the one hand, the art of curing came to be an autonomous science rooted in Greek scientific theories. On the other hand, Christian theology developed into a rationalistic system with the rise of Scholasticism. "As theology became scientific, not only its therapeutic but also its aesthetic and social dimensions were lost."[14] The integration of the spiritual and physical dimensions suffered especially with the dominance of Enlightenment dualism of body and spirit, ensuing secularism, and the more recent development of Western technological pragmatism. In contrast to these, a holistic view of the person within God's providence remained entrenched in popular Catholicism, the healing rituals of which have traditionally sought the person's restoration to health within the family and community.

A wider pastoral context for the meaning of health and illness remains a challenging and necessary precondition for a more integrative view of the Christian ministry of healing. Such a view includes looking at illness, suffering, and health from an inclusive and multifaceted perspective in terms of both science and religion. There is a link between faith and health; the former promotes the latter. They must work together for the person's physical, psychological, emotional, spiritual, and social well-being. Both medical science and Christian healing have to come to terms with the complexity of the person in the community as spirit, soul, mind, and body.[15] As the person cannot be reduced to merely biological functioning or psychological processing, so pastoral healing cannot be limited to a narrow spiritualization of the person. Considering the self from a larger perspective of meaning, Patricia Wismer describes four main dimensions of suffering: physical pain, emotional trauma, social isolation, and spiritual crisis. "If distress is indeed severe (as in case of a serious illness), there will usually be at least three dimensions represented."[16] Many factors (including cultural factors) constitute the human context for the ministry of Christian healing.

*3. Anointing and healing are essentially communal celebrations.*
As a sign of God's reconciling and restoring presence in the world, the Church accomplishes a healing mission: the renewal of the life-giving presence of Christ's ministry to the sick, the suffering, and the aging. They share in the redemptive cross of Christ, whom they also represent: "I was sick and you took care of me" (Matt 25:36). The Christian community is the normal setting of the Church's pastoral care of the sick. The grace encounter of the sacraments, especially the Eucharist, reconciliation, and anointing, is at the center of the Church's healing ministry. Through the sick "Christ continues to 'touch' us in order to heal us."[17] As a pledge of Christ's presence, the Eucharist is the preeminent sign of the unique Catholic identity in healing ministry.

There are many other Christian means of healing, such as the laying on of hands (the principal gesture in the New Testament), the prayer of faith, Masses of healing, healing at shrines, popular Catholic rituals, and various services of prayer for healing. All of these are expressions of charismatic healing. A believer can always expect healing, because the living God is within us. In fact, to some the Holy Spirit has given the gift of healing (see 1 Cor 12:9, 28, 30). Nevertheless, it is important to distinguish between the sacrament of anointing of the sick, reserved to presbyters, and other means of charismatic healing, which could include the use of blessed oil by the laity. The former, according to Charles Gusmer, "would appear to be less directly concerned with physical or emotional cures, but rather aims at a deeper spiritual conformation with Christ through the healing power of the paschal mystery," whereas the latter intends a cure.[18] The sacramental "may appear to mirror the visible, tangible, incarnational side of the

Church, whereas the charismatic reflects [the] more invisible, intangible, pneumatological aspect of the Church."[19]

The situations calling for anointing are extremely varied and arise from different circumstances in the pastoral care of the sick in the parish, the hospital, or home. For this reason, the rites of anointing and Viaticum propose eight different ways of celebration. They favor celebrations, especially within the Eucharist, that involve the community and the family. Periodic celebrations of a Mass of anointing of the sick for the seriously ill and the elderly with their loved ones have become a liturgical hallmark of renewed pastoral care of the sick in each parish. The community's love for the sick climaxes in a liturgical feast prepared for those who hold a special place in God's heart. This celebrative model speaks about the need to strive for the ideals of robust liturgical celebrations as opposed to the sacramental minimalism of "last rites." Anointing is done on the forehead and on the hands while the sacramental form is recited in this way: *(While anointing the forehead)* "Through this holy anointing may the Lord in his love and mercy help you with the grace of the Holy Spirit. *(While anointing the hands)* May the Lord who frees you from sin save you and raise you up."[20]

*4. The sick person acknowledges God's gift of life in encountering the suffering and risen Christ.*
Jesus' miracles were signs of the wholeness of God, which sacramental healing makes present in the recipient believers. This is the fundamental Christian conviction: "I have come that they may have life, and have it abundantly" (John 10:10). Life has to be understood in the comprehensive sense of ultimate healing that transcends, but does not exclude, our welfare in this world. The experience of intimate communion with Christ, the compassionate physician, is manifested in the spiritual as well as in the physical and emotional well-being of sick and suffering people, and in their relationships. They can grow spiritually because suffering accepted with love purifies, enlightens, and transforms. The Roman rite expresses well the vision of the glorified Christ and his gift of the Spirit, whom the sick encounter in faith: "In the splendor of His rising your Son conquered suffering and death, and bequeathed to us his promise of a new and glorious world...Through your gift of the Spirit, you bless us, even now, with comfort and healing, strength and hope, forgiveness and peace."[21]

## Anointing for Divine Glory

After the Vatican II reform, ambiguity in the practice of the sacrament seems to remain. It does not depend primarily on the sacramental complexities, which demand good judgment. The ambiguity has to be seen against the background of the sacrament located historically between two interrelated poles: *healing* (discussed previously) and *passage*. Recent research has paid attention to this ambiguity and emphasized the need of flexible pastoral attitudes and a truthful rite of passage to God. "People are asking vitally and viscerally for a rite of transition, certainly for the last passage."[22] This view of a sacrament of life for the dying also (never for a dead person), does not, however, imply a return to a mentality and practice of "extreme unction." As Vatican II teaches, "as soon as anyone of the faithful begins to be in danger of death from sickness or old age, this is already a suitable time for them to receive this sacrament."[23]

*1. Holy anointing and Viaticum, "the last sacrament," prepare the Christian for the final journey.*
In every religion and society, ritual actions have always surrounded death. The reason is that human existence is shaken to its foundations in the face of death. Nothing so ordinary in human reality can be more extraordinary in a person's life. The symbolic actions of the sacrament engage the Christian believer on two related levels: the anthropological and the christological. On the former level the sacrament functions as a rite of passage, a way of countering the unknown and supporting the grieving process of impending death. The rites fortify the believer with the experience of ultimate meaning. The latter level fully unveils their meaning, pointing to the heart of the Christian mystery of death: a dying person surrendering his or her life to the Father in fellowship with Christ and in the life power of his Spirit. Death is not the end of life: "I am full of joy, I am free!"

The sacrament of holy anointing has to be considered an important rite at the critical moment of preparation for the "passing over" to God. When possible, it is preceded by the sacrament of penance and followed by eucharistic Viaticum. This integrates elements of Christian tradition— healing and dying, body and soul, time and eternity—in a holistic perspective. In the same way, it also relates to baptismal dying with Christ.

This is symbolized by the sprinkling with water and the accompanying prayer (sacramental sign) over the person facing death (existential reality). Anointing celebrates the Christian hope of rising with Christ—an overarching eschatological perspective. As the *Catechism of the Catholic Church* states, anointing of the sick "even more rightly is given to those at the point of departing this life . . . [It] completes our conformity to the death and Resurrection of Christ, just as Baptism began it."[24]

The practice of receiving Viaticum (provision for the journey into eternity) originated in early Christianity. The Eucharist as body of the Lord was seen as the seed of resurrection. The Roman rite offers this beautiful description of Viaticum: "The celebration of the Eucharist as viaticum, food for the passage through death to eternal life, is the sacrament proper to the dying Christian. It is the completion and crown of the Christian life on this earth, signifying that the Christian follows the Lord to eternal glory and the banquet of the heavenly kingdom."[25]

### 2. The Holy Spirit is the pledge of paschal victory.

Doubts and anxiety shroud the person confronted with death. Personal faith is essential. Only through the eyes of faith can the believer see God's mysterious design of grace and salvation. For, "while the imagination is at a loss before the mystery of death, the church, taught by divine revelation, declares that God has created people in view of a blessed destiny that lies beyond the boundaries of earthly misery."[26] The gift of faith through which one enters into the Lord's presence brings to the infirm the unsurpassable strength of his Spirit. This strength is apparent in a deep inner peace experienced in times of trial. In fact, the gifts of the Holy Spirit are the grace of this sacrament given to the person as a pledge of the final paschal victory.

Christ's death on the cross is "the primal sacramental model of Christian dying . . . The anointing of the sick is the confession of the believing Church that the same Spirit which raised Christ also makes Christians' illness and dying, i.e., their earthly end, a sign of consummation."[27]

### 3. The mystery of death is the mystery of life.

What people think about the reality of death necessarily colors their view about the meaning of life, and therefore their religious attitudes. In the same way, their assumptions about death (and its contemporary denial) condition their expectations about holy anointing. Human sciences, such as psychology, describe different approaches to getting a better grasp of the unique person in a state of illness.[28] There are countless differences in how people confront the most radical mystery of human existence—death. Whereas the physician studies its biological causes and the agnostic despairs before the "absurd character" of human existence, the believer fathoms its ultimate meaning and purpose.

Death is our enemy within, the consequence of sin. Naturally, we rebel against it and deny it as an external evil without realizing that this rebellion and denial are *the* evil. This is where the vision of faith can bring a total self-renewal of the person, and, thus, an end to an evil inflicted upon oneself. At this moment, we turn back to our innermost center of existence (where God is), and recognize within this God-given center the seeds of eternity. God's love has planted them in our being. Thus, we come from eternity and return to an eternal destiny.

By God's grace we are now healed ("raised up"), and a great serenity enables us to embrace our enemy within, death: an enemy becomes a friend. We then enter deeply into the mystery of Christ's death and resurrection. His tender touch anoints us in a new prophetic act of compassion. With him and through him, we commit the gift of our life to the Father's hands (Luke 23:46) and accept death in the surrender of that gift—a supreme act of worship of the mortal creature to the eternal One.

A Christian theology of death is essential. The following conclusions draw inspiration from the characteristic terminology found in the ancient Roman and Gallican liturgies.[29] These prayers proclaim a theology of death inextricably linked to a theology of life. In the eyes of faith, the consummation of death is seen, paradoxically, as containing the full meaning of life. This faith vision reaches its apex in the paschal character of Christian death, for death is swallowed up in the victorious passion of Christ. From this perspective, death signifies or becomes for the baptized in Christ, *liberation, rest, passing over (transitus), encounter,* and *transformation.*

Christ "set us free" through baptism, a hope lived in the present and pledged for the promised future. Death becomes the definitive liberation into this future of immortal life from the condition of sin and the oppressive forces of mortality itself.

Through the prism of Christian hope, one sees death as rest for those who have died (1 Cor 15:20), according to the testimonies of early Christianity. In fact, Christians created the terminology of *koime-terion, cimiterium,* meaning cemetery (a sleeping chamber), to counter the Greek concept of necropolis (the city of the dead) for the place of burial.[30] Eternal rest encompasses the profound hope and expectation of bodily resurrection.

The idea of death in the Latin *transitus* (transition, passing over) represents a unique Christian terminology linked to the paschal mystery. It consecrates the passage of the dying to eternal life. Offering the sacrifice of his or her personal life, the believer shares in the *pascha-transitus* of Christ himself.

Death as encounter proclaims the Creator-creature relation of God's saving design for the person who will share forever a divine life in Christ, "the first and the last, and the living one" (Rev 1:17–18). Christian assurance rests in total confidence in God, for "even though I walk through the darkest valley, I fear no evil, for you are with me" (Ps 23:4).

Finally, transformation refers to the radical restoration of the whole person through the mystery of resurrection. The Holy Spirit will effect a completely new mode of existence: "What is sown is perishable, what is raised is imperishable . . . It is sown a physical body, it is raised a spiritual body" (1 Cor 15:42, 44). Christ's Spirit frees and strengthens in the total eschatological sense, and heals the injured soul for divine glory.

## PART FOUR

# The Church at the Service of Communion

# 10
# Orders and Ministries:
# The Priest as Servant-Leader

Over the past three decades ecclesial ministry has undergone para-digmatic shifts in its theology and practice. The spirit and vision of the Second Vatican Council and the flowering of new minister-ial movements have created a sense of renewal and freedom. At the same time, however, an experience of shifting grounds in ministerial models and priestly identity has produced a considerable degree of ten-sion and crises. The pre-conciliar model of priesthood seems to be fac-ing serious challenges. The issues are complex and the problems are deep. They result from cultural and theological shifts, at least in Europe and the United States, after the sixties. While paying attention to these factors, the reflection that follows will focus on a broad and challenging vision of the sacrament of orders within the larger context of ministry from biblical, historical, theological, and pastoral perspectives.

American Catholics and Christians around the world have much to learn from the major turning points of ministry as it evolved at the crossroads of cultural history. The biblical sources of the New Testa-ment will be a primary focus. In them one can find the fundamental direction of the Church's living tradition, which is immensely rich with challenging examples of flowering ministerial charisms and services. One can then envisage from the lessons of history a contemporary view of ministry in *(a) models of ministry: historical shifts.*

The specific calling to and roles of the ordained priesthood and the common priesthood will be explored within the body of the Church and in relation to the mission of Christ, its head. This is the approach of Vatican II. In fact, the council rejected a previous draft, which focused primarily on the clergy. The order was reversed and the theology of the ordained ministry and its roles was incorporated into a broader reality comprising the fundamental priesthood of Christ and of the Church, the whole people of God. This leads to examining *(b) the fundamental priesthood of the Church.*

The vital center of the ministry of the Church—notwithstanding its other dimensions—is in the life-giving power of its sacramental mystery celebrated by the Christian community and lived by its ministers. The Eucharist, gift of divine life, is the bedrock and also the power of the life of those who serve. Consequently, the reflection in the next section focuses on two interrelated aspects: the role of priests—meaning always presbyters—and the call of laymen and laywomen flowing inseparably from *(c) the sacramental foundations of ministry.*

In fact, an understanding of the foundations of the sacrament of orders and the baptismal matrix that defines the role and ministry of the layperson and ministerial priesthood requires theological and spiritual deepening. The recent phenomenon of "the explosion of ministries" together with the opposite trend of a "vocation crisis," resulting in the drastic diminishment of priestly and religious vocations, raises challenging questions. The final section emphasizes the pastoral and spiritual basis for ministerial renewal within the boundaries of a parish in *(d) ministry: building up the Church.*

The last three sections, as indicated above, are thematically interconnected. They focus particularly on the ecclesial, sacramental, and local community aspects. Addressed, although in less depth, are issues relating to the theology of the tripartite orders of bishop, priest, and deacon with their specific roles. Additionally, in the post-Vatican II era, various issues and questions, such as the role of women in ministry, specific challenges facing priestly ministry, and new ecumenical questions, have emerged from further developments in the ministerial life of the Church.

## Models of Ministry: Historical Shifts

Historical paradigmatic shifts provide a key to an understanding of the pastoral office (order) and Christian ministries as these developed from the original wellspring of the New Testament communities. Ministry has always been reshaped historically with the emergence of new religious-theological ideas interconnected with current socio-cultural patterns, for "the blood of the church is history. The church... is eminently historical."[1] What can we learn from the apostolic communities in regard to their spirit and ways of participation in the building up of the community, the formation of a structure of offices appropriate to the community's life, and their link to the apostolic tradition, especially in view of the challenges facing today's Church?

## Apostolic Leadership and Charismatic Ministry

The apostolic Church will always hold the roots and offer fundamental models of inspiration, especially for contemporary churches experiencing a crisis of renewal and growth. For this reason, particular attention will be given to New Testament sources.

### Apostolic Foundations

Ministry will always be the ministry of an apostolic Church. Jesus personally selected disciples, "the Twelve," who followed him more closely and to whom he entrusted the full weight of his ministry with a more complete dedication. The references in the four gospels, Acts, and the book of Revelation demonstrate the constitutive and foundational nature of their call and authority, as unique witnesses not only to Christ's ministry but also to his resurrection (Acts 1:22). The number twelve is symbolic, for it represents the new people of God and has the eschatological meaning of the messianic time of salvation. The term "apostle" that arose in the post-Easter period has the wider meaning of a ministerial function not restricted to the original group of "the Twelve." An example of this can be found in the case of Andronicus and Junias (a female name) who were "prominent among the apostles" (Rom 16:7). Likewise, the meaning and reality of "apostolicity" took on different meanings relative to the process of the development of Christian tradition.[2]

We know little of the concrete mandate of Jesus to the apostolic community in respect to ministerial, communitarian, or sacramental forms. The event of the resurrection gave rise to the early Christian community. Thus, the Church did not create ministry. Rather, it was the Spirit-filled ministry of the apostolic witness to Christ's resurrection that stood at the very beginning of the Church and its mission to the world. Paschal joy pervaded the spirituality of the Christian community. This spirituality of the resurrection, the experience of the liberating grace realized in Christ, impelled the first communities to consider themselves as the people of God in the fullness of time and thus endowed with a new and transforming world vision.

This messianic and prophetic movement bound together "the community of the disciples" (Acts 6:2, NAB), "of one heart and soul" (Acts 4:32). This *koinonia* of discipleship in the risen Lord and in the Spirit-given gifts, rather than the existence of doctrinal lines or institutional models, was the primary basis and empowerment of many to ministry. Referring to this reality in the Fourth Gospel, Raymond Brown draws this summary conclusion: "Church offices and even apostleship are of lesser importance when compared to discipleship, which is literally a question of (eternal) life and death."[3] It is against a wider post-resurrection background that the earliest multifaceted, unplanned, and dynamic Church ministry can be understood.

This Church's missionary movement of men and women "had its source in the baptism of the Spirit, the foundation of all Church life."[4] As baptism initiated Jesus' Spirit-filled ministry, the paradigmatic model of Christian mission, so the community of believers was constituted in a common priesthood through the same baptism in the Holy Spirit. Ministry came from this Spirit of the glorified Lord who endowed the believer with a priestly dignity: "You are a chosen race, a royal priesthood, a holy nation, God's own people" (1 Pet 2:9). The most widespread opinion sees in this text the reality of God's household endowed with a unique dignity. As a body of priests by divine election, the faithful offer corporately a spiritual worship of the whole of life.[5] The community as a whole is priestly and is called, therefore, to the service of apostolic witness, to evangelization, and to full eucharistic participation.

### Charismatic Ministry

In fact, the New Testament speaks only of the *priesthood of Christ* and of the *priesthood of the believer*. Priesthood does not exist in the New Testament as a cultic function or presidential status. Christ is not a levitical priest (Heb 8:4). Rather, his priesthood is of another order as mediator of a greater covenant (Heb 8:6–13), giving "himself up for us, a fragrant offering and a sacrifice to God" (Eph 5:2). Christ "made us to be a kingdom, priests serving his God and Father, to him be glory" (Rev 1:6). The sacred idea of priesthood as a formal function does not actually appear until the third century. Thus, in a summary reflection, Thomas O'Meara describes the four primordial characteristics of ministry in the New Testament: non-sacral office, action, service to the kingdom of God, universality and diversity.[6]

The fountainhead of all the ministries is in Christ, the risen One who is alive in the ecclesial body, and in the power of his Spirit's charisms, the foundation of all ministries. Thus, the presence of the Divine Spirit is the soul of these ministerial communities. From the beginning, there seems to have been a great variety of local models for Christian communities in the New Testament, especially in terms of leadership roles. Envisaged as *diakonia* (service), the words for ministry are varied and secular. Evidently in the earliest days ministries did not develop along institutional lines but in response to the community's life. They were impelled by the same activity of the Spirit for the building up of the community.

The multiplicity of the Spirit's gifts is the fundamental structure of all ministries, particularly in Paul's theology and in the communities he founded. "God has appointed in the church first apostles, second prophets, third teachers; then deeds of power, then gifts of healing, forms of assistance, forms of leadership..." (1 Cor 12:28). These early communities were charismatic, open, and flexible. The panorama of charisms and services was impressive: evangelization, catechesis, healing, prophesy, *diakonia,* presidency, etc. The origin of these gifts of grace is the same—the Divine Spirit; and the goal is identical—salvation through the service of the reign proclaimed by Christ. This ministerial expansion flowed from the baptismal and eucharistic consecration, which calls to life the gift of prophetic power in the Spirit. That same Spirit lives within the believing community.

Not surprisingly, the multidimensional nature of ministry stemming from Christ—the goal and ultimate model of ministry—does not allow worldly competition or individual privilege (Matt 20:25–26). It is founded on the spirit of servanthood taught by the Teacher, prototype of a new way of being in the Church (John 13:2–20). This is the basis for the freedom of a new humanity re-created in Christ and flowing

from the baptismal consecration: "As many of you as were baptized into
Christ have clothed yourselves with Christ. There is no longer Jew or
Greek, there is no longer slave or free, there is no longer male and
female; for all of you are one in Christ Jesus" (Gal 3:27–28). This new
spirit, which today we might call universalist and inclusive, provided
the means of overcoming divisions based on human considerations,
such as culture, status, gender, or sacral office. It inspired a Church of
"co-workers in Christ Jesus" whose unique privilege is that of serving
(Rom 16:3). By the same token, this basic equality in Christ and freedom in the Spirit, which could not prevent tensions among members
and crises in communities (Acts is a telling example), included sound
authority and an inner principle of order.

### Ministerial Office

The oneness of a priestly community of men and women does not
negate either the existence of a plurality of ministries or the exercise of
leadership and authority under an ecclesial commission. Those "baptized into one body" form an organic complexity of diverse functions
animated by the same life principle (1 Cor 12). In a comprehensive
description of ministry in the New Testament, Yves Congar states that
Jesus "instituted an organic community, a holy community, priestly,
prophetic, missionary, apostolic, with its center, the ministers—some
freely sustained by the Spirit, others ordained by the imposition of
hands."[7] The fluid ministerial patterns of the beginning began to take
shape starting from a *collegial* and *charismatic* organization, such as in
the Antioch community (Acts 13:1), especially at Corinth. It moved
toward *presbyteral and episcopal* forms at the end of the first century.

  During the New Testament period in general, beyond the original
leadership role of "the Twelve," the group of "seven," and the "elders,"
the following seem to have been preferred titles and groupings of ministers, although not necessarily in sequential order: (a) *apostle-prophet-
teacher* (before A.D. 70); (b) *bishop-presbyter-deacon.* The elders *(presbyteroi)* were a circle of counselors whose significance derived from the
synagogal elders and who appear several times, especially in Acts, having a variety of regular ministerial roles. The *episcopoi* (overseers) were
elected among them as "first among equals." The pastoral letters to
Titus and Timothy are proof of this grouping of offices. Recent studies
based on the letters written around the year 80 concur in affirming

internal developments and the trend toward institutionalization after the destruction of Jerusalem (A.D. 70). Thus, in subsequent centuries, the wide range of charismatic ministries gradually became a more structured church order, and a greater differentiation emerged between some formal offices validated with a mandate and other charisms or tasks of the community.[8]

In the same pastoral letters the author already reflects a process of institutionalization of presidency of the community. Timothy and Titus, according to the testimony of those letters, received a ministerial power to uphold sound teaching and governing. Officeholders were installed through the imposition of hands, which was probably done by the body of elders and accompanied by prayer. These references and several others of the New Testament (Acts 6:1–3; 13:3; 1 Tim 4:14 and 2 Tim 1:6) appear to be the seeds of an incipient "rite of ordination," which developed fully only after the third century. They celebrate and recognize in some public way God's spiritual gift and the presence of the Spirit in the leaders of the local church endowed with a special authority. These references and other contextual evidence (cf. Acts 20:17–34) make apparent the fact that this is a particular ministerial transmission of the role of office and that this office is indispensably linked to the safeguarding of the apostolic tradition of faith. Thus, "the transmission of office is as much concrete and ecclesial as it is a spiritual and sacramental act."[9]

The appointment of certain members called by God and under the Church's commission (office) is related to two other ministerial issues: the election of local leaders and the presidency of the Eucharist.

The expansion of the church of Jerusalem by means of itinerant missionaries gave place to new Christian communities organized initially after the Jewish synagogal model. The spirit of *koinonia,* or intimate communion in the Spirit and among the members, expressed itself from the beginning in a style of collegial government. The community had an important role in the resolution of conflicts. The community and its leaders had the competency to elect presbyters, although references to the way of their commissioning, often attributed to the Holy Spirit, are few (cf. Acts 1:15–26; 13:2).

As for the presidency of the Eucharist, the New Testament does not speak explicitly of the question. Because the references we find are minimal, the questions raised today on this issue can be only conjectural. A liturgical or priestly leader *(hiereus)* is never mentioned, except for all the baptized. It is the whole assembly that celebrates the liturgy. However, these factors do not preclude a presidency role in the eucharistic thanksgiving celebrated in the house churches. In one of the best researched essays on the theme, Hervé-Marie Legrand makes a conclusive statement when he establishes that those who presided over the Church probably presided at the Eucharist.[10]

The permanent triad of *bishop*—the central unifying figure of authority as in the case of Ignatius of Antioch (martyred in 117), the college of *presbyters,* and the *deacons* would prevail in forthcoming centuries.

## A Christian Priesthood and Ministry

By the turn of the first century, as Christianity spread across the Mediterranean world, the shift from unstructured or itinerant ministries of a charismatic nature to established resident ministries of leadership emerged. The multicultural fabric of the Roman-Hellenistic societies provided a wide context for Christian ministry. Christianity itself was enriched through a dynamic and selectively symbiotic relationship with local cultures. It grew through an ongoing process of transforming integration and established itself by reaffirming its identity as a universal faith.

In their use of religious-technical terminology, in particular Old Testament categories, Christian writers of the second and third century, such as Clement of Alexandria, Justin, and Tertullian, typified this movement. They showed a critical openness to the new cultural matrix, while at the same time safeguarding Christian originality, such as the idea of Christian priesthood. A trend toward a symbolic-sacramental interpretation of the three distinct offices—that is, bishop, or the major Christian community leader, the college of presbyters, and deacons—is evident. These main ministries worked collegially as three different ranks, which Tertullian (d. ca. 225) called *ordo* ("order")—a civic term meaning a social body distinct from the people. They were established through a public ritual and appointment to an office *(ordinatio)* in and for a community.

The major elements of a new theology of priesthood and orders, ministerial patterns, and rites of ordination in use at Rome in the early third century are clearly documented in the *Apostolic Tradition* of Hippolytus. *Episcopoi, presbyteroi,* and *diakonoi* were ordained through the imposition of hands and a consecratory prayer because "ordination is for the clergy on account of their liturgical ministry."[11] The ordination of bishops and presbyters was already connected to the idea of priesthood *(hiereus, sacerdos)*, while many of those in the lesser orders were simply appointed. "It is clear that the conferral of three offices is understood sacramentally and that two of them include a competence related to the Eucharistic liturgy."[12] This most important document served as a model to other churches, Eastern and Western, ancient and modern.

Expressed in the new Greco-Roman cultures, from which the Church took over terminology relating to civic institutions, Christian ministry received a new creative impetus. In fact, the fourth and fifth centuries marked a major turning-point in the development of the baptismal and eucharistic foundations of ministry for both the clergy and the common believer. The Christianization of pagan society and the theological and spiritual development of the institutional Church through the work of the church fathers are telling examples. On the one hand, ministry remained missionary and prophetic, rich and multifaceted. It was neither reduced to just liturgical function nor was it limited to the clergy. On the other hand, ranks already separated the clergy from the laity through a tendency to "clericalize" ministerial tasks, especially after 313. Women's roles, still important to some Eastern churches, were extremely restricted in Rome. The community continued to play an important role in the election of the bishop, as it had in the previous centuries. In Carthage, the bishop Cyprian (d. 258) stated: "The community has the power to elect its bishop and to reject that one which has been imposed upon it by force."[13]

A restructuring of Western church offices and a new shift in the theology of orders came about with the expansion of the missionary movement and the rising of a web of countryside villages, especially after the collapse of the Roman Empire. Up until the sixth century, the bishop led the community in the urban centers and was regarded as a high priest *(pontifex)* and chief presider at liturgical celebrations. In some churches, such as the church in Rome, bishops shared their role with presbyters who became pastoral leaders of emerging "parishes" *(tituli)* from the fourth century onward. A new type of local ministry led by the priest developed due to different factors, especially new pastoral situations. Under the supervision of the bishop, the presbyter became, in those villages, the local leader and priestly figure. From then on, especially with the rising of the royal theocracy of the Carolingian empire (ninth century), the *sacerdos* (priest) becomes synonymous with presbyter.

## Sacramental Ministry as Hierarchy

The medieval division between estates, in particular between holy orders and laity *(ordo laicorum),* is apparent by the end of the first millennium. A process of categorizing all reality in a hierarchical order influenced the theologizing of estates of perfection and ranking within the Church. The Neo-Platonic ideas on hierarchies and the Pseudo-Dionysian subordination of estates were among the most influential factors. These socio-cultural ideas made an impact on the theology of ministry and orders in the scholastic period.[14] Hierarchy, meaning sacred power, represented the whole ministerial and sacramental priesthood of the Church, which was essentially related to the Eucharist.

Thomas Aquinas's theology of priesthood was the most influential in subsequent centuries. His approach drew on the consideration of Christ's priestly mystery and the centrality of the Eucharist. The consecrated priest shared in the most perfect way the priesthood of Christ within the mystical body. "Christ is the source of all priesthood: the priest of the old law was a figure of Christ, and the priest of the new law acts in the person of Christ."[15]

The horizon of ministry and the role of office had shifted dramatically since early Christianity and, in medieval Christendom, its cultural and sacramental context shifted also.

## The Evangelical Minister and the Cultic Priest

The reform of ministry was an important goal for both the Reformation and the Council of Trent (1545–1563). In essence, the "priesthood of all believers" became one of the three great Reformation principles, while Trent insisted on a ministerial hierarchy and priesthood by divine ordinance.

In particular, Martin Luther (d. 1546) rejected the post-biblical tradition of sacramental and priestly mediation and the associated concept of sacrificial cult. There was only grace, an immediate salvific relation with God in the faith of the believer. Through baptism the believer shares in Christ's priesthood, which excludes any hierarchical order, or sacred power, within the Church. The systematization of a more positive view of ministry was left for subsequent Lutheran scholars who took Calvin's right and richer approach of the threefold office of Christ: prophetic, kingly, and priestly.[16]

Trent's theology of order remained within the scholastic-Thomistic framework as a formal counter-position to the Reformation. Thus, the council re-affirmed the three major tenets of late medieval tradition. It recognized a visible and external priesthood with the power to consecrate and absolve; a proper sacrament transmitted by sacred ordination, which imprints an enduring sacramental character; and a hierarchical structure divinely instituted by Christ's mission. However, Trent did not provide a complete theology of orders and ministry.[17] The eucharistic doctrine was its central achievement. Thus, the council was successful in strengthening the ordained priesthood as correlated to a theology of the eucharistic sacrifice. Together with the administration of the sacraments, it stood at the center of a priestly spirituality and ministry in the subsequent four hundred years.

### Ministry as Servant-Leadership in the Priestly Community

A more complete theology of the sacrament is found in the documents of the Second Vatican Council (1962–1965), in particular in its Dogmatic Constitution on the Church (*Lumen Gentium*) and its Decree on the Ministry and Life of Priests (*Presbyterorum Ordinis*). This theology is inclusive of all the ordained ministries (bishop, priest, and deacon) together with the apostolate of the faithful sharing in the priesthood of the baptized in Christ. It is also more thorough, because by establishing a christocentric basis of Jesus as teacher, priest, and pastor—again applied to all members of the Church—it provides an organic structure and a more dynamic vision of the Church's ministry. Ecclesial ministry is considered from the broad perspective of the mystery of Christ and the communion and mission of the Church. The former is the fountainhead and model of all ministry, the latter its womb and setting.

The leadership of priests, co-workers with the bishop, is seen as an apostolic and pastoral office of service, not in terms of status or privilege. "By the anointing of the Holy Spirit [they] are signed with a special character and so are configured to Christ the priest in such a way that they are able to act in the person of Christ the head."[18] The primary focus of the priest's consecration is linked to mission and to the body of Christ (Church). As "apostolic minister" (presbyter), the priest has a triple function of *leadership* (pastoral), *worship* (priestly), and *evangelization* (prophetic). Nevertheless, the Eucharist stands at the center of his consecration and mission. In interpreting Vatican II, the *Catechism of the Catholic Church* states:

> Christ, high priest and unique mediator, has made of the Church "a kingdom, priests for his God and Father." The whole community of believers is, as such, priestly. The faithful exercise their baptismal priesthood through their participation, each according to his own vocation, in Christ's mission as priest, prophet, and king...The ministerial or hierarchical priesthood of bishops and priests, and the common priesthood of all the faithful participate, "each in its own way, in the one priesthood of Christ." While being "ordered one to another," they differ essentially.[19]

The episcopal and presbyteral ministries are a visible sign of Christ —head, high priest, teacher, and shepherd—in the Church and for the world. Within the hierarchical priesthood of the organic body of the Church, bishops have the fullness of the sacrament of orders, as "the summit of the sacred ministry."[20] This sacramental approach was a significant accomplishment of the council. The council also restored the diaconate as a permanent office in the Roman Catholic Church.

Three basic concepts of the role of the laity are found in the vision of Vatican II: (a) the ecclesiology of "the people of God"; (b) the universal call to holiness; and (c) the calling and gifting of the baptized for the life and mission of the Church through the sacraments of initiation. These concepts are of vital importance because they deepen and broaden the organic communion of the body of the Church. In fact the laity, in its own diverse and complementary vocations, are seen not only as sharing in the priesthood of Christ but specifically as participating in his kingly, priestly, and prophetic office, although not in an ordained sense. This threefold mission describes the ministerial life of the whole

Church—both in and outside it—in which the laity participate as subjects of faith and liturgical celebrations, exercising that priesthood, building up the Christian community, and giving witness to a holy life in the family and in the world.

Today the new ecclesial consciousness arising from the council and the ever-changing cultural ways of our society have shaken the dynamics of ministry and remain a continuing challenge to the traditional image and role of the ordained priest. Because the "vocation crisis" is felt mainly in the West, but with substantial differences between various local communities (or religious orders), the problem might clearly depend, at least in general, on two major factors: the cultural dynamics operative in today's secular society and the spiritual vitality of a particular community (or religious order). The social support for the priesthood and tranquil priestly status of the past have largely vanished and in certain quarters modern secularism has become even aggressively hostile to the values that priesthood embodies.

## The Fundamental Priesthood of the Church

An important theological statement of Vatican II begins this investigation: "The common priesthood of the faithful and the ministerial or hierarchical priesthood are none the less interrelated; each in its own way shares in the one priesthood of Christ. The ministerial priest, by the sacred power that he has, forms and governs the priestly people."[21] Thus, a crucial point of focus needs to be the relationship between ministerial priesthood and the common priesthood of the baptized. This approach implies the new ecclesiology of the "organic structure of the priestly community."[22]

### An Organic Communion

The Church as a whole and in its own existence is a priestly community giving itself in obedience to the living God the Father, the Son, and the Holy Spirit for the life of the world. The Church originates from Christ, who through his *Pasch* became the primordial minister and servant, and by way of his Spirit, the source of all gifts and charisms. Therefore, "the fundamental priesthood in the Church is that of the Church, the whole People of God, and...hence the official priesthood, in spite of its institution by Christ—not the Church—finds its immediate theological setting within the priesthood of the Church."[23] Ecclesiology is also key because, as stated above, in our interpretation and response, the varied facets and issues of priesthood and ministry are in some ways conditioned by our understanding of the Church. However, ecclesiology is crucial in that it points to Christ as the ultimate meaning and power of ministry.

Ecclesiology is the starting point, provided that we first understand the Church in the corporate sense of all its dimensions. Second, we must focus on the heart of the mystery of communion in the person of Jesus Christ and his Spirit calling the whole community to discipleship. Since the Second Vatican Council, the concept of models has been used to articulate new ways of being Church: the Church as sacrament, institution, communion, herald, servant. In addition, multiple other ecclesial currents linked to the real life of concrete communities have emerged and resulted in such concepts as the catechumenal, charismatic, and prophetic Church. The new ecclesiological awareness that produced an unprecedented identity crisis in the traditional forms of clerical ministry also gave rise to a historic shift of lay roles in contemporary parish life.

Avery Dulles, who proposed the five major models cited above, has added a sixth model that is inclusive of the others, the Church as "community of disciples."[24] In fact, the mystery of communion into discipleship is the ultimate challenge against which our theological assumptions and practical expectations of ministry must be re-assessed. The different models and visions of Church shape our assumptions and preferences for particular ministerial forms, although this might lead to contrasting ideas and expressions of ministry, especially in today's shifting cultural modes.

> The question is: Can we make room for diverse models of Church? Can we make room for diverse models of priesthood? We have to, because the mystery of Church and priesthood is not defined by only one of these models. Its complete reality is the sum total of all the models... In today's situation, we can ill afford to be polarized, even by healthy differences of opinion

and points of view. We need the support and affirmation of one another.[25]

If the common ground of communion and discipleship (ecclesiology) is fractured, then the full sense of ministerial commitment (priesthood) is weakened.

Fundamentally—in a theological and pastoral sense—our vision of ministry depends on our vision of the Church. As the Church is complex and rich, so is ministry. Furthermore, the power of ministry also depends on the graced vitality of the Church, and this vitality—with God's Spirit—stems from the holiness of its spiritual leaders and the faithful.

The common and the ordained priesthood with its distinct roles are intrinsically related elements of ecclesial communion and discipleship in Jesus Christ. This means that they need and complement each other as they both participate in the saving mission of the Church. For, "there is the communion that exists between priests and people based on the fact that their respective forms of priesthood need each other for the realization of the priesthood of the Church and hence for the ultimate and unified ecclesial worship of God, the purpose for which the human race was created."[26]

## Acting in the Person of Christ

The fundamental priesthood of service of the whole Christian community does not diminish the significance and importance of the indispensable role and core reality of the ordained ministry. The ordained priesthood is defined in relation to Christ's particular, direct call and mission and also in relation to its role of authority within his body, the Church. The body is the image of a vital organism, which in ministerial terms means an organic reality, or structured community, endowed with a directive element, the head. The priest is a servant-leader, and the essential role of priestly service in pastoral leadership is implicit in the will of Christ, who chose particular disciples to act personally in his name.

The unique relationship to Christ and his body configures the spiritual identity and role of ordained priests. Their official and permanent ministry gifted by the Holy Spirit is founded on and related to the apostolic commission of Christ. All ministry arises from the ministry of Christ and the movement of the Spirit that moved the first disciples. This christological basis is of capital importance. Vatican II emphasized the hierarchical and organic nature of sacramental orders, in particular the priestly role, within the body of the Church. As noted earlier, through the sacrament of orders "priests by the anointing of the Holy Spirit are signed with a special character and so are configured to Christ the priest in such a way that they are able to act in the person of Christ the head."[27]

The priest as servant-leader in the Church—according to the presbyter's role of the ancient tradition—is a visible symbol of Christ's headship. All the baptized are consecrated to give witness to Christ's liberating mission, but only the priest/presbyter is empowered for the *diakonia* of spiritual governance as a public representative of the community and agent of Christ's mission and its continuation in and for the Church. This leadership role as head of a priestly office can be translated into the multiple aspects of Christ's prophetic, priestly, and royal mission. The priest's primary function is to preach the gospel. The life of the priest "takes on the likeness of Christ" as he is taken over by him in the most radical way to be a good shepherd and spiritual father, a healer and a teacher, a prophet of God's freedom and a messenger of mercy.

We could add many other different priestly images—all of them flowing from the full measure that is only in Christ. However, in the Christian economy, they all amount to one key word: sacrament. A priest is a living sacrament of Christ—the first and true priest. He stands in his ministry as a representative figure and the pre-eminent bearer of the mystery at the service of communion and reconciliation in Christ's body, an instrument of God's divine mercy and grace in the world. Thus, "the office of priests shares in the authority by which Christ himself builds up, sanctifies and rules his Body."[28] By proclaiming the word of God and living it, presiding at worship (a central role), supporting and directing the various charisms, and serving the poor (in the most inclusive and comprehensive sense), the priest acts sacramentally in the person of Christ *(in persona Christi)*. Therefore, he shows forth the glory and humble service of priesthood as a symbolic and sacramental representation (in the organic sense of body) of Christ, the head and the shepherd.

## Priestly Office versus Common Priesthood

The Church's teaching relating to this subject might be summed up in two important points. On the one hand, there exists an essential difference between hierarchical priesthood and the "common priesthood" of the faithful. On the other hand, each of the faithful is an evangelizer by nature because the Church is essentially on mission, and each member is called to this honor and duty. This raises two issues. One is theological, the other pastoral. How can we explain this essential difference concretely, in relation to Christ as primordial minister? How would we be able to transform passive assemblies "of those merely motivated by religious obligations" into communities accepting and sharing more fully in the mission of the Church?

The special priestly "character" is an issue related to the priest's distinct ecclesial identity just described. Theologians debate whether this priestly character (permanent, according to the magisterium) is ontological or functional, but this might be a false dilemma. In fact, the priestly office is essentially different from the common priesthood, not because of the Christian consecration (the priest is not a super-Christian), or merely because of its different function (the opinion of Küng and Schillebeeckx),[29] but primarily because of what the priest is. As leader and shepherd, he represents sacramentally Christ the head, really and actually. By the grace of his vocation and consecration, the priest embodies the spirit, heart, and entire mission of Christ's unique and eternal priesthood. Thus he has "the character of Christ." This inner reality makes him more than a religious functionary or a ministerial coordinator. Again, the priest is a personal sacrament of a reality that transcends his functions and our world—an in-depth and life-long gift to the Father, with Christ, in the power of the Holy Spirit.

As stated earlier, ministry is not primarily what the Church *does* but what the Church *is*. The Church has a sacramental structure—the universal and historical sign of grace in Christ, the only mediator—in which the priest, in his way of being and ministering, participates as a vital and central figure. This sacramental being of a priest by ordination is a particular charism and personal reality of grace greater than himself. It has the Holy Spirit as its source and the Christian community as its aim. Thus, the priestly character is not a static category (in the scholastic sense of substance), or a merely juridical commission, but a real (ontological) charism of service that, consequently, has to be understood in the relational and personalist sense of communion with others and for others.

## The Sacramental Foundations of Ministry

The sacraments of initiation are the true foundation and cradle of the ministerial Church. Consequently, we will now focus primarily on the fundamental relationship of *sacramental initiation to discipleship*. The Church's theology of ministry began historically with the fundamental reality of Christian initiation. Thus, we will look at the complementary mission of *the laity* and the relationship to the obviously indispensable role of *the ministerial priesthood* in the life of the Church.

### A Baptismal and Eucharistic Foundation

The sacrament of orders, by which the ordained minister shares in the office of Christ, not only as leader-shepherd but also as member of his body, presupposes and builds upon the foundational sacraments of baptism, confirmation, and Eucharist. Holy orders celebrates the same mystery, although through a different sign, in the life of the servant-leader. Ordination links the priest to the original mission of Christ and to the appointment of the apostles. He not only receives the Church's commission, but also becomes a priest with the bestowal of a particular gift of the Holy Spirit.

The fundamental rootedness in baptism and its radical call to discipleship constitutes the common priesthood, the primary vocation of our being incorporated into the body of Christ. It grounds a foundational spirituality as much for ordained priests as for the laity. Both constitute the indivisible priesthood of the Church as expressed in the diversity of functions with their corresponding duties. The analogy of an organic *koinonia* of priests and laity makes possible the understanding of the charismatic structure of the whole Church. The Holy Spirit is the author of this creative richness since "he also distributes special graces among the faithful of every rank. By these gifts, he makes them fit and ready to undertake various tasks and offices for the renewal and building up of the church, as it is written, 'the manifestation of the Spirit is given to everyone for profit'" (1 Cor 12:7).[30] Only the Holy Spirit can guide us toward a greater responsiveness and growth in the ministry of Christ.

Baptism is a call and a gift, a right and a duty, of participation and service of all members *to teach* (experience of faith), *to sanctify* themselves (intimate relation with God), and *to rule* (love leading to service). It is not a simple delegation or concession, but a gift of their baptismal call to be holy for the glory of God and the service of others. It is from here that all Christians, as a community of disciples, have the same dignity and the same call to accomplish the mission and the ministry of Christ. In particular, there is a call to respect and dignify the unique gifts of women that have always been the vital heart of the home and of the Church.

Ministry reaches its culmination in the Eucharist and from this source life flows back into the Church: "Know what you are doing and imitate the mystery you celebrate" (ordination rite of a priest). The observation that follows profoundly grasps the existential heart of priestly spirituality, which stems from the priest's presiding role over a Eucharist that is nurturing:

> Because the Eucharist is the foundation, dynamic force and goal of priestly ministry, priests are both nourished on the servant Christ and offer this same sustenance to others as their greatest service to them. Moreover, inasmuch as all ecclesial service involves participating in the life and mission of Jesus himself, the servant-leadership which is most characteristic of presbyteral ministry is Eucharist both in origin and in expression. The response of the assembly to the priest's Eucharistic ministry can be a profound invitation to union with Christ, as the people evoke and affirm the priestly identity of their ministers.[31]

Thus, the eucharistic foundation—"source and summit of Christian life"—and baptism provide a centering purpose and an integrating factor for the mission of the local church. This is all the more important in our modern, fragmented, and individualistic society, which is characterized by constant and ambivalent change. The unprecedented cultural challenge is reflected in our program-oriented parishes that try to serve disparate pastoral needs. Many of these parishes lack a spiritual vision that would give direction and a sense of identity and purpose to their ministry. They need to listen to the wisdom of Proverbs: "Without a vision, people perish" (see Prov 29:18).

The challenge for a renewed, shared ministerial consciousness will involve changing from a Church of *maintenance* to one of *missionary outreach*. This is not the place to articulate the concrete pastoral implications of this or many other shifts based on a vision for ministerial collaboration between clergy and laypeople. "Pastors are exhorted to acknowledge and foster the ministries, the offices and roles of the lay faithful that find their foundation in the sacraments of baptism and confirmation."[32]

An authentic ministerial community has a corporate vision that unifies the members as an ecclesial body. The richness of ministerial diversity obviously demands respect for ordained and lay competencies and functions. Co-discipleship under the same master should not mean "substitution for" but "collaboration with" pastors. Moreover, ministerial partnership will not demote but will enhance and strengthen ordained ministry. It will demand changing antiquated structures and styles of leadership. It will also require a purification process from attitudes and behaviors inherited from a bygone era, such as paternalism and authoritarianism, and, on a positive note, maturation in priestly spiritual identity that grows from baptismal consciousness. Augustine spoke beautifully of this baptismal and ministerial relationship:

> What I should be for you fills me with anguish; what I can be with you is my consolation. Because for you I am a bishop, but with you a Christian. The first points to my duty, the second to grace. The first shows the danger, the other salvation.[33]

## Ministry: Building Up the Church

We have seen that the concept of ministry has expanded considerably from a monolithic idea that identified ministry with the clergy to a more fundamental and comprehensive concept seen, for instance, in today's multiplicity of lay ministries, particularly in the parish community. A recent Vatican document acknowledges that "the present reality is that there has been an astonishing growth of pastoral initiatives in this area."[34] At the same time, the document raises concerns about the blurring of roles and identities with the consequent confusion that has led in the West to "a reduction in vocations to the (ministerial) priesthood and [could] obscure the specific purpose of seminaries as places of formation for the ordained ministry."[35]

The new conceptual framework for ministry does not pretend to stress the role of the community to the point that the ordained are unimportant, unnecessary, replaceable, or even secondary. Far from it. The concept flows from the clear and compelling vision of Vatican II that the whole Church is called and gifted to share the ministry of Christ: "Therefore there is no such thing as a member who does not have a share in the mission of the whole body."[36] As stated previously, in the early Church, building up the community was the substance of ministry. We will reach that goal not by weakening the priesthood but by empowering the community. And by spiritually empowering the community we will strengthen the ordained priesthood.

This idea of a "ministerial community" might sound utopian because, while all are called to share in the mission of Christ, not all can be expected realistically to participate in collaborative ministry within the parish structure. The laity has the primary function of testifying to the evangelical values in the world, a distinct function and yet intimately linked to that of the priest in service to the fundamental reality of the mission of Christ. The reflection that follows will stress the interrelation of the *spiritual*, *communitarian*, and *sacramental* aspects, which are basic and against which *the collaboration between pastors and laity* will be re-assessed. This in no way offers practical approaches to developing collaborative ministry, which in itself is a complex task and a long-term goal. As discussed previously, the Eucharist is understood as the font and summit of all Christian mission and ministry.

## A Ministerial Vision Spiritually Supported

The impetus of the new evangelization urged all believers to live out the call to discipleship by collaborating with pastors and sharing the faith with others in every human situation. What conditions would make a new baptismal and ministerial consciousness possible? Spirituality is the real challenge, because the mission of the Church is essentially spiritual. Effective ministry does not consist only in what the

Church *does*, but also of what the Church *is*—its signs of love and unity in the living out of God's gifts. In other words, holiness is the only goal of ministry. In the New Testament, "the overarching and unifying purpose of the Church can be expressed in three words: to be holy."[37] Nevertheless, this personal call of Christ cannot be divorced from service and fidelity to the Church's missionary call: "You will be my witnesses" (Acts 1:8).

Communion with God, the source of holiness, and effective ministry are inseparable, because no one can give what he or she does not have. Indeed, participation in the building up of God's reign is a sign of Christian maturity and a sure path to freedom and joy. Our secular world certainly needs the vision of the sacred and transcendent as a living testimony of identification with Christ. This vital communion with God enables us to point others to a view of the transcendent in life and, at the same time, frees us for the mission of bringing God's liberating love to others. Besides helping others, true ministers learn to find God in the ordinary through an awareness of the holy in their personal lives.

Spirituality is life that is born in, and develops from, the baptismal cradle to discipleship and holiness. It feeds itself, grows with, and arises from furthering, with God's grace, the reign of God. It is gospel-centered and eucharistic, nourished in prayer and through awareness of the presence of God in "everyday things." It is less individualistic and more committed to service in the world.

This applies to the priest, the man of faith and prayer called to servant-leadership. Pope John Paul II has spoken about the greatness of the priestly vocation as a "gift and a mystery." He has described the priest as a man completely "for others" and completely "for the Kingdom," whose ministerial effectiveness depends, above all, on being a holy priest.[38] The spirit of fidelity in carrying out pastoral ministry defines a priestly spirituality. It is based on the priest's spirit of servanthood and fidelity. He is the principle of unity and love within the local community. Referring to the necessity for vitality and continuing formation for priests, Donald Cozzens observes: "Only a deep and integrated spirituality grounded in hard thinking and study offers any hope for successfully tending God's word to a people hungry for gospel freedom and holiness."[39]

Christian leadership needs spiritual support and religious formation in order to bring about the growth and complementarity of all the ministries. The Church has laid the groundwork for the flowering of a ministerial spirituality, against the human tendency toward sacramental minimalism, privatistic spirituality, and lay passivity, each of which reinforces the other. To a great extent this is still the case. Believers have to once again become the primordial signs of celebration and evangelization. Only an intense interior life, a genuine spirituality, and faith formation will make this possible. Without this concrete existential reality, it would be meaningless to envision a broad-based participation of parishioners within, and outside of, the community's ministerial life.

A parish community in search of a deeper spirituality and a renewed sense of mission becomes necessarily more aware of the holy in ordinary life (sacramental aspect) and more conscious of the need to transform culture *(consecratio mundi)* through family, professional, and social life (the primary ministry of the laity). At the intersection of both aspects, spiritual life and secular reality—which are always present within a community of faith—the mystery of Christ renews, with the believer's faith, the real foundations of human life.

Speaking from a historical perspective, we can say that at the dawning of a new missionary age, there is always a corresponding spiritual awakening led by an individual or a community. Generally speaking, many of the base groups within the traditional structure of the parish continue to be anchored in three essential realities: word, liturgy, and community. However, many other types of groups in parishes might arise; such groups could be formed to seek more direct and authentic spiritual experience or Christian solidarity with the underprivileged. The actual faces of a ministerially renewed parish are myriad in today's global Church. They all have a common characteristic: a Christian vision that is spiritually supported in an intimate community of faith and prayer.

Relevant spiritual growth, a strong sense of community, and a renewed spirit of mission are integral to Christian ministry. Ministries flower in awakened parishes as a new springtime of the Church. Ministry is Christ within us, with us, and for us. Therefore, this Christian springtime is Jesus Christ alive in the community through his Spirit. As St. Paul said: "There are varieties of gifts, but the same Spirit; and there are varieties of services, but the same Lord; and there are varieties of activities, but it is the same God who activates all of them in everyone. To each is given the manifestation of the Spirit for the common good" (1 Cor 12:4–7).

## Community, Eucharist, and Ministry

In fact, "just as Christian faith is communal, so Christian community is ministerial."[40] A community without ministries atrophies and ministries without community disintegrate. In both cases, the vital energy of a spirituality of communion and of commitment is lacking. The equilibrium between ministries and community has not always been maintained in the past by Catholics or Protestants. In fact, ministries have been placed above or at the edge of the community, that is to say, relegated to the hierarchy or given over to a few interested people.[41]

As the unifying dimension of ministerial participation and of the community's life-rhythms, sacramental liturgy has a central role. In fact, community, sacraments, and ministries are integral to one another. The sacramental liturgy is essentially communitarian and requires, for that reason, a strong sense of community. But community and sacraments cannot exist at the same time without a spirit of conversion and mission. The whole body of the Church is bound together, communally and sacramentally, through the basic threefold mission of evangelization, celebration, and service.

The heart of a ministerial community is the Eucharist, the mystery of the Lord's self-giving presence. All the challenges and longings of a renewed priesthood and Christian leadership intersect in this awesome mystery. It is the paradigm of Christian ministry. A ministerial community has a corporate vision through which the Eucharist is celebrated with concrete references to the daily life of the community. But there is no existential heart if the ecclesial body is not continually built up through apostolic outreach. Nevertheless, even though it is the heart and center, the Eucharist is not the totality of the ministry of the Church.

The truth of the sacramental celebration depends on authenticity of faith and love in service. And the authenticity of service emanates from its strength in the truth of our celebrations. This dynamic relationship between loving service and authentic celebration must, therefore, express itself in a community whose vitality provides a strong eucharistic consciousness. (A related question may arise here: Could Christian communities have such a vital consciousness if they are deprived of the Eucharist for the lack of priests?) A truly eucharistic celebration is the central expression of the Catholic community that bears witness with generosity and holiness to the liberating mission of Christ. In this kind of spiritual environment, priests and laity become co-disciples and co-workers (cf. Rom 16:3; 1 Cor 3:9) of one Master.

## Toward a Ministerial Community

The terminology itself of clergy and laity is ambiguous and nowhere to be found in the New Testament. Yves Congar spoke against a bipolar division of clergy and laity: "It would then be necessary to substitute for the linear scheme a scheme where the community appears as the enveloping reality *within which* the ministries, eventually the instituted sacramental ministries, are placed as *modes of service* of what the community is called to be and to do."[42] The new theology of the sacrament of the Church seen as the fundamental priesthood instituted by Christ has reversed the inherited restrictive view of ecclesial ministries. Both clergy and laity have specific ministries that should respect the ministerial structures of the Church. While recognizing that the secularization of ordained ministries dilutes the holiness of orders, the ministerial community of the baptized needs to give value to the meaning of the sacred rooted in the presence of God, which is at work in family life and in people's lives. Living this presence of God, laity hear the call to holiness in the very heart of their own existence, which, like church ministry itself, is the way to holiness.

John Paul II's apostolic exhortation *Christifideles Laici* envisages the collaboration between the common priesthood and the ministerial priesthood through the dynamic of an organic communion:

> Ecclesial communion is more precisely likened to an "organic" communion, analogous to that of a living and functioning body. In fact, at one and the same time it is characterized by a diversity and complementarity of vocations and states in life, of ministries, of charisms and responsibilities. Because of this diversity and complementarity, every member of the lay faithful is seen in relation to the whole body and offers a totally unique contribution on behalf of the whole body.[43]

To the priest is given the concern of directing and presiding. He is not above the community, but in faithful service to it.

And that means that it does not appertain to the presbyter to accumulate charisms, but to integrate them mutually; it does not belong to him to impede the plurality, but to maintain the unity. All of worship does not pertain to him, but only the presiding action. In a word, it does not belong to him to do all, but to make possible that all be done in fidelity to and communion in the mission of Christ and of the Church. Assistance in directing the community does not consist solely in the duty of animation, coordination and integration of the distinct services and ministries, but also in the service of the complementarity of the diverse ministerial areas. This is so in order to effect an integral realization of the mission, from the level of representation that is characteristic of ordained ministry.[44]

Inspired by the experience of the early Church, new and creative ways for collaboration should not be envisaged as an opposition to the time-honored tradition of ministerial priesthood. On the contrary, the success of future ministry will depend on a strong Christian leadership as well as the continual nurturing of potential vocations to the priesthood and religious life (a topic that cannot be developed here). At the same time, the call to ministry emphasizes the need to rediscover a baptismal consciousness, which means growing in the fullness of Christian life. This growth is the fertile ground for generating ministerial vocations with all the profound implications that follow for the life of the Church. This is already evident in some contemporary spiritual movements.

Empowered by spiritual growth and awakening to the awesome mystery, many local churches around the world, in dialoguing with culture without identifying with it, continue to be seedbeds of Christian vocations. These are God's gifts to the communities, the fruit of their strong Christian identity, and the result of following wholeheartedly through conversion the radical and joyful message of the gospel. All the people of God in communion manifest in the inexhaustible richness of calls and missions the presence of God in the world, the God who is the origin and end of all ministry.

# 11
# Marriage:
# The Call to the Gift of Self

The theology of the sacrament of marriage attained a major watershed in our time, equal in importance to its classical formulation during the High Middle Ages. During the twelfth century the Church defined the canonical components of the "institution" of marriage as a sacrament. Today we are coming full circle, back to the anthropological and theological foundations of marriage that reflect a broader vision of its sacramentality. This view emphasizes the *depth and vitality of the personal relationship* in which two people sincerely give one another the gift of themselves, understandably a decisive factor for true happiness in marriage.[1]

In our contemporary society marriage is a floundering institution, at least in the Western world where it has been subjected to the most radical and rapid changes in the last decades. Lack of cultural support is perhaps the crucial factor. Today, the traditional support of extended families and communities along with the pastoral care of the churches are relatively ineffectual.

Furthermore, a number of theologians, including Karl Rahner[2] as well as members of the Catholic hierarchy, have acknowledged the deficiency of the theology of marriage both in its specific and in its wider sacramental meaning.

The purpose of this chapter is not to provide solutions to particular marital problems, but to offer some suggestions and insights for a new theological synthesis relevant to the marital experience (including divorce and remarriage) in light of today's new religious consciousness and pastoral challenges. A new way forward is proposed and a new vision expressed through five fundamental symbolic models as the foundational basis of a deeper and more personal theology of marriage.

Finally, the meaning of the marriage bond is outlined, both in its ritual celebration and in the challenges presented by the experience of marital breakdown. Throughout the chapter a mystery-centered sacramentality of the experience of married persons (the existential source of theology) provides a fundamental perspective and focus for the integration of the critical issues of marriage, as well as divorce and remarriage.

## Revitalizing the Tradition

The reality of marriage appears to be at a critical juncture today, when it is seen in the context of the evolution of two thousand years of Christian tradition. This development represents two paradigmatic stages, both of which contribute to the Christian vision of marriage. In the first millennium the Church accepted the view of marriage as a secular reality originating in an act of human freedom and expressed in many distinct cultures. Weddings as such were only gradually introduced into the formal sphere and canonical power of the Church from the eleventh century onward and were mandatory only after Trent. This new paradigmatic stage preceded the development of the sacramental concept and the fully developed ecclesiastical definition of the institution of marriage in a formal way.

### First Millennium:
### Secular Marriage and Sacramental Mystery

The references in the writing of the apostolic fathers in this matter point clearly in two directions: First, "Christians marry like everybody else" is quoted from the famous letter of Diognetes of this period.[3] A juxtaposition of familial and popular customs formed the basically secular celebration of the marriage of Christians. The second direction was as important and clear as the first: the marriage covenant must be experienced "in the Lord" (1 Cor 7:39).

The secular character of marriage in the patristic period does not imply in the least that marriage was profane and unholy. On the contrary, marriage, like the whole of life, was considered sacred in the Greco-Roman religious world view as it was in the Christian faith. The incorporation into Christ via baptism founded the Christian matrix of a marital union, which the praxis of the patristic Church understood exclusively from a biblical and ecclesial perspective.

It is important to note an earlier crucial comment by Tertullian (ca. 160–240) in his work *Ad Uxorem:*

> How shall we ever be able adequately to describe the happiness of that marriage which the Church founds, and the Eucharist confirms, upon which the prayer of thanksgiving sets a seal, which angels praise, and to which the Father gives His consent? For not even on earth do children marry properly and legally without their fathers' permission.[4]

Marriage must be according to the Lord; Christ is the foundation of marriage through the all-embracing mystery of the Church. Contracted between two baptized people, marriage receives its confirmation in the Eucharist. Tertullian does not refer to a liturgical ritual blessing, but to a liturgy of thanksgiving of psalms and hymns. He alludes also to the blessing of assent by God the Father. The African writer presents the theological implications and the Christian character of marital covenant "in the Lord." The covenant becomes sacramental by virtue of the faith actualized within a eucharistic community.

At the time of Pope Damasus (366–384), there was already evidence of a liturgical rite in Rome and in Italy. But, in general, from the canonical point of view, the bishops' approval had no bearing on the validity of the marriage. The sacraments of Christian initiation provided the spiritual depth and the sacramental foundation and ecclesial character of marriage. The Eucharist, according to Simeon of Thessalonica, "perfects and seals every sacrament and every divine mystery."[5]

It would be anachronistic to see in patristic terminology the technical category of "sacrament." For Tertullian, conjugal union is an image and symbol of the divine covenant: "If you accept Christ and the Church, you must also accept what is his image, symbol and sacrament."[6]

St. Augustine, who provides the best and most complete patristic synthesis, represents a further development in the theology of marriage, despite the negative influence of Hellenistic dualism on his view of sexuality. His major contribution, which influenced thinking through the medieval period right up until modern times, is his characterization of the threefold goods of marriage: offspring, faithfulness, and sacrament.

St. Augustine understands the concept of sacrament in both the broad sense of "mystery," which includes both the hidden spiritual reality of the saving action of Christ, and the sacramental actions introducing Christians into that reality: "What is celebrated visibly...is understood vitally in Christ."[7] In this regard, marriage, something good given by God and healed by redemptive grace, is seen as a meaningful sign of the mystery of Christ and his Church. The sacramental reality of marriage is the foundation and source of all its other values, including indissolubility, because in Christian marriage "the holiness of the sacrament is more valuable than the fertility of the womb."[8]

The Eastern patristic tradition also conceptualizes marriage from the broad level of sacrament as mystery. Orthodox Christians certainly reached a theological depth, exuberant symbolic celebration, and pastoral realism from a biblico-liturgical focal point unmatched by other traditions. The profundity of their vision of marriage is rooted in the continuum of an ancient tradition based especially in the works of Basil of Caesarea and John Chrysostom. The doctrine of *oikonomia,* or the saving activity of God, centers on the mystery of the *Kyrios*, the Lord, providing a unifying praxis to the theology, liturgy, and experience of marriage. The Orthodox also exercise a healing pastoral ministry toward broken marriages and the possibility of remarriage (a topic that will be explored in the third part of this chapter).

## Second Millennium:
### Ecclesiastical Marriage and Sacramental Contract

Changes in theological understanding come about as a consequence of social transformation and new religious ideas evolving through a complex historical process over the course of centuries. Nevertheless, a comparison between the patristic and medieval understanding of marriage shows a fundamental change. The first centuries of the second millennium overall represented a double paradigmatic shift:

*a) from mystery to sacrament*

*b) from covenant to contract*

In both cases, the emphasis on the *spiritual foundations* of a covenantal marriage changed to an emphasis on the *juridical categories of contract and indissolubility*. At first, marriage was seen as secular, meaning that it was neither considered profane nor made sacred, but was related to the ecclesial community by virtue of Christian dignity. Later, marriage was seen as religious, made holy in a sacred place, and was related to civil society by virtue of a canonical form.

The doctrinal and liturgical context moved from the symbolic and dynamic to the objective and static. Patristic terminology, culturally rooted in Platonism, was now reinterpreted in a more restrictive and rational Aristotelian framework. Within this cultural-religious context, the marriage *in esse*, or marriage as a mode of being, in patristic theology became the marriage *in fieri*, or something to be done, practiced according to scholastic theology (eleventh through thirteenth centuries). The Church followed this new approach down through the centuries. In the long development of scholastic systematization of the sacraments, the emphasis shifted from the *mystery* signified by the sign (the couple) to the *sacramental character* of the sign (ritual consent) understood in a narrow sense.

Gratian's Decree, the first compilation of canon law, appeared around 1140, while Hugh of St. Victor (1079–1141) made a major contribution to the sacramental definition of marriage. The effort to establish the essential element of the sacrament's validity (consent or *copula*) led to a contract-centered theology. Thus, scholastic theologians and canonists formulated the marital bond as combining two types, consent (initiated marriage) and sexual intercourse (consummated marriage). A gradually restrictive and unilateral consideration precluded an authentic spiritual and personal vision of marriage.

Until the ninth century, marriage remained in the Latin churches a civil and familial ceremony. From this century until the Council of Trent the last phase of sacramental evolution opened up the gradual

takeover of the discipline of marriage and the regulations of its ceremonies by the authority of the Church.

The place for those ceremonies was transferred first to the front of
the entrance to the church *(in facie ecclesiae)*, and later to the assembly
in church. Consent remained the essential element, but now the priest
received that consent after a public pre-nuptial investigation. By impos-
ing an ecclesiastical model, the hierarchy aimed to counter abusive
public customs within a wider movement toward a new social order.
With the definitive transfer of the nuptial ceremonies from the home to
the church, the canonical and ecclesiastical character of the marriage
institution developed. The first official declaration of marriage as a
sacrament was made in 1184 at the Council of Verona. The theologians
of Trent (1545–1563) ratified the Augustinian conception, which prevailed from Trent until the present. This council laid the social groundwork for the canonical validity of the sacrament.

Protestant rituals continued the traditions of the Middle Ages,
retaining important religious celebrations. The Protestant Reformation
emphasized the holiness of marriage and family, albeit not from the
sacramental perspective, but from a renewed theology of the Christian
vocation and the covenantal nature of God's plan for the couple.

## The Second Vatican Council: A Dynamic View of Marriage

The Second Vatican Council addressed contemporary challenges in two
constitutions: the Dogmatic Constitution on the Church, *Lumen Gentium* (11, 35, and 41), and especially the Pastoral Constitution on the
Church in the Modern World, *Gaudium et Spes* (47–52). These documents define marriage in terms of the biblical theology of the covenant
and within the inter-personal reality of a "communion of love." Marriage is defined as a personal community within which the partners give
and accept each other (covenant), and also as an intimate partnership
of marital life and love (personal perspective). This Christian understanding of conjugal and familial life is essential from a theological and
ethical point of view.

Consequently, the view of marriage was broadened, not only by
retracing its biblical meaning but also by reformulating the meaning of
marriage with the help of modern human sciences. The council also

rejected the old terminology of primary end (procreation) and secondary end (mutual help), emphasizing instead the centrality of mutual love as the very essence of marriage. The theology of these documents represents a reaction against a contractual mentality, which although inspired by canonical sources, had stressed the objective and natural law components while ignoring the personal dimension of marriage, thus narrowing the scope of the vision of marriage.

Personalism enshrined in a covenant theology became a fundamental key to understanding the theology of marriage in the post-Vatican II era. This line of thinking was reiterated in John Paul II's apostolic exhortation, *Familiaris Consortio,* which is summarized in the conclusions of the Synod on Families (1980) and in the revised Code of Canon Law (1983). Thus, the communion of the faithful and permanent mutual love of the spouses has been slowly replacing the legalist mind-set of past generations.

IN CONCLUSION, a few points may be made about some important lessons of the Christian tradition. First, marriage as *sacramental mystery* is a multi-layered concept in the ancient patristic tradition. Although this tradition needs to be reinterpreted in light of a contemporary view of the person, it has endowed marriage with a deep, analogical, and symbolic meaning rooted in biblical sources of the covenant, especially in the sacramental vision of Ephesians 5:22–32. This ancient tradition stressed the dignity and value of marriage stemming from the creative act of God, *agape* ("life-giving love") and the salvific foundation of Christ manifested in the all-embracing mystery of the Church.

The vision implied a holistic conception of Christian existence, and hence of marriage, not limited by virtue of an efficacious ritual power or sacramental function, but extended to the whole of married life, embraced by Christ. The Orthodox theology and pastoral ministry of the *oikonomia,* or the saving activity of God, is consistent with the ancient patristic theology of sacramental mystery. It is applied to the case of remarriage of divorced Christians, although it has never become part of the Western tradition.

Second, the sacramental foundation does not depend exclusively on the act of marrying itself, but is related to baptismal and eucharistic consecration. Obviously, this initiatory foundation (baptism and Eucharist), which makes possible the essential constant of tradition of a marriage "in the Lord" (1 Cor 7:39) from which Christian marriage originates, reinforces the importance of an authentic ritual celebration of marriage before the community.

Third, the pastoral praxis of the Church is the key to interpreting the rich tapestry of the two thousand years of Christian tradition and a rethinking of the present situation. The dynamic relationship between Church and marriage as a rite of passage has always been an unfinished process and remains so today. The lack of support structures for marriage as a rite of passage in secularized cultures has led to the dramatic crisis in the institution in Western countries. The old models are breaking down. In fact, guided by the teaching of Vatican II, the Church can create a universal vision of new models that is not only rooted in tradition but also reflects modern consciousness. In the following section we propose a set of models that we believe can be helpful toward this end.


## A New Theological Interpretation: Five Models


A theological perspective of marriage must integrate the full complexity of its core values into multi-faceted, *real-life experience*. As Theodore Mackin puts it, "the marriage sacrament, like all sacraments, has as its matrix a complex human experience. And there is no understanding of the sacrament unless we first understand its matrix experience."[9]

In light of this, the comments that follow will be concerned mainly with a contemporary vision of major approaches or "models" of the sacramentality intrinsic to marriage. These approaches will be seen through the lens of the metaphor of *worship,* which allows us to expand considerably the depth and breadth of our perspective.

The analogy of worship allows us to glimpse something of the rich complexity of the marital experience. Moreover, the metaphor of worship provides a foundation for a genuine Christian theology and spirituality of marriage. In addition, a relevant theology of marriage must also integrate its *core values,* which we will refer to as *models of marriage.* The purpose of these models is to allow us to examine the salient realities intertwined in this most complex experience.

## *Worship: A Clue to the Theology of Marriage*

Marriage, like worship, is fundamentally symbolic in nature. While the conjugal partnership is a life experience with complex meanings and levels of reality, it is also the symbolic expression of something deeper and transcendent. We can compare marriage to Christian worship in that both have a *symbolic structure*, which is dialogic and intimate, and which engages the senses and conveys a *deeper meaning* of the human mystery. Both offer the possibility of *self-transcendence*. Their end is *salvation,* both as a hope and a means to it. All four elements are present. Thus, marriage is in itself true worship; it is, in fact, the most basic and original act of worship.

God's touching us deeply and wholly as individuals is related to conjugal intimacy (and also to worship); this correlation is, indeed, the core of marital spirituality. Just as an individual can find his or her "true" self only in God—an outcome of worship—so too, the couple can find authentic validation only in God.

The pledge of the old Anglican wedding rite, "with my body I thee worship," speaks profoundly of the central meaning of the analogy. Like worship, which etymologically means "ascribing worth to another being," marriage is the total validation of the other in the devotion and service to, celebration and mystery of a relationship. Just as the experience of worship engages the whole person, so too marriage is the total gift of self.

While we have merely touched on the analogy of marriage as worship, there are many other dimensions to the comparison that can be played out in all aspects of the relationship. In specific Christian terms, the bestowal of the marital embrace and the sharing of one eucharistic cup and bread intersect in the mystery of the cross, which is the paradigm of Christian worship. Certainly, the salient feature of the analogy points to an inherent sacramentality in marriage, a sacramentality that is both rich and diverse.

Whether in worship or in marriage, sacramentality in the full sense begins with human experience.The marriage relationship embodies both human and divine realities, not only because all creation is potentially sacramental, but also because marriage itself both signifies and makes mystery present. It is, in fact, as Walter Kasper sees it from a biblical perspective, "the grammar that God uses to express his love and faithfulness."[10] In fact, marriage is a sign of Christ's love for his Church because it is, in itself, a sacrament, that is, a natural sign of salvific actualization and self-transcendency that can express the core of the Christian mystery.

David Thomas graphically summarizes the symbolic importance of marriage sacramentality: "Christian marriage is, therefore, a genuine sign/symbol/sacrament that God's presence, love, and power are present in the real world, and that the married can, if willing, make God quite real in bed, board, babies, and backyard."[11]

## Models of Marriage

Since the traditional concept of what we call "sacrament" may be too narrow and/or too static to adequately express an understanding of the rich complexity of marriage, we propose, instead, several overlapping models that taken together embrace the core values and reflect "the heart" of the sacramentality of marriage. Thus, in reflecting on marriage as a dynamic process and in understanding marriage to be all embracing and life-long, we propose the following predominant models that express the inherent symbolic nature of marriage:

*Vocation*

*Communion*

*Covenant*

*Sacrament*

*Partnership*

It is important to note, however, that these models are complementary and open to a variety of legitimate interpretations, especially in light of different cultural contexts. The use of these five models offers a radical shift from the traditional approach in which marriage is emphasized as *sacrament* in the narrow juridical sense. In this new approach, using symbolic models, "marriage as sacrament" is but one dimension. Moreover, these models must be considered together to adequately describe Christian marriage; they cannot be considered in isolation. Thus, it seems preferable to refer to marriage as a *sacramental mystery* rather than simply to state that "marriage is a sacrament."

## THE SACRAMENTAL MYSTERY OF MARRIAGE

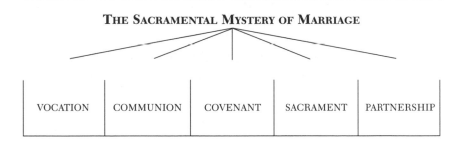

| VOCATION | COMMUNION | COVENANT | SACRAMENT | PARTNERSHIP |
|----------|-----------|----------|-----------|-------------|

The items shown above are distinct (although they are interrelated), and each is equally important in understanding Christian marriage. Note that each opens upward to demonstrate an ongoing process aiming toward full actualization.

In what follows, each symbolic model will be approached as a fundamental dimension of the sacramentality of marriage.

### Marriage as Vocation

Coming together in an intimate partnership and creating a family is a dynamic process whereby a man and a woman separate from their original families, build a shared world, and commit to one another for life. In practice this process, which entails complex human and religious elements, occurs as a gradual transition in two distinct phases: the engagement and the wedding. From a purely anthropological perspective, marriage is a rite of passage; theologically speaking, marriage is a sacrament of initiation.

What follows is a reflection on marriage as a rite of initiation, but seen from the broader sacramental perspective of marriage as vocation; as such, this particular initiation lasts a lifetime. The word "vocation" means call. Thus, theologically speaking, marriage is the divine call by which spouses are fitted and empowered to form an intimate community of persons able to love and serve. John Chrysostom (fourth–fifth centuries) spoke of the sacramentality of marriage as a vocation of spiritual sacrifice in which husband and wife are each ministers in their priestly vocation, offering life and love to each other.[12]

More recently the Church's emphasis on "the universal call to holiness" reminds us that God's call to be holy is not confined to a monastic or celibate elite. Rather, the Church has raised an awareness that marriage (and family life) is indeed a vocation in and of itself. Marriage is just as valid a path to holiness as is a call to the priesthood. In fact, marriage is the vocation *par excellence,* for here the spouses are God's co-creators in the gift of new life, and thus in the child's first experience of love.

In today's foundering secular culture, the Church, by promoting a better understanding of marriage as an ongoing process or an *initiation into a vocation,* can play a decisive role in strengthening the sacrament of marriage. Moreover, the Church can make use of the experiences of married people, and, therefore, of marriage itself, as a major arena for creating a Christian consciousness—in particular for developing an understanding of what it means to be "called" by God and to live out that special "calling." When, for instance, serious problems surface in marriage, the spouses, who understand the nature of their particular calling, can live in the midst of even extraordinary difficulties in a way that brings hope and strength to both partners.

Traditionally, family rituals and customs surrounding courtship and marriage were essentially rites of initiation. Referring to the later development both of the sacramental status and of the initiatory nature of the marriage rite, J. Martos states: "Wedding ceremonies are always sacramental, at least in the broad sense of being celebrations of the sacred value of marriage, whatever it may be in a given culture, as well as in the sense of being rituals of initiation to a new style of life which is honored and meaningful, supported by social custom and religious tradition."[13]

For example, the seminal work of Arnold van Gennep, *Les Rites de Passage,* which became a landmark in cultural anthropology, provides a model of initiation in three parts: *Rites of Separation, Rites of Liminality,* and *Rites of Incorporation.*[14] These rites serve several purposes: helping an individual to become integrated into a cultural community, symbolizing the beginning of a new life, and offering meaning in the process of the transformation. The rites, in fact, correspond to the deep structures of marriage: the *rites of separation* are the betrothal, which involves a provisional commitment to a future marriage; the *rites of liminality* correspond to the engagement, a period of preparation culminating in *the rite of incorporation,* the wedding celebration.

Christian tradition teaches us two important lessons. First, the entire ongoing process of marriage is a rite of passage (an anthropological reality). Second, the nature of the marital union and conjugal life as a whole is sacramental (a theological reality). This stems not from the wedding rite, but from the consecration of the bridal pair at baptism. The gradual shift from the former home-based family rituals to the newer church wedding of the last centuries has "led to a secularization of the domestic and its alienation from the realm of the sacred, now identified with the church," state two experts on historical marriage rites. They rightly affirm that "the renewal of Christian marriage, then, would seem to be inseparable, finally, from the renewal of baptismal consciousness and from the profound consequences that will flow therefrom not only for the life of the family, but for the structures of the Church itself. Thus we shall have come full circle, back to the baptismal foundations of 'marriage in Christ' with which the Church's theology of marriage began."[15]

Bringing to mind an awareness of the baptismal foundations of marriage, that is, as being a "marriage in Christ," requires a shift in consciousness that will depend to a great extent on the Church and on the faith of the couple. The family is too vulnerable in today's secular atmosphere to provide the kind of support and insight required. The recently restored Rite of Christian Initiation of Adults offers the theological model and ritual framework for a three-stage preparation and celebration of marriage. Pope John Paul II echoed this new understanding of the dynamic nature of marriage when he envisioned it as a "journey of faith, which is similar to the catechumenate." Thus, the pastoral care of the family is to be regarded as a progressive action "step by step in the different stages of its formation and development."[16]

Consequently, solemnization of the wedding in church (the rite of incorporation) is not enough, because it is only part of the longer process of *realizing* the marital vocation. While the Church cannot disregard the canonical requirements, its role should be primarily theological and pastoral, so that a total ministry to marriage may offer a concrete, existential vision of the life-long vocation of the spouses.

## Marriage as Communion

Communion—the mutual sharing of the gift of self—is a fairly recent idea in the history of the theology of marriage. The preconciliar theology of the past approached marriage from the point of view of a juridical contract, one that existed solely for the purpose of mutual support and for biological procreation. The notion of marriage as one of the seven sacraments of the faith came about historically as an *extrinsic* addition.

The European existential philosophies, by focusing on individual consciousness, have contributed to the new and more profound perspective of marriage, one that recognizes its sacramentality as an *intrinsic* element. In particular, the philosophy of "existence as dialogue" (where one's existence is predicated on dynamic interchange) has influenced theologians such as Karl Bath and Karl Rahner, for example, who offer a more personal, less objective interpretation of the sacraments. By reaching back to the existential roots of a person's experience and by emphasizing the quality of the personal relationship, marriage becomes, according to a more recent definition, "the intimate community of life and love."[17]

Interestingly, the concept of "marriage as communion" is present in the patristic writings, especially in the Eastern patristic tradition, which understands marriage from the broader level of *sacrament as mystery*. John Chrysostom, who calls marriage the "sacrament of love," sees the intimate union of the spouses as integrated in the eternal redemptive mission of Christ. The African writer Tertullian offers an inspiring, even poetic spirituality of the communion of the marriage partners: "They are brother and sister, both servants of the same master; nothing divides them, either in flesh or in spirit. They are, in very truth, two in one flesh; and where there is but one flesh, there is also but one spirit."[18]

Thus, our present understanding—both through the symbolic model of "marriage as communion" and "marriage as a living sign of salvation" presented by *Gaudium et Spes*—reflects a paradigm shift. The contemporary vision of marriage expands from the covenantal base to interpret marriage as an intimate partnership operating from a center of love; it presents a positive view of sexuality and stresses the dignity and freedom of the human person.

A contemporary perspective of biblical revelation provides the foundation of a theology of "marriage as communion." The archetypes in Genesis where humankind is created in the "image of God" point to the interpersonal nature of the man-woman relationship, as well as to the "goodness" of the body and of the sexual relationship.

The Bible also witnesses in a unique way to the transcendent quality of the origin of human beings. God-*agape* is the source of life and
goodness in the marital communion—the "I-Thou" of dialogue and rec-
iprocity described by Martin Buber—which is dynamically enclosed by
and moves toward the ultimate mystery, God himself: "Extended, the
lines of relationship intersect in the eternal you."[19] The communion
between husband and wife points to innate sacramentality, and thus to
the saving reality of marriage at its very core.

As G. van der Leeuw wrote: "The old primitive world knew marriage as a sacrament in the literal sense of the word. This implies that in
some ways the end of marriage is not mutual comfort or procreation,
but salvation to be found through it."[20]

Finally, communion and sacrament imply one another; neither is
complete without the other. The Church's current theology of marriage,
which stresses the intrinsic connection, can be summarized as follows:
marriage is God's creative reality raised to the dignity of a *sacrament*,
established as a covenant of intimate communion of life and love, by
which the spouses *signify* and *share* in the mystery of love and fidelity
between Christ and the Church by faithfully loving each other.[21]

## Marriage as Covenant

When it is lived as mutual self-giving and intimate sharing between a
man and a woman in faithful love, marriage exemplifies the ideals of
the biblical concept of covenant. Moreover, because the union of the
two partners goes beyond any notion of a human contract, marriage is,
in fact, "a paradigm of human relationship and love"[22] and, thus, is
covenantal in its core.

Inspired by the nuptial symbolism of the covenant, Paul sees in the
marital union an image of Christ's love for his Church (Eph 5:32), and
uses "the language of the sacramental sign-value."[23] Following the same
line of theological thinking, patristic theology drew insights from the
biblical paradigm to describe marriage as the "image and likeness" of
God's covenant with humanity, and perceived in marriage a particular
way of living out the Christ-Church spousal mystery. Thus, the ancient
as well as the patristic view of "marriage as covenant" is based on scriptural revelation, and is, therefore, sacramental, albeit not in the technical sense of later medieval theology.

Since *covenant* is the graced and intimate personal encounter between God and his people fulfilled in Christ, it is the cornerstone of Christian sacramentality, especially the sacramentality of marriage. Marriage is, in fact, *the sacramental covenant.* This covenantal partnership, a human mystery, is in itself a way of holiness, that is, a saving reality, as the Church teaches. "The conjugal covenant instituted by the Creator... already is in a true and proper sense a journey toward salvation."[24] This is expressed by the ritual celebration and living out of the sacrament "in spirit and in truth."

The intrinsic relationship between covenant and marriage is rooted in the history of salvation in a double sense: (1) *symbolic* and (2) *archetypal.*

On one hand, the *symbolic* language opens up a new dimension to the reality of God. By God's initiative people come closer to God and are introduced into the divine mystery. In this way marriage is part of God's transcendent mystery. Certainly, a symbolic perspective cannot be taken literally. But, nevertheless, *the heart of the symbolic message of the covenant*, in light of our faithful interpretation of revelation, can provide a source of meaning and strength for contemporary spouses as they live out their relationship in all its ethical demands. In this regard, the life-creating and salvific message of the biblical covenant is most relevant in contemporary religious consciousness.

On the other hand, the biblical covenant also represents the *archetypal* model of Christian marriage. Conjugal love is modeled on the faithful and compassionate initiative of God's covenantal love, whose ultimate prototype *(in the archetypal sense)* is the marriage of Christ and his bride, the Church, in which Christ sacrifices everything for her, even his life. It is the couple's faith, as expressed in their lives, that renders them a people of the covenant and consequently makes their union a sign and a Christian sacrament of the covenant. This "great mystery" is the foundation of the marriage sacrament. The spouses find here both *the archetype* of their marital spirituality and a source of transforming spiritual power.

### Marriage as Sacrament

What follows is a reflection of the two different, although not separate, dimensions of "marriage as sacrament": (1) *human mystery* and (2) *saving reality*. This discussion will point to those specific elements of marriage that define it as a profoundly Christian sacrament.

## Human Mystery

Faithful love is the very essence of the marital partnership and the heart of its meaning; it is unconditional fidelity that renders marriage a primary and universal symbol. Moreover, since marriage is common to all peoples, regardless of cultural or spiritual orientation, it is the original, universal sacramentality known to human life, and is acknowledged to be such by all religions. Thus, the sacramental mystery of marriage is anchored fully in a human reality; it is a *radically human sacrament*. Its meaning is the salvation of a personal community. It cannot be reduced to a sacred function or ritual, because it is a sign in all its human fullness (the way the spouses live) and transcendent reality.

While the centrality of conjugal love constitutes the human foundation of the sacrament, when two Christians marry, God is present within their human partnership. Thus, the partnership has been subsumed by the redeeming force of Christ, who is part of creation and head of it (Col 1:16). David Thomas extends the sacramental meaning to five distinct, although related, aspects of Christian marriage: the sexual, the creative, the loving, the ecclesial, and the spiritual—which are organically related and mutually interdependent.[25]

From this perspective, the sacramental sign-value of marriage embraces the whole of life. This intimate partnership establishes the couple in a mutual, faithful, fruitful, permanent, and public union. Thus, love and sexuality, procreation and caring, intimacy and communication, and all the hopes and struggles of the intimate and familial lives of the spouses are not just natural phenomena, but are salvific mystery.

## Saving Reality

Marriage is not only a radically human sacrament, it is also a sacrament of faith. It is a saving reality in the specific Christian sense, for the Lord "encounters Christian spouses through the sacrament of marriage."[26] While considering the baptismal character of marriage, Scheeben points out that there is an essential and intrinsic relationship between sacramental marriage and the mystery of the spousal relationship of

Christ and the Church. Marriage participates actively and effectively in that fundamental mystery.[27]

The specific elements of Christian marriage stem from this Christ-Church spousal relationship. Consequently, *faith, baptism*, and *community,* respectively, constitute the personal, ontological, and ecclesial qualifications of the Christian sacramentality of marriage. Baptism is the foundation on which the intimate partnership of the spouses is built in the image of Christ, and through which the partnership becomes (ontologically) a "new way of being" in the Church. (The personal and covenantal orientations of marriage, noted previously, include and presuppose the institutional and contractual aspects, although the latter are subordinate to the personal, covenantal dimensions of marriage.)

## Marriage as Partnership

The Second Vatican Council's well-known definition of marriage as an "intimate partnership of married life and love," cited above, represents a paradigm shift in the Catholic theology of marriage, away from the overly canonical and rationalistic view of the past to today's emphasis on the "whole" person. Contemporary theology thus takes into account what happens in the total life experience of husband and wife and finds here the real sacrament in its own right. Although the models we have previously considered, such as "marriage as communion," have included the partnership aspect, this symbolic model examines the conjugal union against the background of a renewed Christian anthropology, psychology, and historical consciousness, and envisions marriage as *a process.* This model, therefore, includes the whole of family life, that is the marital as well as the parental covenant, for "the family reveals marriage as a social sacrament."[28]

Partnership here does not assign roles or define degrees of responsibility. It is understood in the personalist, not the legalistic sense. Each spouse has full ownership of self and gives her or his total self to the spouse for life. In this sense, the marriage partnership is not a mutual accommodation of fifty/fifty, but one hundred percent commitment from each spouse.

If all of life is "graced," marriage is especially so, because of its nuptial connotations, which are symbolized by the spouses' sexually differentiated bodies. As John Paul II teaches: "The human body, with its sex, and its masculinity and femininity, seen in the very mystery of creation, is not only a source of fruitfulness and pro-creation...but includes right 'from the beginning' the nuptial attribute, that is, the capacity of expressing love in which the man-person becomes a gift [and] by means of this gift...fulfills the very meaning of his being and existence."[29] In their willingness to surrender to one another, the spouses are truly a gift of "grace," a healing sacrament to each other, for they make present God's gift of himself. (Due to human frailty, however, this sacramental potential may remain unfulfilled.)

Finally, from the perspective of *process*, the partnership model provides a vision of the couple as a dynamic entity with a past, a present, and a future. A partnership is sustained and grows—if it does grow—but also, and inevitably, the couple lives with paradox and uncertainty in the process of growing and "becoming." In simple terms, the sacramentality of the partnership is never something fully accomplished, because partnership is a journey, an ongoing, shifting reality, not a static commodity.

This historical vision thus implies the larger, indeed the life-long *process of sacramentality*, which cannot be reduced to the wedding rites. Indeed, the process of sacramentality consists of three phases: *baptismal*, *celebrative*, and *eucharistic*. Baptism (of the believer), the primary and initiatory sacrament, is the foundation of marriage, and thus constitutes the preparatory phase of the sacramentality of marriage; the wedding rite, the public and ecclesial actualization of the dignity and holiness of marriage in Christ, is the celebrative phase; and the Eucharist, "the source and climax of the Christian life," is the continuing, life-long phase that provides nourishment for spiritual formation, "bread for the journey."

As in the case of each of the seven sacraments, the popular language of church ritual conveys the deeper reality of the Christian faith: We are *made* Christians, but we are also to *become* Christians. "Our language of *getting* betrays a *reification* or *thingification* of sacrament. Actually, sacraments are ritual celebrations, steps in a process of growth. Specifically, for our discussion of marriage, one simply cannot *get married*. Two persons can *grow married*, *become married*, or *become divorced* (or, I suppose, *remain stagnant*). The sacramental ritual is a step in a process...again, the goal is to engage in the mystery of *becoming married*."[30]

The contemporary theological perspective that embraces the concepts of *the process* and *the history* of the partnership must also take into account what the human sciences, specifically psychology, have to say about times of change and inevitable crisis in a family's life cycle. In particular, the psychological constructs of *togetherness* and *individuality* offer a common-sense view of how marriages change and mature. "Like the oceans, marriages are dynamic, with tides rising and falling on a consistent, sequential basis."[31] For example, when the couple grows older, eventually the children leave home, and a different kind of partnership emerges. Only a view of the partnership that integrates this dynamic sacramentality of change, or sacramentality which is "in process," with the many other modern aspects of the different stages of the marital, family journey, can approach the wholeness and reality that is the fulfillment of grace.

## Sacrament of Love and Marital Breakdown

Marriage is a rite of initiation in its own right, and today's needed integration of human and Christian values cannot successfully occur without an honest, sustained ritual process of marriage preparation, celebration, and support. This ritual process is, in fact, not only demanded by the personal complexities of marriage but is also integral to the sacramental nature of marriage. Thus, we will first focus on the newly revised Roman ritual for celebrating marriage.[32]

But the event of grace goes beyond the ritual celebration. Those who marry are made sharers of the "great mystery," a mystery of grace for their lifetime marital vocation. Thus, the sacrament establishes a permanent bond between the spouses, a bond that Christian tradition (following the mandate of Christ) calls indissoluble. Regrettably, this ideal of indissolubility is not always realized. Because the Christian community faces today a severe crisis of marital breakdown, it is important to address the problem. Our next consideration will be to attempt to clarify and focus the issues on divorce and remarriage, and second, to propose a way forward.

## *A Grand Feast of Life and Love*

Among all the varied social and ethnic customs that form the cultural context of the wedding rituals, the liturgy of marriage is the centerpiece. It is the event that can evoke the whole range of values and emotions of a communitarian, festive celebration in a faith experience. An attitude of warmth that signals a gracious welcome, "showing that the Church shares their joy" (Rite of Marriage), is very important and will create the right atmosphere for a joyful and prayerful celebration—a grand feast.

Approved by Pope John Paul II and promulgated in Rome in 1990, the new Order of Celebrating Marriage is the liturgical response to recent post–Vatican II theological, liturgical, and cultural developments. The liturgy sees the celebration of marriage as a total giving of mutual service and a sacramental action that integrates the human values of conjugal life. It reflects a cultural sensitivity to the modern world, in that it expresses the idea of the equality and the complementarity of the spouses. The new Roman Ritual will be analyzed in the light of: (a) its catechetical and formative components; (b) liturgical rationale and structure; and (c) the new features of the liturgical celebration.

*Components*

In teaching the spouses something concrete about the heart of their marriage journey, sacramental liturgy provides a foundational conjugal spirituality, namely, the central form of their freedom to faithful and fulfilling love. But all this cannot happen without regaining the primacy of the spiritual element in church weddings. This paramount theme of the biblical model of the covenant provides an integrated vision of the spirituality of marriage. Specifically, the following themes can be drawn from the introduction to the Roman Ritual.

First, marriage is seen in its divine source from which its goodness, unity, purpose, force, and strength are derived. The idea of a sacred and sanctifying bond, originating in God and effected by the irrevocable consent of the spouses, is stressed throughout.

Second, this human and divine bond forms an indissoluble covenant that presents the image of God's creating and redeeming relationship with us and raises it to sacramental dignity and holiness by the Bridegroom Jesus. The created reality of marriage is a major theme of the marriage liturgy where it is presented not simply as a historical fact but in relation to the "great mystery" (Eph 5:32).

Third, all these essential aspects converge in the same covenantal unity, Christology. A sacramental marriage signifies and shares in the sacrificial and transformative, healing and fruitful mystery of grace by which Christ encounters the spouses.

The liturgical reform brought about an awareness of the creative presence of the Spirit in the eucharistic and sacramental actions. In the 1990 ritual the function of the Holy Spirit has been made explicit in five new prayers of the nuptial blessing. The Holy Spirit will remain the pledge of God's provident care in the couple's marriage journey of inevitable human failures, joys, trials, and triumphs.

*Framework*

Ritually, two centers of the celebration are key to the rite's structure: the exchange of consent and the nuptial blessing. They are the two high points of the liturgy. A constant in the historical rituals of marriage during the eleventh and twelfth centuries, they express two essential aspects of the celebration: the human root of love manifested by the parties' consent and the covenantal and eucharistic summit that seals the Christian character of marriage. The consent of the spouses received by the presider and the nuptial blessing remain the two specific features of all Roman Catholic marriage rituals.

The nuptial blessing evokes God's salvific events exemplified by the saving reality of marriage. The liturgical content of this blessing centers on the reality of biblical symbolism, the heart of which is Christ's Easter, reenacted in the present conjugal bond. This blessing is placed at the eucharistic summit following the Lord's Prayer. According to tradition, the eucharistic covenant is the seal of the covenant of marriage.

By way of summary, we can broaden the liturgical framework and interpret the sacramental mystery of marriage by envisioning marriage in terms of three poles: the *biblical revelation* of the covenant, which becomes an actual saving event in the lives of the spouses: the *conjugal partnership* of full ownership of each spouse, which constitutes its sacramental root; and the *ritual celebration* in church, which is the symbolic expression of its mystery of love and life.

*Celebration*

Planning and preparation are demanded, not only because this is a sacrament of faith but especially because the couples are the ministerial principles of the ritual. A meaningful liturgy in a truly prayerful atmosphere should become a high point in the religious journey of the couple and serve as a wellspring for growth in their conjugal spiritual life. In this case, liturgy becomes central, not only expressing the essential value of faith, but also as the paradigm for the spirituality of conjugal beginning and development. The assembly celebrates not to make marriage holy, but because it is already holy and requires a public and ecclesial expression as a sign of faith.

The eucharistic liturgy is the preferred way to celebrate marriage, since both realities are intimately connected. As the ritual states: "The Eucharist is the very source of Christian marriage . . . In this sacrifice of the New and Eternal Covenant Christian spouses encounter the source from which their own marriage covenant flows, is interiorly structured and continuously renewed."[33] "Through the sacrament of the Body and Blood of Christ, the Lord will unite in love the couple he has joined in this holy bond."[34] The symbolic action in which the core meaning of marriage and Eucharist intersect is the couple's sharing in the Lord's eucharistic body and blood—the nuptial banquet of Christ's love.

## Reconsidering Divorce and Remarriage

Most cultures and religions consider marriage a life-long sacred bond. Stability is still the reality in many countries untouched by the Western culture of modernity. Here divorce is non-existent, because in traditional cultures marriage rests on the solid foundation of a network of family relationships and societal support. The outcome is unity and permanence in marriage. In contrast to this pre-modern world view characterized by strong family relationships, marriage in modern and secularized societies is a foundering institution. Without support even from fragile families in a fragmented social system, married life suffers the effects of erosion and possible disintegration. When divorce is widespread, the pastoral challenges to the Christian community are enormous.

However, while cultural factors may be crucial, stable and healthy families are possible in any given culture. Marital breakdown and wounded relationships are real manifestations of the stark reality of sin in human existence. Jesus, who stood in the prophetic tradition of renewing the covenant's ideals, called for reestablishing God's primordial plan of an unbreakable pledge of a lifetime fidelity between husband and wife: "But from the beginning of creation, God made them male and female...the two shall become one flesh. So they are no longer two, but one flesh...Therefore what God has joined together, let no one separate" (Mark 10:6–9).

This *logion* of Jesus against divorce is consistent in the apostolic tradition, because it appears in the Synoptics and in the letters of Paul, albeit in two complementary traditions applying it as absolutely (Mark 10:2–12; Luke 16:18; 1 Cor 7:10–11) or qualified: "except on the ground of unchastity" (Matt 5:32), and also in the exceptional case of an unbeliever's spouse (1 Cor 7:12–16). The interpretation of this apostolic mandate gave rise to two different Christian traditions. On one hand, the Latin and Roman Catholic tradition maintains the absolute indissolubility of sacramental *and* consummated (canon 1142) marriages even in the case of the sin of adultery. On the other hand, the Greek Orthodox tradition, affirming its belief in indissolubility, applies a praxis of flexibility in dissolving "dead" marriages. The former tradition developed the tribunal discipline which, using a legal procedure, has the authority to declare the sacramental bond null and invalid. The latter originated out of the guiding principle of *oikonomia*, which calls for an exercise of pastoral ministry based on God's everlasting mercy.

Both ancient traditions will be the starting point and the basis of our approach to the following topics: (1) the bond of marriage in its unity and indissolubility; (2) the Church's response to marital breakdown; and (3) admission to the Eucharist of civilly remarried people. Each of these implies very complex issues, which the following reflection will attempt to approach only summarily.

## The Bond of Marriage

The marital bond can be considered from the triple perspective of the nature of love, the gospel ideals, and the sacramental pledge. These are tied together and grounded in marital unity and indissolubility.

Fidelity is the foundation of love, not vice versa. True love is unconditional and lasting. These qualities are at the core of marital fidelity. They create the one-body partnership of a grace-filled interpersonal communion that is in itself indissoluble. This unconditional one-body existential reality is at the heart of the creation narrative (Genesis) and the basis of humanity itself. Other considerations could be added in support of the definitive and exclusive surrender of the spouses to each other, such as the raising of children who would also be able to love and trust.

The gospel ideals enshrined in Jesus' own unambiguous teaching restore and reaffirm the call to total personal self-giving inscribed in the human heart. These ideals do not permit withholding something, spiritual estrangement, or the betrayal of abandonment. Finally, the sacrament renders marriage indissoluble because it is an actual symbol, that is, a permanent reality of grace flowing from the transforming and unifying love of the Spirit of Christ—bridegroom of the Church—into the hearts of the spouses. Therefore, the sanctity and permanence of marriage are God's will for all, but especially for the Christian couple who, sealed by the Spirit and grace, make present the never-ending love of God.

The above considerations perhaps reflect lofty and unrealistic ideals that neglect the fragile side of human nature. Marriage can fail, for despite the good intentions for a lifetime commitment of love, the ideal might tragically never be able to be realized. Translating this into canonical terms using the personalist theology of Vatican II, we could say that in such a case the couple's giving love to each other, of its nature indissoluble, did not mature, and consequently was barely "consummated." The fact that marriage shares in the contingencies of the ever-changing and unpredictable human journey, especially in today's cultural upheaval, provides a realistic vision of a potentially fallible human symbol of God's everlasting infallible love.

A balanced consideration integrates the institutional and subjective aspects of marriage. The emphasis on the quality of the personal relationship, which is evolving, is not opposed to the ecclesial dimension of marriage. This "becoming" aspect, or the call to *become* holy (vocation), does not render the covenantal bond less "real," but rather revitalizes it. It does not deny, but reaffirms the ontological foundation of the sacramentality of marriage. From the consideration of marriage as process,

Bernard Cooke examines the question of the indissolubility of Christian marriage:

> To put it in biblical terms, a Christian marriage, like any other created realities, does not exist absolutely; like anything in creation, particularly anything in human history, a marriage exists eschatologically; it is tending toward its fulfillment beyond this world. However, the fact that it does not yet have in full fashion the modalities—such as indissolubility—that should characterize it does not mean that it is devoid of them. A Christian marriage is indissoluble, but short of the *eschaton* it is *incompletely indissoluble*...[It] already realizes to some degree the indissolubility which can mirror the divine fidelity to humans, but it cannot yet lay claim to the absoluteness which will come with the fullness of the Kingdom. Similarly, two Christians can be very genuinely and sacramentally married, but they are still being married to one another; their union can always become richer and stronger.[35]

## The Church's Response to Marital Breakdown

Divorce means the end of a dream and of a future, often accompanied with pain and anguish, and in some cases an experience comparable to the death of a loved one. The statistics are well known and alarming. Divorce affects millions of men and women in distress, many of whom feel unsupported and cut off from their Catholic roots. How can the Church promote and affirm sacramental marriage while at the same time reaching out effectively to those living through the trauma of a marital breakdown? While this brief discussion cannot address particular pastoral options and specific canonical implications, it can provide a focus for understanding the Western discipline of annulment and the Orthodox tradition of *oikonomia*.

The Roman Catholic position on the indissolubility of marriage is summarily reiterated in the *Catechism of the Catholic Church*:

> Thus *the marriage bond* has been established by God himself in such a way that a marriage concluded and consummated

between baptized persons can never be dissolved. This bond, which results from the free human act of the spouses and their consummation of the marriage, is a reality, henceforth irrevocable, and gives rise to a covenant guaranteed by God's fidelity. The Church does not have the power to contravene this disposition of divine wisdom.[36]

*Annulment*

From the twelfth century onward the Church developed from Roman law the canonical principles of a marriage contract and the process of annulment. This process applies juridical criteria to a very complex human reality. Marriage with a non-baptized person can be dissolved in favor of the faith of the baptized spouse, as in the case of converts, or a divorced Christian spouse (Pauline privilege, 1 Cor 7:15). The Church declares non-existent and annulled the bond of a sacramental marriage found to be invalid, but it cannot dissolve a valid and consummated marriage contract between baptized persons. The debated questions raised in regard to this long-standing practice are too many to list here, and they are well known. Thus, Timothy Buckley's enlightening book on the plight of divorced Catholics speaks of a theological impasse: "The present discipline of the Church is not based on a sound theology of sacrament and Church . . . the discipline codified in the law does not reflect [the] theological development [of Vatican II]."[37]

Marital breakdown is a human tragedy that challenges the Church to a supporting, healing, and compassionate ministry toward those who experience it. In fact, diocesan tribunals have been undergoing a substantial change in approaches and attitudes toward those seeking a human and evangelical transition from an irretrievably lost marriage. On one hand, the 1983 Code of Canon Law adopted the new theology of Vatican II (canons 1055, 1057) and paid more attention to the insights of behavioral sciences (cf. canon 1095). On the other hand, the annulment system became more efficient (in 1985, 36,180 annulments were granted in the United States) and jurisprudence in the area of marriage, at least in the United States, developed into a more spiritual pastoral ministry of healing, recovery, and reconciliation. Thus, the Canon Law Society of America has stated that the threefold mission of diocesan tribunals is: to judge, to heal, and to educate.

*Oikonomia*

The 1980 Rome Synod on the family presented a request to Pope John Paul for the exploration of the Orthodox tradition of *oikonomia*. This may contribute to a more compassionate ministry to divorced and remarried Catholics. The importance of the Orthodox approach stems from the fact that the celebration and pastoral ministry of marriage was developed from an eminently spiritual perspective, parallel to a profound theology of marriage. We now turn to the Eastern tradition.

The theological term *oikonomia* is used to refer to God's ongoing and saving relationship with us and for us. It also refers more specifically to the pastoral economy of the Church which, interpreting the Father's loving compassion, gives dispensation from its law in particular cases. The Orthodox theology of marriage is profoundly rooted in the divine mystery and its doctrine is enshrined in the writings of the Greek fathers of the Church, such as Origen (d. ca. 254), and especially St. Basil (d. 379). This patristic basis with a firm belief in indissolubility as doctrinal principle provides the greatest hope for creative exchange and mutual enrichment, especially at the theological level, between the Eastern and Western traditions. Both traditions have much to learn from each other. The latter followed Jerome's (d. 420) and Augustine's (d. 430) teaching of opposition to remarriage after divorce. By contrast, the former adopted an individualized approach of compassion and forgiveness, which characterized most patristic writings in readmitting to the Eucharist a remarried person after divorce.

Pastoral leniency and a flexible praxis prevailed in the interpretation of the teaching of scripture with regard to the application of the evangelical ideal of the marriage bond. The Orthodox approach discourages remarriage, because of the belief that marriage is "not dissolved by the death of one of the partners, but creates between them an eternal bond."[38] Nevertheless, Christ's teaching cannot be reduced to legal prescriptions and his mandate cannot be adequately translated into a "juridical" formulation. Thus the gospel *oikonomia* of grace came to be a guiding principle for tolerance and flexibility on account of human weakness, for God's compassion supersedes human law. Only the first marriage is blessed in Church during the Eucharist. Annulments and permissions to remarry are given after some kind of penance and based on a broad interpretation of grounds (flowing from Matt 5:32

and 19:9), which are all reducible to the reality of actual death of the sacramental union and binding love in the spousal relationship.

## Admission to Communion after Divorce and Remarriage

Christian marriage originates in the paschal mystery of Christ, and the Eucharist is the sacrament of the paschal mystery of Christ. Thus, the Eucharist is key to the meaning of marriage and its progressive realization during the entire life of the couple. The spouse who, sustained by a living faith, remains loyal in times of turmoil, and even spiritual and emotional darkness, rises up to the height of the cross and experiences in the process spiritual transformation and growth. This spouse shares in hope, sometimes heroically, in the eucharistic and freeing cup of Christ's paschal mystery (cf. Matt 20:22–23).

In fact, most couples start out feeling the promise of faith. But often after a time, when problems arise, the promise appears to be broken. Instead of a place of love, the home becomes a place of anger where hurt is piled on top of hurt. At this juncture, many couples split up (this is true for at least 40 percent in the United States). However, it is at this point that the *covenantal* aspect of marriage becomes most significant. Courageous trust—not that the wife, for example, trusts in her husband, but that she places her trust in the *larger meaning of the marriage*—allows one to live in the *transcendent* dimension of the relationship, believing that God is somehow present in the brokenness. It can be a time of active "waiting" for the Lord, albeit a painful time when counseling may be essential, but it can also be a profound spiritual experience, even a time of healing.

## Need for Outreach and Discernment

This stance is counter-cultural and many people fail to measure up to this Christian ideal. In spite of the promise of "forever," many couples do experience a disintegration of the relationship for complex reasons. But to deny them participation in eucharistic communion means that they will be excluded from a main source of nourishment for their spiritual life. This might come at a critical moment when the divorced person, recovering from a traumatic experience of loss, guilt, and rejection, is able to establish a new family and even develop a deeper religious maturity and commitment to the Church. Our mandate is to reach out to such persons by embodying Christ's healing ministry of compassion. His table companionship with the excluded—sinners and outcasts— remains a prophetic sign of God's present grace of mercy.

However, in an attempt to protect marriage indissolubility "the Church reaffirms her practice, which is based upon sacred scripture, of not admitting to Eucharistic communion divorced persons who have remarried."[39] The reasons for entering a second marriage are many and diverse. There are those "who are sometimes subjectively certain in conscience that their previous and irreparably destroyed marriage had never been valid."[40] The situations of divorced people are each unique, and although the cases reach epidemic proportions today, the Church still calls for an exercise of careful discernment of these situations. Staying together seems to be impossible in many cases. Thus, the Church calls divorced persons to reconciliation in the sacrament of penance, which would admit them to the Eucharist if they agree to "take on themselves the duty to live in complete continence."[41] This appears to be in most cases humanly impossible in light of the dynamics and meaning of marital sexual fulfillment and love.

This painful situation is the reason for the greatest number of defections from the Church's membership. Most people ignore its teaching. Others, more mature in the faith, seek reconciliation, believing in their hearts that God's compassion has forgiven them, and that in "good conscience" nothing prevents them from receiving the Eucharist. In this particular case, the principle of internal forum has been invoked. An individual makes a conscientious judgment on a personal basis, ideally after careful discernment with a priest. In recent years, three German bishops proposed this option, which is within the context of traditional Catholic moral teaching, calling upon pastors "to exercise careful discernment of situations." However, a clarification of the issue came in 1994 from Cardinal Ratzinger of the Congregation for the Doctrine of the Faith condemning the use of the internal forum and calling for observance of the current discipline of the external forum, arguing that marriage "is essentially a public reality."[42] Obviously, a balance between both forums is needed.

We will never find a perfect pastoral solution. The complete answer only comes from God, who knows how to "write straight with our crooked lines." At any rate, these complex issues cannot be reduced to the ecclesiastical framework or even to the question of admission to the sacraments. In fact, the two questions of indissolubility and participation in communion should be distinct (according to such theologians as Kasper, Ratzinger, and Örsy). Although the available pastoral options, such as annulment, are crucial, divorced couples also have other ways to cope with their situations, including support groups and other pastoral initiatives involving faith conversion and growth to Christian maturity. Clearly, this is a time to reexamine the psychological and spiritual factors required in forming a genuine Christian conjugal community.

## Sacramental Mystery

The law of Christ cannot be reduced to ecclesiastical law. Going far beyond the polarization between simple leniency and harsh inexorability, the sacramental mystery of marriage itself as interpretative key remains central. It is impossible to understand either New Testament writings or the Christian tradition on marriage without reading the issues raised today through the lens of the celebrated and lived sacramental mystery. The following example, which a canon lawyer provides, illustrates the implications of this approach. The 1983 Code of Canon Law avoids notions of love and intimacy, which the marriage liturgy portrays as essential to marriage. "But even beyond the somewhat narrow tribunal implications...there is also a broader implication here; it would bring into harmony the *lex orandi* and the *lex credendi*...The liturgy, in short, is a teacher of doctrine."[43] The sacramental mystery of marriage (we have already presented in this chapter the theological implications) is a foundational source of inspiration for the Church as it confronts severe dilemmas and seeks an enriching vision.

Therefore, we need a paradigmatic shift from the sacramental *contractual* mind-set to a deeper theology of sacramental *mystery*. Making the tribunal's process more pastorally oriented will not be enough. Likewise, in aiming for the Christian ideal, we need a preventive strategy through the whole journey of marriage (preparation, celebration, support, as well as reaching out to the divorced) rooted in true theological principles of sacramentality. Canon law and the tribunals, though important, should have an ancillary role. In truth, the essential indissolubility of Christian marriage must be safeguarded in today's climate of moral fragmentation, but an undiscerning and external observance of the law, which is alienating in itself, amounts to a denial of God's forever abiding compassion and a blatant contradiction of the Spirit of Christ.

In summary, one wonders whether the juridical, conceptual framework will ever adequately respond to an extremely complex existential and spiritual problem. Canon law has been predominant in the Catholic theology and pastoral practice of marriage and remarriage. This centuries-old process originated not from a truly theological inspiration of Christian sacramentality, but from the lack of it. The gap between an all-embracing Christian view of the human values of marriage and a corresponding appropriate pastoral policy can be bridged coherently only by going back full circle to the broad meaning of marriage as *sacramental mystery* rooted in scripture and tradition. This primal frame of reference has profound implications. From the beginning, this has been our thesis and the heart of the conceptual context of the present chapter on marriage.

# Conclusion:
# The Signs of Christian Freedom

The quest and struggle for freedom remains characteristic of our times. Even though a longing for freedom is always present in human existence, the pursuit of freedom changes with situations and cultures. What does freedom mean in our world of rationalism, secularism, and individualism? On the one hand, the culture of modernity with its critical social thinking has enhanced freedom. On the other hand, the same culture has compromised freedom through the loss of a sense of communal solidarity, a crisis in moral values, and a weakening of the sense of God's mystery in the world.

From the theology of the Christian sacraments, this book comes full circle to a re-consideration of the Christian meaning of sacramentality. It looks at the sacramental interplay involving *Christian praxis, prophetic symbolism,* and *the human person in Christ* from the perspective of their social relevance and their wider spiritual implications. These three dimensions are the essential means by which sacraments become the living signs of Christian freedom as they interpret the fundamental experience of what it is to be a Christian. The reflections that follow will focus on the importance of sacramental life and sacramental imagination as a central source of the Church's prophetic action in society.

Sacraments, God's self-giving embrace of the whole of life, are both signs and vehicles of freedom. They represent four interrelated levels of the Christian world view: (a) *Christ*, the embodiment of God's freedom to the world; (b) *Church*, the historical sign of Christ's salvific freedom; (c) the *person*, the bearer of the gift and responsibility of freedom; and (d) *society and cosmos*, the entire creation "groaning" to be set free.

A consideration of authentic freedom is necessary for an integral and broad-based understanding of the sacraments. Spiritual hunger for true and joyful personal, ecclesial, and social freedom, should find satisfaction through a liberating experience of faith in genuine sacramental celebration and praxis. Such a consideration can be framed under three headings: sacraments are (1) signs of the prophetic mission of the Church; (2) signs that speak the Christian freedom; and (3) signs of the liberating presence of the risen Lord.

## Signs of the Prophetic Mission of the Church

Sacraments touch the deepest mystery of human life and freedom. They draw their power from the heart of the mystery of Christ. Thus it is that St. Augustine, who saw the world filled with sacraments, rightly envisaged them as "sacraments of Christian freedom."[1] They exist for the spiritual transformation and self-realization of the human person in the fullest possible sense.

Sacramental celebrations, the self-giving of God, that One in whom we find the absolute freedom and the experience of wholeness, are liberative actions of God for his people. In fact, "All that God is and means as a liberating presence in human life has become visible in Jesus. But it was by particular, concrete actions that Jesus made God's love clear to his contemporaries. So it is today: in and through his Church he gives visible signs of his liberating presence in the concrete details of our lives. Among these signs are the sacraments."[2] Christ is the symbolic and real expression of God's liberating presence. Nothing less than Christ can bring true freedom to the world. The key to a liberative praxis is consequently a regaining of the impact of the "good news" of sacraments.

Sacraments are actions of the Church. By their inner dynamism they bring about freedom and transform the human person. As the actualization of the Church, sacraments express symbolically the fundamental experiences of its treasure of faith. They call for celebration in a believing and challenging environment in which the person is reborn, nurtured, reconciled, healed, and given joyful hope. Here the experience of freedom is already at work in the hearts of believers and in their attitudes toward life.

Sacraments, however, are more than private matters in the religious practice of the individual, more than mere sacred signs of a community centered on itself. Alive with the Holy Spirit directing it toward missionary outreach, the Church cannot live unconnected to social reality and apart from the world. Personal experience and a communal spirit, necessary as they are, cannot preclude a wider role for the sacramental Church that by its nature looks outward. They should point beyond liturgy toward the universal mission of the transformation of society from within. They call forth "the new heaven and the new earth." In fact, sacraments are not only signs of community; they also signify the Christian community's calling to be itself "a sign and instrument ... of communion with God and of the unity of the entire human race."[3] The Church's sacraments and the Church become prophetic signs of freedom for people and their history.

In the background there lies a new vision of total reality about God, the world, the Church, and the sacraments, a vision introduced by Vatican II. One cannot think of these dimensions separately and statically. They enjoy an intrinsic and dynamic relatedness within which the saving presence of God's self-gift embraces all humanity and all human history. From a symbolic perspective, we call this overall created reality "cosmic sacramentality," since it reveals God. Inherent in patristic tradition, these visions are today more relevant than ever for a world of heightened social and global consciousness.

In seeing the world as a sacrament of communion with God, Alexander Schmemann tries to retrieve the ancient sacramental world view. He attempts "to relate the world's problems, hopes and difficulties to the sacramental experience which has always constituted the very heart of the Orthodox world view, to indicate the cosmic and catholic, i.e., the all-embracing, all-assuming and all-transforming nature and scope of Christian *leitourgia* [liturgy]."[4]

The broadening of the Christian vision of sacramental symbolism and content from the realm of the private to an ecclesial spirituality of social and cosmic corporate responsibility does not weaken the traditional "sacramental principle." It affirms it. This principle, embedded in the mystery of the incarnation, perceives God's presence in every person and in all created reality. Furthermore, seeing a sacrament as a societal symbol does not devalue its contemplative dimension and the sense of awe and transcendence that should be present in every celebration. On the contrary, prophetic praxis substantiates the sacramental mystery. Personal piety and the sense of an awe-inspiring rite do not oppose social consciousness; interior listening does not preclude active participation; an atmosphere of fiesta does not negate the need for reverence.

In recent church teachings, this emphasis on solidarity has shown itself in language about preferential yet not exclusive love for the poor. Vital corporate sacraments are the very matrix of a freeing evangelization. They are the answer to "the great aspirations to liberation of the contemporary world."[5] Still, the language of our sacramental celebrations often corresponds to another social order; it does not voice a spirituality relevant to the actual world's social realities. It frequently fails to proclaim a dramatic outcry for justice, peace, and other aspirations of today's world.

The problem of freedom, then, and the reality of salvation are closely connected. Christian Duquoc points out that the title "free man" best describes the historical impact of Jesus. He is the one whom early Christian communities came to proclaim as the Christ in their liberating experience of faith.[6]

Spirituality is crucial to sacramental participation if it is to bring about freedom. To search for God means to journey toward a freedom—or, better, be drawn to a freedom—that has as its point of departure encounter with Jesus Lord.[7] Such freedom is the Spirit's work in individuals and in communities of manifest love and active faith. True spirituality is holistic and already liberative in itself. The primacy of this radical and interior liberation, however, must not deter Christians in their social and historical task of "restoring everything in Christ."

Christian sacramentality emphatically rejects false dichotomies between sacraments or spirituality and secular involvement. Worship is the larger context of the sacraments. Indian theologian Aloysius Pieris rightly stresses the importance of regarding worship as flowing from what he calls "the liturgy of life." He names this liturgy of life "the matrix of all sacramental expressions, for it is the context of a living encounter with God in Christ. Sacraments, life and mysticism cannot be artificially reconciled if they are uprooted from their natural environment, which is the paschal mystery of Christ continued in the (secular) lives and struggles, in the deaths and triumphs of his members."[8]

The concrete steps of the process of freedom in sacramental praxis change in the all-but-infinite variety of historical contexts. We name now just a few contextual considerations associated with liberation: (a) the interpretation of expressions and symbols of popular religious expression; (b) the relation between service as a consequence of faith and celebration of "the feast"; (c) the concept of life and a people's key religious traits; and (d) the experiences of women and their role in the Church.

The proponents of liberation theology gave serious consideration to the problem of freedom in the context of oppression. This theology developed after the council in Latin America; its effects are felt globally today. Liberation theology sees salvation taking historical form in the process of authentic liberation. Emphasizing the social implications of Christian praxis and the need for a process of inculturation for sacramental celebrations, liberation theologians stressed the sacraments' prophetic dimension and historical efficacy. The Latin American bishops also indicated a liberating understanding of sacramental praxis: "the privileged moment of communion and participation for an evangelization that leads to integral, authentic Christian liberation."[9]

There will always be a need for Christians to struggle to bring about a society grounded in love because new forms of alienation falsely claiming self-liberation will emerge. Whether social or political, psychological or moral, they ultimately derive from the mystery of sin in the world. A sacramental spirituality unmasking these forms of slavery by responding to the prophetic, liberating, and healing character of God's reign in the world is crucial. Sacraments, living signs of the new covenant community that lives for the world's transformation, are the embodiment of that spirituality.

## Signs That Speak of Christian Freedom

We can approach sacraments as signs that speak of Christian freedom in two complementary ways: first, from the perspective of full symbolic expression of the Christian message as it is proclaimed in the sacraments, prophetic signs of Christ, and, second, from the perspective of the community's sacramental practice. Both speak of commitment to the "full sign" of the sacrament. The Christian community as historical and symbolic real entity, local and universal, is itself a sign that speaks signs.

*1. Sacraments are the full symbolic expression of the Christian message of freedom.*

Sacraments are prophetic and effective signs of the presence of the reign of God. They actualize the concrete actions and spirit of Jesus' prophetic ministry and the impact of his "good news." They announce freedom of life in its fullness, through the visible signs of word, community, and symbol. An interpretation of sacramental freedom begins in the saving mystery of Christ. All prophetic expectations of definitive and universal liberation originate in the arrival of the reign of God. Jesus' message heralds a new age of freedom and human solidarity according to God's plan, for "God is with us": "The Spirit of the Lord is upon me . . . He has sent me to proclaim release to the captives . . . to let the oppressed go free, to proclaim the year of the Lord's favor" (Luke 4:18–19). His ministry of liberation embraces every sphere of human existence—body and spirit, humanity and cosmos, time and eternity. As essential signs of the reign of God's presence, sacraments proclaim integral liberation. Though they may be fragile in terms of human experience, yet they are anticipatory of the full establishment of the reign to come.

Freedom's call is to live the spirit of humanity's new relationship with God, a relationship that touches all dimensions of life. The Christian's vocation is a summons to freedom: "For freedom Christ has set us free. Stand firm, therefore, and do not submit again to a yoke of slavery" (Gal 5:1). Christ's freedom is all-embracing and diametrically opposes the slavery from which he definitively liberated the world. As God's gift, freedom finds full expression in Christ's discipleship and committed faith, for "where the Spirit of the Lord is, there is freedom" (2 Cor 3:17). Sacraments celebrate God's communion with believers through personal conversion and call them to live in the same communion with others through signs of human solidarity. Witnessing to God's oneness, the disciples become credible witnesses to Christ's mission (John 17:21–23).

The call to an authentic liberation celebrated by the sacraments derives from the salvific work of Christ. This message pervades the New Testament, especially when associated with the faith-communities of Paul and John: "You were called to freedom" (Gal 5:13); "The truth will make you free...So if the Son makes you free, you will be free indeed" (John 8:32, 36). Paul characterized the historical impact of Jesus of Nazareth in the faith of the early Christian communities by calling their members "free persons." For him the liberation effected by Christ is multidimensional.

The significance of this liberating spirit within the early New Testament communities for today's Church and world is clear. It is a spirit that pervades the early disciples' sacramental praxis. Christian initiation establishes a new relationship of unity, obedience, and service through the consecration of baptism, by which we are all "one in Christ Jesus" (Gal 3:28). Some theologians have translated this biblical perspective into modern terms by saying, as for example: "baptism is the sacrament of equality." Similarly, the Eucharist invites the believer to enter the reality of Christian freedom through "drinking the cup" in a spirit of servanthood (Matt 20:20–23) and "discerning the body" in the organic unity of discipleship (1 Cor 11:29). The Eucharist is a festive memorial of Christian freedom in that it is the paschal sacrament of Christ's victory over the ultimate slavery of sin and death.

Freedom, therefore, expresses a fundamental reality of the specifically Christian experience. As signs of the freedom of Christ who confronted the reality of evil, sacraments are both the present celebration of that freedom by God's grace in the power of the Spirit and the individual's commitment to the same freedom. It is a freedom that opposes any historical form of slavery, whether personal or social, internal or external, psychological or political. These slaveries, which degrade the dignity of God's children, especially the weak and the marginalized, are manifestations of the reality of evil. Although sacraments are not the total expression of God's liberating presence in the world, nevertheless through them as signs of Christ's freedom the believer "affirms life over death, love over hatred, justice over injustice, freedom over slavery."[10]

In order for the sacraments to act as means of liberation, they themselves must be liberated from captivity. As Gérard Fourez states: "The sacraments today seem to be in captivity, their power is not easily revealed in the technological society which is out of step with the rites and symbolic language. Our society prefers rational discourse and univocal processes."[11] In past generations, the symbolic universe supported a religious and sacramental world view. As observed earlier, within the secularized climate of modernity there has been a loss of the sense of the symbolic, a sense that enables people to see the larger sacramentality of the divine in the world, "as in a mirror."

*2. Sacraments express Christian freedom from the perspective of practice.*
From the perspective of genuine participation in the sacraments, two things are central: symbolic relevance and committed faith. The history of sacramental participation shows how often it has reduced itself to bare minimums of both personal and social relevance. We can say the same about the sacramental signs themselves. Like the very concept of sacramentality, they have suffered a progressive shrinking of meaning. These two problems—symbolic reductionism and spiritual minimalism —still persist and underlie the present sacramental crisis.

Instances of symbolic reductionism, the pauperizing of the truth of the content and use of symbol, may disappear more and more in light of the biblical, prophetic, and festive praxis gaining ground today in Christian communities. Life is the heart of a sacrament. Individuals impacted by sacramental freedom become themselves genuine signs/symbols/sacraments of God's baptismal deliverance, Eucharist for a hungry world, or a reconciling freedom of forgiveness. One telling example of renewal is the process found in the Rite of Christian Initiation of Adults (the RCIA), a process that is gradually becoming pastorally normative. It makes perfunctory rites for even infant baptism implausible. The biblical depth and rich imagery of baptism—such as, for example, Paul's paschal symbolism of the bath, new creation, or mystical union—are beginning to prevail in the West over the more restrictive concept of baptism as dominantly deletion of original sin. A covenantal understanding of the sacrament of marriage is transforming overly canonical and contractual approaches to marriage celebration and to "preparation" for it. Sacramental renewal is under way and is laying the groundwork for a flowering of sacramental spirituality.

Behind today's sacramental crisis, we see the spiritual crisis of current religious consciousness. Perception of the underlying mystery and the possibility of genuine sacramental participation depend on religious consciousness. Although sacraments are means of spiritual empowerment through invisible grace transforming personal lives, they demand a faith commitment expressing itself in the individual's living out of Christ's discipleship.

Sacraments function as effective signs of a liberative spirituality when their praxis includes some of the following characteristics: (1) *catechetical symbolism*, rooted in the word that empowers the person by God's grace and the call of the Spirit to conversion (it forms and transforms the person); (2) *ritual symbolism*, rooted in a sense of mystery, awe, and contemplation that makes God real to the assembly (it gives spiritual profundity to the celebration); (3) *prophetic symbolism*, rooted in God's reign and in the liberative paschal experience that leads to the Church's communion with Christ (this gives the believer a Christian world view); and (4) *ecclesial symbolism*, rooted in an inclusive sense of *ekklesia* that links Church, sacraments, and local mission (it penetrates and transforms culture).

## Signs of the Liberating Presence of the Risen Lord

Passover, which celebrates the exodus of God's people from slavery, means essentially liberation. The Jewish Passover is the "sacramental" memorial of the exodus, the fundamental experience of Israelite deliverance through God's mighty works. As Herbert Vorgrimler writes, "the presence of God is also realized, according to the 'sacramental principle,' in historical events and dimensions. God's will aims at justice and freedom. God wishes to participate in the festive memorial of liberation, so that the *whole nation* may see the glory of the Exodus God who is present in its midst, and welcome this God in praise and gratitude."[12] This liberative experience gives rise later to eschatological expectations and to the hope of messianic fulfillment as an irreversible exodus (cf. Isa 65:22–25).

Christ is the Christian Passover of universal deliverance. The origin, meaning, and power of sacramental actions flow from the Easter event: the redeeming death of Christ and the faith-experience of the disciples with the liberating love of the risen Lord. In the mind of the church fathers, the sacraments and the "admirable sacrament" of the Church were born from the pierced Christ. From him flowed blood (Eucharist) and water (baptism), which signified the sacraments of our redemption.[13]

Sacraments are, in fact, the historical extension of the mystery of the incarnation and the paschal mystery through which Christ became Lord and Savior to free humanity. In the words of Pope Leo I, "What was visible in our Savior has passed over into his mysteries."[14] The sacramental humanity of the risen Christ, the primordial sacrament, realizes our total human and Christian potential. His living presence in the Spirit, the guaranty of the Church's freedom, makes it possible for the sacraments to be God's gift flowing from life and leading us back to life. Elaborating on the language of mystery, Karl Rahner shows the intrinsic relationship between the word of God and the sacraments in their liberating reality. He writes: "Sacraments are nothing but God's efficacious word to man, the word in which he offers himself to man and thereby liberates man's freedom to accept God's self-communication by his own act."[15]

"There is no other possible liberation of humanity but the sacrament by which Christ through his death and resurrection established the universal kingdom,"[16] writes Henri Denis. In reality, we humans are not born free, and therefore we experience our call to freedom both as gift and as responsibility for our lives. Not yet fully free, the pilgrim Church can live this hope for that integral and universal liberation we call salvation through sacramental encounters. This is so because Christ is risen. Sacraments empower us to achieve authentic freedom. They demand, however, an attitude of Easter tested with the cross. In fact, as vital signs of freedom sacraments depend on the paschal vision that inspires their praxis.

Today's cultural signs and global dynamics certainly speak of human hunger for authentic liberation. Christian freedom is essentially freedom to hope. As Christians wait in hope for Christ's coming, we shall always see new strides toward liberation of the person and society, humanity and the universe, the present moment and the future in God. Through these divine-human encounters, God invites the Christian community to the ultimate freedom of "new heavens and a new earth, where righteousness is at home" (2 Pet 3:13). Thus a creative tension develops between the human experience of fragility and the fulfillment of a future promise. In fact, every movement toward authentic liberation is already a historical form of salvation. Marching to its fulfillment, the people of God experience historically in the sacraments the continuing liberative symbolic action of the risen Christ, the beginning and the end, here and now, and in the reign that is to come.

# Notes

## 1. A Sacramental Universe

1. DS 1639.

2. Dogmatic Constitution on the Church, 34. This and all other quotations from Vatican II documents are from *Vatican Council II, Constitutions, Decrees, Declarations,* ed. Austin Flannery, O.P. (Northport, N.Y.: Costello Publishing Co., 1996).

3. Constitution on the Sacred Liturgy, 10.

4. Literature treating the symbolic nature of the person comes from many and different fields of the human sciences. The following are only two examples of interest for affirmation of symbolic ritual in the context of current secularism: Paul Ricoeur, *A Ricoeur Reader: Reflection and Imagination,* ed. Mario J. Valdes (Toronto: University of Toronto Press, 1991); Bernard Lonergan, *Myth, Symbol and Reality,* ed. Alan M. Olson (Notre Dame, Ind.: University of Notre Dame Press, 1980).

5. Karl Rahner, *Theological Investigations* #4 (Baltimore: Helicon, 1966) 235.

6. John Macquarrie, *A Guide to the Sacraments* (New York: Continuum, 1997) 14. See also Kevin Irwin, "A Sacramental World—Sacramentality as the Primary Language for Sacraments," *Worship* 76 (2002) 197–211.

7. William Barclay, *The Lord's Supper* (London: SCM Press, 1967) 12.

8. Irenaeus, *Adversus Haereses* 4, 21; SCh 100, vol. IV, 685.

9. Diverse human sciences share this interest in the study of symbols. They have been the central concern for the renewal of contemporary sacramental theology and at the forefront of theological investigation and renewal. A symbolic model of a foundational theology of sacramentality is proposed by Louis-Marie Chauvet in *Symbol and Sacrament: A Sacramental Reinterpretation of Christian Existence* (Collegeville, Minn.: The Liturgical Press, 1995); see also a textbook version of this work, *The Sacraments: The Word of God at the Mercy of the Body* (Collegeville, Minn.: The Liturgical Press 2001).

10. Cf. Ernst Cassirer, *An Essay on Man* (New Haven, Conn.: Yale University Press, 1944) passim.

11. Leonardo Boff, *Sacraments of Life, Life of the Sacraments* (Washington, D.C.: Pastoral Press, 1987) 1–2. Boff provides an excellent introductory synthesis of a sacramental spirituality based on understanding the presence of God in creation.

12. Ibid., 2.

13. Karl Rahner, *Theological Investigations* #14 (London: Darton, Longman & Todd, 1976) 169.

14. Alexander Schmemann, *For the Life of the World: Sacraments and Orthodoxy* (New York: St. Vladimir's Seminary Press, 1973) 139–40.

15. See the chapter "Du Symbole a la dialectique," in Henri de Lubac, *Corpus Mysticum* (Paris: Aubier, 1944) 255–84.

16. Irénée H. Dalmais, "Theologie of the Liturgical Celebration," in *The Church at Prayer, Vol. 1, Principles of the Liturgy,* ed. Aimé Martimort (Collegeville, Minn.: The Liturgical Press, 1987) 257.

17. The following are just three examples coming from an Eastern Orthodox background: Yannis Spiteris, "L'Eucaristia e il sacramento nella teologia ortodossa. Status questionis," in *Il mondo del sacramento: Teologia e filosofia a confronto,* ed. Nicola Reali (Milano: Paoline, 2001) 59–80; B. Bobrinskoy, "Mystagogie trinitaire des sacrements," in *Mystagogy: Pensée liturgique d'aujourd'hui et liturgie ancienne,* ed. A. M. Triacca and A. Pistoia (Rome: Edizioni Liturgiche, 1993); Jean Corbon, *The Wellspring of Worship* (New York/Mahwah, N.J.: Paulist Press: New York, 1988).

18. Chauvet has been quoted above. Kenan B. Osborne, *Christian Sacraments in a Postmodern World: a Theology for the Third Millennium* (New York/Mahwah, N.J.: Paulist Press, 1999), offers an excellent critical synthesis of the fundamental contributions of the twentieth-century sacramental movements, as well as new directions for a future sacramental theology consistent with postmodern thought. David N. Power, *Sacrament: the Language of God's Giving* (New York: Crossroad, 1999), focuses on a sacramental interpretation as language event and as gift in a thorough examination of the historical tradition and a visionary integration of diverse liturgical dimensions toward a future sacramental theology.

19. Paul Ricoeur, *The Symbolism of Evil* (Boston: Beacon Press, 1967) 247–48.

20. Paul Tillich, *The Shaking of the Foundations* (New York: Charles Scribner's Sons, 1948) 86.

21. Bernard Cooke, *Sacraments and Sacramentality* (Mystic, Conn.: Twenty-Third Publications, 1983) 45.

22. Roger Haight, *Dynamics of Theology* (New York/Mahwah, N.J.: Paulist Press, 1990) 156.

23. Frederick H. Dillistone, *The Power of Symbols in Religion and Culture* (New York: Crossroad, 1986) 136.

24. Paul Tillich, *Systematic Theology* #3 (London: SCM Press, 1978) 130–31.

25. Karl Rahner, "How to Receive a Sacrament and Mean It," *Theology Digest*, 19 (1971) 227–34.

26. Michael G. Lawler, *Symbol and Sacrament: A Contemporary Sacramental Theology* (New York/Mahwah, N.J.: Paulist Press, 1987) 28.

27. Antoine de Saint-Exupéry, *The Little Prince* (New York: Harcourt, Brace & World, 1943) 21.

28. Paul Tillich, *Ultimate Concern* (London: SCM Press, 1965) 149.

29. See my article, "Secularization and Worship," in *The New Dictionary of Sacramental Worship*, ed. Peter E. Fink (Collegeville, Minn.: The Liturgical Press, 1990) 1156–61.

30. Anthony C. Thiselton, "Sign, Symbol," in *The New Westminister Dictionary of Liturgy and Worship*, ed. J. G. Davies (Philadelphia: The Westminister Press, 1986) 491.

31. Cooke, *Sacraments and Sacramentality*, 53–54.

32. Cf. Gilbert Durand, *L'Imagination Symbolique* (Paris: Presses Universitaires de France, 1968).

## 2. The Development of Christian Sacramentality

1. The modern origins of this sacramental terminology of the "primordial sacrament" *(ursakrament)* are studied by H. Vorgrimler, *Sacramental Theology* (Collegeville, Minn.: The Liturgical Press, 1992) 30–40. He quotes the following (p. 30): "Without losing his personal character, says Augustin Schmied, Jesus as the Christ attracted to Himself the power of primal human symbols (light, wellspring, shepherd, door, bread). He could be called the icon, the image of God pure and simple (2 Cor 4:4; Col 1:15), the visible epiphany of the invisible essence of God (Heb 1:1–2; 1 John 1:1; also John 14:9)."

2. Texts written by two of the most influential Roman Catholic theologians before the Second Vatican Council in the sixties and afterwards are Karl Rahner, *The Church and the Sacraments* (New York: Herder and Herder, 1963) and Edward Schillebeeckx, *Christ the Sacrament of the Encounter with God* (New York: Sheed and Ward, 1963).

3. Cf. John 1:29–34; and the Synoptics: Mark 1:9–11; Matt 3:13–17; Luke 3:21–22.

4. Dionisio Borobio, *La Celebración en la Iglesia: Liturgia y Sacramentología Fundamental* (Salamanca: Sígueme, 1987) 380.

5. Walter Kasper and Gerhard Sauter, *Kirche-Ort des Geistes* (Freiburg: Herder and Herder, 1976) 39–40.

6. Michael Quesnel, *Aux sources des Sacraments* (Paris: Cerf, 1977) 128.

7. For the biblical roots of *mysterion,* see the thorough study of Gunter Born-Kamm, "Mysterion," in *Theological Dictionary of the New Testament,* ed. G. Kittel and G. Friedrich (Grand Rapids, Mich.: Eerdmans, 1967) 802–28.

8. Theodore Schneider, *Signos de la cercanía de Dios* (Salamanca: Sígueme, 1986) 32.

9. See Alexander Ganoczy, *An Introduction to Catholic Sacramental Theology* (New York/Mahwah, N.J.: Paulist Press, 1984) 7–15.

10. Some of the ideas that follow are derived from my article, "Cult and Culture: The Structure of the Evolution of Worship," *Worship* 64 (1990) 406–32.

11. *Protrepticus,* 12, 119; SCh 2, 181–83. See A. Ganoczy, *An Introduction to Catholic Sacramental Theology,* 16.

12. Jean Galot, "Eschatologie, Eschatologie patristique," in *Dictionnaire de Spiritualité* (Paris 1960) vol. IV, col. 1046. See Germán Martínez, *La escatología en la Liturgia Romana Antigua* (Madrid: Instituto Superior de Pastoral, 1976) 13–17.

13. Eusebius, *Demonstratio evangelica* V, 3; PG 22:368. See E. Evans, *Tertullian's Homily on Baptism* (London: SPCK, 1964).

14. R. Hotz, *Los sacramentos en nuevas perspectivas: La riqueza sacramental de Oriente y Occidente* (Salamanca: Sígueme, 1986) 75.

15. Augustine, *Epistle* 55, to Januarius, 7, 13; PL 33:210, quoted by Maurice Jourjon, *Les Sacraments de la Liberté Chrétienne* (Paris: Cerf, 1981) 139.

16. Augustine, *Epistle* 138, 7; PL 33:527.

17. Augustine, *Sermo* 10, 2; PL 38:93.

18. Leo the Great, *Sermo* I, 2; SCh 74, 136–37.

19. Ambrose, *De Spiritu Sancto* 2, 10; PL 16:796.

20. Regis A. Duffy, "Sacraments in General," in *Systematic Theology: Roman Catholic Perspectives,* ed. F. Schüssler Fiorenza and J. Galvin (Minneapolis, Minn.: Fortress Press, 1991) 195.

21. Thomas Aquinas, *Summa Theologiae* III, 99, 60–65.

22. Alexander Schmemann, *For the Life of the World: Sacraments and Orthodoxy* (New York: St. Vladimir's Seminary Press, 1973) 150.

23. Josef Jungmann, *La Liturgie des premiers siècles jusq'à l'époque de Grégoire le Grande* (Paris: Cerf, 1962) 380.

24. Paul Tillich, *A History of Christian Thought,* ed. C. E. Braaten (New York: Simon and Schuster, 1967) 145. "The Pope who can be said to be the

Church," stated Giles of Rome, theologian of the fourteenth century. (Yves Congar, *L'Église: De Saint Augustine a l'époque moderne* [Paris: Cerf, 1970] 272–73.)

25. Theodor Klauser, *A Short History of the Western Liturgy: An Account and Some Reflections* (London: Oxford University Press, 1969) 94.

26. Josef Jungmann, "The State of Liturgical Life on the Eve of the Reformation," *Pastoral Liturgy* (1952) 79–80.

27. James White, *Sacraments as God's Self-Giving: Sacramental Practice and Faith* (Nashville: Abingdon Press, 1988) 118.

28. Ibid.

29. Tillich, *A History of Christian Thought*, 53.

30. James White, *Introduction to Christian Worship* (Nashville: Abingdon Press, 1981) 229.

31. John Calvin, *Epître à Sadolet*, in *Trois Traités*, 53, quoted by J. De Wattleville, *Le Sacrifice dans les textes Eucharistiques des premiers siècles* (Neuchatel: Delachaux et Niestlé, 1966) 220.

32. Dogmatic Constitution on the Church, 48.

33. Pastoral Constitution on the Church in the Modern World, 45.

34. Constitution on the Sacred Liturgy, 59.

35. Ibid., 61.

36. Ibid., 59.

37. Odo Casel, *The Mystery of Christian Worship* (Westminister, Md.: Newman, 1962).

38. Edward Schillebeeckx, *Christ, the Sacrament of the Encounter with God* (New York: Sheed and Ward, 1963).

39. Karl Rahner, *Theological Investigations* #14 (Baltimore: Helicon, 1966) 143–44.

40. Michael Skelley, *The Liturgy of the World: Karl Rahner's Theology of Worship* (Collegeville, Minn.: The Liturgical Press, 1991).

41. Pastoral Constitution on the Church in the Modern World, 58. See Instruction on the Roman Liturgy and Inculturation, *Origins* 23 (1994) 745–56.

42. Christopher Dawson, *Religion and the Rise of Western Culture* (Garden City, N.Y.: Image Books, 1958) 43.


### 3. Basic Dimensions of Christian Sacramentality

1. *Catechism of the Catholic Church*, 1113–1130.

2. Ibid., 1115; St. Leo the Great, *Sermo* 74, 2; PL 54, 398.

3. Most modern European theologians, like Schillebeeckx, Semmelroth, and Schulte, agree on this approach. It is important to consider also the

approach of Eastern Orthodox theologians, such as Evdokimov and Afanasieff, who stress the sacramental foundations of the Church-Eucharist based on the reality of the risen Christ.

4. Karl Rahner, *The Church and the Sacraments* (New York: Herder and Herder, 1963) 38.

5. Edward Schillebeeckx, *Christ the Sacrament of the Encounter with God* (New York: Sheed and Ward, 1963) 118.

6. Melito de Sardis, *Homily on the Pasch,* 2; F. L. Cross, *The Early Christian Fathers,* I (London: Duckworth, 1961) 104.

7. Jean Corbon, *The Wellspring of Worship* (New York/Mahwah, N.J.: Paulist Press, 1988) 34.

8. J. Betz, "Eucharistie als zentrales Mysterium," in *Mysterium Salutis* 4/2, ed. J. Feiner and M. Lohrer (Madrid: Cristiandad, 1975) 189.

9. Regis Duffy, "Sacraments in General," in *Systematic Theology: Roman Catholic Perspectives,* ed. F. Schüssler Fiorenza and J. Galvin (Minneapolis, Minn.: Fortress Press, 1991) 187.

10. Peter Lombard, *Book of the Sentences* iv, dist. I, 1; PL 192:839.

11. Thomas Aquinas, *Summa Theologiae* III, 65, 1.

12. Alexandre Ganoczy, *An Introduction to Catholic Sacramental Theology* (New York/Mahwah, N.J.: Paulist Press, 1984) 52.

13. Albertus Magnus, *De Sacramentis,* i.q. 4 ad 12; ed., *Opera Omnia* (Westfal 1958) XXVI, 11.

14. *Catechism of the Catholic Church,* 1210; see Thomas Aquinas, *Summa Theologiae* III, 65, 1.

15. Bernard Cooke, *Sacraments and Sacramentality* (Mystic, Conn.: Twenty-Third Publications, 1983) 7.

16. Leonardo Boff, *Sacraments of Life, Life of the Sacraments* (Washington, D.C.: Pastoral Press, 1987) 57–58.

17. Kenan Osborne, *Sacramental Theology: A General Introduction* (New York/Mahwah, N.J.: Paulist Press, 1988) 77.

18. Irénée Dalmais, "Theology of the Liturgical Celebration," in *The Church at Prayer, Vol. 1, Principles of the Liturgy,* ed. Aimé Martimort (Collegeville, Minn.: The Liturgical Press, 1987) 243.

19. Alexander Schmemann, *For the Life of the World: Sacraments and Orthodoxy* (New York: St. Vladimir's Seminary Press, 1973) 144.

20. Cf. Ph. Béguerie and C. Duchesneau, *How to Understand the Sacraments* (New York: Crossroad, 1991) 59.

21. Thomas Aquinas, *Summa Theologiae* III, 65, 3.

22. *Catechism of the Catholic Church,* 1121; cf. Council of Trent (1547): DS 1609.

23. For Augustine, sacrament is a "sacred sign" in which one thing is the bodily reality seen, and the other is the spiritual fruit not seen. (*Sermo* 272).

24. Béguerie and Duchesneau, *How to Understand the Sacraments*, 5.

25. *Catechism of the Catholic Church*, 1116; cf. Luke 5:17; 6:19; 8:46.

26. Constitution on the Sacred Liturgy, 59.

27. *Catechism of the Catholic Church*, 1124.

28. Juan Luís Segundo, *The Sacraments Today* (Maryknoll, N.Y.: Orbis Books, 1974) 38.

29. See Odo Casel, *The Mystery of Christian Worship* (Westminister, Md.: Newman, 1962) 6–8.

30. Dogmatic Constitution on the Church, 11.

31. Thomas Aquinas, *In IV Sent.*, dist. 13, q. 1, 5.

32. DS 1608.

33. DS 1529; see also DS 1532.

34. Karl Rahner, "Considerations on the Active Role of the Person in the Sacramental Event," in *Theological Investigations* #14 (New York: Seabury Press, 1976) 166–67.

35. Pastoral Constitution on the Church in the Modern World, 22.

36. Dogmatic Constitution on the Church, 16.

37. Thomas Aquinas, *Summa Theologiae* III, 60, 3; quoted by the *Catechism of the Catholic Church*, 1130 (italics mine).

38. Raymond Vaillancourt, *Toward a Renewal of Sacramental Theology* (Collegeville, Minn.: The Liturgical Press, 1979) 119.

39. Pastoral Constitution on the Church in the Modern World, 43; see also Dogmatic Constitution on the Church, 48.

## 4. Sacramental Mystery and Christian Spirituality

1. Karl Rahner, *Meditations on the Sacraments* (New York: Seabury Press, 1977) ix–x.

2. See R. Hotz, *Los sacramentos en nuevas perspectivas: La riqueza sacramental de Oriente y Occidente* (Salamanca: Sígueme, 1986) 225.

3. Karl Rahner, "Considerations on the Active Role of the Person in the Sacramental Event," in *Theological Investigations* #14 (New York: Seabury Press, 1976) 169.

4. Michael Skelley, *The Liturgy of the World: Karl Rahner's Theology of Worship* (Collegeville, Minn.: The Liturgical Press, 1991) 158.

5. Aloysius Pieris, "Spirituality in a Liberative Perspective," in *An Asian Theology of Liberation* (Maryknoll, N.Y.: Orbis Books, 1988) 3–14. See also German

Martinez, "Secularization and Worship," in *The Dictionary of Sacramental Worship*, ed. Peter E. Fink (Collegeville, Minn.: The Liturgical Press, 1990) 1156–61.

6. Constitution on the Sacred Liturgy, 2.

7. Regis Duffy, "Sacraments in General," in *Systematic Theology: Roman Catholic Perspectives*, ed. F. Schüssler Fiorenza and J. Galvin (Minneapolis, Minn.: Fortress Press, 1991) 183.

8. Peter Fink, *Worship: Praying the Sacraments* (Washington, D.C.: Pastoral Press, 1991) 9.

9. Constitution on the Sacred Liturgy, 10.

10. Robert Taft, "What Does Liturgy Do? Toward a Soteriology of Liturgical Celebration: Some Theses," *Worship* 66 (1992) 210.

11. Jean Corbon, *The Wellspring of Worship* (New York/Mahwah, N.J.: Paulist Press, 1988) 185.

12. Donald Senior, "God's Creative Word in Our Midst: The Mystery/ Sacrament of Divine Love from Genesis to Jesus," in *The Sacraments: God's Love and Mercy Actualized*, ed. Francis A. Eigo (Villanova, Pa.: Villanova University Press, 1979) 21.

13. *Catechism of the Catholic Church*, 1127.

14. Among other examples, see *Martirium Policarpi*, 14; *Letter to Flora*, 3; SCh 24; Tertullian, *Apolog.*, 30, 5; Augustine, *De Civitate Dei*, 10, 6; PL 41, 183ff.

15. Alexander Schmemann, *The World as Sacrament* (London: Darton, Longman & Todd, 1965) 16.

16. Philip Pfatteicher, *Liturgical Spirituality* (Valley Forge, Pa.: Trinity Press, 1997) 1.

17. Ambrose, *Apologia proph. David* 1, 2; CSEL 32:339.

18. Constitution on the Sacred Liturgy, 12; Secret for Monday of Pentecost Week.

19. Taft, "What Does Liturgy Do?" 204–205.

20. Decree on the Ministry and Life of Priests, 5.

21. Walter Kasper, "The Mission of the Laity," *Theology Digest* 35 (1988) 136.

22. Karl Rahner, "The World and the Eucharist," in *Theological Investigations* #5 (Baltimore: Helicon, 1965) 267.

23. Michael Schmaus, *The Church as Sacrament* (London: Sheed and Ward, 1975) 17.

24. Groupe des Dombes, "The Episcopal Ministry," *One in Christ* 14 (1978) 267–68. Studied by D. Salado, "Un modelo de sacramentología integral: el Espíritu Santo, la Iglesia y los sacramentos," *Ciencia Tomista* 356 (1981) 469–501; 357 (1982) 3–40.

25. *Commentary in Isaias, Prologue;* PL 24:17; Constitution on Divine Revelation, 25.

26. Constitution on the Sacred Liturgy, 24.

27. Pfatteicher, *Liturgical Spirituality,* p. 22.

28. *Sermo* 229; PL 38:342.

29. *Sermo* 272; PL 38:1246.

30. Robert Browning and Roy Reed, *The Sacraments in Religious Education and Liturgy* (Birmingham, Ala.: Religious Education Press, 1985) 61.

## 5. Baptism

1. Joseph Fitzmyer, "The Letter to the Romans," in *The New Jerome Biblical Commentary,* ed. Raymond E. Brown et al. (Englewood Cliffs, N.J.: Prentice Hall, 1990) 847–48.

2. Reginald Fuller, "Christian Initiation in the New Testament," in *Made, Not Born: New Perspectives on Christian Initiation and the Catechumenate* (Notre Dame, Ind.: University of Notre Dame Press, 1976) 7–31.

3. Kenan Osborne, *The Christian Sacraments of Initiation: Baptism, Confirmation, Eucharist* (New York/Mahwah, N.J.: Paulist Press, 1987) 31.

4. See John 4:2, which disagrees with John 3:22, 25–26. Other authors favor the idea that Jesus himself baptized.

5. Cf. Mark 6:7–13; Matt 10:5–25; Luke 10:1–16.

6. Daniel Harrington, *The Gospel of Matthew* (Collegeville, Minn.: The Liturgical Press, 1991) 414.

7. Gerhard Lohfink, "Der Ursprung der christlichen Taufe," *Theologische Quartalschrift* 156 (1976) 38.

8. "Baptism would have been performed in a river or pool or in a domestic bath-house." K. W. Noakes, "From New Testament Times until St Cyprian," in *The Study of Liturgy,* ed. Ch. Jones et al. (New York: Oxford University Press, 1992) 117.

9. Aidan Kavanagh, *The Shape of Baptism: The Rite of Christian Initiation* (New York: Pueblo Publishing, 1978) 25.

10. Cf. Acts 11:16; 1 Cor 12:13; 2 Cor 1:22; Titus 3:5.

11. Regis Duffy, "Baptism and Confirmation," in *Systematic Theology: Roman Catholic Perspectives,* vol. 2, ed. F. Schüssler Fiorenza and J. Galvin (Minneapolis, Minn.: Fortress Press, 1991) 217.

12. Louis Villete, *Foi et sacrement,* vol. 1 (Paris: Bloud et Gay, 1959) 31.

13. Pheme Perkins, "The Gospel According to John," in *The New Jerome Biblical Commentary,* 955.

14. R. Schnackenburg, *Das Johannesevangelium* (Freiburg: Herder, 1965) 383.

15. Duffy, "Baptism and Confirmation," 188.

16. Theodor Schneider, *Signos de la Cercanía de Dios* (Salamanca: Sígueme, 1979) 81.

17. Alexander Schmemann, *The World as Sacrament* (London: Darton, Longman & Todd, 1965) 16.

18. William Dalton, "The First Epistle of Peter," in *The New Jerome Biblical Commentary,* 905.

19. E. Käsemann, "The Beginnings of Christian Theology," in *New Testament Questions of Today* (Philadelphia: Fortress Press, 1969) 82–107.

20. Robert Grant, "Development of the Christian Catechumenate," in *Made, Not Born,* 32.

21. Hippolytus, *Apostolic Tradition;* Gregory Dix, ed., chapter 16 (London: SPCK, 1968). Cf. Jones et al., *The Study of Liturgy,* 130–31.

22. St. John Chrysostom, *Baptismal Instructions* II, 15–16; SCh 50, 141–43.

23. Robert Cabié, "Christian Initiation," in *The Church at Prayer, Vol. 3, The Sacraments,* ed. Aimé Martimort et al. (Collegeville, Minn.: The Liturgical Press, 1987) 35.

24. Cyril of Jerusalem, *Catecheses mystagogicae* II, 4; 126, 110; quoted by Cabié, "Christian Initiation," 48.

25. St. Ambrose, *De mysteriis* 43; SCh 25bis, 179–80; quoted by Cabié, "Christian Initiation," 61.

26. Josef Jungmann, *La Liturgie des Premiers Siècles jusqu'à l'époque de Grégoire le Grand* (Paris: Cerf, 1962) 216.

27. See Edward Yarnold, *The Awe-Inspiring Rites of Initiation* (Collegeville, Minn.: The Liturgical Press, 1994).

28. Wallafrid Strabo, *De ecclesiasticarum rerum exordiis et incrementis,* c. 27; quoted by Mark Searle, "Infant Baptism Reconsidered," in *Alternatives Futures for Worship,* vol. 2, ed. Mark Searle et al. (Collegeville, Minn.: The Liturgical Press, 1987) 23.

29. See M. Andrieu, *Le Pontifical Romain au Moyen-Âge,* I: *Le Pontifical Romain du XIIe Siècle,* Studi e Testi 86 (Vatican City, 1938) 246–47.

30. *Summa Theologiae,* III, 63, 3 sed contra.

31. John Calvin, *Epître à Sadolet* in *Trois Traités,* 53, quoted by J. De Wattleville, *Le Sacrifice dans les textes Eucharistiques des premiers siècles* (Neuchatel: Delachaux et Niestlé 1966) 220.

32. Duffy, "Baptism and Confirmation," 34.

33. This topic was addressed in the first part of chapter 3 on "The Origin of the Sacraments."

34. This subject has been treated at length in other chapters; see especially the end of chapter 2 on "The Development of Christian Sacramentality: Vatican II and Beyond."

35. On this point, I am indebted to the insights of Kenan Osborne in *The Christian Sacraments of Initiation*, 79–89.

36. *Catechism of the Catholic Church*, 1257.

37. The New Testament background explains the use of the idea of the seal in reference to baptism in ancient Christianity. The following is one of the most relevant quotations: "In him you . . . were marked with the seal of the promised Holy Spirit; this is the pledge of our inheritance towards redemption as God's own people, to the praise of his glory" (Eph 1:13–14). Thus it is clear that early Christians referred to baptism as "the seal."

38. Cf. *Summa Theologiae*, III, 63, 3.

39. *Catechism of the Catholic Church*, 1274; cf. St. Augustine, *Ep.* 98, 5: PL 33, 362; *Eph* 4:30; cf. 1:13–14; 2 Cor 1:21–22; St. Irenaeus, *Dem ap.* 3: SCh 62, 32; *Roman Missal*, EP I (Roman Canon) 97.

40. *Rite of Christian Initiation of Adults*, General Introduction, Nos. 1–2.

41. Thomas Morris, *The RCIA: Transforming the Church. A Resource for Pastoral Implementation* (New York/Mahwah, N.J.: Paulist Press, 1997) 67–68.

42. Mircea Eliade, *Rites and Symbols of Initiation* (New York: Harper & Row, 1965) x.

43. Frank Sokol, *The Rite of Christian Initiation of Adults* (Collegeville, Minn.: The Liturgical Press, 1984) 8.

44. *Rite of Christian Initiation of Adults*, No. 47.

45. *Rite of Christian Initiation of Adults*, No. 244.

46. Morris, *The RCIA* (1989 edition), 135.

47. *Rite of Christian Initiation of Adults*, No. 245.


## 6. Confirmation

1. See, for instance, the excellent study of a Lutheran scholar that reevaluates confirmation as part of the unified complex of initiation rites: Maxwell Johnson, *The Rites of Christian Initiation: Their Evolution and Interpretation* (Collegeville, Minn.: The Liturgical Press, 1999). Among the American Catholic bishops, see a recent pastoral letter by Bishop William Skylstad of Spokane, Washington, "Confirmation and the Sacraments of Initiation," *Origins* 28 (1998) 274–78.

2. Constitution on the Sacred Liturgy, 71; Paul VI, apostolic constitution *Divinae Consortium Naturae*, in *The Rites of the Catholic Church* (New York: Pueblo Publishing, 1976) 290–97.

3. Kenan Osborne, *The Christian Sacraments of Initiation* (New York/Mahwah, N.J.: Paulist Press, 1987) 135.

4. *Code of Canon Law* (1983), canon 891.

5. Kieran Sawyer, *Confirming Faith* (Notre Dame, Ind.: Ave Maria Press, 1982) 9.

6. Johnson, *The Rites of Christian Initiation*, 373.

7. *Divinae Consortium Naturae*, in *The Rites of the Catholic Church*, 292.

8. Aidan Kavanagh, "Unfinished and Unbegun Revisited: The Rite of Christian Initiation of Adults," in *Living Water, Sealing Spirit: Readings on Christian Initiation*, ed. Paul Bradsaw et al. (Collegeville, Minn.: The Liturgical Press, 1995) 256.

9. Thomas Marsh, "Confirmation in Scripture," in *The New Dictionary of Sacramental Worship*, ed. Peter E. Fink (Collegeville, Minn.: The Liturgical Press, 1990) 257.

10. Richard Dillon, "Acts of the Apostles," in *The New Jerome Biblical Commentary*, ed. Raymond E. Brown et al. (Englewood Cliffs, N.J.: Prentice Hall, 1990), 743, 756.

11. Herbert Vorgrimler, *Sacramental Theology* (Collegeville, Minn.: The Liturgical Press, 1992) 125.

12. See Ch. Jones et al., *The Study of Liturgy* (New York: Oxford University Press, 1992) 121–24.

13. Robert Cabié, "Christian Initiation," in *The Church at Prayer, Vol. 3, The Sacraments*, ed. Aimé Martimort et al. (Collegeville, Minn.: The Liturgical Press, 1987) 51.

14. Aidan Kavanagh, *Confirmation: Origins and Reform* (New York: Pueblo Publishing, 1988) 69–72.

15. Quoted by Robert Cabié, "Christian Initiation," 57.

16. Quoted by Aidan Kavanagh, "Confirmation," 69.

17. DS 1628.

18. Dogmatic Constitution on the Church, 11.

19. Salvatore Marsili, "Il simbolismo della iniziazione cristiana all luce della teologia liturgica," in *I simboli dell'iniziazione* (Roma: Studia Anselmiana, 1983) 280.

20. Letter to a boy preparing for confirmation by Carlo Maria Cardinal Martini, in *Communicating Christ to the World* (Kansas City, Mo.: Sheed & Ward, 1994).

21. Herbert Vorgrimler, *Sacramental Theology*, 129–30.

22. *The Rites of the Catholic Church*, Confirmation, No. 58.

## 7. Eucharist

1. Edward Kilmartin, "The Catholic Tradition of Eucharistic Theology: Towards the Third Millennium," *Theological Studies* 55 (1994) 404. See also

Kilmartin's book, *The Eucharist in the West: History and Theology,* ed. Robert Daly (Collegeville, Minn.: The Liturgical Press, 1998).

2. See Joachim Jeremias, *The Eucharistic Words of Jesus* (Philadelphia: Fortress Press, 1977) 41–84.

3. Constitution on the Sacred Liturgy, 47.

4. Herbert Vorgrimler, *Sacramental Theology* (Collegeville, Minn.: The Liturgical Press, 1992) 139. See also "Key Foundational Images" in the second part of this chapter.

5. Xavier Léon-Dufour, *Sharing the Eucharistic Bread: The Witness of the New Testament* (New York/Mahwah, N.J.: Paulist Press, 1987) 82–95.

6. Joachim Jeremias, *New Testament Theology* (New York: Charles Scribner's Sons, 1971) 115.

7. *The Jerusalem Bible,* The Gospel According to Saint Luke (New York: Doubleday, 1966) 131, footnote 22 e.

8. Raymond Moloney, *Problems in Theology: The Eucharist* (Collegeville, Minn.: The Liturgical Press, 1995) 13.

9. See the excellent work by Manuel Gesteira, *La Eucaristía, Misterio de Comunión* (Salamanca: Sígueme, 1995) 33–49.

10. Alexander Schmemann, *For the Life of the World* (New York: St. Vladimir's Seminary Press, 1973) 26.

11. Alexander Schmemann, *The Eucharist: Sacrament of the Kingdom* (New York: St. Vladimir's Seminary Press, 1988) 43–44.

12. Vorgrimler, *Sacramental Theology,* 145.

13. Léon-Dufour, *Sharing the Eucharistic Bread,* 283.

14. David Power, "Eucharist," in *Systematic Theology: Roman Catholic Perspectives,* vol. 2, ed. F. Schüssler Fiorenza and J. Galvin (Minneapolis, Minn.: Fortress Press, 1991) 27.

15. Oscar Cullmann, *Early Christian Worship* (London: SCM, 1953) 118.

16. For a complete study of eucharistic themes, see Eugene LaVerdiere, *The Eucharist in the New Testament and in the Early Church* (Collegeville, Minn.: The Liturgical Press, 1996) 37. I am also indebted to the research done on this subject by Luís Maldonado, *Sacramentalidad Evangélica: Signos de la Presencia para el Camino* (Santander: Sal Terrae, 1987).

17. LaVerdiere, *The Eucharist in the New Testament and in the Early Church,* 37.

18. Patrick Reardon, "Sacraments, Martyrdom and the Sons of Zebedee," *Touchstone* (7–8/1998) 40.

19. Cf. Michel Quesnel, *Aux Sources des Sacraments* (Paris: Cerf, 1977) 59–78.

20. Heinz Schurmann, *Das Lukasevangelium. Erster Teil* (Freiburg i. b., 1969).

21. Maldonado, *Sacramentalidad Evangélica,* 183.

22. Philippe Béguerie and Claude Duchesneau, *How to Understand the Sacraments* (New York: Crossroad, 1991) 21.

23. Raymond Brown, *The Gospel According to John I–XI, XIII–XXI*, The Anchor Bible 29, 29A (New York: Doubleday, 1970).

24. Salvatore Marsili, *I Segni del mistero di Cristo: Teologia liturgica dei sacramenti* (Roma: Edizioni Liturgiche, 1987) 283–91.

25. Oscar Cullmann, *Early Christian Worship*, 117. Xavier Léon-Dufour also addresses the sacramental meaning of John's Gospel (*Sharing the Eucharistic Bread*, 248–77).

26. LaVerdiere, *The Eucharist in the New Testament and in the Early Church*, 114.

27. See several references in Kilian McDonnell, *The Baptism of Jesus in the Jordan: The Trinitarian and Cosmic Order of Salvation* (Collegeville, Minn.: The Liturgical Press, 1996) 209.

28. The historian Thomas S. Kuhn applied the concept of paradigm to the evolution of scientific ideas. Paradigm "stands for the entire constellation of beliefs, values...shared by the members of a given community." Paradigms are "employed as models or examples." *The Structure of Scientific Revolutions*, 2nd ed. (Chicago: University of Chicago, 1970) 237. Here the concept of paradigm used in approaching the nature of scientific revolutions is analogously applied, *mutatis mutandis*, to the evolutive nature of ritual worship, specifically to the liturgy of the Eucharist, through different cultural periods.

29. Paul Jones, "The Meaning of the Eucharist: Its Origins in the New Testament Texts," *Encounter* 54 (1993) 169.

30. Xavier Léon-Dufour, "Jesus' Understanding of Death," *Theology Digest* 24 (1976) 294.

31. David Power, *The Eucharistic Mystery: Revitalizing the Tradition* (New York: Crossroad, 1992) 51.

32. Léon-Dufour, *Sharing the Eucharistic Bread*, 10–14. See also, "Christological Origins: Pasch, Reign, and Praxis," in the first part of this chapter.

33. Theodor Schneider, *Signos de la cercanía de Dios* (Salamanca: Sígueme, 1986) 160.

34. Léon-Dufour, *Sharing the Eucharistic Bread*, 110. According to Jeremias, divine remembering is an integral part of ritual worship in the Bible, *New Testament Theology*, 244.

35. This is according to Cesare Giraudo, *Eucaristia per la Chiesa: Prospettive teologiche sull'eucaristia a partire dalla "lex orandi"* (Rome: Editrice Pontificia Università Gregoriana, 1989) 162–86. Edward Kilmartin in *The Eucharist in the West* follows this viewpoint.

36. Max Thurian, *The Eucharistic Memorial*, 2 vols. (London: Lutterworth Press, 1960–1961) was a pioneer work. It stressed the concept of "memorial" as

the key to understanding the idea of sacrifice rejected by the reformers. For a systematic outline of the more recent contributions of Catholic theologians to the idea of eucharistic sacrifice, see Edward Kilmartin, *The Eucharist in the West*, 339–83.

37. Quoted by Herbert Vorgrimler in *Sacramental Theology*, 145.

38. Jones, "The Meaning of the Eucharist," 179.

39. *Sermo* 229; PL 38:342.

40. Jean-Jacques von Allmen, *The Lord's Supper* (London: Lutterworth Press, 1966) 86, 96.

41. Henri de Lubac, *Corpus Mysticum: L'Eucharistie et L'Église au Moyen Age*, 2d rev. ed. (Paris: Aubier, 1949) 89–115, 248–77.

42. Lanfranc, *De corpore et sanguine Domini*; PL 150:430.

43. *Summa Theologiae* III, 73, 3.

44. Ibid., III, 75, 3.

45. Ibid., III, 22, 2–3.

46. DS 1651.

47. DS 1734.

48. William Crockett, *Eucharist: Symbol of Transformation* (New York: Pueblo Publishing, 1989) 124. In the last decades, there has been a growing ecumenical consensus on eucharistic faith and practice. An example of a major document is *Baptism, Eucharist and Ministry*, Faith and Order Paper No. 111 (Geneva: World Council of Churches, 1982).

49. James White, *Sacraments as God's Self Giving* (Nashville: Abingdon Press, 1988) 54.

50. *Baptism, Eucharist and Ministry*, 11.

51. J. G. Gibbs, "The Cosmic Scope of Redemption According to Paul," *Biblica* 56 (1975) 29; see also Kilian McDonell, *The Baptism of Jesus in the Jordan: The Trinitarian and Cosmic Order of Salvation* (Collegeville, Minn.: The Liturgical Press, 1996).

52. Karl Rahner, "The Hermeneutics of Eschatological Assertions," in *Theological Investigations* #4 (Baltimore: Helicon, 1966) 331.

53. Aidan Kavanagh, *The Shape of Baptism: The Rite of Christian Initiation* (New York: Pueblo Publications, 1978) 122.

54. *Eucharisticum Mysterium*, 1; in *Vatican Council II: The Conciliar and Post Conciliar Documents*, ed. Austin Flannery (Northport, N.Y.: Costello Publishing Co., 1996) 107.

55. Kenan Osborne, *The Christian Sacraments of Initiation: Baptism, Confirmation, Eucharist* (New York/Mahwah, N.J.: Paulist Press, 1987) 231.

56. Simeon of Tessalonica, *Dialogos*, Ch. 282; PG 155:512.

57. *Catechism of the Catholic Church*, 1324; cf. Dogmatic Constitution on the Church, 11; Decree on the Ministry and Life of Priests, 5.

58. *Didache* 10:6. *Maranatha* is an Aramaic expression found also in 1 Cor 16:22; see Geoffrey Wainwright, *Eucharist and Eschatology* (London: Epworth Press, 1973) 68–70.

59. Gustave Martelet, *The Risen Christ and the Eucharistic World* (New York: Seabury Press, 1976) 136.

60. Pierre Nautin, *Homelies pascales* 1; SCh 27, 159.

61. Cf. J. Betz, "Eucharistie. In der Schrift und Patristik," in *Hanbuch der Dogmengeschichte* IV/4c (Freiburg 1979).

62. Martelet, *The Risen Christ and the Eucharistic World,* 137.

63. Paul VI, *Mysterium Fidei* (1965); DS 1580.

64. DS 1642. See Osborne, *The Christian Sacraments of Initiation,* 193–209.

65. Schmemann, *The Eucharist: Sacrament of the Kingdom,* 144. For the most recent approach to the question of transubstantiation, see Kilmartin, *The Eucharist in the West.*

66. Jean Corbon, *The Wellspring of Worship* (New York/Mahwah, N.J.: Paulist Press, 1988) 184.

67. Jones, "The Meaning of the Eucharist," 177.

68. de Lubac, *Corpus Mysticum,* 168–75.

69. Gustave Martelet, *The Risen Christ and the Eucharistic World,* 161.

70. *Sermo* 63, 7; PL 54:377 C.

71. Augustine, *On the Merits of Sinners,* I/I, 36, 60; PL 44:145.

72. *Sermo* 272; PL 38:1246.

73. *Sermo* 131; PL 38:720; Cf. *Sermo* 9, 14; PL 38:85.

74. Osborne, *The Christian Sacraments of Initiation,* 210.

75. See a summary of Betz's approach in "Eucharist," *Sacramentum Mundi* (New York: Seabury Press, 1975) 447–59; "La Eucaristía, misterio central," in *Mysterium Salutis* IV/2, ed. J. Feiner and M. Lohrer (Madrid: Cristiandad, 1975) 185–310.

76. George Maloney, *The Cosmic Christ: From Paul to Teilhard* (New York: Sheed and Ward, 1968) 181.

77. Pierre Teilhard de Chardin, "Pantheism and Christianity" (1923) in *Christianity and Evolution* (New York: Harcourt Brace Jovanovich, 1971) 74.

78. Cf. G. W. H. Lampe, *A Patristic Greek Lexicon* (New York: Clarendon, 1961) 859–61.

79. *Adversus Haereses,* IV, 18, 5; SCh 100, vol. II, 40.

80. Moloney, *Problems in Theology,* 96.

81. Martelet, *The Risen Christ and the Eucharistic World,* 188.

82. Pierre Teilhard de Chardin, *Le Milieu Mystique* (1917) 23, cited in Natham Mitchell, *Eucharist as Sacrament of Initiation* (Chicago: Liturgy Training Publications, 1994) 122.

83. Pierre Teilhard de Chardin, *The Divine Milieu* (1926) (New York: Harper and Row, 1960) 125–26.

84. Dogmatic Constitution on the Church, 48.

85. Decree on the Ministry and Life of Priests, 5.

86. Karl Rahner, "Considerations on the Active Role of the Person in the Sacramental Event," in *Theological Investigations* #14 (New York: Seabury Press, 1976) 169–70.

87. Pope John Paul II, encyclical *On Social Concerns,* 48.

## 8. Reconciliation

1. Hans U. von Balthasar, *A Theology of History* (New York: Sheed & Ward, 1959) 93.

2. Kenan Osborne, *Reconciliation and Justification: The Sacrament and Its Theology* (New York/Mahwah, N.J.: Paulist Press, 1990) 19.

3. Karl Rahner, *Theological Investigations* #10 (New York: Seabury Press, 1977) 134–137; *Theological Investigations* #15 (New York: Crossroad, 1982) 19. Regarding the historical approach to the question, see the classic work of Bernhard Poschmann, *Penance and the Anointing of the Sick* (New York: Herder and Herder, 1964).

4. Schnackenburg, "Die Stellung des Petrus 27," in *Theologisches Wörterbuch zum Neuen Testament* 3: 749–751, quoted by M. Garijo-Guembe, *Communion of the Saints: Foundation, Nature, and Structure of the Church* (Collegeville, Minn.: The Liturgical Press, 1994) 70.

5. Isaac of Stella, *Sermo XI* (In dominica III post Epiphaniam); PL 194:1729.

6. *Catechism of the Catholic Church,* 1428; see Dogmatic Constitution on the Church, 8, §3.

7. Dietrich Bonhoeffer, *Life Together* (New York: Harper and Row, 1954) 90.

8. *Catechism of the Catholic Church,* 1431.

9. Cf. for instance, Jer 18:8; 31:19; Mal 3:7; Amos 5:24; 4:4–5; 5:4,15; Isa 1:10–20; Ezek 18:5–9; Joel 2:12; Zech 1:3.

10. James Dallen, *The Reconciling Community: The Rite of Penance* (Collegeville, Minn.: The Liturgical Press, 1986) 271.

11. "On the dominical day of the Lord come together to break bread and give thanks, after having also confessed your sins so that your sacrifice may be pure" (*Didache* 14, 1; SCh 248, 192–93).

12. *Didascalia apostolorum,* c.6; R. Connolly, *Didascalia Apostolorum. The Syriac Version Translated* (Oxford: Clarendon, 1929) 52–53.

13. *De paenitentia* and *De pudicitia,* in *Ancient Christian Writers* 28, ed. William P. Le Saint (New York: Newman Press, 1959).

14. "Vel si presbyter repertus non fuerit et urgere exitus coeperit, apud diaconum quoque exomologesin facere delicti sui possint..." (Cyprian, *Epistle* 18; ed. G. Hartel; CSEL III, 2, 524).

15. For more complete documentation of the above, see my article, "Perspectivas histórico-teológicas del sacramento de la penitencia," *Antonianum* 56 (1981) 86–100.

16. Quoted by J. Ramos-Regidor, "'Reconciliation' in the Primitive Church and Its Lessons for Theology and Pastoral Practice Today," *Concilium* 61 (1971) 79.

17. L. Ligier, "Il sacramento della Penitenza secondo la tradizione orientale," *Rivista Liturgica* 8 (1967) 603.

18. Thomas Aquinas, *Summa Theologiae* III, 79, 3; also, 84–90; *Supplement* 1–28.

19. See the pastoral role of the confessor in DS 813.

20. DS 1743.

21. H. Jedin, "La nécessité de la confession privée selon le Concile de Trente," *Maison-Dieu* 104 (1970) 115; see his work on *A History of the Council of Trent* (St. Louis, Mo.: Herder Book Co., v. I, 1957; v. II, 1958).

22. *Catechism of the Catholic Church*, 1849; cf. St. Augustine, *Contra Faustum* 22: PL 42, 418; Thomas Aquinas, *Summa Theologiae* I–II, 71, 6.

23. Pope John Paul II, apostolic exhortation on *Reconciliation and Penance*, n. 14 (12/2/1984).

24. Thomas Aquinas, *Summa Theologiae* I–II, 106, 1.

25. A seminal work on the renewal of the concept of sin is Louis Monden's *Sin, Liberty and Law* (Kansas City, Mo.: Sheed and Ward, 1965).

26. Pastoral Constitution on the Church in the Modern World, 16–17.

27. St. Augustine, *Confessions*, 10:27; ed. Henry Chadwick (New York: Oxford University Press, 1991) 201.

28. Declaration of the American Bishops prior to the 1983 Synod of Bishops in Rome on "Reconciliation and Penance in the Mission of the Church," *Origins* 13 (1983), nos. 18–22.

29. Osborne, *Reconciliation and Justification*, 253.

30. *Catechism of the Catholic Church*, 1428; cf. Dogmatic Constitution on the Church, 8, §3.

31. Ibid., 1465.

32. James Dallen, "Theological Foundations of Reconciliation," in *Reconciliation: The Continuing Agenda*, ed. Robert J. Kennedy (Collegeville, Minn.: The Liturgical Press, 1987) 14.

33. Dogmatic Constitution on the Church, 11.

34. Francis Buckley, *"I Confess": The Sacrament of Penance Today* (Notre Dame, Ind.: Ave Maria Press, 1972) 21.

35. Pastoral Research and Practices Committee, National Conference of Catholic Bishops, "Reflections on the Sacrament of Penance in Catholic Life Today: A Study Document," *Origins* 19 (1990) 618.

36. Joseph Favazza provides good background on these issues in "Forum: The Fragile Future of Reconciliation," *Worship* (1997) 236–244.

37. Ladislas Örsy, "The Revival of the Sacrament of Penance: A Proposal," *Chicago Studies* 34 (1995) 140.

38. Ibid., 138.

39. Dallen, *The Reconciling Community,* 354.

40. Osborne, *Reconciliation and Justification,* 3.

41. Thomas Aquinas, *Summa Theologiae* III, 79, 3; also, 84–90; *Supplement* 1–28.

42. John Quinn, "The Lord's Supper and Forgiveness of Sin," *Concilium* 61 (1971) 231.

43. Osborne, *Reconciliation and Justification,* 254.

44. DS 1638.

45. *Catechism of the Catholic Church,* 1439.

## 9. Anointing

1. John P. Meier, "Jesus," in *The New Jerome Biblical Commentary,* ed. Raymond E. Brown et al., (Englewood Cliffs, N.J.: Prentice Hall, 1990) 1321.

2. Ibid.

3. Betty J. Lillie, "Suffering," in *The Collegeville Pastoral Dictionary of Biblical Theology,* ed. Caroll Stuhlmueller (Collegeville, Minn.: The Liturgical Press, 1996) 961–63.

4. Bernard Botte, ed., "La Tradition apostolique de saint Hippolyte. Essay de reconstitution," *Liturgiegeschichtliche Quellen und Forschungen* 39 (1963) 18–19.

5. Paul Palmer, ed., *Sacraments and Forgiveness,* Sources of Christian Theology II (Westminster, Md.: Newman Press, 1959) 288.

6. Ibid., 1321.

7. Thomas Aquinas, *Summa Contra Gent.,* IV, 73.

8. Thomas Aquinas, *Summa Theologiae,* III, 65, 1c.

9. Paul VI, apostolic constitution, *Sacrament of the Anointing of the Sick,* 1972.

10. *Pastoral Care of the Sick: Rites of Anointing and Viaticum,* General Introduction, 8–15.

11. Ibid., 60.

12. Ibid., 125b.

13. James Empereur, *Prophetic Anointing: God's Call to the Sick, the Elderly, and the Dying* (Wilmington, Del.: Michael Glazier, 1982) 73.

14. Eugen Biser, "The Healing Power of Faith. Outline of a Therapeutic Theology," *Concilium* (1998/5) 71.

15. There is an enormous body of literature offering valuable insights into medicine and spiritual healing. The following are three examples that provide

both spiritual and medical perspectives: Francis MacNutt, *Healing* (Notre Dame, Ind.: Ave Maria Press, 1974); Larry Dossey, M.D., *Prayer Is Good Medicine: How to Reap the Healing Benefits of Prayer* [with bibliography] (New York: HarperCollins, 1996); Herbert Benson, M.D., *Timeless Healing* (New York: Simon and Schuster, 1996).

16. Patricia Wismer, "For Women in Pain: A Feminist Theology of Suffering," in *In the Embrace of God,* ed. Ann O'Hara Graff (Maryknoll, N.Y.: Orbis Books, 1995) 140.

17. *Catechism of the Catholic Church,* 1504.

18. Charles Gusmer, *And You Visited Me: Sacramental Ministry to the Sick and the Dying* (Collegeville, Minn.: The Liturgical Press, 1984).

19. Ibid., 158.

20. *Pastoral Care of the Sick,* 124.

21. Ibid., 145.

22. Kristiaan Depoortere, "Recent Developments in the Anointing of the Sick," *Concilium* (1998/5) 96.

23. Constitution on the Sacred Liturgy, 73.

24. *Catechism of the Catholic Church,* 1523.

25. *Pastoral Care of the Sick,* 175.

26. The Church in the Modern World, 18.

27. W. Simonis, *Glaube und Dogma der Kirche: Lobpreis seiner Herrlichkeit,* #6 (St Ottilien, 1995) 540; quoted by Gisbert Greshake, "The Anointing of the Sick: The Oscillation of the Church between Physical and Spiritual Healing," *Concilium* (1998) 79–88.

28. Elisabeth Kübler-Ross did extensive research on the stages of dying. See for instance, *On Death and Dying* (New York: Macmillan, 1969).

29. The patristic and liturgical theology of the ancient sources offer excellent resources for a theology of death. See my research on *La escatología en la Liturgia Romana Antigua* (Salamanca, Spain: Universidad Pontificia de Salamanca, 1976) 133–203. See also, Bernard Botte, "The Earliest Formulas of Prayer for the Dead," in *Temple of the Holy Spirit: Sickness and Death of the Christian in the Liturgy* (Collegeville, Minn.: The Liturgical Press, 1983) 17–31.

30. See Cyrille Vogel, "The Cultic Environment of the Deceased in the Early Christian Period," in *Temple of the Holy Spirit,* 259–76.

## 10. Orders and Ministries

1. Thomas O'Meara, *Theology of Ministry* (New York/Mahwah, N.J.: Paulist Press, 1983) 16.

2. Cf. Edward Schillebeeckx, *The Church with a Human Face: A New and Expanded Theology of Ministry* (New York: Crossroad, 1985) 115–19; Kenan Osborne, *Priesthood: A History of the Ordained Ministry in the Roman Catholic Church* (New York/Mahwah, N.J.: Paulist Press, 1988).

3. Raymond Brown, *The Churches the Apostles Left Behind* (New York/Mahwah, N.J.: Paulist Press, 1984) 95.

4. Schillebeeckx, *The Church with a Human Face*, 35.

5. William Dalton, "The First Epistle of Peter," in *The New Jerome Biblical Commentary*, ed. Raymond E. Brown et al. (Englewood Cliffs, N.J.: Prentice Hall, 1990) 905.

6. O'Meara, *Theology of Ministry*, 87–90.

7. Yves Congar, *Lay People in the Church* (Philadelphia: The Westminister Press, 1967) xvi.

8. See Raymond Brown, "Episkope and Episcopos: the New Testament Evidence," *Theological Studies* 41 (1980) 322–38.

9. H. von Capenhausen, Kirchliches Amt und geistliche Vollmacht in den ersten drei Jahrhunderten (Tubingen, 1953) 126; quoted by Miguel Garijo-Guembe, *Communion of the Saints: Foundations, Nature, and Structure of the Church* (Collegeville, Minn.: The Liturgical Press, 1994) 49.

10. Hervé-Marie Legrand, "The Presidency of the Eucharist according to the Ancient Tradition," *Worship* 53 (1979) 413–38.

11. *Apostolic Tradition* 9, 5; see Bernard Botte, "Christian People and Hierarchy in the Apostolic Tradition of St. Hippolytus," in *Roles in the Liturgical Assembly* (New York: Pueblo, 1981) 61–72.

12. Herbert Vorgrimler, *Sacramental Theology* (Collegeville, Minn.: The Liturgical Press, 1992) 251.

13. St. Cyprian, *Epistle* 67, 4; ed. G. Hartel; CSEL III, 2, 738.

14. Cf. Guntram Bischoff, "Dionysius the Pseudo-Areopagite: The Gnostic Myth," in *The Spirituality of Western Christendom*, ed. Ellen Rosanne Elder (Kalamazoo, Mich.: Cistercian Publications, 1976) 13–40.

15. Thomas Aquinas, *Summa Theologiae* III, 22, 4.

16. John Calvin, *Institutes of the Christian Religion*, ed. J. T. McNeill (Philadelphia: The Westminister Press, 1960) book 4, p. 1053.

17. Kenan Osborne provides a thorough presentation on the sacrament of orders and the Council of Trent, *Priesthood*, 248–79.

18. Decree on the Ministry and Life of Priests, 2.

19. *Catechism of the Catholic Church*, 1546–1547; cf. Rev 1:6; 5:9–10; 1 Pet 2:5, 9; Dogmatic Constitution on the Church, 10, §2.

20. Dogmatic Constitution on the Church, 21.

21. Ibid., 10.

22. Ibid., 11.

23. F. Wulf, "Decree on Priestly Ministry: Commentary on the Decree," in *Commentary on the Documents of Vatican II* (New York: Herder and Herder, 1969) 4:220.

24. Avery Dulles, *Models of the Church* (New York: Doubleday, 1978) 204–26.

25. Basil Pennington and Carl Arico, *Living Priesthood Today* (Huntington, Ind.: Our Sunday Visitor, 1987) 32–33.

26. David Coffey, "The Common and the Ordained Priesthood," *Theological Studies* 58 (1997) 236. See also Jack Risley, "The Minister: Lay and Ordained," in *The Theology of Priesthood*, ed. Donald Goergen and Ann Garrido (Collegeville, Minn.: The Liturgical Press, 2000) 119–39.

27. Decree on the Ministry and Life of Priests, 2.

28. Ibid.

29. Hans Küng, *Why Priests? A Proposal for a New Christian Ministry* (Garden City, N.Y.: Doubleday, 1972) 53–69; Schillebeeckx, *The Church with a Human Face,* 203–208.

30. Dogmatic Constitution on the Church, 12.

31. Robert M. Schwartz, *Servant Teachers of the People of God* (New York/Mahwah, N.J.: Paulist Press, 1991) 145.

32. Instruction of Eight Vatican Offices, *Some Questions Regarding Collaboration of Non-ordained Faithful in Priests' Sacred Ministry,* Foreword, *Origins* 27 (1977) 399; see *Christifideles Laici,* 23.

33. St. Augustine, *Sermo* 340; PL 38:1483.

34. Instruction of Eight Vatican Offices, Foreword, 399.

35. Ibid., 2, 401.

36. Decree on the Ministry and Life of Priests, 2.

37. Avery Dulles, *The Priestly Office: A Theological Reflection* (New York/Mahwah, N.J.: Paulist Press, 1997) 59.

38. See John Paul II, "Letter to All the Priests of the Church on the Occasion of Holy Thursday 1979," in John Paul II, *Letters to My Brother Priests,* ed. James P. Socias (Princeton, N.J.: Scepter Publishers, 1994).

39. Donald B. Cozzens, *The Changing Face of the Priesthood* (Collegeville, Minn.: The Liturgical Press, 2000) 139.

40. O'Meara, *Theology of Ministry,* 3.

41. Greg Ogden provides a challenging analysis of the historical and theological aspects of the Reformation's view of ministry, *The New Reformation: Returning the Ministry to the People of God* (Grand Rapids, Mich.: Zondervan Publishing House, 1990).

42. Yves Congar, "My Path-Findings in the Theology of Laity and Ministries," *The Jurist* 32 (1972) 181.

43. Pope John Paul II, *Christifideles Laici,* 20, *Origins* 18 (1989) 570.

44. Dionisio Borobio, "Fundamentación sacramental de los servicios y ministerios," *Phase* 27 (1987) 503–504.

## 11. Marriage

1. This chapter is new in its conceptual framework. It also includes some important theological insights. It derives much of its content from the author's book, *Worship: Wedding to Marriage* (Portland, Ore.: Catholic Press, 1993) and from his chapter, "Models of Marriage: a New Theological Interpretation," in *Perspectives on Marriage: A Reader,* ed. Kieran Scott and Michael Warren (New York: Oxford University Press, 2001) 59–79.

2. Karl Rahner, *Theological Investigations* #10 (New York: Herder and Herder, 1973) 199.

3. *Epistle to Diognetus* 5:6; SCh 33, 62–63.

4. *Ad Uxorem* 2, c. 8, 6–9; *Corpus Scriptorum Selectorum Latinorum* 1:393.

5. Simeon of Thessalonica, *Dialogos,* ch. 282; PG 155:512. According to early Christian writers, "It is the Eucharist which gives to marriage its specifically Christian meaning." John Meyerdorf, *Marriage: An Orthodox Perspective* (New York: St. Vladimir's Seminary Press, 1970) 24.

6. Tertullian, *De Monogamia Xa,* 1–2; PL 2:994.

7. Augustine, *Sermo* 10, 2; PL 38:93.

8. Augustine, *De Bono Coniugali,* ch. 18, 21; PL 40:388.

9. Theodore Mackin, "How to Understand the Sacrament of Marriage," in *Commitment to Partnership: Explorations of the Theology of Marriage,* ed. W. P. Roberts (New York/Mahwah, N.J.: Paulist Press, 1987) 34.

10. Walter Kasper, *Theology of Christian Marriage* (New York: Crossroad, 1983) 27.

11. David Thomas, *Christian Marriage: A Journey Together* (Wilmington, Del.: Michael Glazier 1983) 203.

12. John Chrysostom, *Homily 9 on 1 Timothy;* PG 62:546.

13. Joseph Martos, *Doors to the Sacred: A Historical Introduction to Sacraments in the Catholic Church* (Tarrytown, N.Y.: Triumph Books, 1991) 386–87.

14. Arnold van Gennep, *Rites of Passage,* originally published in 1909 (Reissued by University of Chicago Press, 1981) 10–11.

15. Mark Searle and Kenneth W. Stevenson, *Documents of the Marriage Liturgy* (Collegeville, Minn.: The Liturgical Press, 1992) 270–71.

16. John Paul II, *Familiaris Consortio* (On the Family) 65; *Origins* 11 (1981) 459.

17. Pastoral Constitution on the Church in the Modern World, 47–51.

18. Tertullian, *Ad uxorem* 2, VIII, 6; CCSL 1:395; English tr. by J. Quasten, *Patrology,* vol. 2 (Westminster, Md.: Newman Press, 1983) 303.

19. M. Buber, *I and Thou* (New York: Charles Scribner's Sons, 1970) 123.

20. G. van der Leeuw, *Sakramentales Denken* (Kassel, 1959) 152.

21. *Ordo Celebrandi Matrimonium, Editio Typica Altera* (19 March 1990) Introduction.

22. Bernard Cooke, *Sacraments and Sacramentality* (Mystic, Conn.: Twenty-Third Publications, 1983) 20.

23. Denis O'Callaghan, "Marriage as Sacrament," *Concilium* 55 (1970) 107.

24. *Familiaris Consortio* 68; *Origins* 11 (1981) 459.

25. David Thomas, *Christian Marriage: A Journey Together* (Wilmington, Del.: Michael Glazier, 1983) 203.

26. Pastoral Constitution on the Church in the Modern World, 48.

27. Matthias Joseph Scheeben, *The Mysteries of Christianity* (St. Louis: B. Herder, 1946) 601, n. 13. The work of this nineteenth-century German theologian still remains profound and modern.

28. Peter Elliot, *What God Has Joined . . . The Sacramentality of Marriage* (New York: Alba House, 1990) 222.

29. John Paul II in *L'Observatore Romano* (21 January 1980).

30. Patrick Brennan, *Re-Imagining the Parish* (New York: Crossroad, 1991) 121.

31. Patrick and Claudette McDonald, *The Soul of a Marriage* (New York/ Mahwah, N.J.: Paulist Press, 1995) 14.

32. *Ordo Celebrandi Matrimonium* (1990).

33. *Familiaris Consortio,* 57.

34. *Ordo Celebrandi Matrimonium,* 73.

35. Bernard Cooke, "What God Has Joined Together . . ." in *Perspectives on Marriage,* ed. K. Scott and M. Warren (New York: Oxford University Press, 1993) 358.

36. *Catechism of the Catholic Church,* 1640; cf. canon 1141.

37. Timothy Buckley, *What Binds Marriage? Roman Catholic Theology in Practice* (London: Geoffrey Chapman, 1997) 168. See also William Roberts, ed., *Divorce and Remarriage: Religious and Psychological Perspectives* (Kansas City, Mo.: Sheed & Ward, 1990) and Michael Lawler, "Divorce and Remarriage in the Catholic Church: Ten Theses," *New Theology Review* 12 (1999) 48–61.

38. John Meyerdorff, *Marriage: An Orthodox Perspective* (Crestwood, N.Y.: St. Vladimir's Seminary Press, 1984) 54.

39. *Familiaris Consortio,* 84.

40. Ibid.

41. Ibid.

42. Timothy Buckley, *What Binds Marriage?* 136–138.

43. Lawrence Wrenn, "Refining the Essence of Marriage," *The Jurist* 46 (1986) 550.


**Conclusion**


1. *Epistle* 55, to Januarius, 7, 13; PL, 33:210, quoted by Maurice Jourjon, *Les Sacrements de la Liberté Chrétienne* (Paris: Cerf, 1981) 139.

2. Bakole wa Ilunga, *Paths of Liberation* (Maryknoll, N.Y.: Orbis Books, 1984) 184.

3. Dogmatic Constitution on the Church, 1.

4. Alexander Schmemann, *The World as Sacrament* (London: Darton, Longman & Todd, 1965) 7.

5. *Instruction on Christian Freedom and Liberation* (Vatican City, 1986) 1, 81; in *Liberation Theology: A Documentary*, ed. Alfred T. Hennelly (Maryknoll, N.Y.: Orbis Books, 1990) 461, 488.

6. Christian Duquoc, *Jesus, homme libre* (Paris: Cerf, 1978) 27–39.

7. Gustavo Gutiérrez, *We Drink from Our Own Wells* (Maryknoll, N.Y.: Orbis Books, 1985) 35.

8. Aloysius Pieris, *An Asian Theology of Liberation* (Maryknoll, N.Y.: Orbis Books, 1988) 5.

9. "Evangelization in Latin America's Present and Future," No. 895; in *Liberation Theology*, 232–49.

10. Dionisio Borobio et al., *La Celebración de la Iglesia* #1 (Salamanca: Sígueme, 1987) 496.

11. Gérard Fourez, *Sacraments and Passages: Celebrating the Tensions of Modern Life* (Notre Dame, Ind.: Ave Maria Press, 1983) 7.

12. Herbert Vorgrimler, *Sacramental Theology* (Collegeville, Minn.: The Liturgical Press, 1992) 14.

13. John 19:34; cf. Augustine, *In Johan. ev.* 9, 10; *Epistle* 54, 1; PL 33:200.

14. *Sermo* 74, 2; PL 54:398.

15. Karl Rahner, *Foundations of Christian Faith* (New York: Seabury Press, 1978) 415.

16. Henri Denis, *Les Sacrements: ont-ils un avenir?* (Paris: Cerf, 1971) 83.

# Bibliography

(This bibliography presents key works in English on sacramental theology. It confines itself to a few principal references. These references are helpful for both scholarly research and pastoral ministry.)

Austin, Gerard. *The Rite of Confirmation: Anointing with the Spirit.* New York: Pueblo, 1985.

Beguerie, Philippe, and Claude Duchesneau. *How to Understand the Sacraments.* New York: Crossroad, 1991.

Bermejo Luis. *Body Broken and Blood Shed: The Eucharist of the Risen Christ.* Chicago, Ill.: Loyola University Press, 1987.

Bernier, Paul. *Ministry in the Church: A Historical and Pastoral Approach.* Mystic, Conn.: Twenty-Third Publications, 1992.

Boff, Leonard. *Sacraments of Life and Life of the Sacraments: Story Theology.* Washington, D.C.: The Pastoral Press, 1987.

Browning, Robert, and Roy Reed. *Models of Confirmation and Baptismal Affirmation.* Birmingham, Ala.: Religious Education Press, 1996.

Buckley, Thomas. *What Binds Marriage?* London: Geoffrey Chapman, 1997.

Casel, Odo. *The Mystery of Christian Worship.* Westminster, Md.: Newman Press, 1962.

*Catechism of the Catholic Church,* 1066–1130.

"The Catholic Tradition of Eucharistic Theology," *Theological Studies* 55 (September, 1994).

Chauvet, Louis-Marie. *The Sacraments: The Word of God at the Mercy of the Body.* Collegeville, Minn.: The Liturgical Press, 2001.

————. *Symbol and Sacrament: A Sacramental Reinterpretation of Christian Existence.* Collegeville, Minn.: The Liturgical Press, 1995.

Cooke, Bernard. *The Distancing of God: The Ambiguity of Symbol in History and Theology.* Minneapolis, Minn.: Fortress Press, 1990.

"Current Theology, Sacramental Theology: A Review of Literature," *Theological Studies* 55 (1994) 657-704.

Dallen, James. *The Reconciling Community: The Rite of Penance.* Collegeville, Minn.: The Liturgical Press, 1986.

de Lubac, Henri. *Corpus Mysticum.* Paris: Aubier, 1944.

Driver, Tom F. *The Magic of Ritual.* San Francisco: Harper Collins, 1991.

Drumm, M., and T. Gunning. *A Sacramental People: Initiation into a Faith Community.* Mystic, Conn.: Twenty-Third Publications, 2000.

Duffy, Regis A. *Real Presence.* San Francisco: Harper & Row, 1982.

Empereur, James. *Prophetic Anointing: God's Call to the Sick, the Elderly, and the Dying.* Wilmington, Del.: Michael Glazier, 1982.

Fink, Peter E., ed. *The New Dictionary of Sacramental Worship.* Collegeville, Minn.: The Liturgical Press, 1990.

————. *Praying the Sacraments.* Washington, D.C.: The Pastoral Press, 1991.

Galot, Jean. *Theology of the Priesthood.* San Francisco, Calif., Ignatius Press, 1984.

Goergen, J. Donald, and Ann Garrido, eds. *The Theology of Priesthood.* Collegeville, Minn.: The Liturgical Press, 2001.

Gusmer, W. Charles. *And You Visited Me: Sacramental Ministry to the Sick and the Dying.* New York: Pueblo, 1989.

Johnson, Maxwell, ed. *Living Water, Sealing Spirit: Readings on Christian Initiation.* Collegeville, Minn.: The Liturgical Press, 1995.

————. *The Rites of Christian Initiation: Their Evolution and Interpretation.* Collegeville, Minn.: The Liturgical Press, 1999.

Kasper, Walter. *Theology of Christian Marriage.* New York: Crossroad, 1983.

Kavanagh, Aidan. *Confirmation: Origins and Reform.* New York: Pueblo, 1988.

Kilmartin, Edward. *The Eucharist in the West: History and Theology.* Collegeville, Minn.: The Liturgical Press, 1998.

Lawler, Michael G. *Symbol and Sacrament.* New York/Mahwah, N.J.: Paulist Press, 1987.

Luther, Martin. *Word and Sacrament,* vol. 35-38 of Luther's Works, ed. E. Theodore Bachman. Philadelphia: Muhlenberg Press, 1960.

Macquarrie, John. *A Guide to the Sacraments.* New York: Continuum, 1997.

Martelet, Gustave. *The Risen Christ and the Eucharistic World.* New York: Seabury Press, 1976.

Martinez, German. *Worship: Wedding to Marriage.* Washington, D.C.: The Pastoral Press, 1993.

Martos, Joseph. *The Catholic Sacraments.* Wilmington, Del.: Michael Glazier, 1990.

McCauley, George. *Sacraments for the Secular Man.* New York: Herder & Herder, 1969.

Moloney, Raymond. *The Eucharist: Problems in Theology.* Collegeville, Minn.: The Liturgical Press, 1995.

Morris, Thomas H. *The RCIA: Transforming the Church: A Resource for Pastoral Implementation.* New York/Mahwah, N.J.: Paulist Press, 1997.

The Murphy Center for Liturgical Research. *Made, Not Born: New Perspectives on Christian Initiation and the Catechumenate.* Notre Dame, Ind.: University of Notre Dame Press, 1976.

Noll, R. Ray. *Sacraments: A New Understanding for a New Generation*. Mystic, Conn.: Twenty Third Publications, 1999.

O'Meara, Thomas F. *Theology of Ministry*. New York/Mahwah, N.J.: Paulist Press, 1999.

Osborne, Kenan B. *The Christian Sacraments of Initiation: Baptism, Confirmation, Eucharist*. New York/Mahwah, N.J.: Paulist Press, 1987.

―――. *Christian Sacraments in a Postmodern World: A Theology for the Third Millennium*. New York/Mahwah, N.J.: Paulist Press, 1999.

―――. *Sacramental Theology: A General Introduction*. New York/Mahwah, N.J.: Paulist Press, 1988.

Poschmann, Bernhard. *Penance and the Anointing of the Sick*. New York: Herder and Herder, 1964.

Power, David. *The Eucharistic Mystery: Revitalizing the Tradition*. New York: Crossroad, 1992.

―――. *Sacrament: The Language of God's Giving*. New York: Crossroad, 1999.

Powers, Joseph. *Spirit and Sacrament*. New York: Seabury Press, 1973.

Rahner, Karl. *The Church and the Sacraments*. New York: Herder & Herder, 1963.

―――. *Meditations on the Sacraments*. New York: Seabury Press, 1977.

Schillebeeckx, Edward H. *Christ, The Sacrament of the Encounter with God*. New York: Sheed & Ward, 1963.

―――. *The Church with a Human Face: A New and Expanded Theology of Ministry*. New York: Crossroad, 1985.

Schmemann, Alexander. *For the Life of the World: Sacraments and Orthodoxy*. New York: St. Valdimir's Seminary Press, 1973.

Schüssler Fiorenza, F., and John P. Galvin, eds. *Systematic Theology: Roman Catholic Perspectives*. Minneapolis, Minn.: Fortress Press, 1991.

Segundo, Juan L. *The Sacraments Today.* Maryknoll, N.Y.: Orbis Books, 1974.

Semmelroth, Otto. *Church and Sacraments.* Notre Dame: Fides Publishing, 1965.

Skelley, Michael. *The Liturgy of the World: Karl Rahner's Theology of Worship.* Collegeville, Minn.: The Liturgical Press, 1991.

Stasiak, Kurt. *Return to Grace: A Theology of Infant Baptism.* Collegeville, Minn.: The Liturgical Press, 1996.

Theological-Historical Commission for the Year 2000. *The Eucharist, Gift of Divine Life.* New York: Crossroad, 1999.

Triacca, Achille, ed. *Temple of the Holy Spirit: Sickness and Death of the Christian in the Liturgy.* New York: Pueblo, 1983.

Von Balthasar, Hans Urs. *Gloria. The Glory of the Lord: A Theological Aesthetics.* Ft. Collins, Colo.: Ignatius Press, 1984.

Vorgrimler, Herbert. *Sacramental Theology.* Collegeville, Minn.: The Liturgical Press, 1992.

White, James F. *Sacraments as God's Self Giving.* Nashville: Abingdon Press, 1983.

Wilkes, Paul. *Excellent Catholic Parishes: The Guide to Best Places and Practices.* New York/Mahwah, N.J.: Paulist Press, 2001.

# Index